FREE RANGE LEARNING

FREE RANGE LEARNING
How Homeschooling Changes Everything

Laura Grace Weldon

HOHM PRESS
Chino Valley, Arizona

Cover design: Adi Zuccarello, www.adizuccarello.com

Layout and Interior Design: Zachary Parker, Kadak Graphics, www.kadakgraphics.com

Library of Congress Cataloging-in-Publication Data

Weldon, Laura Grace.
Free range learning : how homeschooling changes everything / Laura Grace Weldon.
    p. cm.
Includes bibliographical references and index.
ISBN 978-1-935387-09-1 (trade paper : alk. paper)
1. Home schooling. I. Title.
LC40.W45 2010
371.04'2--dc22

                    2010006787

Hohm Press
PO Box 4410
Chino Valley, Arizona 86323
800-381-2700
www.hohmpress.com

This book was printed in the U.S.A. on recycled, acid-free paper using soy ink.

With love to Benjamin, Claire, Kirby and Sam.

Acknowledgements

I'm honored to present contributions from people around the world on these pages, making this work a mutual conversation about authentic learning experiences. Thank you to each person who shared their words and photos with me. My gratitude to Helen Hegener for this book's beginnings and all she does for educational freedom each day. Many thanks to the kindest editor ever, Regina Sara Ryan, and to everyone at Hohm Press for bringing this book into being. Boundless appreciation to my extended family and my friends, each one an inspiring example of life's possibilities. I give thanks for the parents life gave me, Earl and Grace Piper. Their support and strength of spirit continues to bless me daily. And to Mark, love of my life, thank you for believing.

Contents

Part Two

Introduction

"We all have the extraordinary coded within us, waiting to be released." —Jean Houston

A child's wonder is a precious thing. Kept alive, it remains a lifelong wellspring of curiosity, awe and heightened awareness. The challenge is to live in such a way that wonder is not smothered.

Each baby is born with unique capabilities. Ideally the child grows toward his or her potential as children have throughout time—through observation, exploration and hands-on learning. Learning happens constantly. Naturally. The inborn drive to gain meaningful first hand experience is often at odds with the predetermined course set before today's students. Many styles of homeschooling foster greater comprehension than the typical school environment. That's because experiential learning, along with the guidance of parents and other elders, is precisely the education known throughout the majority of human history. This is how we as a species learn best. Schooling is the experiment.

As homeschooling parents we can take into account individual learning styles, innate skills and interests to bring out the best in each child without being restricted by the dictates of any institution. We can educate as easily as we breathe simply by remaining fully present to our children's questions and enthusiasms. The homeschooling child's life is filled with conversation, music, play, stories, struggles and overcoming struggles, chores, laughter and the excitement of examining in depth any of the rich wells of knowledge that humanity has to offer.

Each of us needs to feel we belong, that our relationships are of value and our efforts have purpose. We can't expect any one institution to meet these needs. Homeschoolers take responsibility for learning back to the family realm but do so in the context of the larger community where each child grows whole and strong within a vibrant network. As we nurture children who learn eagerly we help them to mature into adults fully suited to meet the challenges of the future.

Homeschooling families have time for quiet days at home as well as time for community involvement. We know that new endeavors spark enthusiasm and develop confidence. As we seek out wider ways of learning, we collaborate with people and organizations in ways that benefit all of us. Those benefits include civic engagement, volunteerism, environmental awareness, cultural growth, entrepreneurial reinvigoration and more.

Studies indicate that adults who were homeschooled:
- Are more likely to vote, volunteer and be involved in their communities than graduates of conventional schools.
- Read more books than average.
- Are more likely to have taken college level courses than the population as a whole.
- Tend to be independent and self-reliant.

Nowadays homeschooled youth are gaining recognition as innovative, self-directed thinkers with diverse experiences. By the time they reach adulthood they are blessed with an appetite for lifelong learning.

This book helps you see the potential in meaningful, real-life learning. It builds trust in your child's abilities. It encourages you to network with others so that the possibilities for enrichment continue to grow, making your community a better place for everyone. And it speaks to the wider implications of free range learning for the individual as well as society. Perhaps you'll agree that homeschooling is a form of collective intelligence, even a sign of cultural awakening.

First-hand accounts from homeschoolers around the world can be found throughout this volume, generally identified by name and country or state. These contributions provide the wisdom gained from experience, and will hopefully serve to encourage and inspire you.

PART ONE

CHAPTER ONE

Natural Learning Happens Everywhere

Overview of Natural Learning

"To be surprised, to wonder, is to begin to understand."
—Jose Ortega Y Gasset

Children want to be involved in the fullness of life around them. That's the way they naturally learn. As they imitate what they see, they gain greater understanding. A tribal child will fashion a fishing net from the same fibers she's seen her mother use. A suburban child will use hammer and nails to make repairs as his father does. Throughout time, children have become capable adults by observing and participating in real work.

Children develop deeper understanding through stories, religion, art and conversation with their elders. They are drawn to what is meaningful. Often they like to hear the same things over and over, as if recognizing what they need even if they cannot fully grasp the richness of these traditions until they are older.

And, of course, children play. Play is generative, transforming the ordinary into something unique. It also imparts advanced social skills and a creative approach to life.

These many ways of learning are ingrained, a human legacy from prehistory.

If learning is imposed by hours of worksheets or computer curricula, children are separated from rich stimuli that inspire them to connect ideas and to develop meaningful competence beyond test readiness. This doesn't imply that using curricula is always wrong, it simply means that children need more. Much more. Real experiences help them build understanding, incorporate new information, and make the "aha" connections that are the hallmark of insight.

John Holt describes the process of natural learning in *How Children Learn*.

> The child is curious. He wants to make sense out of things, find out how things work, gain competence and control over himself and his environment, do what he can see other people doing. He is open, receptive and perceptive. He does not shut himself off from the strange, confused, complicated world around him. He observes it closely and sharply, tries to take it all in. He is experimental. He does not merely observe the world around him but tastes it, touches it, hefts it, bends it, breaks it. To find out how reality works, he works on it. He is bold. He is not afraid of making mistakes. And he is patient. He can tolerate an extraordinary amount of uncertainty, confusion, ignorance, and suspense.

The growing brain hungers for stimulation. An estimated 100 billion neurons make trillions of connections. New neural pathways are developed constantly as information and perceptions are linked. Children literally rewire their brains while learning. The observations and insights made are unique to each learner.

For example, a field trip to a potato chip factory will be a different experience for every child. One child may be so intrigued by the machinery she is loathe to continue with the group and would rather look at each moving part to understand its function. The second child may notice distinct jobs performed there, focusing on how the workers' efforts make the factory operate. Another child might be enthralled by conveyor belts and giant fans, wishing only to translate those motions into a spinning dance of his own. And the fourth child might marvel at the tons of potatoes waiting for processing and want to know what calculations factor into converting these raw materials into the final product. Each child is inspired by the experience in entirely different ways.

It's worth noting that many adults would chastise a child who prefers to look at a machine rather than continue with the group, who stares too long at the workers, who asks potentially intrusive questions about profits, or who cannot stop himself from excited movement. Good behavior is essential on a field trip. But it's also important to recognize that what children make of learning is truly their own work.

Children are busier than we imagine. They listen to conversations, look for patterns in random occurrences, search for meaning, and perpetually seek to understand their place in a larger context. It can be exhausting, confusing work. It takes imagination and energy. No wonder they need more sleep than adults.

Issa has been "wide awake" since infancy. Nothing escapes her notice. At six she is our reference point for occurrences we can't remember. I'm no longer surprised that she pulls up something we'd forgotten and applies it to something she's just learned. —Kelly

---

It's non-stop and all the time. Bath time, bedtime, playtime—my children are absorbing, observing, imitating no matter where we are … Learning is facilitated all the time.

—Hema A., Bharadwaj, Singapore

Sometimes I think Jiann (five) isn't interested in what we are doing until I pay attention to what she plays. The other day Jiann and her friend were making a

lot of noise in the basement ... When I went down later to do laundry I noticed that they were pounding on old cornmeal canisters from hideouts they'd made on opposite ends of the basement. I asked what they were doing with all that racket. They told me they were talking with drums. I remembered that maybe two months ago we learned about how drums were a kind of language that their ancestors used. For my girl to remember that and play at that brought me to tears. —Tisha, Maryland

Young children seem to recognize that knowledge is an essential shared resource, like air or water. They demand a fair share. They actively espouse the right to gain skill and comprehension in the way that is necessary for them at the time. This is not only an expression of autonomy, this is a clear indication that each child is equipped with an educational guidance system of his or her own.

In our culture such fervent curiosity is more common in early childhood. Why does it lessen with age? The world doesn't become less tantalizing. In fact, as children get older, their opportunities increase as their abilities improve. Something else must have an effect. Often the change has to do with the coercion involved in what we call education. There's no need to look for external "motivators" when children remain eager. Curious children will learn more than any external reward, punishment or praise can compel them to learn. Artificial inducements actually interfere with the process. The key is preserving their right to learn in their own way, according to their own interests.

My four-year-old daughter's ... abilities to represent human figures are now very sophisticated. She includes plenty of detail, including hair on those with hair and no hair for those without. Again, she did this without us directing her drawing. It seemed that the more she drew the more she learned how to draw. This should not be surprising.

Now, another important thing in all of this is that we never told her to draw, write or read and so on. She just did it when she felt like it. Interestingly, my daughter attended a play program one morning a week with several of her neighborhood friends. What I noticed was that when she would be asked to paint or draw while in the program, it would be merely a slab of paint on the page. It probably would take her seconds to do ... I suspect that the reason why her paintings when she was in the program looked so unsophisticated is that she was doing it not because she wanted to paint but because she was made to paint. I suspect that she would rather be playing with her friends than painting, and so she complied because she had to, but resisted by doing as little as was required for her to do. I believe she did this so that she could get it over with and move on to do what she really wanted to do, which was go off and play with her friends.

—Dr. Carlo Ricci, Canada

Children are drawn to explore the world with a sensory approach. When they are fully involved, what they learn is entwined with the experience itself. A child's whole being strains against the limitations of curricula meant only for eyes and ears, or that assigns closed-ended tasks.

A typical school or school-at-home lesson intended to teach a child about worms may have diagrams of a worm's body to label and a few paragraphs about the importance of worms, followed by comprehension questions. If the child musters up enthusiasm to learn more about worms despite this lackluster approach, there's no time to do so because directly after the science lesson the child must go on to the next subject. When education is approached in this disconnected manner, the brain doesn't process the information in long-term storage very effectively. It has no context in the child's experience and no connection to the child's senses.

On the other hand, a child encountering a worm while helping in the garden gains body memories to associate with the experience. The heft of a shovel, sun on her face, fragrant soil on her knees, and the feel of a worm in her hands provide her with sensory detail. She also encodes the experience with emotion. Her father likes to read books about soil health and sometimes she looks at the pictures. When she asks about worms he answers the few questions she has. And when she is satisfied he doesn't go on to give her more information than she can handle. Next time they go to the library or log on to the Internet they may decide to find out more about worms. She may be inspired on her own to draw worms, save worms from the sidewalk after the next rain, or otherwise expand on that moment in the garden. She is much more likely to retain and build on what she has learned.

The difference between these two approaches is worlds apart. Separating children from meaningful participation, as in the first example, doesn't simply impair comprehension. It changes the way learning takes place. The child is made a passive recipient of education designed by others. Then the excitement of learning is transformed into a duty.

Any form of education that treats the brain apart from the body will ultimately fail. Our senses cannot be denied. They inform the mind and encode memory. We must see, hear, smell, touch and, yes, taste to form the kinds of complex associations that make up true understanding. We humans are direct "hands-on" learners.

Frank R. Wilson points out that brain development and hand use have always been inextricably intertwined in *The Hand: How Its Use Shapes the Brain, Language and Human Culture*. When interviewing high achievers to understand this connection, he found that people credit their success to attributes learned through hands-on activities. Wilson writes,

> I was completely unprepared for the frequency with which I heard the people whom I interviewed either dismiss or actively denounce the time they had spent in school. Most of my interview subjects, although I never asked them directly, said quite forcefully that they had clarified their own thinking and their lives as a result of what they were doing with their hands. Not only were most of them essentially self-taught, but a few had engineered their personally unique repertoire of skills and expertise in open retreat from painful experiences in a school system that had dictated the form and content of their education in order to prepare them for a life modeled on conventional norms of success.

Hands-on effort toward long-term goals has a significant impact. Whether we paint, weld or sail something greater can come into play. We gain a sense of effortlessness, of becoming one with the movement. Then it seems we're longer working with objects, but with material partners in a process of co-creation. It's what musicians, athletes and artists seek out. Wilson calls it "a powerful emotional charge" and says that people are forever changed by such pursuits.

Wilson's interest in direct learning led him to study the work of Seymour Sarason, an eminent researcher in educational psychology and author of over forty books. Sarason was concerned with restoring creativity to education. He concluded that learning at any age takes place best and most quickly when the student's self-interest drives the search for comprehension and skill. Wilson says, "What this means, if Sarason is right, is that any student who chose spontaneously and voluntarily, on the basis of his or her own inclinations and experience, to become a brain surgeon could probably prepare adequately to enter that career by the age of twenty if those in a position to support that ambition provided the necessary assistance or at least did not stand in the way."

Direct learning comes alive. Principles of geometry and physics become apparent while children work together figuring out how to stack firewood. They develop multiple layers of competence as they solving tangible problems. Their bodies are flooded with sensation, locking learning into memory. Such experiences develop a stronger foundation for working with abstract postulates, theorems and formulas.

It appears we do stand in the way. High school graduates heading to college are woefully unprepared to comprehend university level reading assignments in core subjects, according to a report by the Alliance for Excellent Education. In the U.S. about a third of all college freshman need at least one remedial course. Those are the successful students.

One-third of U.S. students drop out before high school graduation. Fewer than half graduate in many inner-city districts. The Gates Foundation conducted focus groups with high school dropouts across the country to find out why. A majority of these young people had grade averages of C or better, as well as career aspirations requiring higher education. Although there were personal reasons for leaving school, such as needing to work full time or care for a family member, still nearly half of the former students said that they felt bored and disengaged by classes they did not find interesting. The rates are not necessarily better in other countries.

Twenty percent of Belgian students, a quarter of Irish students, and a third of Swedish students drop out, too. Current forms of education must change.

According to a report on BBC News, "One of the most intriguing statistics from international comparisons is the lack of relationship between hours in the classroom and educational achievement." This turns conventional thinking upside-down. We assume that more time "hitting the books" translates to smarter students. But it turns out some pupils who spend a smaller amount of time in school end up achieving the highest educational standards. Children in Finland don't start formal education until the age of seven. They enjoy longer summer holidays and are spared the sort of standardized testing so popular in the U.S. During the school year Finnish children gather in small classes where they are provided a rich variety of activities, including art, music, woodworking and crafts. From early grades through the midteen years, they go outdoors for a recreation period after each forty-five-minute lesson. A young person's need for free time, fresh air and play is understood. By the age of fifteen, Finnish students rank at the top of the world in knowledge and skills.

Education as it has been perpetrated on children the last few hundred years places value almost exclusively on the intellect; in fact, emphasizing one hemisphere of the brain over the other. When rational and analytical functions are elevated in importance over all else, we effectively devalue emotion, intuition, creativity, physicality—indeed the whole person. Clearly, suppressing body, heart and soul in favor of the intellect is not a good idea. A cursory look at the state of the planet will convince anyone that a head-based approach hasn't been working. It seems to have caused many of the problems in the first place. All the obedient, high-test-scoring students our schools churn out haven't solved the big crises that face humankind. As Benjamin Franklin said, "The definition of insanity is doing the same thing over and over, and expecting different results."

Ironically, some schools in the U.S. have cut down on recess and physical education classes in order to promote academics. This is phenomenally counterproductive. As John J. Ratey, MD, explains in *Spark: The Revolutionary New Science of Exercise and the Brain*, "In addition to priming our state of mind, exercise influences learning directly, at the cellular level, improving the brain's potential to log in and process new information." When children run and play, actually when any of us exercise, our muscles generate proteins that enter the brain and support the learning processes. One such protein is called brain-derived neurotrophic factor, which promotes the sort of brain development necessary for learning, long-term memory and higher level thinking. Exercise also increases blood flow to the brain, essential to thought processes. And we know that an active lifestyle stimulates neurotransmitters such as serotonin, dopamine and norephinephrine that are required for attention, learning and positive emotions. When young people get their heart rates up as they play a fast-paced game or challenge themselves to master complex martial arts moves, they are also readying themselves to focus their attention on learning. Physiology proves this connection.

Our school systems already know this. Over a million California school children in grades five, seven and nine were rated as either fit or unfit in the following categories: aerobic capacity, body composition, abdominal strength and endurance, trunk strength and flexibility, upper body strength and endurance, and overall flexibility. A student score of six indicated healthy fitness in all areas. These fitness levels were compared with student achievement. Across all socioeconomic boundaries, students who were more fit showed correspondingly higher achievement. Those who were fit in at least three areas showed the greatest gains in academic achievement. Clearly, an active body correlates with a lively mind, even if most images of mainstream education call to mind a student sitting still.

One of the main reasons we started homeschooling was that it didn't seem right to take an active little boy who loved being outside and force him to be in school all day. He learned about nature through playing in the woods and the creek behind our house, having pets and hands- on experiences. We've had aquariums containing all sorts of interesting creatures through the years, such as praying mantises, tadpoles and turtles. If he wanted to learn about something, we checked out books from the library. These books would be read while he was sprawled out on the floor or couch or wherever the mood hit him. He learned what he was interested in and ready to learn at the time. Not what the school curriculum said it was time to learn. —Lori Scelina

I can't conceive of restricting Skye's education. She learns as she has since birth: fully in body and mind ... This morning we read a book set in an earlier time in which the character was around her age. Skye was asking some questions that got us talking about decisions made in that time. I could see how much this stimulated her thinking and feeling for the past. When we got to a part that mentioned the jitterbug, I got up to show her the steps. She tried it with me and we danced until we fell down laughing.
—Mari, Oregon

There's no getting around the fact that we humans have mastered everything from fire to the most technologically advanced communications systems by making full use of our learning capacities. That involves a meaningful pursuit, engaged awareness, openness to intuition, caring interaction and hands-on work. When mastery is reduced to something less, it makes those involved feel lessened. What is fully human in us cries out for more.

Developing an optimal learning environment means restoring a gentler, more holistic approach to our lives. It also means nurturing children in closer proximity to nature. Child development expert Joseph Chilton Pearce believes that early

exposures to unnatural, intense stimulation have caused significant damage to children. He cites a study from Tubingen University in Germany. After analyzing twenty years of data from four thousand subjects, it was found that the children had 20 percent less sensory awareness of their environment compared to children just two decades earlier. Pearce believes this is due to the type of stimuli in the lives of most children. Rather than developing subtle yet multifaceted awareness by playing in natural settings, young children accommodate to intense bursts of sound, light and color during their early years. Their brains and nervous systems become wired for massive overstimulation. Without it they are bored. But what they lose is incalculable. A child accustomed to blinking, beeping toys and rapidly changing screen images may not be attuned to more complex nuances in the natural world. In fact, the same study noted that the first group of children could differentiate 360 shades of red, but twenty years later children could distinguish only about 130 shades.

Your eyes adjust inside and get used to dreary. Going from drab colors, it's a wonderful change to be outside where there's a variety. Being outside even changes my view of colors. Then coming in from the outside it's amazing that it physically brightens things up inside too. If you are exposed to the extraordinary you get a new perspective on things. It's like a physical effect on your body.
—Sam, 15

Our nervous systems and emotional states appear to be set at nature's wavelength. Research shows that people benefit enormously from exposure to natural settings, finding them physically and emotionally restorative. Children are less impulsive and aggressive, handle stress better, and are more able to concentrate when they are in contact with nature. We see this in our own experience. The child who has spent the whole day shut up indoors, even with plenty of room to play, does not show that same indefinable joie de vivre as the child who has been ambling alongside a stream or running with friends through backyards. The proportion and inherent rightness of the natural world seems to inspire a sense of well-being.

I tell my son that we are not separate from nature, but if we forget and separate ourselves, we end up forgetting who we are. —Erin M., Maine

---

I think the freedom to go outside helps a lot. I can't focus on one thing for too long. If I really lose my train of thought, I go outside and think about something else for a while. —Allison, 14

Learning indoors, especially with nature-related topics like biology, is way too static and one dimensional. For example, I don't think I truly understood how to apply the basic principles of what I was taught in my college biology courses until I started an internship that involved fieldwork and showed me how to really use what I had learned in school to investigate and hypothesize on things I was doing and seeing. A textbook or a lab procedure can't teach you how to really think in the way that getting out and dirty can. And, in my experience, what you learn when you are enjoying yourself sticks around and makes a far bigger impression than when you are at a desk or sitting at a table taking notes. —Claire, 22

Everything about natural settings, from the vitamin D provided by sunshine to the aural pleasures of wind and rain, has an impact beyond our conscious awareness. Even simple dirt holds a clue to happiness. A specific soil bacterium has been found to increase serotonin in the brain and improve mood. This soil bacterium is so common that we can get a dose of it from hiking in the wild, working in the garden, or eating fresh produce.

Biologist Edward O. Wilson explains that the affiliation we subconsciously seek with other living beings, plants as well as creatures, is in our genes. Wilson writes, "To the extent that each person can feel like a naturalist, the old excitement of the untrammeled world will be regained. I offer this as a formula of reenchantment to invigorate poetry and myth: mysterious and little-known organisms live within walking distance of where you sit. Splendor awaits in minute proportions."

Studies have measured the amount of green space surrounding a child's home or play area and found that it is positively linked to how well the child is doing in terms of mental health. Even indoor plants have a beneficial effect. One study of 337 children assessed the child's exposure to nature based on his or her home. The variables included nature viewed through windows, the number of indoor plants, and whether the child's home was surrounded by concrete, dirt or grass. Children living in homes with more nature inside and out were better able to handle stress and adversity in their lives. This result was found for rural as well as urban children. The greater the exposure to natural surroundings the better, particularly in terms of reducing stress, strengthening resiliency and promoting attention. This makes sense. Through every era of human history our ancestors adhered to natural rhythms. Their hardships and blessings all came through the same primal, essential connection to the earth.

Whether we recognize its effect or not, the natural world immerses us in what is aesthetically appealing and deeply restorative. We center ourselves when we notice the progress of leaves unfolding each day in the spring, when we smell an approaching thunderstorm, when we step beyond pavement onto textures our soles recognize. We feel rooted in something greater than what is manufactured for us. As Rachel Carson says, "Those who contemplate the beauty of the earth find resources of strength that will endure as long as life lasts."

Creating a more natural childhood of outdoor play, hands-on involvement, and attunement to individual interests is the most promising orientation for learning. Yet educational standards increasingly focus on measurable outcomes that make learning an indirect rather than direct experience. This translates into rigid curricula with regular drills to ensure passing grades on mandatory tests. And this approach takes children farther away from what we know actually promotes long-term learning.

Some of the recent evidence indicating that we are direct learners comes from neuroscience, which shows that it isn't possible to transmit reams of cultural, ethical and practical learning from one generation to another on a flat page or screen. We comprehend in a much deeper and more complete way when learning from one another. Intriguing details about how we learn through first-hand observation and imitation has accelerated with the discovery of mirror neurons.

When a person is performing a task or expressing an emotion, it activates certain areas in the brain. We now know that specific neurons in the brain of someone who is simply observing this individual are also activated. The cells responding in this way, called *mirror neurons*, are essentially duplicating the action or emotion being observed. This means there is a physical basis for feeling what others feel.

As a toddler plays in the kitchen and watches a parent prepare vegetables for dinner, she observes the activities of washing, peeling and cutting. This activates her mirror neurons. Her brain simulates the actions she sees, even though her muscles are not performing those same tasks. She is gaining dinner-making experience that will hold her in good stead when she is old enough to help. Because she observes this regularly, she is forming a mental template for this activity. Mirror neurons help all of us form a mental framework for the minutiae of everyday life through observation. Any variation on familiar patterns captures our attention, and we respond in a learning mode. So if this child's family has a party and prepares unusual foods, her attention is heightened and the mental template enlarges.

Mirror neurons are intrinsically related to emotions such as empathy. If the child's father accidentally cuts his finger, the child's mirror neurons will cause her to respond immediately. Based on the activity of mirror neurons, it's clear we don't think first, we feel. Her brain will light up with surprise and pain similar to his experience. The child will then adapt the mental template she's developing to include the danger of sharp knives, made more real to her through observation than any cautionary statement might accomplish.

This has tremendous implications for the way we learn. We are constantly practicing, passively, as we observe. As we watch other people, our mirror neurons are reacting. That's why starting a job or trying out new skills can be stressful, because we may not have a template that fits directly in that situation. It's also why following written instructions for an unfamiliar physical task can be so daunting.

Mirror neurons clarify many aspects of social behavior as well. A child recognizes when a hand is raised a certain way that a wave goodbye will inevitably follow. But if that child is saying farewell to a new friend from a different cultural background, a casual wave may not be met with a wave. Instead, the friend may bow with hands clasped together. In response, the child's brain duplicates those motions. This helps convey the intention and emotion behind an action even when seen for the first time. We are wired to understand down to the cellular level. Nothing can replace direct observation and experience.

A natural education is complex and purposeful. When each person is empowered to learn as it suits him or her, the process of discovery is invigorating.

I like to figure things out and do stuff. That's how I get good at things. I'm going to be a chef or a game designer when I grow up, so I have a lot to learn. I'm making a sprite from scratch for a RPG. I'm really good at making pasta dishes that I add things to. —Tyler, 9

I do better watching someone else, like over their shoulder, and then trying for myself ... When we're learning something new, my guitar teacher copies the songs down on my iPod. He'll show on his guitar you play this, this and this. Then he'll have me play it, then tell me how I can do it better. We work on it till I've got it right. —Josh, 12

I'm very bookish, so I take things in with a book, but hands-on experience seems to help more. —Allison, 14

When I get into something, I just want to keep going when there's more to know about it. Lately I have been writing knitting instructions to go with projects that my mom and I sell on Etsy.com, and that got me looking up how to do technical writing because I want to make it easy to understand, and then I started reading different instructions that got me going in other directions I didn't expect ... I think it's awesome when my friends call me "brainy girl." —Carlee, 15

I do best following my own direction. Left to my own devices I've managed to find my way into studying every necessary subject without touching a traditional textbook. —Kirby, 19

Young people are perfectly attuned to learn. They are drawn to what is fully authentic in life. Their bodies, minds and spirits nearly shimmer with the intense urge to discover. Every meaningful experience, each revelation shines greater light on this dawning awareness.

Education as Life, for Life

"The young do not know enough to be prudent, and therefore they attempt the impossible—and achieve it, generation after generation."—Pearl S. Buck

It's a stretch of logic to think a young child's education can be put into a distinct category apart from play, chores and family time. Learning is constant. The child's wondrous progress from helpless newborn to a remarkably sophisticated five-year-old happens without explicit teaching. In fact, most of a child's learning is so continual that it goes unnoticed. Toddlers experiment like enthralled scientists. They rapidly develop a grasp of everyday physics. They master nuances of social interaction long before they can speak in sentences. Sometimes they are frustrated because their comprehension expands much more quickly than their growing vocabulary. Often, children seem to ignore what they aren't ready to learn, only to return to the same skill or concept later with ease. What they do is intrinsically tied to why they do it, making the learning process purposeful. Young children tend to be playful and very curious. They are confidently in charge of their own instruction. They require little fanfare for their achievements, as mastery gives them more than enough satisfaction.

Then we start educating them. With great optimism, we set learning aside from ordinary life. We talk about the fun they'll have in school. In an effort to motivate them, we explain they need to apply themselves and that their job now is to learn, just as adults have to go to work. Some children seem to adjust well to a conventional education; others do not. But school irrevocably alters the natural process of learning for every single child.

The very structure of school makes the child a passive recipient of education designed by others. No longer is he or she permitted to charge ahead fueled by curiosity. There are rules about following the curriculum and doing assignments exactly as expected. Very quickly the child discovers that despite what he or she wants to contribute, value is given to what can be evaluated. The most passionate and caring teachers still have to work within the system. There is precious little time to humor a girl's urge to observe a bird outside the window, to listen to a boy's idea for a story, or to let children experiment.

The subject matter in school, even when taught well, isn't necessarily what the child is ready to learn. The way it is presented tends to be indirect, inactive, removed from the fibers that connect it to everything else. It may cover material the child has no interest in, or be so remote from the child's life that it has no relevance. Schoolwork repeatedly emphasizes skill areas that are lacking, or goes over skills already mastered with stultifying repetition. The brain and body seek novelty when an experience is deadening, but a child's attempts to enliven the day by talking to a friend, tapping on the desk, or getting up too often are reframed as behavior problems. Even the child's natural inclination to seek collaboration is defined as cheating.

Schoolwork clearly separates what is deemed "educational" from the rest of the child's experience. This indicates to children that learning is odious and confined to specific areas of life. A divide appears where before there was a seamless whole. Absorption and play are on one side in opposition to work and learning on another. This sets the inherent joy and meaning in all these things adrift. The energy that formerly prompted a child to explore, ask questions, and eagerly leap ahead becomes a social liability. Often this transforms into cynicism or disobedience.

Other divides appear as well. School keeps the child from family and community for much of the waking day, segregating him or her with others of the same age. The models for behavior and maturity then orient toward the peer group. Even when it is not an overt aim, schools lean toward categorization. Every student quickly recognizes they are ranked by criteria such as high test scores and acquiescent behavior.

The result? When students are frustrated, when they are insufficiently challenged or pushed to achieve, they do learn, but not necessarily what they're being taught. What they learn is that the educational process is boring or makes them feel bad about themselves. They see that what they achieve and how they achieve it is relentlessly judged. They learn to quell independent thought and value-laden questions that normally bubble up in those growing whole selves. Gradually, children's natural moment-to-moment curiosity is distorted until they resist learning anything but what they have to learn. The life force is drained from education.

Some children who don't fare well in these educational environments face powerful pharmacological interventions. Every day in the United States about 8 percent of elementary school-aged children take a medication prescribed for a mental health problem such as attention deficit disorder, depression or anxiety. This is a much higher rate of medication than is seen in most other countries. Entire classes of these drugs have not been tested on young people. The side effects can be dangerous. Medication may be warranted in serious cases, along with appropriate therapy and improvements in the child's diet and circumstances. Experience, however, shows that when children diagnosed with attention deficit disorder, anxiety or similar mental health issues are homeschooled, especially when their families carefully tailor the homeschool environment to the child, these problems often become less significant or disappear altogether. Clearly, changing the education milieu can work as well or better than medication.

As homeschoolers, we're not immune to the school mindset that prescribes conformity to certain standards. Or, for that matter, to a homeschooling mindset that prescribes conformity to other sets of standards. Many homeschooling parents know the struggle to find a homeschooling style appropriate for our children. We try to keep our spirits up while doubting ourselves or questioning our children's abilities. Formerly schooled students ourselves, some of us find it difficult to think of education in wider terms. Many times we resort to educational products promoted as "fun" although they provide little more than added glitz to material that is rote and lifeless.

Although there are many homeschool educational programs, experience shows that parents don't strictly adhere to such materials. Some parents combine learning products based on what works for their children. Many other homeschooling families don't rely on prepackaged curricula at all. Overall, most tend to combine educational materials along with real life experiences, independent projects and other activities to meet the needs of their children.

Manuals for those who homeschool in a school-like style advise us to deprive our children of what they like to do until they've met the standards we set for them. Do the work, get the grade, pass the test. Some children live up to such expectations. But other children struggle to finish their lessons, never spending much time on what best stimulates learning. Their interests.

Although homeschool curricula packages do sell, some of these products do more to stymie the learning process than invigorate it. Rote education actually interferes with true learning whether in school or at home. How?

- The child's natural inclination to explore and experiment is steered instead toward completing assignments. Gradually the child's need for full sensory learning is supplanted by less meaningful ways of gathering information.

- Children recognize that coming up with the correct answer leaves little room for trial and error. Thinking too carefully or deeply may result in the wrong answer. The right answer from the child's personal perspective may actually be the opposite of the correct answer, but to get a good mark the child cannot be true to his or her experience. The grade becomes more important than reality. No curriculum is perfectly accurate nor able to reflect a child's life.

- The emphasis on the correct answer squeezes out unconventional thinking. The fear of making mistakes squelches creativity and innovation. After years of being taught to avoid making mistakes, the child has also learned to steer clear of originality.

- The desire to produce meaningful work, the longing to make contributions of value, the need to belong, and other complex interpersonal factors are diminished in importance by the child's overriding obligation to complete assignments.

- Children who must hurry to finish assignments or change subjects before making any real sense of them, exactly the type of education that has long been in vogue, have no way of fully comprehending what they are expected to learn. The information is stuffed into their short-term memories in order to get good grades and pass tests, but they aren't provided with a means of relating the material to something they already understand. They aren't learning to use the information for real life activities or, worse, generating any real wisdom from it. The very essence of learning is thereby ignored.

If children spend their formative years in a back-to-basics environment that has left them little time to foster their own talents or preserve their innate curiosity, they may seem ready for success. But they are not well prepared to face a rapidly changing world. Young people raised to focus on conventional standards of academic overachievement, whether in school or in an overly rigid school-like home situation, are receiving the sort of education that works against the unique gifts they bring to the future.

In *Windows on the Future: Education in the Age of Technology*, authors Ian Jukes and Ted D. E. McCain quote former Secretary of Education, Richard Riley, as saying the top jobs that will be available in the next few years did not even exist ten years ago. Riley says that such careers will necessitate the use of cutting-edge technology to confront the newest issues. Jukes and McCain write,

> We are entering an era that increasingly will demand just-in-time learning. This contrasts dramatically with the just-in-case model currently used in most schools—just-in-case it's on the test, just-in-case we might need to use it on the job, just-in-case it might be important. This is because the amount of information coming at us grows almost as quickly as the new technologies. By the time children who are now in kindergarten graduate from 12th grade, a conservative estimate is that information will have doubled itself seven times, and technological power will have doubled itself nearly nine times, producing 256 times more power. Students will still need to learn things, but there will be much less emphasis on the amount of material memorized and much more emphasis on making connections, thinking through issues, and solving problems.

Overemphasis on left-brain analytical thinking at the expense of right-brain ability may be a prescription for failure, according to Daniel H.

Pink in *A Whole New Mind: Why Right-Brainers Will Rule the Future.* He notes that studies attempting to link IQ with career success find that it accounts for only between 4 and 10 percent. Pink explains that capabilities such as creativity, humor, intuition, empathy and social dexterity are increasingly necessary in the professional world. He says, "We are moving from an economy and a society built on the logical, linear, computerlike capabilities of the Information Age to an economy and a society built on the inventive, empathic, big-picture capabilities of what's rising in its place, the Conceptual Age."

> Confronting today's serious issues in medicine, business, ecology, justice, transportation and dozens of other areas requires a broader concept of what it means to be educated. The long era of the educated *knowing* more than the uneducated is over. In an age of digital information, this is more a matter of access. When education is weighted toward measurable outcomes, the meaning of learning is diminished. True education has more to do with nurturing critical thinking, innovation and lifelong openness to learning.

Business advisor John Kao says that classrooms have churned out students who are not up to the challenges of a global economy, leaving the U.S. farther behind in a rapidly changing and ever-flattening world. In *Innovation Nation: How America Is Losing Its Innovation Edge, Why It Matters and What We Can Do to Get It Back,* Kao observes that the educational system is highly resistant to change. When improvements take place they do so at a "frustratingly glacial pace." His prescriptions for change include highlighting creative diversity and structuring education "around learners and learning processes rather than around the bureaucratic convenience of a model of scheduling still optimized more for agricultural production than for the information age."

Our homeschooling lives already offer that solution.

> One periodical, *The Journal of College Admission,* reports that homeschooled students are not only well prepared for college, they also have developed distinctive qualities. Joyce Reed, associate dean of Brown University, comments, "They've learned to be self-directed, they take risks, they face challenges with total fervor, and they don't back off." The article also noted that Stanford University admission officers are impressed by the high incidence of a trait they call "intellectual vitality" among homeschooled students and link it to the prevalence of self-teaching.

J. Gary Knowles, a University of Toronto professor, has been researching home education for twenty-seven years. He and his wife chose to homeschool their own children as well. Knowles finds that homeschoolers bring certain broad advantages to adulthood. Their backgrounds foster autonomy, resourcefulness and independence. They tend to be highly motivated and are less susceptible to peer pressure. He says that home-educated people are less likely to work for institutions, many choosing self-employment.

But Knowles points out that a complex interplay of factors must be taken into account. "Some homeschooled children have very narrow views of the world. That all goes back to the fundamental philosophy that guided their learning and worldview," he says. "I think it's the tone of the home, the openness to surprise and to the rest of the world that will be reflected in the young people."

Knowles stresses the importance of embracing the community and culture around the child. Too often he's seen curricula written thousands of miles away being used even though it makes no sense to that family.

After years of teaching, researching and homeschooling, Knowles has a clear perspective on what provides the best outcome for children. "For me, the more unstructured, the more open and collaborative programs that parents facilitate are more appropriate," he says. "The programs that honor experiential learning or self-directed learning are always preferential to top down methods no matter who is at the top. I'm very much of the opinion that community based, exploratory, experiential [approaches] are best for kids."

Studies repeatedly show that homeschooled students rank well ahead of their schooled counterparts on standardized tests. That shouldn't matter. Such studies may have a political agenda or unreliable methodology. Of more importance, no grades or tests can possibly encompass the meaning enfolded in the learning experience. Our culture's heavy reliance on test scores is a trap—the exact trap contributing to the current crisis in education. Basing education on these measurements cheapens the richness of learning. In schools, this emphasis on grades and test scores leads to rebellious or depressed students, those who believe that school achievement determines self-worth or feel that school is meaningless, those who endanger themselves in order to assert their individuality, or those who will do anything to conform. Homeschoolers are not immune. Homeschooled children who are relentlessly pushed to achieve lose, too. There is no objective way to measure something as subjective, as deeply personal, as an individual child's learning. Regardless of the noise and money tossed at "standards" and "outcomes," it is obvious that these models only work in a limited way. The message given to young people? That who they are and what lights them from within doesn't matter quite as much as what their final test scores indicate.

In remarks to a Cato Institute Policy Forum, Alfie Kohn said, "Research has repeatedly classified kids on the basis of whether they tend to be deep or shallow thinkers, and, for elementary, middle, and high school students, a positive correlation has been found between shallow thinking and how well kids do on standardized tests. So an individual student's high test scores are not usually a good sign."

It's widely assumed that national test score rankings are vitally important indicators of a country's future. To improve those rankings, national core standards are imposed with more frequent assessments to determine student achievement (meaning more testing). But twisting education to improve test scores diminishes higher-level skills such as critical thinking, creativity, problem-solving, initiative and persistence.

Do test scores actually make a difference to a nation's future?

Results from international mathematics and science tests from a fifty-year period were compared to future economic competitiveness by those countries in a study by Christopher H. Tienken. Across all indicators he could find minimal evidence that students' high test scores produce value for their countries. He concluded that higher student test scores were unrelated to any factors consistently predictive of a developed country's growth and competitiveness.

In another such analysis, Keith Baker, a former researcher for the U.S. Department of Education, examined achievement studies across the world to see if they reflected the success of participating nations. Using numerous comparisons, including national wealth, degree of democracy, economic growth and even happiness, Baker found no association between test scores and the success of advanced countries. Merely average test scores were correlated with successful nations while top test scores were not. Baker says, "In short, the higher a nation's test score 40 years ago, the worse its economic performance ..." He goes on to speculate whether testing itself may be damaging to a nation's future.

Why then do adults push standardized tests if it has been shown that the results are counterproductive? Well, we've been told that this is the price children must pay in order to achieve success. This is profound evidence of societal shallow thinking, because the evidence doesn't stack up.

> The criteria for academic success isn't a direct line to lifetime success. Studies show that grades and test scores do not necessarily correlate to later accomplishments in such areas as social leadership, the arts, or the sciences. Grades and tests only do a good job at predicting how well youth will do in subsequent academic grades and tests. They are not good predictors of success in real-life problem solving or career advancement.

A survey of the research related to the link between grades and accomplishment—appropriately titled "Do grades and tests predict adult accomplishment?"—was conducted back in 1985. The conclusion? No.

Since that time, the emphasis on quantifying education has increased. This makes no practical sense. In your town, what are the chances that the business owner down the street, the police chief, or any enlivened person you know happened to ace standardized tests back in school? In fact, some Nobel Prize winners were not high achievers in school. William Faulkner was described as an indifferent student. He dropped out of high school at the age of fifteen. That didn't stop him from later winning the 1950 Nobel Prize in Literature. Joseph Brodsky also left school at the age of fifteen. In 1987 he won the Nobel Prize for Literature, and in 1991 he became Poet Laureate of the United States. Peter Agre dropped out of high school in his senior year. His final grade in chemistry was a D. He went on to win the 2003 Nobel Prize in Chemistry.

While these top achievers are mentioned for comparison's sake, what most parents want for their own children is simple. Happiness. A major contributor to happiness is healthy relationships. Yet one of the most common objections to homeschooling is that children will be insufficiently socialized. This may be due to the term "homeschooling," which implies that children somehow remain cloistered at home, separated from interaction with anyone other than their own families. There is no basis in fact for these concerns.

> Homeschooled children have more opportunity to regularly and actively socialize with many different people in their communities. Research backs that up, also indicating that homeschoolers engage in more extracurricular activities than their schooled counterparts. In fact, studies show homeschoolers ahead in socialization skills. This may be due to a number of factors, including more one-on-one time with adults and a wider range of role models than is found in the peer culture typified by school.

One study tested homeschooled as well as schooled children using the Vineland Adaptive Behavior Scales, a measure of social development. On this test, the homeschooled children scored higher in socialization, communication, daily living skills and maturity. Overall, the mean score of the schooled children stood at the 23rd percentile. In contrast, the mean score for the homeschooled children stood at the 84th percentile.

Another study compared 140 children matched in age, socioeconomic status, gender, race and frequency of extracurricular activities. Half had been entirely homeschooled, the other attended school. Each child was rated on a checklist of ninety-seven behaviors by observers who did not know who among the children were homeschooled. The Direct Observation Form of the Child Behavior Checklist includes problems such as shows off, isolates self from others, disturbs other children, argues, brags or boasts, shy or timid, doesn't pay attention. When the results were tallied, it was found that the mean problem behavior score for schooled children was more than eight times higher than that of homeschooled children. Lead researcher Larry Edward wrote that the schoolchildren were "aggressive, loud and competitive," while, in contrast, the homeschooled children sought common interests, cooperated, and invited others to play.

That doesn't mean homeschooled children never tease, bully or fight. But the conditions surrounding them may be less conducive to those behaviors.

I don't fault schools necessarily. The kids get pent up sitting in a classroom, then watch out at recess. They learn by example. If the example of how to act and reason is 25 other kids versus one teacher, then teasing and coercion are likely to rule. One difference for homeschoolers is the ratio. When we get together, my son has peers of all ages. The small ones look to the older ones, choosing more mature behavior. Parents are right there if someone needs a better way to get along. Most of the time that means a few carefully chosen words.

A few weeks ago at a skate day, a new family joined our group. Their little girl couldn't stop pointing out a boy whose hair was in braids. Another mother said cheerfully to her how great it is that everyone is different and asked her if she would like her own hair braided. Something that could have turned into a negative judgment was transformed.

—E. Williams, New Jersey

My son always looks forward to Fridays because that's park day. The number of homeschooled kids there on any given week varies from thirty-five to sixty. They have a blast ... The older kids organize their own games. They're pretty good about including everyone who can play ...

Everyone gets along really well. We've had some disruptive kids over the years but we (parents) have learned to handle that as a group. We tell the kids to intervene on behalf of one another. If they see another kid being ordered around or teased, they should object. We have decided that this is more helpful than having a parent rush in to fix problems. It's like peer pressure to be civil to one another. Most of the time it works great. The kids are very accepting of each other's differences too.

—Mandy, Iowa

I homeschool my seven-year-old son. He was born with spina bifida. Homeschooling has been such a wonderful experience for us. There are definitely those days that are more challenging than others, but it has given me the opportunity to take care of my son's special needs at home, which gives me such a peace of mind. It is also amazing to me how incredibly accepting homeschool children are of my son's differences. He wears braces on his legs to help him walk. Never once has a homeschooler questioned him about it. He has made such great friends in the homeschool community. —Angie, Alabama

It may be impossible to sort out exactly what factors benefit homeschoolers. We do know that whatever the homeschooling style, our children have more freedom to explore their own interests and to enjoy close relationships with family and friends simply because they have more time available to them. No lesson provides the sort of enrichment found in hiking in the woods, no homework can improve on an evening playing board games and talking together. Our instincts tell us that children flourish when they are raised with loving guidance and celebrated for who they are.

As homeschoolers we watch our children grow into caring, capable adults without the strictures of formal education. We hearken back to what has worked throughout time even as we latch on to the latest great idea. In that way, learning informs the widest realm of our days together. And it seems that we're on to something. In *Magical Parent, Magical Child: The Art of Joyful Parenting,* Michael Mendizza and Joseph Chilton Pearce contend that up to 95 percent of learning occurs through the natural processes of observing, playing, and participating in ordinary activities. The authors state, "Only 5 percent of what we learn, lifelong, is acquired through formal instruction, training, or schooling. Of the 5 percent of information we learn through instruction, only 3 to 5 percent is remembered for any length of time. State-specific learning, what we refer to as 'primary learning,' is remembered for a lifetime." In other words, all the structured efforts to enforce learning with school-like activity do not have the same beneficial effect as the inborn mechanisms that have made us a successful species. In fact, natural learning is compromised by these efforts.

We need to pay attention to what has always worked well for our species. That means giving children time to play, allowing them to model the behavior of elders, providing learning that is purposeful to them, and weaving their growing talents into the lives of family and community.

Innate Gifts

"You always carry within yourself the very thing that you need for the fulfillment of your life purpose."
—Malidoma Somé

Parents come to know their children as highly distinct individuals soon after birth. In part, that's because babies arrive with unknown traits and talents waiting in a raw state of potential. Each young person's drive to explore his or her possibilities is inborn. Sometimes this leads them in directions that don't meet with approval. What we often don't recognize is that these exact idiosyncrasies or problems may indicate the child's gifts.

As James Hillman explains in, *The Soul's Code: In Search of Character and Calling,*

> I want us to envision that what children go through has to do with finding a place in the world for their specific calling. They are trying to live two lives at once, the one they were born with and the one of the place and among the people they were born into. The entire image of a destiny is packed into a tiny acorn, the seed of a huge oak on small shoulders. And its call rings loud and persistent and is as demanding as any scolding voice from the surroundings. The call shows in the tantrums and obstinacies, in the shyness and retreats, that seem to set the child against our world but that may be protections of the world it comes with and comes from.

It can be difficult to recognize these gifts. Sometimes they unfold in mysterious ways. Oftentimes we can't see the whole picture until long after the child has grown into adulthood. Sometimes we can't see our own gifts either, even though they have whispered to us of destiny or wounded us where they were denied.

A little girl creates chaos with her toys. This child won't put blocks away with other blocks nor put socks in her dresser drawer. As a preschooler she creates groupings that go together with logic only she understands. One such collection is made up of red blocks, a striped sock, plastic spoons and marbles. She sings to herself while she rearranges these items over and over. The girl is punished when she refuses to put her puzzles away in the correct box or her tea set dishes back together. She continues making and playing with these strangely ordered sets but hides them out of sight to avoid getting in trouble until the phase passes when she is about nine years old. Now an adult, she is conducting post-doctoral studies relating to string theory. As she explains, her work as a physicist has to do with finding common equations among disparate natural forces.

A young boy's high energy frustrates his parents. As a preschooler he climbs on furniture and curtain rods, even repeatedly tries to scale the kitchen cabinets. When he becomes a preteen, he breaks his collarbone skateboarding. He is caught shoplifting at thirteen. His parents are frightened when he says he "only feels alive on the edge." Around the age of fifteen he becomes fascinated with rock-climbing. Reluctantly his parents let him get involved. His fellow climbers, mostly in their twenties, also love the adrenaline rush that comes from adventure sports but help him gain perspective about his responsibility to himself and other climbers. His ability to focus on the cliff face boosts his confidence on the ground. At nineteen he is already certified as a mountain search and rescue volunteer. He is thinking of going to school to become an emergency medical technician.

Few young people have clear indications of their gifts. Most have multiple abilities. A single true calling is rarely anyone's lot in life, as it is for a legendary artist or inventor. Instead, a mix of ready potential waits, offering a life of balance among many options. Education emphasizing the child's particular strengths allows that child to flourish, no matter if those gifts fall within mainstream academic subjects or broader personal capacities. Traits such as a highly developed sense of justice, the knack for getting others to cooperate, a way with animals, a love of organization—these are of inestimable value, far more important skills than good grades on a spelling test.

A learning situation that nurtures each child's unique abilities must leave ample space for these gifts to unfold. This takes time and understanding. The alternative deprives not only the child, it also deprives our world of what that child might become. Acknowledging that each person is born with innate abilities ready to manifest doesn't imply that our children are destined for greatness in the popular sense of power or wealth. It means they are waiting to develop their own personal greatness. This unfolding is a lifelong process for each of us as we work toward our capabilities for fulfillment, joy, health, meaning, and that intangible sense of well-being that comes from using one's gifts.

A child's passions often reveal many of their natural gifts.
—Tamara Markwick, California

I believe that we are all gifted in some way, but the current definition is too narrow. My twins are basically ordinary boys who like hockey and bike rides to the ice cream store. But in my love for

them I also see talents developing that might not be noticed by someone who didn't know them as well. Aaron has been struggling with some aggressive kids on the hockey team. A few times he acted like them. He was penalized on the ice and had to deal with his parents after the game. As a result he's been thinking through his own beliefs about fair play and honesty while learning to be true to himself. This has been a good learning experience for him. I see that he is very interested in issues of right versus might, whether in current politics or in movie plots. His struggle with fair play has led to interests in policing, legislation and rights. We signed him up for a weeklong camp this coming summer that explores law and public service. Aaron is really interested in going.

His brother Alex is totally different. He's laid back and plays hockey only for fun. Everyone thinks that he's a goofball. And it's true that he's fun to be around. He's also one of those kids who worries about pollution and climate change. He doesn't even want us to fly for vacation this year because it's bad for the ozone, and there aren't too many teens who would cut into their own fun out of concern for something like that.
—Enid, Canada

Left to their own devices, children act quite a bit like geniuses. What are traits associated with geniuses?
- They don't learn in a straight line.
- They are highly individual.
- They may not be all that interested in what others think of them and don't necessarily apply common sense to their pursuits.
- When their concentration is interrupted, they may react with frustration.

Notice that these traits are more common in the youngest children, before we "teach" them.

Although society confuses genius with IQ scores, such scores don't determine what an individual will do with his or her intelligence. In fact, studies have shown that specific personality traits are better predictors of success than IQ scores. Genius has more to do with *using* one's gifts. In Roman mythology, each man was seen as having a genius within (and each woman its corollary, a juno) which functioned like a guardian of intellectual powers or ancestral talent. What today's innovators bring to any discipline, whether history or art or technology, is a sort of persistent childlike wonder. They are able to see with fresh eyes. They can't be dissuaded from what they want to do, and often what they do is highly original. Sometimes these people have a difficult personal journey before using their gifts, either because of their strong ethics or low tolerance for frustration. Their paths are not easy or risk-free, but the lessons learned from making mistakes can lead to new strengths.

A brief look at two innovators provides inspiration for those of us raising today's children.

Unable to engage in strenuous play, a sickly French child named Jacques-Yves Cousteau developed an interest in photography. Cousteau was a mediocre student who was expelled from high school after throwing rocks through the school windows. He was sent to a military boarding school and later entered the Navy. His lifelong fascination with the sea led him to develop the Aqua Lung, a revolutionary method for breathing underwater. Cousteau's films of sea life became documentaries seen around the world. This former hunter's efforts stopped pet food companies from using dolphin meat and helped foster the early environmental movement.

R. Buckminster Fuller's early years were marked with struggle. As a college student he hired an entire dance troupe to entertain a party, and in that one night of excess he squandered the tuition money his family saved to send him to school. In his twenties he was a mechanic, meat-packer and Navy commander before starting a business that left him bankrupt. After his daughter died of polio, he began drinking heavily. Contemplating suicide, Fuller decided instead to live his life as an experiment to find out how one penniless individual could benefit humanity. He called himself Guinea Pig B. Without credentials or training, Fuller worked as an engineer and architect inventing such designs as the geodesic dome and advancing the concept of sustainable development. He wrote more than thirty books. Fuller once said, "Everybody is born a genius. Society de-geniuses them."

We don't intentionally deprive anyone of manifesting his or her gifts. Yet somehow many people end up long after formal schooling has ended without using or even understanding what their gifts might be. Surely there are many reasons why this is so. One reason may be a limited understanding of equality. It's a given that we deserve equal rights. But the concept of equality is educationally misapplied, muffling many students' abilities and strengths in a misguided effort to build up areas that have been determined to be "weaknesses." Children are expected to attain certain measurable outcomes in all subject areas at each grade. This negates the uneven and distinctly individual ways in which children develop. It also stratifies them by ability and willingness to conform, inevitably impacting their personalities. No matter whether at school or at home, if children are held accountable to this limiting version of uniform achievement, they will judge themselves harshly. No one is an intellectual jack-of-all-trades in each subject at every age. This expectation can cause a once trusting child to hide the true self within because his or her emerging potential doesn't conform to the sameness these standards impose. All that focus on left-brain outcome-based standards can squelch a child's unique form of expression. Even children who love the subject being taught may find their interest dimmed. As Henry David Thoreau said, "What does education often do? It makes a straight-cut ditch of a free, meandering brook."

In the quest to educate equally, we have simplified who students are. They are not empty fields to be planted and sowed with seeds of knowledge. They are living ecosystems unto themselves. Some savannahs, some deserts, some woodlands, some oceans. All with unique capacities, needing a unique balance of nurturance and guidance to flourish. We are equal, yes. But nature teaches us that diversity works. Imagine a world in which each child's gifts were allowed to manifest in their own time. One in which we taught mutual respect while celebrating differences. One where we let our children awaken fully to their potential in body, mind and spirit. In this world, the highest expressions of equality could flourish.

Surely this is the first and foremost job of education: Awareness of the majesty of creation, the beauty of nature and the ever unfolding wonders of the self.
—Urmila, India

CHAPTER TWO

Nurturing the Learner

Trust

"We have a cultural notion that if children were not engineered, if we did not manipulate them, they would grow up as beasts in the field. This is the wildest fallacy in the world." —Joseph Chilton Pearce

A key factor in homeschooling is trust. Children have the innate ability to learn and an inborn sense of how they learn best. It is difficult for adults to accept this concept. It is liberating to recognize it and live it.

When we first started homeschooling, I did not believe that a child could possibly learn without my or my husband's help. I learned very quickly that nothing could be further from the truth. When given the right environment and resources, children love to learn and will learn with or without you.

The greatest lesson that I have learned is that it is not a tragedy for one child to be a little behind in math and a little ahead in reading than her peers. The difference is that she is being allowed to take the time to learn each lesson in its entirety rather than being forced to move on to the next lesson before she is ready. I have one child who reads very well and one who struggles. They both have weaknesses and strengths in other areas. When observing their public schooling friends and family, I have noticed that these same strengths and weaknesses are present … The best part about homeschooling is that there is no failure.

—Laurel Santiago, Texas

Homeschooling books, magazines and blogs often have accounts of children who do not read or perform math calculations at the same ages that they are expected to master these tasks in school. According to mainstream educational thinking, this is an emergency. Sometimes homeschooling parents agree. They enforce tougher standards or try one approach after another with increasing desperation. But this is an emergency only to a school-oriented mindset. In school, the longer a child goes without achieving the norm, the more poor grades and negative reinforcement he or she gets. The subject itself becomes an exercise in misery and futility. Then the chances of success are even more limited. Many students go on to suffer math anxiety or serious reading problems as a result.

It's different for homeschoolers. Parents provide an enriching environment that stimulates learning without pushing a child before he's ready. In many countries around the world it is recognized that the brain simply does not mature sufficiently for abstract concepts until the child is older. When homeschooling, there is no need for pressure or negative reinforcement. Failure doesn't belong on this horizon. Math, reading and other topics can be folded into activities of the day and learned with gradual ease.

Many homeschoolers try instructional methods with differing degrees of success, gradually discovering on their own that children learn easily once they are ready. Some children are ready much earlier than the "norm," while others do best when they are older. Pushing reading or writing too early results in no greater achievement than waiting a few months or years until the child eagerly absorbs the necessary skills, often as a side result of an engaging project. Eventually most homeschooling parents recognize that their children are intrinsically able to learn. They realize that adults function best to aid, not mandate, this process. Force, intimidation and coercion in the name of education sullies the honorable work entrusted to us.

These same homeschooling books, magazines and blogs describe children who do not read, write or calculate until much later than their schooled peers, some not until they are ten or twelve years old. These children learn reading or math in their own way, for their own reasons. In a matter of months they pass where they "should" have been if they'd started years before. And they love what they are doing.

A pioneering educator proved back in 1929 that delaying formal instruction, in this case of mathematics, benefits children in wonderfully unexpected ways. Louis P. Benezet, superintendent of the Manchester, New Hampshire, schools, advocated the postponement of systematic instruction in math until after sixth grade. Benezet wrote, "I feel that it is all nonsense to take eight years to get children thru the ordinary arithmetic assignment of the elementary schools. What possible needs has a ten-year-old child for knowledge of long division? The whole subject of arithmetic could be postponed until the seventh year of school, and it could be mastered in two years' study by any normal child."

While developing this rationale, Benezet spoke with eighth-grade students. He noted that they had difficulties putting their ideas into English and could not explain simple mathematical reasoning. This was not only in his district; he found the same results with fourteen-year-old students in Indiana and Wisconsin. Benezet didn't blame the children or teachers, he blamed introducing formal equations too early.

So Benezet tried an experiment of abandoning traditional arithmetic instruction below the seventh grade. To start, he picked out five classrooms, choosing those districts where most students were from immigrant homes and the parents spoke little English. Benezet knew that in other districts the parents with greater English skills and higher education would have vehemently objected, ending the experiment before it started. In the experimental classrooms, children were exposed to what we would call naturally occurring math. They learned how to tell time and keep track of the date on the calendar. The students played with toy money, took part in games using numbers, and when dimension terms such as "half" or "double" or "narrower" or "wider" came up incidentally, they were discussed. Instead of math, the emphasis was on language and composition. As Benezet describes these children, "They reported on books that they had read, on incidents which they had seen, on visits that they had made. They told the stories of movies that they had attended and they made up romances on the spur of the moment. It was refreshing to go into one of these rooms. A happy and joyous spirit pervaded them. The children were no longer under the restraint of learning multiplication tables or struggling with long division."

At the end of the first school year, Benezet reported that the contrast between the experimental and traditionally taught students was remarkable. When he visited classrooms to ask the children about what they were reading, he described the traditionally taught students as "hesitant, embarrassed and diffident. In one fourth grade I could not find a single child who would admit that he had committed the sin of reading." Students in the experimental classrooms were eager to talk about what they'd been reading. In those rooms, an hour's discussion went by with still more children eager to talk.

Benezet hung a reproduction of a well-known painting in the classrooms and asked children to write down anything the art inspired. Another obvious contrast appeared. When he showed the ten best papers from each room to the city's seventh-grade teachers, they noted that one set of papers showed much greater maturity and command of the language. They observed that the first set of papers had a total of 40 adjectives such as nice, pretty, blue, green and cold. The second set of papers had 128 adjectives, including magnificent, awe-inspiring, unique and majestic. When asked to guess which district the papers came from, each teacher assumed that the students who wrote the better papers were from schools where the parents spoke English in the home. In fact, it was the opposite.

Those students who wrote the most masterfully were from his experimental classes.

Yet another difference was apparent. It was something that Benezet had anticipated. He explained, "For some years I had noted that the effect of the early introduction of arithmetic had been to dull and almost chloroform the child's reasoning faculties." At the end of that first year, he went from classroom to classroom and asked children the same mathematical story problem. The traditionally taught students grabbed at numbers but came up with few correct results, while the experimental students reasoned out correct answers eagerly, despite having minimal exposure to formal math.

Based on these successes, the experiment expanded. By 1932, half of the third- to fifth-grade classes in the city operated under the experimental program. Due to pressure from some school principals, children were started on a math book in the second half of sixth grade. All sixth-grade children were tested. By spring of that year, all the classes tested equally. When the final tests were given at the end of the school year, one of the experimental groups led the city. In other words, those children exposed to traditional math curricula for part of the sixth-grade year had mastered the same skills as those who had spent years on drills, times tables and exams.

In 1936, the *Journal of the National Education Association* published the final article by Benezet. His results showed the clear benefits of replacing formal math instruction with naturally occurring math while putting a greater emphasis on reading, writing and reasoning. The Journal called on educators to consider similar changes. As we know, schools went in the opposite direction. However, homeschoolers can easily take this more natural course, aware that the concepts can be readily grasped in short order, just as Benezet proved.

I've come to trust the process ... that they WILL learn all they need to know. It might not look the same as their publicly schooled peers, but when the time is right, and the need is there, they will learn it. My husband and I have as one of our greatest goals that our children learn how to learn. That when they need the information they know how to go about getting it.

—Angie Beck, Kansas

Child development experts are aware that when adults are highly directive and exert control over a child's activities, they weaken the child's natural motivation. This changes the way the child learns.

In one study, three groups of children were given the same passage to read from a social studies book. The first group was informed they would be tested on the material for a grade. The second group was told they would be asked questions about the material. The third group was asked to read the passage to see what they thought of it. Afterwards, it was found that those who read for a test and grade had the poorest conceptual grasp of the material. Although the children weren't forewarned, two weeks later they were asked about the material again. Again it turned out that children under the pressure of being tested and graded had forgotten more information than those who read for pleasure or simply to respond to questions. This is common sense. When any of us is expected to learn for a specific measurable outcome like an exam or grade, we don't absorb the information as naturally, as eagerly, connecting it to other areas of interest or retaining it in long-term memory. We're left with a surface imprint of knowledge rather than the kind of understanding that sinks in and stays with us.

Pressuring a child to learn diminishes the meaning and importance of what is learned. In fact, research shows that the influence of rewards or evaluations undermines a whole range of endeavors, including creative writing, artistic expression, understanding literature, and grasping scientific concepts. One study looked at mothers writing a poem with a child. It was found that the more controlling the mother was during the task, the less able the child was to write creatively on his or her own. This is important for parents to remember. Guiding children is invaluable. Controlling and judging children hinders them in ways that we cannot readily see but which harm them nonetheless.

When my son was five I had it in my head that he should learn to read since that's when children in school learned to read. I bought a reading curriculum and sat down and tried to teach him to read. He immediately struggled with it. He would get more frustrated each time I would try to teach him to read. After a few lessons I said to myself, "What are you doing? Why does he have to learn to read now? He will eventually learn to read when he is ready. I just need to trust that. There is no way I am going to continue to try to force him to learn to read and cause him to have negative feelings about reading."

I put that reading program away and never mentioned it again. Over the next year I became more comfortable as I trusted that he would read when he was ready ... I used that lesson to trust as the base for all future learning.

—Tamara Markwick, California

Homeschooling has been a tremendous blessing, but it certainly hasn't come without many struggles and discoveries. I discovered that my youngest daughter has ADHD after a year of struggling with traditional "book" teaching. I also discovered that she has dyslexia ... I found that although I need total and complete structure by utilizing schedules and books, that she needed something different. I discovered that if I read her material to her she succeeds, but as long as our routine called for her to sit and read it herself, she suffers. I discovered that my oldest daughter is very independent, and that she has to read her material herself in order to comprehend and understand it. The fact that she is so independent gives me freedom to spend more time with her sister. It took several years of trial and error to find the right curriculum for both of my girls' learning styles, but trial and error worked. I have witnessed trust grow with leaps and bounds not only in myself, but in my girls.

We finally have it figured out, and it's wonderful. I wouldn't trade this chance to teach and learn with my girls for anything in the world ... My husband and I feel extremely blessed that God has granted us the resources, wisdom, and desire to teach our children.

—Joane, South Carolina

There is no exact prescription for raising a child. Each child, each situation is different. We provide them with shelter and nurturance, and with our loving guidance we help them discover the confounding, glorious clamor that is the world beyond. What our children make of their lives is ultimately their own doing.

As we begin to trust that our children are learning, we start to relax. This process takes time, sometimes years, because most of us who are parenting homeschooled children were not homeschooled ourselves. We have a mindset about what defines education based on our own background, even if we fully intend to change those experiences for our children. Most of us need evidence of achievement to help us recognize that our children are learning, especially at first. Gradually we recognize the strengths our children are developing. We acknowledge the uniquely purposeful way they are maturing as they explore, argue, question, play and participate in the world around them. And parental intuition is at work as well, letting us know on a gut level that our children are not only okay, they are thriving.

As we truly relax in our homeschooling lives, something nearly magical starts to happen. We not only demonstrate trust to our children, we feel it. We are more centered. We are better able to be joyful and present to each other without the constant pressure to meet school-like expectations. That makes all the difference. Through these eyes of trust we are more readily able to see, really see, how much learning is taking place.

The image of how I wanted to homeschool has changed greatly from "doing school at home" to a more fluid form of family learning.

Early on, I noticed that my son did not like to be told what to learn ... I was proud of him for being different but it also confirmed a growing conviction that traditional schooling, even "traditional" homeschooling, was not our path ...

I've realized all of the family's interests are equally valid to explore, whether his, his sister's, his father's, or mine. Mine! Unschooling freed me to write a list of all the subjects I wished I'd studied and now hope to tackle. I thought this was about educating my kids but now I see that "interest-led learning" describes how we approach life. —Karen, Texas

Trust goes the other way as well. We raise our children with confidence that learning will unfold. In doing so, we not only empower this natural process, our words and actions also teach our children to trust themselves. This is a continuum that begins at birth. When a parent is consistently responsive to a baby's cries, the infant forms a sense of security. Psychologist John Bowlby developed the now widely accepted attachment theory based on work done over several decades. Bowlby and others, including Mary Ainsworth, focused on the mother-child relationship. According to their research, when a mother delays in responding to an infant's cries and shows less sensitivity to her child's temperament, in subsequent months the baby becomes more demanding, insecure and clingy. However, when the mother is tender in her interactions and does not let crying go unheeded, in the following months her securely attached baby cries less, explores more confidently, and begins to engage in other forms of communication such as gesturing and vocalizing. Mary Ainsworth wrote, "An infant whose mother's responsiveness helps him to achieve his ends develops confidence in his own ability to control what happens to him."

Infancy is the first pivotal stage of development identified by psychiatrist Erik Erikson. Trust versus mistrust is life's initial challenge, faced from birth to eighteen months. In Erikson's view, a baby held and soothed develops secure attachment and the lifelong asset of hope. As infants grow into toddlers and children, parents' behavior toward them continues to demonstrate trust or lack of trust. This stems in part from parenting styles. The concept of trust does not simply mean trusting the child, it implies that the parent is able to recognize that each child is on a unique path of learning.

Too often we are not aware of the way our day-to-day behavior might influence a child. Studies overwhelmingly show that children who are raised with warm and consistent parenting practices are most likely to mature into capable and motivated young people. Starting in the 1960s, developmental psychologist Diana Baumrind observed interactions between parents and children using three categories to describe parental behaviors. Years later she followed up to determine the results of different parenting approaches. Other longitudinal studies have reinforced her conclusions.

Authoritarian parents put a high value on a child's unquestioning obedience to the parent's absolute standards and dictates. The parent does not encourage discussion of these rules. The child's choices are restricted. His behavior is judged and punishments are punitive. The outcome? Children raised by authoritarian parents may do as they are told but they have less social competence. They are followers rather than leaders and let others make decisions for them. They don't handle frustration well; in particular, the girls are prone to passivity and boys to hostility.

Permissive parents put a high value on a child's autonomy. The parent has few rules and attempts to use reasoning to elicit the child's compliance, yet rarely enforces control over the child's behavior. The parent is warm but lax. The child has minimal responsibility. Children of permissive parents have little ability to persist when they face challenging tasks, making them less likely to achieve their potential. They tend to be selfish and react defiantly when they don't get their way. They are more likely to be antisocial.

Authoritative parents represent a middle ground between these two extremes. They value the child's autonomy but they use their authority to elicit compliance with a balanced, rational approach. These parents welcome dialogue, explain the reasons behind rules, but maintain the rules. They are positive and warm. As a result, their children are confident, emotionally stable and optimistic. The children are also socially mature.

Ongoing research continues to affirm that these parenting approaches have the same effect as children grow toward adulthood. One study looked at teens of different ethnic backgrounds using measures that ranged from self-reliance and academic competence to substance abuse and delinquency. The authors concluded that aloof parenting with lax discipline was "universally harmful to adolescents." On the other hand, responsive parents who maintained firm expectations were found to be helpful well into adolescence.

What do these parenting styles look like in action? Mothers reacted differently as their one-year-olds played with a new toy in a study. Some mothers actively instructed the toddler in what she perceived as its proper use. They intruded on the child's exploration, corrected and criticized, sometimes without regard to the child's frustration level. These mothers were considered "controlling," similar to authoritarian. Other mothers acted as a resource for the child, encouraging and helping only if the child solicited assistance. These mothers were termed "autonomy supportive," similar to authoritative. When these same toddlers were then given an absorbing challenge to tackle alone, children raised by controlling mothers were easily frustrated and tended to give up. The youngsters of autonomy supportive mothers behaved very differently. Already they showed high motivation to persist and accomplish challenges.

This study lets us see the relationship between parenting styles and learning behavior. Relaxed and supportive mothers gauged their responsiveness to the child's reactions, and as a result the child was secure enough to persist in learning. Controlling mothers halted the natural process of discovery, teaching the child to ignore personal observations and look to others for answers.

I have learned that forcing a child to learn something will never work. If it is worth learning it, they will. When they want to learn something they will do it to the fullest and develop strong interests. Children are different and should not be forced to fit into the same molds. Life is what we make of it, not what we make others do. I feel my job as a parent is to protect my children and see that they have the necessary tools they need to develop their own interests.
—Jessie Mato Toyela, Florida

Living our trust as more than a concept can have a lasting effect. Demonstrating our trust in our children sends them a potent message. As Albert Einstein said, "I think the most important question facing humanity is, 'Is the universe a friendly place?' This is the first and most basic question all people must answer for themselves."

Our children, confident and empowered to learn, are our own resounding answer to that question as we send them toward the future. How did Einstein go on to answer that question?

For if we decide that the universe is an unfriendly place, then we will use our technology, our scientific discoveries and our natural resources to achieve safety and power by creating bigger walls to keep out the unfriendliness and bigger weapons to destroy all that which is unfriendly and I believe we are getting to a place where technology is powerful enough that we may either

In *Raising Self-Reliant Children in a Self-Indulgent World,* H. Stephen Glenn and Jane Nelsen contrast parenting behaviors. Some behaviors build trust and self-reliance, while others are unintentional barriers to trust and self-reliance.

The barriers?

- Making limiting assumptions about children, often for our own expediency. Such attitudes imply, according to Glenn and Nelsen, "What you were yesterday is all I will allow you to be today."
- Stepping in to rescue them or explain things instead of allowing them to wonder, figure things out and come up with their own solutions. When a child has difficulty, parents assume they should help or provide answers, but the consequence is often a child who needs more help next time.
- Directing and controlling, sometimes down to every detail, rather than inviting participation, ideas and cooperation. At any age, the desire for independent action is strong. When children are overly directed, chances are they will react with frustration, resistance or aggression.
- Imposing unrealistic standards instead of encouraging capabilities. When standards are well beyond the child's ability, it can make her feel unaccepted or inadequate.
- Expecting a child to understand an adult's perspective while forgetting what it feels like to be a child.

The builders?

- Checking. Instead of assuming, ask to find out what is needed for the situation at hand. Rather than assuming a child will forget a coat and hat and directing him to take those things, check in with him by asking what he'll need or what weather he'll be facing during the day. If he chooses to skip a hat and later regrets his decision, chances are he will remember it next time. Instead of reacting to a perceived error, ask, "How do you think we can handle this?"to initiate dialogue.
- Exploring. Allow children to deal with experiences directly. Encourage them to reflect on the experience. Don't lead them toward any particular answer, but demonstrate your belief in their resourcefulness and problem-solving abilities.
- Encouraging/Inviting. Children are responsive to the needs of others when their cooperation is solicited and their input is seen as an asset.
- Celebrating. Recognize small achievements, show appreciation, and remain positive about incremental success rather than pointing out negatives. This helps to build optimistic children.
- Respect. When we show respect for a child's perceptions, experiences, ideas and the growing knowledge gained through mistakes and problem solving, we demonstrate our belief in the unique value of all individuals.

completely isolate or destroy ourselves as well in this process ...

But if we decide that the universe is a friendly place, then we will use our technology, our scientific discoveries and our natural resources to create tools and models for understanding that universe. Because power and safety will come through understanding its workings and its motives.

The Nature of Interests

"You cannot teach a man anything; you can only help him find it within himself."—Galileo Galilei

It remains a mystery exactly how interests develop. But it is certain that they set us aglow. They kindle enthusiasm like tinder catching flame. When pursuing their interests, children know for sure that the world offers adventures perfectly suited to them.

My five-year-old son has been very interested in frogs for two years or more. I don't know whether this started with Kenneth Grahame's Wind in the Willows or the other way around, but basically, frogs and amphibians have taken over our lives! Following this passion we have taken all sorts of books out of the library on frogs, beginning in the children's section with storybooks and picture books on frogs (which has allowed us to access the alphabet and numbers)[and proceeding] to heavy tomes on amphibians and reptiles from the natural history section. Finding this section of the library on his own, my son discovered other books of interest in the natural world … We now know the names of literally hundreds of types of frogs and where they come from, how to identify a poison frog and why we mustn't touch a frog. We know that frogs only eat live prey and will eat anything that will fit in their mouths. We've discovered that even spiders will eat a frog, if they can catch one! We have been frog hunting at night and in the daytime. We are currently learning to identify different Australian frog calls.

… There is talk around the table of making a purpose-built pond in our garden; what is required, how much it will cost, what plants we need and where we can get tadpoles from to inhabit the pond. This takes us into discussion on the need to keep fish in the pond to reduce the mosquito population and how we can care for the fish.

The main character in Wind in the Willows being a toad, my son was rather keen on cane toads for some time, only to be rebuffed by everyone he mentioned it to. We have since looked at the problem the cane toad poses in Australia and why it is not a welcome amphibian in this country. We have also looked at its country of origin and seen that it is not a pest there. This has led to discussions on why we shouldn't move animals from one place to another …

Following the literary trail; we have been discussing all winter the need to go on a Ratty and Mole's picnic (Chapter 1) and recently did this to celebrate Father's Day. We know a good place at the local botanic gardens where frogs abound and this is where we set up camp for the day. All the ingredients for the picnic had to be those mentioned in the book (with great sadness that we couldn't source any "cold tongue"). There were many forays to find frogs, tadpoles and spawn and much conversation about whether water rats are found in Australia and why you could only find moles in other continents. It has been a great opportunity to try new foods (pickled gherkins and potted meat-pate).

We've discussed the seasons in the Northern Hemisphere, particularly England, where the story is set, and how they differ from the Australian seasons. This passion shows no sign of abating and we are riding the wave with great pleasure! —Kendal, Australia

---

Rewards, bribes and grades can't provide the sort of motivation that children find in their own increasing competence. There is intrinsic satisfaction to be found in achievement when it results from meaningful efforts. What provides that meaning varies from person to person and can change over time. It may be a desire for independence, or the longing to strengthen relationships. It may be competition or cooperation. Whatever elements work best, the child who follows the stimulus of his or her own interests is likely to meet with success. And we know that success tends to breed more success.

In the late 1970s, educational researcher Benjamin Bloom wearied of the emphasis on testing to assess a student and predict future school grades. He was sure that the environment could bring out each child's talent and ability and he wanted to determine how innate potential was best nurtured. This resulted in a study called The Development of Talent Research Project. One hundred and twenty adults were identified as highly successful in fields such as mathematics, sports, neurology, art and music. Interviews were conducted with these adults, as well as with those significant to them—teachers, family and others—to determine what factors led to their achievements. What Bloom found in nearly every circumstance was that, as children, these successful people had been encouraged by their families to follow their own interests. The adults in their lives believed time invested in interests was time well spent. These children were not steered toward specific careers but toward a strong achievement ethic. As a result of this research, Bloom emphasized learning for mastery.

This makes sense. We recognize that children gain immeasurably as they pursue their interests. And not only in terms of success. When caring adults support a child who loves to play baseball, study sea turtles, and read comics, that child realizes, "I am okay for who I am." The interests well up from within him and are reinforced by those around him, so there is a feeling of coherence between his interior life and exterior persona. This reinforces a strong sense of self. Sturdy selfhood helps him to internalize values and beliefs, which will hold him in good stead even when other cultural forces may try to sway him toward unhealthy or negative behaviors.

The interests themselves also have a great deal to do with promoting a child's feelings of worthiness. There is an enhanced quality of life, a sense of being completely present that is hard to name but recognized by those who "find" themselves within a compelling pursuit. A girl may love speed skating, or writing short stories, or designing websites. When she's engaged in her interests, she knows herself to be profoundly alive. That feeling doesn't go away afterward, even when she has to deal with other tasks which are not as entrancing. Everyone strives to belong, contribute and feel significant. The child who has learned that his or her interests and unique abilities lead to fulfillment is already aware that self-worth doesn't come from popularity or possessions.

You know what little kids are like? They are into everything, wanting to figure stuff out all the time. Well, that's what Jake is like. Except he's 12. There's no stopping him. One minute he's asking questions and the next thing you know he's come up with some project of his. He built a ham radio last year and talks to people from all over using his equipment. He rigged up a better system to get garbage to the incinerator for our apartment complex that the custodian still uses. There's no way I can answer most of his questions but that doesn't matter. If I don't know, he finds out and tells me about it. I think a lot of kids would still be like Jake if they didn't have to go to school where learning is turned into a chore. —Christiana, Georgia

---

*Lego® was a favourite toy in our house, though we quickly realised that our children weren't simply playing. They started early and grew up with Lego®. As a construction block it was a great tool for expressing their developing interest and skills across the curriculum. In their teenage years I began to see how constant "playing" with Lego® had developed a range of skills. * It complemented the skills and knowledge they "absorbed" from living with owner builders. Each child took on building jobs (fences, sheds, helping with building the house) with ease, understanding the importance of accurate measurements, angles, perspective, function and aesthetics; they each drew on the design and planning skills from their Lego® play to build items of furniture; *Two of our children delved into electronics, building and fixing computers, and then took on problem solving and installing all aspects of wiring in cars, fixing mobile phones, remote controllers and other gadgets as needed. * Lego® and Lego Technics® helped them get a better understanding of how things go together. All of my offspring can pull a car apart and put it together, fixing any problems.*

—Beverley Paine, Australia; author of Learning Without School < http://homeschoolaustralia.com>

Cassidy became interested in origami at about age seven. He soon was advancing in the instructional booklets and making models that require high skill levels. He went to NYC twice each year to gatherings of the International Origami Society and met people who were advanced in the craft and who had lives that interested him.

—Ned Vare, Connecticut author with Luz Shosie of *Smarting Us Up, The Un Dumbing of America: Homeschooling How and Why*

Youth easily gain competence as they build on their capabilities and interests. Sometimes child-led learning is like a dance. Children ask for help, make their own attempts, then back off. They try later, and this time they are energized by the challenge, pushing themselves until they succeed. They want to be fully engaged as active participants. When their interest wanes, they want the freedom to move on to something that delights them more. The adults in their lives help them make sense of this process. A person who is available to answer questions, point out related topics, and explain new ideas, a person who can demonstrate concepts and assist in finding resources without undue intervention—this person is truly a teacher.

Of course, children need guidance in order to act safely, understand consequences and show compassion for others. They need consistent and reasonable rules as they learn about many kinds of

> Children flourish when they are not the center of attention. Instead, they want to center their *own* attention. They learn by watching, imitating, helping and doing for themselves. It's best if adults don't overly focus on a child's efforts because the child wants to be part of the process, not the sole reason for the process.
>
> It's natural for children to be drawn to people whose activities are competent and purposeful. If the only adults a child sees tend to sit in front of a television or computer after a long day away, the child doesn't have activities to model. If, instead, people in the child's life engage in activities such as gardening, making repairs, preparing food, talking with friends, practicing music and so on, the child has enlivening examples of adulthood.

boundaries. And part of a parent's role is choosing what limits to place on their children's access to potentially detrimental influences. Each family determines to what extent they will reveal painful issues to their young children. Many parents carefully gauge a child's readiness for information and the form this information takes, preferring, for example, to gently introduce difficult realities to young children through personal discussion and carefully selected books rather than sensationalized media. This feeds the desire to learn while guiding them away from what is not nourishing to their bodies or minds. But it also means steering them to the most beneficial and appropriate resources. Your seven-year-old may be fascinated with whales. Among all the books, documentaries, interactive websites, field trips, podcasts, museum displays and other resources

relating to whales, you will also find educational materials for her age group about the potential extinction of some whale species and the ongoing decline of the world's oceans. You may prefer to avoid inundating her with dire predictions.

A survey of children ages six to eleven found that more than half worry that Earth will not be as good a place to live when they grow up. More disturbing yet, a third of the children surveyed admit they fear the planet won't even be in existence by the time they reach adulthood. It's important to balance difficult truths about ecological devastation, war, crime, child labor, or any tragic realities with information about individuals and organizations working to help improve those situations. This helps children develop optimism, an invaluable trait.

We don't put the evening news on at our house. I have been known to hide the front page of the paper if the headlines involve something I don't want our children to worry about. Now that our children are teenagers we talk a lot more about events in the world but try to stress that they can make an impact through how they vote and live. —Lori Scelina

---

Optimistic people expect that their efforts will be effective. They are more confident that they can overcome difficulty, solve problems and remain in control of their lives. These characteristics lend them resiliency, helping them weather adversity better and work toward positive change. After all, hope is empowering, despair is not.

Learning isn't effortless even when following an interest. It's time consuming, challenging and often frustrating. Recall something you set out to work on, the obstacles you surmounted, and the resulting sense of achievement. Maybe running a marathon, designing a website for the first time, forming a support group to help children like your autistic son. You faced setbacks, but overcoming them felt exhilarating. These are important moments, times we revisit in our minds again and again. Working toward a goal is one of the many pleasures of human existence.

Talk within your child's hearing about your short-term and long-term aims and how you plan to accomplish them. Your example of self-motivation and reasonable self-assessment is vital. It's particularly important to avoid disparaging yourself or blaming others. You model for your child continually how to take responsibility for mistakes with grace and humor.

Our efforts say something about who we are. They provide a context for the meaning in our lives. You might refresh your ability to play the piano in order to accompany a soloist at church; help your uncle fix his old motorcycle so he can take a cross-country trip; attend poetry readings to inspire your own writing; design a bench to fit in the front hall; practice a foreign language to better welcome an exchange student. You will notice that purpose is connected with what you do and learn.

Point out that you seek help from people who have already succeeded at the tasks you have now taken on. You either do so in person or from wisdom shared through conversation, books, websites and classes. We humans draw from what has already been learned.

When children are working in an area of passionate interest, they often find that a whole range of related topics opens up, each new topic fueling their interests even more. They develop related skills almost unwittingly. These skills are transferable to many other fields.

A girl who likes reading about horses starts sketching pictures of herself on a horse. To hone her drawing skills she looks up skeletal structure. Gradually she applies careful mathematical analysis in order to draw more exacting studies of horses. She moves on, studying examples of fine drawings and paintings, then becoming interested in stylized representations of horses found in early art. This stimulates interest in history as well as mythology. Although her interest in horses does not persist, her love of history remains. Now an older teen, she has gone beyond researching the effect horses have had on different cultures to deeply appreciating the way the past impacts the present.

A boy who watches a bridge under construction from his apartment window turns everything he can find into building equipment. First he uses couch cushions balanced between bookcases, then he makes suspension bridges fashioned from cut-up cereal boxes and paper clips. At the age of eight he begins asking questions about force, stability and load strength. He is frustrated when the answers he gets are too simple. Finally, his mother seeks out architects, construction foremen and engineers to answer his questions. Their use of applied mathematics, science and design inspire him to pursue his own endeavors. He now draws futuristic cities, complete with transport systems of his own devising. At twelve years of age he still corresponds with an architect.

Who knows what sparks an interest? Most of these phases don't last, but they do deepen the child's sense of competence as well as teach many new, often interrelated concepts. When children have a drive to find out, they learn and retain what they've learned. Think of your education. You studied and were tested on volumes of material each year. Yet, what do you remember? Your

> When children initiate learning, they are ready. Motivated. If a child could describe what the state of curiosity feels like, chances are it would have something to do with highly focused energy. That's why children whose curiosity is thwarted so often get in trouble, intentionally or otherwise. That frustrated energy is seeking an outlet. Curiosity is akin to awe, a sense of enhanced aliveness. To staunch it repeatedly is to snuff out the wonder that accompanies it.

recall is best for those areas that fascinated you. You delved into intriguing questions for answers you wanted. That wanting to know, that hunger, in itself has power. As Tom Brown Jr. writes in *The Tracker*, "This mystery leaves itself like a trail of breadcrumbs, and by the time your mind has eaten its way to the maker of the tracks, the mystery is inside you, part of you forever."

In the Flow

"Flow with whatever may happen and let your mind be free. Stay centered by accepting whatever you are doing." —Chuang Tzu

---

Children are energized by their interests. They can concentrate so fully that they lose sense of themselves, of time, even of discomfort. Psychologist Mihaly Csikszentmihalyi terms this experience "flow." He says, "It is what a painter feels when the colors on the canvas begin to set up a magnetic tension with each other, and a new thing, a living form, takes shape … ."

When pulled by the current of any project, we are more likely to experience flow. In this marvelous state the boundary between you and your experiences seems fluid, as if you are merging with what it is you are doing. The more opportunities any of us has to immerse ourselves in activities we love, the more capable and centered we feel in other areas of our lives.

What does this feel like?

I believe this is where your passion is defined. —Karen Streator Smith, Ohio

---

My children play many pretend games into which they completely disappear. They make large constructions with bedsheets and/or blocks and chairs. Since they do not go to school, they can carry on through to ages when school children in India are bogged down with books, bags, memorizing, and after school tuition and extra classes.

They make up names for made-up games like Zigzag Hydoon in which they stalk the adults working around the house and silently leap out from one hiding place into another, disturbing no one, but stifling giggles and signing to each other their next plan!

—Urmila, India

The summer after third grade my family drove to Prineville, Oregon, for a visit with my grandparents and uncle. Shortly after we arrived, my grandfather showed me the child-sized rowboat he had built for me to use in their irrigation ditch as often as I wanted. Of course I spent a great deal of time in that rowboat over the next three weeks! I can still feel the dry desert air. I recall the feeling of rowing my boat back and forth for hours at a time and I can still picture the arid landscape behind their house. I felt alone in a strange land, but not in the least bit afraid. Truth be told I was just floating in a little irrigation ditch, but to me, that ditch was as big as the Mississippi and my grandpa had made me the captain of my own ship … Those weeks were definitely a time when I was totally absorbed in my interest …

I think a child's natural curiosity results in that state of immersed passion, but I think a nurturing environment helps that inspiration to take place. Speaking as a child who was nurtured, I was free to be myself and confidently follow the interests that pulled me.

—Mary Nix, Ohio

Children demonstrate amazing reserves when they are caught up in pursuits like drawing, reading, building, playing games and pretending. Their focus makes a mockery of what is supposedly a child's developmental handicap—a short attention span.

The characteristics of flow mean that an individual is concentrating with such engaged awareness that he or she has gone beyond a sense of time or external obligations. Flow truly puts a person in the moment. It's easy to see why some children have difficulty transitioning to other activities.

Adults often regard children's pursuits as irrelevant. We call them away from their interests to what we deem more important. We chastise them for not paying attention to the time. Our dreary grown-up preoccupation with schedules and planning can teach a child to block his or her experience of flow if we aren't careful. It's possible to handle regular obligations with respect for all family members' differing needs. Posting schedules everyone can read, reminding children that an obligation is coming up in a few minutes so they have time to finish an activity, and allowing choices whenever possible are some ways to ease these problems.

I remember reading some of Mihaly Csikszentmihalyi's books and realizing that children are in the flow all the

time. We obstruct their flow with our rigidity and requirements.

—Hema A. Bharadwaj, Singapore

Being mindful of flow doesn't mean that we should never interrupt children. There are marvels in everyday life too important to bypass. Call your child to the window to see songbirds chasing a hawk away from their nest. Hurry down the street to hear a band performing in the park. Hop in the car to observe monks create a sand mandala in the next town. These opportunities awaken fresh perspectives. According to Albert Einstein, "Curiosity has its own reason for existing. One cannot help but be in awe when he contemplates the mysteries of eternity, of life, of the marvelous structure of reality. It is enough if one tries merely to comprehend a little of this mystery every day. Never lose a holy curiosity."

I remember when my young son first developed an interest in puzzles. Finally I had ten straight minutes of peace! When he gave up his afternoon nap, we warred over having a "quiet time" in his room every afternoon. Now he spends hours alone in his room working on Legos® or other building toys and often complains when I tell him that quiet time is over. I wish I could tell you what I did to help him achieve flow, but he just figured it out on his own.

Loving what you do and being able to do it are what produce flow. If something is just beyond what we're comfortable with, not too hard, not too easy, it has the best chance of producing flow. When I was in teacher training we called it "controlled frustration." You want to make sure an experience hits just above ability level. If it's too easy, then what's the point? If it's too hard, then the child gets frustrated. Like tennis, flow is about hitting the sweet spot where interest and the willingness to be stretched intersect. As a teacher I thought I was responsible for crafting an experience where the

kids could achieve flow. As a parent I've learned my job is to support him in discovering how to get there on his own.

—Karen, Texas

Free Range Learning

"A joyful life is an individual creation that cannot be copied from a recipe."—Mihaly Csikszentmihalyi

Most childhood interests aren't the all-consuming variety. They are, however, wide ranging. They take the child on a journey of exploration that provides competency and understanding.

Observe a six-year-old child playing alone in the backyard for a half hour. His imagined super powers give him a lesson in the limits of make-believe when his cape refuses to provide lift-off even after a running start. His interest in gravity, however, is stimulated. As he drops objects from the sliding board, he observes the different ways a leaf, stick and rock fall. The leaf inspires him to try climbing a nearby tree. His attempts to reach the lowest branch incorporate problem-solving techniques ranging from acrobatics to leverage. When it's clear he's too small, he lies under the tree envying the birds their easy access to every branch. He remembers bits of a poem his grandmother likes about birds. Sometimes she lets him use her binoculars when they go to the park. He wonders if the birds know that people give them names like "warbler." What if birds want to be called something else? Maybe their names are songs? He spies a lumbering beetle near the roots and watches its halting progress, suddenly feeling much more capable in comparison. The beetle's sharp mouthparts remind him of some implements in the kitchen drawer and he's off to ask if he can use them in the sandbox. He's hoping to link them together with twist ties and make

a robot with nutcracker legs and corkscrew arms. Maybe two robots! He runs to the house even faster with the urgency of this new quest, his legs energized as he pictures the possibilities of tongs, measuring spoons and whisks.

Notice in the example above how naturally this boy is guided by what he finds intriguing. Frustrations give him reason to reflect or try new solutions, but he doesn't linger over them as failures. He absorbs what he is ready to learn and moves on. Earlier in the day this boy played at a steady pace making roads in the dirt, picturing a tiny city. All of his activities have an element of imagination and adventure. He is fully absorbed in the work of play.

This child is responsible for his own learning in a situation of freedom and safety. He plays out scenarios that incorporate information and stories others have shared with him. He knows that he can ask questions or receive help when he needs it. His educational life is rich. While his mother works, his grandmother stays with him. She reads with him, they play card games, and sing as she plays guitar. She speaks Spanish to him and tells him about her girlhood in Argentina. His enthusiasm revitalizes her longtime interest in photography, and he has been helping her organize her pictures. He has daily chores and weekly visits to the library. Recently, he has started a rock collection. His grandmother found a few local resources

for him to learn more about rocks and geology. That's basic early childhood homeschooling. Uniquely customized to the child, it's wonderfully flexible and balanced between freedom and responsibility.

Children find optimum nurturance when adults are able to adapt the learning situation to the needs of the child rather than force the child to meet institutional requirements. Too often this isn't the case. We know children who are dulled or oppressed by a system that makes them feel lesser. Any highly controlling top-down structure, whether school or authoritarian family, has difficulty adapting when faced with someone as changeable, promising, infuriating and loving as a growing child.

The school didn't know what to make of Jerod. He was just being himself, a very inquisitive and caring little boy. When he asked a question about the teacher's rules, it infuriated her ... He got his work done early and tried to help nearby children who had difficulty with the same assignment. The teacher punished him for "promoting cheating." He

already knew how to read, but every day the teacher made him fill out sheets to practice the same sight words the rest of the class was learning until he got bored and messy, then she gave him poor grades. The teacher passed out candy to kids for reading books, and as a result we noticed that Jerod got less interested in reading on his own. The phys ed teacher said that Jerod was reluctant to play games. Jerod told us he was sad to make the other side lose because the kids who won made fun of the kids who didn't win.

We tried to explain to Jerod what was expected of him. We had several conferences with the teacher. She did admit that the curriculum was too slow for him, but she also made it clear that he had to do what was expected of him without questioning or he'd be a rule breaker his whole life. Every day when he came home from school we could see by the way he played with his younger brother and sister that he was working out his frustrations. He had trouble sleeping and getting up in the morning. And his personality started changing. He was acting cocky and cynical. This was all in first grade!

So we took him out of school to give homeschooling a try. Jerod is a good big brother again. He loves going everywhere, and yes, he still constantly asks questions. I think this morning already he has read about, asked about or looked up these topics— St. Francis, a recipe for making apple butter, how long bugs live (which led to a muddy project making a bug sanctuary in the backyard because he aspires to be St. Jerod these days), Vikings, an explanation of the term "homogenous," and finally, as I'm writing this, some help with his math.

I understand that it would be too hard to have this much learning energy in a classroom. To have twenty-five or more Jerods in one room would be impossible without limiting them somehow.

—Leslie Ann

From day one we homeschooled Jose and Rosalina. Rosa does fine as long as I let her do the work at her own pace. Sometimes she already understands the math so I let her skip every other problem or some pages. And lots of times I let her skip the sections that have her read and then answer questions because she would rather read a real book and I think that's better for her. She can get all her work done in an hour or two, and that leaves her time to go skating with her friends and other things she likes.

Jose did not like the program we had used with]Rosa. It was expensive but we got a different one. He still got angry or upset every day. At seven years of age he couldn't read much, and we were worried. We put up a chart with rewards and punishments for getting his work done. That helped for a while. My husband threatened to put him back in school. That helped but not too long. Every day Jose and I fought about his schoolwork.

I talked to some friends and they told me to back off of him for a while. That didn't seem fair when Rosa was doing schoolwork every day. So Jose and I made up our own schoolwork, except it was what he wanted to learn. First thing he wanted to learn was about bugs. That seemed funny to me, because he was kind of afraid of bugs. His sister teased him about it. Anyways, we looked at books about bugs and looked them up

on the computer. We went to the museum, where he saw insects from everywhere. I told Jose he had to have at least two papers each day so we could show the state at the end of the year that he was learning, and that was his job, to come up with those papers. He took that job on pretty well most of the time. Sometimes he had me write some math problems for him. Sometimes he drew a picture and had me write a story underneath what he told me. But for a while we did bugs, and sometimes Jose did a lot more than two pages a day some days. We turned those papers into his bug book. He has math story problems I wrote for him about bugs, magazine pictures labeled with bug names, stories about bugs that he made up and a list of books we read about bugs. Now he's not afraid of them. He's pretty proud of how much he knows about bugs.

I'm sorry that I forced him to do so much schoolwork that he hated when he's doing a lot better now doing his own schoolwork. And he is starting to read really well without me teaching him to read because the papers he has been doing recently are cartoons he's drawing and he wants sentences on them. He likes to type the words and cut them out so they fit on the page better. Then he makes copies of his cartoons for his grandparents. Rosa says she likes what she's doing better, and Jose says he likes what he's doing better.

—Maria, Arizona

Surely no system or person overtly tries to lessen a child, but that can be the end result when academics are overemphasized. That doesn't happen only in school. Many homeschool curricula are also modeled on certain types of thinking, while shortchanging wider learning. The focus on one hemisphere of the brain effectively diminishes expression of other capacities. It is well-known that engaging children in art, music, storytelling, volunteerism, dance, spiritual pursuits, meditation or athletics adds to academic enthusiasm while more fully expressing wider abilities.

Unlike school, it doesn't take the slow gears of educational initiatives, governmental funding, or a new grant for homeschoolers to adapt. Change can happen as soon as a need is recognized. If a child constantly seeks movement, she can be encouraged to express her kinetic energy in worthwhile work, sports, play or dance. Then, as her active nature is fulfilled, she is more likely to find reflective moments when she will be receptive to quieter forms of learning. If a child is shy and prefers to spend much of his time in solitary play or drawing creatures of his own invention, this self-expression will likely leave him more at ease and able to respond from a place of strength to interact with others.

My daughter has been all over the place with her interests. For a while she was going to be a clothes designer. She tired us all out. She sewed us clothes that she had designed herself. That almost made up for all her criticism of what we usually wore! She dragged us across the state to the Kent Museum of Costume and got interested in reproducing historical designs. Then she was going to be a historian. She loved big heavy history books, documentaries and plays set in certain eras. That got her started sewing for the kids' theater. Then she was going to work in the theater. She acted a few times but mostly loved the plays themselves and chances to create outfits for the actors. She's my youngest homeschooler, so by the time I got around to her I was expecting less in
terms of daily assignments of math and writing, which was good because she did so much of her own work. She read all the time. She learned lots of math as she did her designs, with measurement and transposing different elements from paper to fabric. She studied history and literature to be more exacting in her costume design and because she loved it. I used to think that she was fickle with her interests since she was so hot and heavy on a topic only to drop it for something else. But she was really making her own wide circles around the same thing. She's already built up dressmaking and alterations clients. She has the confidence and skills to be anything she wants to be, but we know she'll always be designing things her way.

—Anna, Michigan

There's an element of uncertainty involved in education. An analogy can be found in art. A painter approaches the canvas, but rather than push himself to begin, he pauses, allowing impressions and sensations to fill him. When he surrenders to the process, he is ready. Then he is able to forget himself and bring forth the waiting image. These same steps work as we encourage learning.

1. Embrace the possibilities.
2. Step back slightly, allowing the learning situation to unfold.
3. Remain present without exerting undo control over the outcome.
4. Be comfortable with what is unmeasurable.

A child's desire to learn is a light that shines from some inner part of his or her being. As adults, we are guardians of that light. Many times we find that it illuminates us as well when a child's awe and wonder reinvigorates our own lives.

It wasn't until I became a father that I recognized how much I had given up over the years. Kids are like ambassadors from somewhere mysterious. Each one brings with them certain traits that are ready to be lived. We parents are here to keep them safe and teach them a modicum of civilization and hopefully not dull their sense of adventure. With their enthusiastic trust in me, I've gone back to my early love of music. Every night I play the fiddle. My kids dance or sing or read or wash dishes to the music. I'm thinking about forming a band. They don't know why I haven't done it already. My kids go right ahead and leap into what they want to learn. I hope they always do. —Gus and Kiley's dad

Here we have some structure for the comfort of routine, but mostly we let Madeline (8) explore as she wishes. When she is excited by something, there's no stopping her. At a recent dinosaur exhibit she literally hopped up and down because she was so happy to see an Astrodon (named for its star teeth, she informed us). When she's on a roll, all we have to do is help her find out the answers and learn more. Other times she just goes along with whatever we have for her to do, happily learning and asking questions about everything. It's so much fun being part of a new learner's life! —Kari and Jake Warner

I give my girls, ages five and seven, a lot of time to laze in bed in the mornings when they are half awake. I believe a lot of inspiration takes place during this time, and I want them to be comfortable with silence and not doing anything. I give them time to think, to experiment with most things in the house, especially water and clay. They play all the time ... in fact, the whole day, as long as they're done with the four compulsory homeschool activities. They don't watch TV (only movies during the weekends), no computer or electronic games, and no Internet.

Once a week, we go to a patch of nature to sketch anything we want to—a pebble, an ixora, the clouds ... I encourage them to do a lot of hands-on activities: sewing/beading/hair plaiting/stenciling/constructing Lego®, etc. At times, I read a story and ask them to draw on a big piece of paper their thoughts/feelings/ideas while listening to me.

Math facts/times tables are written on big sheets of paper and pasted on the wall in front of the toilet bowl. Grammar rules are pasted above the sink where they brush their teeth. Poems and Bible verses are pasted on the wardrobe door. Science ideas and new concepts are pasted on the big mirror in our dining room. The kids are not taught nor drilled these facts but absorb them like sponges. There's lots of space on these papers for the girls to add on their own facts and drawings ...

We have relatives and foreign friends staying at our place throughout the year and the girls learn a lot from them. We want them to learn from as many teachers as possible.

—Linda Goh, Singapore

The complex process of learning is beautifully intertwined with the growing child's urges to explore, interact, ask questions, try new things, and seek time to reflect. The child isn't aware why she wants to help Grandpa in the workshop or wade in puddles, she only knows how strongly she wants to do these things. The child longs to do these things, in part, to incorporate greater understanding and higher-order skills. Childhood is a time of major neuroplasticity, when thought and action actually change the brain's functional anatomy. Adults often intrude with activities they deem more worthwhile or safe. But the activities imposed by adults may provide a great deal less for the child from a developmental standpoint. Parking children in front of a wildlife documentary or sending them off to organized sports practice may seem advantageous, but not if these things do not flow from or sustain the child's interest.

Our incidental daily conversations are extremely valuable. Conversation is in short supply in the lives of many children. It has been estimated that, once directives are taken out of the equation, the average parent spends less than five minutes a day talking with a child. Discussion stimulates children to use language to think, remember, reflect, and imagine aloud. This builds connections in the brain. More important, conversation builds relationships. We come to know each other more completely when this is a priority.

Conversation helps us to understand our children and helps children recognize the perspective of others. Even a few words can express complete understanding between people who care deeply for one another. It's crucial to be seen and accepted for who you truly are.

That's rare outside of the shelter of a loving relationship. Philosopher Ralph Waldo Emerson wrote, "To be yourself in a world that is constantly trying to make you something else is the greatest accomplishment." Perhaps it doesn't have to be that difficult after all. The strength to be oneself can emerge from a childhood where the self isn't masked, tenderness isn't hidden, and acceptance is mutual.

Our son was part of a book group that included four other boys. I remember one time the boys and moms were all sitting around talking and one of the kids said that if they were in regular school they would have been labeled geeks. The boys seemed very proud of their supposed geekiness and not the least bit embarrassed by it.

I felt like I had to put up an emotional barrier to keep from getting hurt in public school and was always trying to fit in. I feel like our kids never felt that pressure. They are happy just being themselves.

—Lori Scelina

As we all do, children learn from experience. If a boy runs outside without gloves on a snowy day, he will quickly recognize the wisdom of going back inside to find them. If a girl takes a friend's toy home without asking permission, she will suffer that friend's indignation later on. The lessons are remembered because they have impact and meaning for that particular child. No nagging about bundling up or excuses for forgetting to return a toy have the same impact as cold fingers or a friend's heated rage. It's when we deprive children of the consequences of their actions that we short-circuit learning.

Children's experiences may teach what we don't intend. For example, when a child gets his way by whining, he learns to perpetuate that behavior even if he is chastised for it. Each time a busy, distracted parent gives in, the child is being taught to continue, even though his tactics increasingly annoy his parents. What he is learning with each success is that a parent's irritated voice is often followed by exactly what he wants. He's not only learning to act self-centered, he is learning to associate a parent's negativity with his gratification. Hardly a prescription for family harmony. We need to pay attention to what the child is learning by noticing the bigger picture. Look at situations from the child's perspective. After all, we parents have been children before, but children have a limited ability to understand an adult's frame of reference.

A significant portion of childhood experience in our society comes in a prepackaged format. Some studies find that youth are exposed each day to eight and one-half hours of screen time, i.e., television, computers and video games. We know that young children take in content with minimal filtering. They absorb media messages uncritically. Most commercial media, in both advertising and content, are cleverly designed to influence thinking patterns and behavior. The emphasis falls toward materialism, aggression and superficial thinking. Even caring, attentive families find it challenging to balance these influences despite limits on the use of technology.

Yet balance provides security so that our children can actively proceed with the hefty tasks of learning, growing and maturing without the problems engendered by violent entertainment or excessive consumerism.

Life is school. Any time there is something in the news, or someone asks a question, we explore it. Real life learning means that you try to be as well-informed as possible in those things that interest you or impact on your life.
—Karen Pennebaker, West Virginia

Life is learning and learning is life is a motto of our family's. We truly believe life is your best textbook. You learn most by simply living life day to day. We can find many math, science, history, social, art and more lessons simply by walking into the grocery store—just as one very basic example. While going shopping we may talk about how much the food costs and how it works in a budget, where various foods originate from, how certain foods are looked at in various cultures, irradiation, organic vs. conventional, the artwork on various packaging, marketing strategies and more. —Tamara Markwick, California

Free range learning has parallels to the growing movement toward sustainable diets. More and more of us seek out the essential nutrients found in whole foods. We try to fill our plates with meals made humanely and with the least impact on the environment. Consumer awareness is the engine driving increased demand for organic, locally grown foods. The agriculture and food industries aren't the ones sounding alarms about unsound policies that are damaging to human health or the environment. No, a flawed system is being changed by the concerns of ordinary people. Although there aren't exact parallels, it is interesting to note that both agriculture and education systems are divided by similar principles: small, local and diverse models versus large-scale, top-down, expediency-driven models. Learning is an organic process that resists mechanistic control. Measurements and codes are legislated onto education the same way that agricultural regulations are passed. We see education sold like an expensive product with no warranty. Those who love to teach and those who wish to learn can be trapped in such a system.

Thankfully, we can make conscious decisions not only about the food we eat but also about the sort of education our children receive. We feed our growing children wholesome food and encourage them to try new tastes because we know their bodies are built by what goes into forming each cell. It's the same with the elements that build their experiences. We want our children's lives built on meaningful influences. What relationships and activities each family chooses will be unique. That uniqueness is precious. By filling our days with what is important to us, we take charge of our own lives. We don't have to fit cherished moments into the time left after school hours and homework. Nor do we have to confine our bodies and minds to processed educational materials if we choose to find our own way. Beyond the adage, "You are what you eat," we are also aware that "You are what you think, feel and do."

We don't want our children left in a system that espouses the best ideals but can't possibly educate in ways that are relevant to each child, each family and each community. Our choices matter. Collectively, our decisions may change what it means to be educated in the years to come, just as current choices by consumers are now making the relationship between land, grower and life-giving nourishment part of our global conversation.

I love the term "Free-range Learners!" That's just what it is. Looking at any baby or preschooler playing or asking

Nature operates complex systems with awe-inspiring success. None of these systems can be fully understood when examined in isolation, as they function as part of a larger whole.

Any self-organized system, including a human being, is exquisitely cued to maintain equilibrium. Yet that equilibrium can't be maintained for long. And that's good. An overly stable system is rigid, unchanging and eventually collapses. Even our heart rates fluctuate unpredictably. Interestingly, the heart rates of young healthy people are highly variable. In contrast, the beat of a diseased or elderly heart is much more regular.

We are attuned to minute fluctuations in our bodies as well as in the world around us, and we are capable of almost infinite responses to regain balance. Some of these responses occur at a level we can't consciously detect. Other responses are sophisticated maneuvers by choice. Change or disturbance at any level functions as a stimulus to create new options. Each time we are destablilized, these elegant and complex processes at our disposal give us ways to regain balance. The more potential responses we have, the greater our adaptability. That means we are perfectly suited to expand our learning infinitely outward as long as we are not confined to sameness and inflexibility.

Modeling education on the natural world makes it more viable. After all, we are living natural systems ourselves. What principles are found in sustainable ecosystems? Cross-pollination, diversity, self-assembly, interdependence, adaptation, balance, and the undeniable tendency toward beauty. Such principles sustain and enhance life. These principles can form the core of a living system of education as well. All we need to add is the very human need for meaning and love.

questions will give you a strong impression of what free-range learning is about. The term also subtly connotes that someone is "free-range" until somebody else makes them otherwise. The mind may be resilient but it is also heavily influenced by the atmosphere that surrounds it daily. School teaches, out of necessity, that it is more important to follow the group than to explore. I'm not a subscriber to the idea that all children, left to themselves, will pick challenge over laziness, but I do believe that most of us would do better on our own with the guidance of a wise,

loving mentor than put into school factory farms. —Karen, Texas

---

We love every day spent with our kids. Life is such a joyous process with kids who love to learn, who aren't being forced or coerced into learning what someone else says they need to know. And the things they learn stick with them! Nothing is quickly learned for the "test" and then promptly forgotten. My kids remember it all—sometimes to my downfall! —Angie Beck, Kansas

---

Interests in Perspective

"No child on earth was ever meant to be ordinary."—Annie Dillard

---

As you and your child search out activities which build on interests, you'll find the possibilities for learning continue to expand. The saying, *The more you know the more you find out how much more there is to know*, becomes apparent. One question builds on another, and soon a whole world of interconnections opens up. Thankfully, parents don't need to have all the answers. They sustain a child's curiosity best as facilitators. They provide a home environment rich with reading materials, learning supplies, and ample time for discovery-based learning. They support the child's interests with resources in the community. And they empower the child to find answers.

Perhaps you attend a play with your child and she's intrigued by a character's ability in swordplay. Afterward, you might check out library books and movies based in the feudal era, attend a Renaissance fair, visit a display of armor at the history museum, try out a few fencing

lessons, whatever seems enticing. Just remember to let your child's enthusiasm guide the depth of exploration.

Search out related areas only as far as your child's interest warrants. Much as you want to provide encouragement, you don't want to take over and thereby dampen the child's eagerness. It is easy to do this unintentionally. To illustrate how this can happen, say you become energized about a political issue. You watch a few interview shows and read an interesting analysis of the issue. You enjoy talking to people who share your interests, if not your opinions. Those conversations are lively. You see how the topic dovetails with other issues and want to learn more. You may hope to act on it by volunteering to work on a local campaign or by e-mailing your legislators. Now imagine that someone with the best intentions leaps in to help you learn more. You may welcome this at first. She discusses it with you, provides you with relevant articles, and takes you to meetings about it. She expects you to watch specific documentaries and books on the topic. But you begin to feel disengaged. As your interest falters, she tells you how much you've accomplished while reminding you to appreciate her efforts on your behalf. That makes you feel self-conscious or manipulated. Then she takes you to a day-long event to learn about the history of the issue. You are ready to quit. There are other things you want to do. The interest has become hers and not yours. And that's before she asks you to take notes, write a paper, or take a test on the subject!

Today, I am more convinced than ever of the uniqueness of all children and their natural ability to learn what they need to know. As support group leaders, we are frequently asked to reassure parents that, yes, their kids are learning all the time, especially when you, the parents, are NOT trying to teach them something. Teaching can be beneficial, but ONLY if the learner requests it.

—Ned Vare, Connecticut

I believe that children who are expected to want to learn new things will be inspired by everything from the newspaper to movies to learn new things. My younger granddaughter is dyslexic and loves books on tape. Her passions are ancient history and "spooky literature." She is also interested in art and architecture. I have lots of books on both subjects, having majored in art in college, and she loves books—even those she is unable to read. She does 4H independent projects on historical figures.

My older granddaughter is interested in animals. We have used 4H animal

and veterinary science projects as her science lessons, as she is interested in learning everything she can about improving her herd and agriculture as a business. She designs her own spreadsheets for record keeping, set up her own website and keeps it updated, and loves to take her goats to county fairs and show them.

Homeschooling gives children the opportunity to run with a project. Rather than spend minutes a day in each subject in school, they can learn and use math, science, English, history, etc., all at the same time in their research and exploration. Children learn to use proper English by reading and writing. They can learn spelling the same way. "Going with the flow" allows them to proceed at their own rate, which is not always possible in a public school setting. One child may be on a college level in one subject and still at middle school level in another; but if they are in charge of their own progress, they realize that "I have to learn Algebra if I want to … " or "ratios and percentages are really important when figuring out proper nutrition for a dairy goat."

—Karen Pennebaker, West Virginia

Learning is intertwined with meaning that is unique to the learner. None of us comprehends or remembers in quite the same way as the next person, and this very human feature gives us the sort of diversity that no computer can match. We don't simply take in and store data. We attach meaning as we learn. We link new information with what we already know. Every second, sensory impulses flow to our brains, coloring the moment of learning with an imprint that is particularly notable if we attach emotional or physical impressions to it. Gazing at the constellations with one's family from the comfort of a blanket on a hillside or playing a game while laughing uproariously are learning experiences filled with memorable emotion and sensory detail.

Not all emotions help cement learning in place. When experiencing anxiety, anger or fear, the body produces stress hormones that impair comprehension and memory. No wonder so many of us resisted forced educational objectives, yet learned topics of interest eagerly. As the polymath Johann Wolfgang von Goethe wrote, "I educated myself in my own way without adopting any given or traditional approach. This allowed me to take up every new discovery with enthusiasm and pursue the investigation of things I myself had come upon. I profited from the useful without having to bother with the odious."

You learn all the time but your brain isn't processing that you're "learning." I think that's a good thing. You aren't thinking "oh great, here's another thing I have to learn." You think "this is cool."

—Allison, 14

I'm not, never have been, one of those highly organized homeschool parents. We're very casual, and somehow my boys learn in leaps and bounds.

Today my boys decided to construct a trap for a squirrel. They think they'll catch one and train it to do tricks. Except to give permission for tool use, I'm not involved. I know that if I intruded with my opinions or made the project into a teaching opportunity that I'd rain on their parade. I know that they'll end up asking me a question or two. I'll just answer, not go into more detail than they need. I won't try to figure out what they've gained from this project either, even though if I were organized I'd write down that this was a unit study with science and math. Above my desk is a quote from John Taylor Gatto. "The truth is that reading, writing, and arithmetic only take about one hundred hours to transmit as long as the audience is eager and willing to learn. The trick is to wait until someone asks."

That's my motto. *—Lucia, Ohio*

Parents demonstrate by example that learning is a lifelong pleasure. When a child sees adults in his or her life continuing to develop their own skills, the child understands that a person's interests can capture the imagination at any age. The young person often develops a fascination with the same subject as well. An adult and child may grow to share a love of sailing, drumming, motocross racing or archeology. Even if the child moves on to other preoccupations, something invaluable has been transmitted. It's like giving off a spark. When an adult and child who care about one another have an interest in common, the child lights up with the importance of that shared enterprise.

The lessons learned while sharing a parent's interests don't always carry over the same way to the child's interests. Some children are thrilled that their parents are enthusiastic partners in model rocket building or movie making; other children prefer to take the active role and go to adults for guidance only as needed. This is a matter of age as well as personality. As youth get older, they want to take greater charge of their pursuits. The adults in their lives can provide support without directing or controlling. After all, young people push themselves to accomplish their own goals in ways their parents might never have considered.

> Many of us are quite proficient in areas our own parents knew little about. Something about chemistry or fly-fishing or cooking intrigues us. We may not know why. What we do understand is that the mastery has a flavor all its own when gained by our own initiative. It is strong and distinctive. It is ours. A wise parent allows a child the honor of owning his or her passions.

Our son has become an expert in fields his father and I know nothing about.
—Olga, Germany

For my oldest daughter, simply having time gave free rein to her interests. Of course, at the time, we had a TV only for video, and had no video games in the house. During the school year, she spent a fair amount of time doing math and writing assignments, but once summer hit, look out!

She immersed herself in art, which she had no formal instruction in. She joined a theater group. She read and read and read. She babysat to earn money and spent her earnings on materials to build a tree house, independently seeking out plans and techniques before starting. She checked out library books on HTML coding and Javascript, and put together her first web pages.

Interestingly enough, when she chose fields to study in college, none of them were the "required" subjects, but instead were extensions of the passions she pursued during her free time. She majored in web design and theater costume design, and got degrees in both. Since then, she has also worked for a time in a library, and has considered getting a graduate degree in library science. —Kim O'Hara, Washington

---

There are many ways to provide enrichment without taking over. Homeschooling parents actively seek out books, articles and movies on topics of interest and introduce the materials matter-of-factly: "Oh, I found this tape on deep sea diving at the library" or "Did you know there's a cookbook based on the Little House on the Prairie books?" Often the child shrieks with delight at these announcements if they are in line with a current learning fad. Other times we simply leave these items where the child might encounter them: near the computer, in the car, by the couch. This is popularly known as "strewing."

We seed our homes with a variety of learning materials. Art supplies, magnifying glasses, puzzles, musical instruments, maps, dress-up clothes, and microscopes can be important tools for children. The world around us is also an essential element in learning, so we indulge in field trips, hikes, workshops and other programs as they suit our needs.

Dialogue is another vital way to open a child to new aspects of learning. We answer questions and ask about the child's perspective, demonstrating that there are many viewpoints and ever more enticing things to learn. We also help the child find others who share a particular interest by seeking out organizations, clubs and perhaps professionals in the field who may become mentors.. The key is to whet the child's appetite.

Often, young people take control of their interests as a natural progression of maturity. For example, a homeschool science club formed for boys between the ages of ten and twelve initially relies on the parents. On the day of science club, each hosting parent provides a project and supplies, explains the procedure, discusses the science behind the results, and provides extra links and information. If the project doesn't work, the parent helps the boys find out why or search for alternative approaches.

As the boys get older, they simply assume control of the science club. They look for their own projects in advance, often debating among themselves the merits of each, and find ways to get their parents to agree to permit more ambitious undertakings. The boys share responsibility for getting supplies. On the day of science club, they work on the agreed project together, without parental help. If it fails, they look up parallel projects. They like to find online videos showing new approaches. Then they try again. They often strategize between science club meetings. It's their own science club now, and they learn more on their own.

It's a common perception that children should "stick" with an interest once they have begun in order to help them develop the sort of staying power necessary for more difficult adult challenges. This is true for household chores, not for interests. Child development expert David Elkind writes in *The Power of Play*, "Children may not have a good idea of where their talents or passions lie. They may want to take drum or guitar lessons but then, after a few lessons and often some expense, may decide to stop. We may feel that the child has made a commitment and needs to keep it. Because we are worried about the child's future we think this will set a bad precedent in the struggle to learn responsibility … The common assumption that commitment transfers from one activity to another is wrong."

In other words, permitting a child to stop art lessons she once begged to take does not teach

her to be a "quitter" in the way parents might assume. It's helpful, however, to talk over what the problems are when the child wants to stop. Sometimes there are side issues that can be solved. It's also important that a child understands about commitment to others before joining a group activity such as a team or theatrical troupe. Responsibility to others until the end of a game season or performing cycle is an important obligation.

Children naturally have extended slack times between interests. Sometimes a boy doesn't want to act in any more plays even though he always loved being on stage, or a girl chooses to skip soccer sign-ups just when she seemed to be the team's best player. These are times when the child needs to incorporate the gains made in growth and understanding before charging ahead, sometimes toward totally new interests. The hiatus may be lengthy. These youth are showing us they need time to process, daydream, create and grow from within. They need to be bored and resolve their own boredom.

Many long-term homeschooling families notice that youth accustomed to self-initiated learning really take off in their teen years. Comfortable with their ability to find out what they need to know, they often look for ways to meet their own goals. Some add ambitious job schedules to previously unstructured days, others seek out heavy doses of academic work of their own volition, still others do not appear to be doing educational activities in any conventional sense. They are creating new pathways for themselves.

Recently my son, Cody, who is 14, made the decision to take advantage of the Running Start Program through our local college. Clark College lets juniors and seniors take classes for free. In order to do this the kids must pass an admission test. Part of the test is algebra. Cody has two years to learn this and a couple of other things. We've never approached algebra, so he asked how I could help him learn it. I picked up a great pre-algebra book which is a self-learning type, Pre-Algebra DeMystified. He didn't think that was all he needed, so he asked if he could take a class as well. I loved that he wanted to do this on his own. He was looking at his future wants and needs and made the right decision.

He loves music. He practices his guitar daily and is taking voice lessons with a friend. This is also something he has done on his own. Another thing is comedy. Cody wants to be a stand-up comic. The only improv type group here is through Christian Children's Theater and Cody would need to take a few of their classes before he can be included in the group. We simply can't afford their prices, so he and I together have started a free comedy group. We meet with others twice a month. Everyone is invited to join in, which was his idea also. Although he does get a little upset with his five-year-old sister wanting to do everything!   —Kim Railey, Washington

———————————————

Homeschooling teens is much easier than younger kids. The kids have the tools they need to learn anything and to do it mostly independently. My job, aside from hauling them to ball practice and SCA, is to balance things. In our house that means healthy food and no phone or screen time till mid-afternoon. I'm amazed by how my kids learn in big gulps. I don't think it's in their nature to learn a little bit about one subject over a period of months in dribs and drabs.

When they want to know something, that's all they do for the day or the week or longer. I'm okay with the slow periods because I've come to recognize that they are learning a lot.

—Sarah Brill, New York

———————————————

My daughter had what I considered a very lazy senior year. Except for her job at the golf course she didn't do much at all. I complained about the papers she should be writing and the math she needed to catch up on but she didn't worry because she was accepted at MSU. At the time I figured she needed some time to sort herself out before college, but I was dreading her freshman year because I thought she'd be stuck in remedial courses. Turned out she needed no remedial classes. She got A's and B's her first semester and will be graduating with honors. Sometimes she e-mails me papers she wrote. One of them was about her last year at home, and reading it I found out she spent a lot of time in her senior year rereading her favorite books and trying to write a novel. I never knew she had any interest in that. She's majoring in international finance, so I guess her math skills must be strong too.   —R.K., Michigan

———————————————

I look to the older kids from our group for inspiration when I'm not sure that what I'm doing with mine will turn out okay. These teens are great. They have part-time jobs, take early college courses and find all kinds of cool programs to get involved in. Two of the boys who are around 19 started up a business of their own a few years ago and now it's making enough money to support them. I *called to offer a desk we have and found out that they have an office in the city already.* —Unsigned

---

Honoring a young person's interests goes hand in hand with reasonable behavior guidelines. The child's right to follow his or her interests does not in any way abrogate family or community obligations to be respectful of others, to follow reasonable safety rules, or to act in ways that are developmentally appropriate. Nor does it imply that all daily activities are based on the child's whim. Regular obligations are important. A sense of responsibility, along with a feeling of belonging and purpose, leads to the development of higher-level character traits. It's a balance. The child who has the security of limits and the freedom to share his feelings is one who can emerge from the cradle of childhood with a strong sense of self.

CHAPTER THREE

Work, Play & Other Essentials

Meaningful Work, Authentic Roles

"Inspiration usually comes during work, rather than before it."
—Madeleine L'Engle

Too often youth in our society are entertained and educated by adults whose main function is to keep them busy. Adults drive them places, provide lessons, maintain their homes and cheer them on at soccer games. From a child's perspective it might seem that adults work for, even pander to, children. That puts youth in an uncomfortable position of power. Somehow we have placed children in the spotlight, the pivot around which activities revolve. Considering this fact, it's astonishing that more children aren't obnoxiously self-centered and imperious.

Making children into a family's entire raison d'etre confounds the dynamic of an adult relationship while at the same time empowering children in an unhealthy way. It is contrary to the role children have played throughout most of human history. Childhood in earlier cultures was generally left to children. They worked, played and learned without intense adult attention. As they matured, their contributions became increasingly necessary. Often a ritual of some kind welcomed them from childhood to adulthood. Although these rituals differed across cultures and eras, this passage acknowledged the young person as a fully contributing member of the community. The limitations of childhood were left behind. Becoming an adult and taking on responsibilities was a goal young people were eager to achieve.

While they are often subject to adult hyper-focus, today's youth conversely have little opportunity to participate in the community in any meaningful way. Events requiring people of all ages to contribute effort, such as a barn-raising, don't seem to happen anymore. Typically, young people are told their only "job" is to do assigned schoolwork. Youth have more material possessions in our society than ever before, while at the same time their parents are more indebted than in any previous generation. What motivation does a child have to grow up when his age group has the most perks and adulthood seems to mean more work and less fun?

Culturally, we are replacing a young person's burgeoning desire for autonomy with consumer goods. This is the logical outgrowth of heavy exposure to media, with its emphasis on instant gratification, easy solutions and violent disregard for others. When children are denied activities that give them hands-on lessons in taking initiative, practicing cooperation, demonstrating tolerance, deferring gratification, and working toward a goal, they don't always build essential personal strengths they can rely on. The effect may be an emerging sense of self defined more by appearance, acquisition and cynicism than by competence and independence.

At a time when young people are establishing an identity, they are denied a real role in their families and communities. Their efforts aren't needed as they once were on the farm or in the shop. In fact, many children do not help out on a daily or even weekly basis in the home because parents don't consistently expect them to manage household chores. Why? Some think their children have too many time constraints due to education, sports, music lessons and socializing. Some feel guilty expecting a child or teen to take on chores. And many parents find it easier to do the work themselves, not recognizing that their children can make real contributions to the household while learning how to cook, make repairs, clean, launder, mow and do other tasks which will later become essential for an independent adult life.

All young children learn through observing and working alongside older youth and adults. They want to gain useful skills. That's because it's a human drive to be needed, to know one's efforts are important. When a preschooler begs to help in the kitchen, he doesn't want to play with a toy cooking set, he wants to participate in the real work he sees taking place. It slows down a parent to pull up a stool and let him cut fresh mushrooms with a butter knife (and it takes restraint to avoid criticizing or recutting the resulting vegetable pieces) but the child recognizes that he is contributing effort toward making dinner. When a girl wants to help wash the car, she isn't satisfied playing in the sandbox instead. She would rather be given tasks such as mixing the soap in the bucket, rinsing the doors and shining the hubcaps. Staunching a young child's eagerness to help often results in an older child who is reluctant to do chores.

As children grow, they can take on larger, more responsible jobs. Families have relied on children throughout history for two reasons—their work was reliable and their work was essential. These days their efforts may not be vital to continued survival, but we can still expect them to be reliable. Household tasks are not glamorous or even interesting, but they are important. When the whole family is involved in cleaning the house, raking leaves or canning pickles, it gives everyone a feeling of shared resolve. It isn't always possible to do chores together. That's why families divide work in whatever way is most effective. They may rotate chores among family members, post job lists with due dates and rely on sign-ups, assign chores by ages, or allow children to negotiate among themselves for work sharing.

Paying children for chores in money, toys, candy or privileges is counterproductive. Anything more than expressing thanks tends to backfire. Children may expect greater gains for the same tasks or refuse to help out without perks provided. Older siblings may "bribe" younger children to do chores for them. Payment or other perks for chores is a sort of bribe. Regular household and yard chores should not be likened to a parent's career, which brings in a paycheck, but to the sort of regular obligation found in cooking a meal, changing a lightbulb or caring for a pet—the ordinary work of living. The effort contributed by each person is simply part of being alive and functioning. "It's the way we do things in our family" is a sufficient reply to complaints. This is more succinct than bargaining and more effective than begging children to finish their chores.

When children are held responsible for the outcome, they are much more likely to recognize the importance of their work. If a ten-year-old plays video games instead of taking his turn to do the family's laundry, he knows his sister will miss the next day's lacrosse practice because her team shirt is still dirty. He'll have to get up early to finish the task, and the resulting weariness will remind him that it's not worth putting off his duties the next time. A girl may not enjoy helping her parents unload and stack firewood, but the warm house will be due, in part, to her efforts. Chores demonstrate to a young person that he or she is a valuable contributor to the well-being of the family. Even when work isn't fun, it leads to a sense of purpose and belonging. And hearing, "Thanks, we couldn't have done it without you," feels good, too.

Research bears out the wisdom of giving children responsibility in their earliest years. Longitudinal studies starting in the late 1930s followed men from young adulthood until death. Only one factor stood out as a predictor of adult happiness and stability: having chores in childhood. The men who helped out with regular tasks starting at a young age were also likely to enjoy good mental health later in life. This fact held true even though the men in the study had very different lives. Some were affluent Harvard graduates, others were impoverished inner-city residents.

Studies continue to prove the positive impact of chores. Marty Rossmann analyzed twenty-five-years' worth of data gathered by Diana Baumrind. What she found surprised her. Factoring in all measurable influences, such as parenting styles, gender, types of chores, attitudes, inducements used, and amount of time spent on chores, she discovered that success in young adulthood is best predicted by participating in household tasks at age three or four. Even I.Q. scores had a weaker correlation with adult success than starting chores at a young age. The study found that getting children used to household responsibilities is best done early. Parents were met with resistance when they suddenly expected children to help out once they were older.

These studies have resounding significance. Parents devote untold hours and spend enormous sums driving children to lessons, sports practice and camps. They buy them the newest learning gadgets. They assume such efforts promote success. They may provide wonderful hours of enrichment in reasonable doses, but if children don't have time to help out with chores around the house they are being deprived of key components of adult competency and achievement.

It can be daunting for children to take on new responsibilities, but becoming a contributing member of the family develops confidence. It also helps to internalize motivation—doing a chore not to avoid punishment or to get a reward but doing it well because it's the right thing to do. Increasingly challenging tasks build the child's skills, including the ability to delay gratification. It takes certain inner resourcefulness to stick with an unpleasant but necessary task before going on to something more enjoyable. That's a vital life skill in short supply. Ask any employer.

Helping out with household tasks happens to be one of those things that our family just does. I'll never forget a nephew who was staying with us walking into the house without helping carry in groceries. When I asked him to get some, he told me he didn't want to. I told him that I guessed I didn't want to feed him either. I looked him square in the eye and said, you are part of this family and this family helps each other. My nephew went back out and brought in groceries. To this day (a good decade and a half later), he always asks me if I need help with anything.

My children have watched our family become a well-oiled machine. As a child matures and works outside of our home, younger children help pick up the slack. It gives us all a bigger appreciation for what that person did/does in our household. Because each of my children has a strong sense of work, they've held onto outside jobs much longer than other children their age. Some of their employers have told me what a joy it was to work with them and how they value their work ethic.   —Beth Whitson, Ohio

---

We learn by doing. My daughter likes to help cook. When she does this, she learns math, science and reading. She also learns practical skills. These everyday things are what life is all about. Things that are real.

—Jessie Mato Toyela, Florida

Working out in the hay fields gives you a sense of accomplishment because you know without that assistance you wouldn't be drinking an ice cold glass of milk. You don't really appreciate someone's assistance unless it's not available. For example, no one really notices when you clean the house, but when you don't it's plenty obvious that someone hasn't done their job. It's kind of like

a "for the greater good" situation. Even though your individual part may not be immediately recognized, you know in your heart you made a definable difference.   —Sam, 15

If you make the chores fun, you can enjoy doing the chores. Whenever my sister and I do laundry we watch a movie and it makes it fun. We've worked out a system; she'll sort and I'll fold. Some chores are fun and some aren't. I like mowing.   —Josh, 12

My children go almost everywhere that we go. They have gained some positive, and maybe even some negative, but realistic, experiences this way. There was a time when we were having to help my elderly mother during the final stages of her life. This was hard for the children, but they rolled up their sleeves and helped with household chores and anything else that their Grammy needed, as much as possible. They were with me while their beloved Grammy was in the nursing home and the hospital, and when they were not directly helping us, they were there to observe. Even though it was a sad time, the things that they learned about health, healthcare, eldercare, death and dying could never have been taught as effectively in a textbook. They also learned that grieving is normal and expected.

On a more positive note, they have learned to help care for or babysit younger family members because they were home to help when I would babysit. By being asked to do simple shopping without my help, they have learned that there is a cost for things that they want, *and sometimes they have to wait. They are often asked to help devise solutions to minor household problems such as unexpected expenses, overlapping schedules, etc. Often, because the children are allowed to see how the household runs, they have no trouble coming up with wonderful ideas to save money or to use our time more efficiently.*

Basically, we just wake up in the morning and jump into life. Some days we spend more time with our noses in books, and other days we are out and about, doing things that make our lives easier. In the process, their exposure to different ideas and people is endless.

—Laurel Santiago, Texas

The lack of meaningful work and authentic responsibility hits hardest in the teen years. Just at a time when the body is streaming with vibrancy and the mind is awakened by questions, teens are beset with additional pressures such as additional schoolwork, rote jobs, career planning and the strain of fitting in socially. Most youth are more than ready to prove themselves. A quick Internet search will provide examples of highly competent young people in history. The Marquis de Lafayette, educated by his aunts and members of the church, entered the French Army at age fourteen, married at age sixteen, and was commissioned

as a United States Major General at the age of nineteen in 1777. Benjamin Franklin's schooling ended when he reached the age of ten. At twelve, he was apprenticed to his brother as a printer's assistant. At fifteen, Franklin began writing under a pseudonym in the first independent newspaper in the colonies, published by his brother. When his deception was discovered, he left the apprenticeship. By age twenty-one Franklin had created a lively discussion group which later gave rise to the formation of the nation's first public library. These stories hint at the energy of countless other youth who set out to claim homesteads, start businesses, marry, go to sea, learn trades or otherwise lead independent lives. This is not to romanticize earlier eras, when oppression, disease and other hardships often made life harsh. But it does acknowledge that young people, given increasing responsibility and corresponding freedom, have gladly met adult challenges.

It's common wisdom among homeschoolers that a child leaving the school environment needs time to relax and settle in to homeschooling. Often it takes months to rediscover a zest for learning on his or her own terms. Homeschoolers call this "decompression." During decompression, parents are advised to leave young people with days as unstructured as possible.

This period often proves fruitful, especially for young children who have had little time to play and daydream and for youth who have lost their autonomy to homework, tests and scheduled activities. But for some teens, this or any other prescribed step, however well intentioned, is another barrier to assuming fully meaningful roles. For those teens the antidote is action. A challenging job, apprenticeship, mentoring opportunity, serious volunteer position, service travel or other way to engage the wonderfully edgy, questioning and reflective energy of youth is the road forward and at the same time a healing balm for what has been imposed on them in the past. This is true of many teens, homeschooled for years or not. The itch to do more, to prove themselves, is natural. Condemning them to stay within comfortably safe routines is too confining. This sort of interference with their independence tends to backfire in ways commonly seen in our society.

We pulled Jason (14) out of school this year, right after he got in trouble for breaking a window at the middle school. My wife and I tried everything the school suggested over the years to get Jason to buckle down. If he didn't get his homework done we kept taking away his privileges as they recommended. As a result, most of the time Jason was deprived of the activities that made him happy and had nothing left to do but schoolwork. Not the best boyhood. That broken window was a wake-up call.

At the time I was coincidentally reading a new book, In Defense of Childhood: Protecting Kids' Inner Wildness, by Chris Mercogliano. That book pointed out exactly what Jason was trying to tell us all along. I finally saw that the kind of consequences the school insisted we enforce at home went against Jason's character.

Jason has been homeschooled for three months. After he earned money to pay for the window, we gave all his privileges back. His home education has accelerated him much more quickly than school ever did, plus he showed interests that we'd never known he had. He started apprenticing at a bike repair shop because he wanted to learn how to fix bikes. After a few sessions the owner offered to pay him to do repairs. We let him work two afternoons a week there. He is starting to "mod" bikes with special parts and features that he sometimes makes on his own. We've never seen

him display the maturity this job brings out in him … At his age he needs to prove himself. —Eric Faustini

---

Our daughter loves horses. She took lessons, read all about horses, both fiction and nonfiction, and went to many horse shows and events. She saved her money for years doing various jobs (babysitting, lawn mowing, pool cleaning) until she saved up enough money to buy her own horse at the age of sixteen. Part of the deal when we let her get the horse is that she had to make enough money to also pay the monthly board. Our daughter has always been very shy, but I have seen her blossom through her love of horses. She is becoming a confident young woman, and I really believe that her love of horses has been a big part of this. —Lori Scelina

---

Although work is valued largely for its monetary worth, work is a pursuit that has inherent worth, even pleasure. It's the attitude brought to the task, whether shoveling manure or performing a sonata, that elevates its meaning. When our children spend time with adults who hold different jobs, they have the opportunity to develop a mature attitude about work. When youth work alongside adults both at home and in their communities, they have the opportunity to see the honor that exists in doing a job well, no matter if it consists of pushing a broom or designing a better broom.

Young people are undervalued community resources. Given a measure of respect for their ideas, they respond with dignity. A group of pre-teens who toured a rural historical society noticed that the attic and basement were stuffed with uncataloged documents. They offered to digitally scan and reference these materials with the volunteer coordinator of the museum. Teens who interned with the mayor researched the standards for a dog park and petitioned the city council for a permit, eventually seeking a grant to construct the appropriate fencing. Children who visited an assisted living facility suggested a collaborative gardening project with the residents. These examples demonstrate the energy and enthusiasm children can bring to authentic community participation.

Doing real work and taking responsibility builds maturity. No purchase or amusement acknowledges children's worth as powerfully as giving them the right to take on meaningful roles.

Challenges

"Life's challenges are not supposed to paralyze you, they're supposed to help you discover who you are."—Bernice Johnson Reagon

Interesting problems and exciting risks are life's calisthenics. They stretch us in directions we need to grow. Children are particularly oriented this way. They think up huge questions and search for the answers. They face fears. They puzzle over inconsistencies in what is said and done around them. They relentlessly challenge themselves to achieve social, physical or intellectual feats that, from a child's perspective, seem daunting. They struggle for mastery even when dozens of attempts don't provide them any success. It's a testament to courage that they continue to try. Sometimes children are accused of "looking for trouble" when they simply yearn to vanquish dragons of their own making. A child's desire to challenge him- or herself is at times as unrelenting as physical growth.

As adults we do this in our own way. If we don't have enticing challenges, we may develop a state of mental friction to compensate. It seems to be a very human trait to clutter up our days with trouble if we have no more engaging prospects. We worry, rehash old issues, overreact, find complications where there may be none. As the roots of a plant become more tightly entangled once they are pot bound, an individual without the freedom to take on greater challenges often gets caught up in the same confining struggles.

One thing we can learn from children is the way they are attracted to dilemmas that help them learn and grow. Children who are nurtured in a healthy, free range learning environment are invigorated by the challenges they seek out. They expand their own frontiers on a comfortable, self-regulating timetable. Perhaps people of all ages define themselves, in part, through the challenges they take on and the way they resolve those challenges.

Oftentimes we deprive our children of normal day-to-day challenges because of our own time constraints. As adults we are often distracted and focused on moving forward. It takes considerable tolerance to keep from stepping in and doing for our children what will take them much longer to do for themselves, such as solving problems, making choices and completing tasks. But when we recognize that even these small challenges are catalysts for growth, it is easier for us to step back and let our children face them as they occur. These are normal stressors. Dealing with them gives our children the critical experiences that lead to self-reliance.

> We hear a lot about the damaging effects of stress. But stress itself is not necessarily negative. We see this everywhere around us in nature. Pressure exerted on any living system encourages it to develop. In fact, organisms protected from all stressors stagnate. That's true of our individual lives as well.

Stress is inherent in growth-producing situations. The challenge of mastering a difficult musical instrument is a form of stress. Taking a personal risk such as learning to assert oneself is a difficult but ultimately important step in maturing. And it requires bodily stress to reach new levels of physical ability, whether you are a runner, tennis player or dancer. These forms of positive stress have been called "eustress," a term made by adding the Greek prefix "eu," meaning "good, healthy," to the concept of stress, defining something that is fulfilling even though difficult.

The amount of stress that is helpful depends on the person and situation. If your child is preparing for an upcoming geography bee, the built-in pressure to study can enhance his performance. But too much stress during this highly intellectual task—perhaps constant interruptions by younger siblings or parental admonitions to win—will impair his memory and attention. If he is performing a different task, say white-water rafting, the stress level will be very high, but in this case may heighten his performance.

A scientific principle called the Yerkes-Dodson law demonstrates that one's performance improves with a certain degree of stress or pressure. There is an optimal level of excitement or stress in performing any task well; an increase in pressure after that will result in deteriorating performance.

One challenge I've seen my children deal with head-on were those dealing with academics. Not being in a public school with a lab, or a sports team, or other public school resources, they often sought out other avenues to meet their needs. Both loved sports, so they played ball on the local city teams and also took classes so they could learn to umpire as well. When one started college, he was pleasantly surprised to find that all the independent self-education that sometimes challenged him during high school was just the type of study skills he needed to succeed in college.
—Mary Nix, Ohio

My son joined up with the Royal Air Force cadets program when he was 13. It was the perfect age for him to prove himself to himself. The RAF Adventure Training offers hang gliding, target shooting, fieldcraft and survival methods. He is in line to become a junior leader next year. He's gained immeasurably from the challenges.   —Fiona, England

The words we choose when talking to our children about the challenges they face have a significant impact. Most of us tell our children that they are bright and talented. Yet it's best to avoid implying that any such fixed traits are tied to meeting with success. Because they aren't.

Decades of studies show that putting the emphasis on intelligence or talent is actually counterproductive. According to Carol S. Dweck, author of _Self-Theories: Their Role in Motivation, Personality, and Development_, when we assure children that they are capable because they have innate ability, eventually they tend to react poorly to challenges. Perhaps they fear mistakes will disprove their abilities. Children who show early promise in any endeavor often become accustomed to expending little effort. Then when the process becomes more difficult, they feel threatened and lose confidence.

Imagine if your friends say, "Oh, you are such a talented cook, everything you make is perfect," or "You're such a natural, you can fix anything." The pressure to live up to those expectations might make you feel any failure would disprove who you are in their eyes. It would be easier to avoid cooking or tinkering except when you were sure you could perform up to those standards. In the same way, children feel judged when we tell them, "You're smart, so this math shouldn't be any problem for you," or "You were born to pitch; no one else on the team has your arm." We think we're encouraging them, but we're putting the emphasis on talent or intellect. That gives children the impression that these traits are set in place. Such a concept leads them to regard challenges, setbacks and even extra effort as proof that our trust in their abilities is mistaken. When children believe that their performance is due to hardwired traits, they blame any poor outcome on a lack of ability rather than a lack of effort. This creates a downward spiral in motivation.

According to research by Dweck and many others, the solution is what is called a "growth mindset." This puts the emphasis on effort. When children recognize that no matter how much intelligence or talent they have it's what they put into the effort that counts, they build an upward spiral of motivation. Adults help children orient toward this attitude by focusing on persistence and love of learning. It's helpful to reframe our remarks by talking about behaviors rather than any inborn trait. Emphasize effort, such as, "You've been practicing your math facts and it shows," or "You were really watching the ball in the game today." This focus on strategies also provides feedback about doing better. All of us need to recognize that improving over time leads to true achievement. When adults promote this viewpoint, children can learn to recognize

that mistakes are necessary. They come to enjoy confronting increasingly difficult challenges. In this way our children build the inner mettle for lifelong achievement.

Adults can also promote mastery behavior in children by explaining exactly what happens as people learn. The sort of stimulus that strengthens brain connections has a physical basis. The process, called *neural branching*, creates more synapses between nerve cells in a way similar to the way in which exercise strengthens muscles. The opposite process, called *neural pruning*, occurs in order to eliminate unused neurons. Children are often excited to find out that they actually multiply brain connections every time they solve problems, read, debate, explore or figure out something new. This gives them a greater impetus to take on new challenges. It can also help them recognize that current performance is not a measure of their overall intelligence or talent, nor is it an indicator of their worth. Children who understand how the brain works realize that they have options. They can work harder, learn from mistakes, try a new strategy, practice, study, and gain skills. The person who is willing and eager to overcome obstacles is the sort of person who is capable of extraordinary things.

Success stories can be highly motivating. Through such tales, young people learn that mastery is reached after steady persistence. Delve into success stories in documentaries, books and plays. Remember to tell your children about people you know. Share the story of a cousin who used to be a troublemaker but now runs his own landscaping company, the neighbor who taught herself to craft intricate weavings she sells in art galleries, the college roommate who hiked the Appalachian Trail after recovering from a combat injury. Accounts of people who overcame odds help to keep us going when our own resolve falters.

When we expose our children to great ideas, deeply moving artistic works, and ingenious inventions, these accomplishments show them what humanity can do. They call out to the best in us.

Children can take steps to help them attain their dreams. The same steps are helpful whether the goal is getting a black belt in karate or becoming an astronaut.

- **Write down goals.** Describe objectives in detail in order to picture them as a likely eventuality. Make the aims specific.
- **Learn more.** Research goals by talking to people, reading books and magazines, finding information online and contacting organizations. As children understand their dreams clearly, they are empowered to turn them into reality.
- **Develop a personal plan.** Determine what needs to be achieved, such as specific skills and basic learning objectives. Sketch a rough timetable, keeping youth in charge of their own progress.
- **Notice the effect of focus and perseverance.** Emphasize positive results of persistence. As children grow into young adults, they are likely to modify or completely change their original goals, but the steps remain the same.

Occasionally, children may react to great works differently; they see them as representing insurmountable challenges to their own potential. The girl who has great hopes of becoming an architect may despair at the wondrous designs already found in cities throughout the world. The boy who longs to write novels may not be inspired by the best writers among us, believing instead that he will never be as good. This is not an unusual response. Individuals with strong personal reactions such as awe or sorrow when encountering masterful works may be responding to a calling of their own. It's important to recognize that a youth who feels diminished or challenged by great accomplishments of others is reacting normally. Many of us begin to recognize our own inherent promise through the work of others. Eventually, those who feel overwrought when faced with works of mastery will measure their stride in more reasonable steps. Pivotal works don't have to diminish what each of us can accomplish. They show us how deeply we long to demonstrate our own mastery.

To us the most masterful thing of all is the beauty of nature. I think my daughter's interest in studying environmental science is inspired by some of the beauty she's seen in the world.

— Lori Scelina

We don't want to remove challenges from our lives nor protect our children from normal stressors. Challenges develop a strong, resilient outlook akin to the developing immune system. Immunologists know that children build healthy resistance, in part, by dangers posed to the immune system. Studies continue to find that some exposure to infectious agents and bacteria in childhood actually helps to mature the immune system. This supports the rationale behind what has been called the "hygiene hypothesis," which explains why children raised in a very clean environment with little exposure to pets, other children and the accompanying germs are more likely to develop allergies or other autoimmune disorders than children raised in less hygienic environments. Protecting children from personal challenges can have a parallel effect on the mind and spirit.

Even learning to wait has critical long-term consequences. Although advertisers tell us the opposite, providing children with what they want right away can be a mistake. This may seem counterintuitive, but the benefits of affluence can impair a vital form of maturity. Giving children what they want when they want it doesn't help them learn to delay gratification.

In a series of experiments in the late 1960s, Walter Mischel and his colleagues at Stanford University measured this ability. Four-year-olds were asked to wait in a room that had a treat such a marshmallow on a plate. Experimenters told each child they would return in fifteen minutes. The child was permitted to eat the treat while waiting, but was told that if he managed to save the treat, the experimenter would reward him with an additional marshmallow. Some children couldn't wait and ate it immediately. Other children used a variety of coping mechanisms to ward off the temptation, such as looking away, closing their eyes, talking to themselves or making up games. But the most interesting aspect of the study was the follow-up. Researchers tracked down these same children when they were in high school. They found that the children who had difficulty delaying gratification as preschoolers in that simple test continued to have low self-discipline. They were easily frustrated and less academically successful. In contrast, the children who had demonstrated an ability to wait fifteen minutes for an extra treat were found to have more social responsibility, better concentration skills, greater self-assurance and higher academic standing as teens. In fact, the ability to delay gratification is highly predictive of future success.

Too many children are deprived of normal challenges. They don't learn early on the connection between their actions and the consequences of their actions. If a parent helps a child on and off playground equipment for fear of falls, the child is taught that she can't trust her own body. If a parent takes over building a model when a child becomes frustrated, the child is taught that he is incompetent. If a parent refuses to let a child take the blame after hurting another child, she is being taught to avoid responsibility. These are not the messages the parents intend to convey. They are hoping to make things safer, easier and happier for their children. But frustration, embarrassment and a few bruises are normal and important aspects of growing up. Attempts to make childhood frictionless are misguided.

The child who wants a new gadget is best served if he is told to put it on his birthday wish list or to obtain it himself by earning and saving until the purchase price is met. In this way he has the benefit of anticipation and the reward of waiting. Privileges and possessions obtained too easily have little allure compared to hard-won or long-hoped-for rewards. And they don't foster the resilience that children need to develop for later challenges.

We just don't have the money that a lot of people do in this neighborhood. I used to feel bad that my kids didn't have the same stuff other kids did around here. But now that they're older I can see a big difference in the way they behave. The kids who have everything want more all the time and nothing is ever enough. For my kids it's a big deal to them if they go to a movie theater and out for pizza a few times a year. It's nice to see how excited they get. And they know how to save their money if they want something. —Debbie

Our five children are ages 9 to 24 currently. We lived in remote areas doing mission work for eight and a half years. My husband and I had to find time to school our own children while doing God's work. Although I knew my children had a good grounding in Scripture, I was sure we were shortchanging them in academic areas because we simply could not afford to have textbooks and educational materials flown in. The children did learn many practical skills, the oldest ones in particular. The children helped us and the villagers build a dock, a small storehouse and an addition to the church. On a daily basis they were a help to us both with their physical energy and their optimism. Most of all, they put our family on the villagers' hearts because they made everyone into a friend.

We have been back in the States for four years. The oldest three are in college or technical school and doing very well. My prayers that they would not be hindered by their years without educational materials have been answered. I'm homeschooling the younger two and miss the effect that mission work had on our family. I've come to realize that children benefit from doing real work more than they do from schoolwork.

My 21-year-old daughter recently said she had been thinking about the villages where she spent so many of her growing-up years. She said, "My friends here [in the U.S.] would think of those kids as poor because they don't have new clothes or electronics, but the kids here are poor in a way too. They're poor because they are all worried about what other kids think of them, they barely know their families, and they don't have any bigger purpose in life. The village kids all had to do things like haul water … But they knew why they were doing that and they knew their families."

She said that she'd miss us, but for the sake of her younger brother and sister she thought we should rededicate ourselves to mission work for a few more years. She felt her growing-up years were the best even without schoolbooks and wanted to give her brother and sister the start she had. —Jordan, Jennifer, Justin, Jonathan and Julia's mom

---

At times all families face major stressors such as divorce or remarriage, unemployment, illness or death. These are not reasons to discontinue homeschooling, even if such difficulties may cause us to slack off on enriching activities. How a family copes together during this time is itself a process of learning for everyone involved. Struggle, however onerous, is a normal part of life. When we accept life's challenges and permit our children to do so as well, we are on the path to authenticity. This helps us to live beyond those surface values so prized by our culture: appearances, possessions, status, popularity and wealth. These superficial attainments leave many people ignorant of their inner vitality and uniqueness. Real challenges force us to go deeper, to honestly reveal who we are and creatively access reserves that might otherwise go untapped.

Oftentimes those who have faced trials discover their own strengths. They may gain a heightened sense of justice, compassion or insight. What is trying or painful may provide motivation for their life's work. Sometimes it's hard to see that difficulties have any positive side. We despair at each extra challenge our children face. It takes a larger perspective to see that when children grow up with challenges or life experiences more arduous than the norm, they are also enabled to develop different and often more innovative abilities.

It's heartening to recognize that many fulfilled, caring adults were once the very same youngsters who were characterized as "difficult" or "different." Some children face adversity in the conditions around them and some in the conditions within. Children dealing with serious issues such as autism, developmental delays, disease and birth defects face not only their own suffering but also societal strictures. Their situations challenge us to bring about inclusive and positive changes.

It takes a wider lens to accept our children exactly as they are, to find purpose where others may see only problems. There's a lesson to be found in certain traditional healing arts from around the world. The lesson is part of a profoundly different worldview in which each person is seen as a whole being designed in perfection. A healer or shaman often regards an issue within the context of the person, community and environment. Focusing on the "brokenness" only accentuates illness, pain or disability. Instead, the focus is on reestablishing harmony. The healer treats a person with an illness but may do so in a way that accentuates greater strengths, pulling what is unwell into a healthy alignment. Disease and disability may be accepted as an integral part of the person's story. In some cultures, a person who is "different" is thought to be in greater contact with the spirit world or dream world, and may be treated with high regard. Our current focus on what is wrong with a person may miss a bigger picture. It may also miss the purpose behind these difficulties.

With any challenge we have an element of choice—our attitude. No matter the difficulty, we can choose how we react. In any crisis, a person can constrict or grow. Sometimes personal growth takes place slowly, in fits and starts, and often with much sorrow, before something invaluable is gained. As Frank Warren, editor of the PostSecret books has said, "The children the world almost breaks become the adults who save it."

Children are eager to face the ultimate challenge of growing up, adulthood. So much about today's "managed childhood" has been developed in order to prevent young people from making mistakes. We think we know the prescription for success, but as we've seen, a one-size-fits-all approach doesn't allow individuals to thrive. It also denies them the very human right to learn in the

way best for them and to listen to the callings that prompt them. The "right way" to proceed in our culture usually means health, popularity, good grades, attractiveness, college degree, career, marriage, mortgage and so on. We've created these societal expectations largely to cushion youth from mistakes. But error is inevitable even if we avoid all risks. That narrow, preordained path is anathema to genuine experience. Setting rigid standards for our children sends a message. It says to them that failure is the worst outcome, that our acceptance is conditional. What we might do instead is recognize that courage is required to go one's own way, that mistakes are inevitable, and that the outcome is authenticity. The real challenge lies in accepting each person's possibilities. That's how activists work for change, musicians compose, and each of us does what we can with what we have in order to live our lives fully. The path not taken may be the journey regretted forever. That's why we need to honor mistakes as important passages in our lives too. They help us face the next challenge with a wry smile and new determination, knowing another lesson has been learned.

Creativity

"The world is but a canvas to the imagination."—Henry David Thoreau

Imagination springs from nowhere and brings something new to the world—games, art, inventions, stories, solutions. Childhood is particularly identified with this state, perhaps because creativity is rarely regarded as necessary or even desirable for adult life in our society. The trait is shuffled off into a separate category as something possessed by the artistic few.

Nurturing creativity in all its forms recognizes that humans are by nature generative beings. We need to create. The best approach may be to get out of one another's way and welcome creativity as a life force.

Surfing is a creative effort. It's just me and the ocean mediated by a board. I define myself this way. That quest for stoke is the same thing a poet goes after when he writes. —Corey, 15

If we are familiar with the process that takes us from vision to expression, we have the tools to use creativity throughout our lives. When we honor the expressiveness our young children demonstrate as they dance around the room, talk to imaginary friends, sing in the bathtub, draw with anything at hand, and play made-up games, we validate their unique pursuits. Children who are comfortable with the creative approach can apply this skill to any endeavor in the adult world. Creativity is necessary in handling an architectural dilemma, new recipe, marketing campaign, environmental solution, personal relationship or musical composition. In fact, it's essential.

The child who paints freely and unreservedly at the age of five probably won't grow up to be a painter. But her experiences contribute to character development as well as talent. The satisfaction she feels as she chooses green tempera paint, dips her brush into the shiny fluid, and spreads a thick arc of color across the paper is greeted by her family's casual, non-intrusive acceptance of her work. If she retains an interest in painting, she will learn a great deal about applying knowledge and discipline to her artwork. She will also gain insights about herself. It's likely she will grow up with the confidence and innovative approach that will hold her in good stead no matter what she chooses to do. That's true of most creative endeavors. The lessons are valuable throughout life.

All four of my girls have loved scrapbooking ... They have a complete sketch of their unschool years caught on film that they have put together into multiple books ... I have gone to bed at midnight or later, and one or more of the girls would still be wide-awake cutting and designing pages in their scrapbooks until the wee hours of the night. Their scrapbooks are like mini chronologies of their lives.

Another thing my girls have all enjoyed has been homemade movies. My girls have a camcorder and they make homemade movies with the neighbors, their friends, their nieces and nephews, and they have a blast. They have even posted small clips recently on YouTube. The girls have been writing and acting out their own skits since they were very small. Everywhere we went, whether to a friend's house, relatives, even my husband's boss's house for a cookout, the girls would get the other kids around them mobilized to put together skits and then all the adults would have to come watch their play. They are still doing this even though they are young adults. They have even filmed their toys in action and have made some really cute and innovative skits. The girls have also acted in church plays, community plays, and skits/films at the library (teen department). They do not seem to mind being silly, dressing up as characters, doing voice-overs, and really having fun with what they are doing. —Lori Smith, Ohio

Teens need to find something they are passionate about. When I was younger, I only cared about what others thought of me, and that got me into some bad situations …

I make sure my own kids are hooked into things that get their creative juices going. My son works with his dad sometimes in the welding shop learning to fabricate designs and is really proud of the work. He also is really good at skateboarding and the last two years has entered some competitions.

My daughter used to do hip hop dancing, but then she took a class and ever since then she has been involved in stilt dancing. She's performed at festivals and stilt-walked in costume for parades. —Rhynn

Our dream life is a commonly overlooked source of creativity. We can encourage our children to use the images and ideas that arise from their dreams, to talk about their dream stories, and to find the meaning that waits to be unlocked from within the quiet mystery of sleep. This avenue of exploration gains credence when we remember that luminaries such as Harriet Tubman, Albert Einstein, author Mary Shelly, and mathematician Srinivasa Ramanujan found inspiration through dreams.

Homeschooling itself can be an ongoing work of creativity. As our children spend their days in exploration based on their own interests, they access their potential naturally, perhaps not in the linear fashion expected by a test-obsessed society but in a way well suited to their needs. This style of education is self-created and flows from a generative impulse. The child, family and community form a unique set of learning circumstances to co-create education organically as the child matures.

Allowing a child to engage in creativity means that they have to figure out their own way. A huge part of learning is the "figuring out" process, not just memorizing the end result. Learning through creativity means mistakes will be made alongside the typically accepted correct answers. Sometimes, the mistakes are the most important part of the learning process.

I encourage my children to be creative throughout each day, whether through play or typical learning tasks. I am convinced that our modern global society functions through creative thinkers. It will be the creative thinkers who will help solve problems that plague us today and will plague us tomorrow. It will be the creative thinkers who will help make advancements in our increasingly technological and global world. Creativity cannot be separated from learning, it IS the learning! —L.C., Ohio

---

The act of creating is so natural in all of us. Yet through social conditioning and to some degree even too much praise, over time we can come to view art (visual, musical, movement, etc.) as something we do to please others ...

In my experience, art in a traditional school setting is not seen as a way to deepen learning about the world around us and certainly is not seen as a tool to express what is within. Art is separate from learning about math, writing, history and science so we gradually learn that it is yet another skill to master. Slowly, as time goes by, it becomes something only those with "talent" do and you either "have it or you don't."

Creating is a deeply individual experience, and in my opinion is quite sacred. I feel if a child is allowed to deeply connect with their own unique creative process, they will simply continue to create because it is part of how they relate to life—it is THEIRS. If a child begins to see artistic endeavors as separate from themselves or something that is done to please another, true self-expression is highly unlikely and will dwindle or disappear over time. I hear so many adults say, "I am not creative at all ... just don't have it in me." I say hogwash; it just lies dormant under layers of negative conditioning waiting for you to connect to it once again.

Creating an environment that is truly supportive of individual self-expression is challenging and requires much introspection on the part of teacher/parent. I still have to watch that my ideas and my expectations do not limit my children's spontaneity and their need to express themselves. It can be hard to know when to show techniques, when to inspire them to stretch, and when to just step away.

We learn writing and reading through fairy tale, legends and well-written stories. We often act out the story with clay figures, puppets or by becoming the characters. The writing comes later, once things have really been felt deeply. We learn math through stories and movement ... we focus a lot on the way in which math reflects the physical world (A Beginner's Guide to Constructing the Universe is great reading) so that it is relevant and felt all around. We paint a lot—sometimes to observe color and sometimes just for painting what needs to be painted. We allow for lots of free time to play, observe nature and to find the questions which are really springing forth naturally. We have even chucked carefully planned lessons to explore the woods in search of wooly bears to watch over winter. Creativity seems to require space, time and freedom, something we have to be willing to give ourselves and our children.

Great books that touch on this are Kids Play *and* Point Zero *by Michelle Cassou,* The Artist's Way *by Julie Cameron, and* Spirit Taking Form *by Azara.*

—Jody

Imagination and inspiration have fueled human progress throughout time. These creative powers have brought marvelous innovations and continue to expand the boundaries of progress. But creativity isn't always positive, visionaries aren't always compassionate, and progress isn't always beneficial. After all, a clever mind is required to craft a conspiracy as well as to negotiate a peace accord.

Today's world requires a greater understanding of creativity. We need individuals who are accustomed to learning and living as self-directed homeschoolers do—with inventive, resourceful and joyfully focused creativity. Creativity is a life force when it arises as a healing impulse, as a truth-telling impulse, as an impulse to approach mystery. The energy underlying the creative act is life sustaining and honors the work of others. That's one reason why it's so essential to encourage a creative, self-aware approach from the earliest ages. And that's something that can be done easily in the homeschool environment, where children are free to express themselves without undue stricture and without the negative peer culture so rampant in today's schools. The fertile imagination all young children display can stay alive to invigorate learning and inspire problem solving throughout life.

Slowing Down

"The question is not how we can move faster so we can do more; the question is how we can use our time wisely so we can live a good life." —Carlo Petrini

---

Ask any child. Standard questions from adults who meet them for the first time include, "What do you want to be when you grow up?" right after classics like, "What grade are you in?" and "What's your favorite subject?"

These questions, intentionally or unintentionally, gauge a child's progress toward adulthood. That's because adults tend to be future oriented. We're distracted from the present moment by the need to plan and work toward any number of goals—what to do about dinner, how to juggle next month's schedule, when we can get some bills paid off. These distractions take our attention away from what is in the here and now. When we think ahead so often, we have less time to notice, let alone appreciate, what makes up our lives minute by minute. What is impatience except denying the value of the present moment? The watercolor effect of rain on the window, the meandering quality of a child's conversation, the long wait for a pot to boil—these can be occasions to experience impatience or opportunities to breathe deeply and experience gratitude.

Leaning so often toward the future unconsciously demonstrates to our children that later is more important than now. Yet, as we know, later never comes. As long as we're alive there's always "later" to strive toward. Worse, we are surrounded by media-driven messages telling us that we aren't there yet, that we need to do more or become something more in order to have friends, be successful, find love.

The nature of early childhood is the perfect antidote to this hurry-up attitude; that is, if adults truly pay attention to the lessons the youngest model for us. Young children who are not yet pulled by the adult world's messages are oriented to the present moment. When forced to disregard what is vital to their bodies and spirits—pretending, daydreaming and playing—they rebel. They are who they are, where they are. They are not caught up in the future tense which diminishes the here and now.

Homeschooling can be a solution to our cultural overdrive.

Homeschooling days provide ample opportunities for a mix of multisensory activities that anchor us to the moment. Practicing a new piece on the guitar, forming a juggling troupe with friends, birdwatching, reading on the couch, volunteering at the Head Start center down the street, growing heritage vegetables, competing in a robotics tournament, putting out a zine—homeschoolers can engage their creative energies as they choose. Providing children with a range of opportunities while leaving plenty of space for relaxation allows each family member to find his or her balance. It gives us the time to know one another as whole human beings.

There's no need to make homeschooling into a daily hustle of events. Some well-intentioned parents overload their children with so many lessons, field trips, sports and clubs that everyone feels tense. Admittedly there are more enticing prospects for children's activities than ever before. But what is learned here is larger. We show our children by example that we know how to savor life. Each day is a microcosm of the lessons we teach them about our values and priorities.

My five-year-old likes it most when I listen ... That seems to be the activity in the shortest supply. He loves the trips to the museums and playing with his friends. He loves crafts, blocks, and puzzles. He loves singing, dancing together and gymnastics. But mostly, he asks for me to listen to his wild stories, to cuddle and often to read a book. —Karen, Texas

I have learned that each child is very different. Not only in how they learn, but in what interests them. To be honest I am much more structured with my younger daughter than I was with the older two. In many ways she is an only child and wants someone to be with her. She loves to play school and sit down to do workbooks and academics, which the older ones seldom cared to do, but then they had each other to play with. Children need down time and independent play time way more than they need field trips and group activities.
—Betty K., Tennessee

It's about finding a happy medium. One of my teens likes to be on the go all the time, the other is more a homebody. I love that my kids are free to be who they are and follow their (sometimes weird!) interests. It's like they are fueled by generous amounts of time at home with people who love and support them, and with that they can take on anything.
—Sarah Brill, New York

Throughout most of history, childhood was entirely different. Children provided significant help to their families, and otherwise they were left to their own devices. This left them with ample time to reflect, imagine, play and understand themselves in relation to the world around them.

The Slow Movement is part of a cultural shift toward reconnecting with a simpler way of life, such as locally grown food, slower-paced work and closer relationships. Savoring rather than rushing. Homeschooling makes up part of this trend. We are taking back time with our families, and choosing to spend that time in ways that are personally meaningful to us.

These days, parents are urged to boost their child's achievement by starting them early in activities designed to help them succeed. Pick-up games with kids of all ages from the neighborhood are replaced with organized sports. Building a fort, wading in a creek, or watching bugs on the sidewalk are replaced with enrichment programs designed to boost scientific understanding. The resulting heavy schedules cause tension as youth rush back and forth, with little time to enjoy an unplanned moment. It also unbalances the family, making the child's activities more important than the well-being of the entire family.

When we allow real learning to unfold, we actually have more time. Our daily lives offer the exact sort of hands-on, complex, open-ended learning that our children need. Hours of top-down instruction and carefully orchestrated experiences are not only more work for us, they are less stimulating experiences for our children.

As Carl Honore writes in his book, *In Praise of Slowness: Challenging the Cult of Speed,*

Children increasingly pay a price for leading rushed lives. Kids as young as five now suffer from upset stomachs, headaches, insomnia, depression and eating disorders brought on by stress. Like everyone else in our "always-on" society, many children get too little sleep nowadays. This can make them cranky, jumpy and impatient. Sleep-deprived kids have more trouble making friends … When it comes to learning, putting children on the fast track often does more harm than good. The American Academy of Pediatrics warns that specializing in a sport at too young an age can cause physical and psychological damage. The same goes for education. A growing body of evidence suggests that children learn better when they learn at a slower pace.

There is no "age appropriate" development or activity in our family. One read at 4, the other at 9. Two hardly write. My husband and I and other adults join in the children's games.

… Now, 15 years down the line, I realize that lazing is an important aspect of creativity. In fact, now I don't see it as lazing. It is space-ing. Adults today suffer from stress because they just cannot keep still—in mind, body or spirit. Constant activity is a habit forcibly created while growing up and is very hard to break. Structured games and some attention to academics (for the boys) happen during September to November. My daughter studies in fits and bursts all the year around. Very intense—nothing—very intense—nothing …

—Urmila, India

The biggest issue we have run into is learning with three children of different ages. Because we are family oriented, rather than peer oriented, I don't like many drop-off activities where I have to leave one child because the other is not old enough to attend. This limits some theater, music, museums and other activities in which I think my older ones would benefit but my three-year-old is not yet welcome. The awe I feel when I see the kids so excited about learning has me wanting to do all I can to further this. The resolution has been to have my husband be available a little more—which has been good

for everyone—and also to simplify our lives and not try to do so much. Both of these are a work in progress, but are making an obvious difference.
—Margaret S., Texas

As we slow down, we have time to truly know each other and ourselves. We have time to recognize the messages our bodies send us and act on those signals, before they turn into symptoms. We have time to reflect. Time to remember our dreams. After all, time is the only true wealth we have to spend.

Slowing down means that boredom can be welcomed. Recognize that the child who complains of boredom is one who has the blessing of free time. Rather than turning to video games or television, encourage your child to experiment with boredom. Let it fester for a while. For many children this feels frustrating at first. They are ready to quit and may beg for something to do. But as a child goes into the heart of boredom, the experience feels, in the words of one girl, "dreamy, as if I'm not there." That's fertile space. The child may range around outside or lie on the couch, but gradually he or she may come into contact with something deeper, a focus that seems beyond the ordinary reality. And all of a sudden inspiration hits. The child finds something to do that he or she wouldn't have thought of a moment before. That inspiration couldn't have come from outside the child.

Stillness

"We all need a certain amount of fallow time … Watching the grass grow, sitting on the hillside, staring out the window daydreaming. When we don't have it, there is a deeper intelligence that won't come forth."—Sue Bender

Everyone needs time to simply "be." The quiet center of one's being is where we are fully present. The constant activity of obligations and entertainment can easily crowd our thoughts and feelings into a jumble of surface impressions. Our busy schedules may hardly leave time for introspection. Even when we are mindful of the need to downshift, constant intrusion from media can deter us from becoming self-aware. Yet we know contemplation flourishes best in solitude. Notice that when children are left in peace they tend to daydream, a natural form of meditation. Choosing inner stillness for even a short time each day helps to establish it as a priority.

Parents naturally recognize that a long bath settles a restless child and snuggle time brings serenity to a child's day. Even the most active youth will make time to swing in the backyard or sit looking out the window. Many families include a daily ritual of prayer or meditation that, in addition to the spiritual purpose, also teaches a child to find an essential stillness within.

For some of us, a specific place helps us to gather what is fragmented in ourselves and find peace. We might be drawn to sit on the porch step each evening and watch dusk turn to darkness, we may make a ritual of drinking tea in a certain comfortable chair each morning, we may notice that time alone in nature strengthens our spirits. Many children like making their own realms under blankets, in closets, behind furniture. Outdoors they will find hideouts and forts.

Here children do more than play, they command their own worlds of imagination away from adult view, often listening to silence by choice. When a child asks an adult to enter one of these tiny places, it is an honor.

Every morning of my son's life we have started the same way. We sit at our big wide window seat with bay windows where we have lots of pillows and a spot to put mugs next to us. When he was a baby I used to nurse him there, watching the boats out at the harbor. Nate is nine this year. When he gets up we sit here snuggling with blankets to read our latest chapter book. He has cocoa and I have tea. After we read, we talk or look out at the boats. This is very special time. I won't answer the phone or make doctor's appointments or sign up for anything in the morning that would make us rush. The mood we create stays between us the whole day.

—Erin M., Maine

Most of us have distinct sensitivities. Children may have difficulty coping with overstimulation, they may object to certain foods, or they may refuse to play at a new friend's house. These sensitivities or inclinations aren't wrong. They are among the many indicators of who we are as individuals. In a world that unrelentingly pushes us to fit in by denying our feelings, a measure of stillness and acceptance at home leaves the child space to know him- or herself. By reacting mindfully we draw the child's conscious awareness to these differences.

Many of us were taught as children to ignore our inner promptings. We may have felt instinctive revulsion when served particular foods, but were told we had to clean our plates. We may have known that we weren't ready to sit at a desk practicing math facts over and over, but were told that if we didn't behave we'd be punished. We may have heard a small voice inside warning us to stay away from a particular person, but were told to obey grown-ups.

Instead we want our children to recognize that they have an internal system of communication known as intuition. They can tune in to their own impressions, perhaps learning that they get grouchy when they are thirsty or feel a stomachache coming on when they aren't being true to themselves, giving these signs credence when making decisions. The child whose gut feelings are taken seriously will learn to respond to the form his intuition takes. Security expert Gavin de Becker explains in *Protecting the Gift: Keeping Children and Teenagers Safe*, that this is imperative for safety because intuition is a hardwired trait warning us of danger. If the child is aware of his inner warning system, he will trust himself well enough to recognize the indicators that something is wrong. As de Becker says, this could save the child's life.

Incorporating tranquil interludes into our daily lives is one way to nurture calmness. This holds us in good stead for stressful times when we need to rely on a sturdy sense of self and the inner reserves found beyond that self, in stillness.

School for Ethan was like having a pointless job at a young age. We finally started homeschooling when he was in sixth grade. Slowly his personhood underwent a renaissance. I guess we never knew how much alone time he had needed but never got. Especially that first year or two he spent a lot of each day reading, walking the dog and listening to music by himself. Those hours alone seemed to restore something in him that had been suppressed.

The whiny and often selfish little boy turned into a great teenager. He has great friends. He and I have been reading works of philosophy recently. When we talk over what we're reading, I'll say this for him, he can see right through bullcrap. The best part of homeschooling is the way it permits Ethan to be himself. —Jeff, New York

Simplicity

"Be content with what you have, rejoice in the way things are. When you realize there is nothing lacking, the whole world belongs to you."—Lao Tzu

Many homeschooling families choose to live simpler lives. Seeking to do more with less reduces the economic burden on parents. Some of us practice simple living due to religious, social justice or ecological concerns. We recognize that daily decisions continually demonstrate and reinforce the values underlying our consciously chosen lifestyle. Simplicity, especially in concert with other like-minded people in the community, helps our children develop traits like generosity, frugality and altruism—traits often deemphasized in a consumer-driven society.

Homeschooling itself can be an integral aspect of a decision to live more sustainably. Educating in a holistic fashion upholds our connection to family and community. It also affirms the importance of nurturing body and spirit in relation to our beliefs, our culture and the cycles of nature.

Taking responsibility for our children's learning impacts household income for some of us. A wage earner may decide to work from home, change careers, or forego income-producing activities, especially while children are young. Rather than fretting over these choices, we can celebrate the larger implications. Often homeschooling parents are the lifeblood of a community. They connect with people throughout their neighborhoods. They volunteer, direct plays and develop programs with local businesses. If homeschooling causes a parent to pare down working hours, find better working conditions, or leave employment, such decisions have a powerful ripple effect. They orient us to what matters right now. They put us in sync with our own priorities, despite the prevailing tendency to place high income and career status above other values. And they allow us to cherish slower, naturally paced days.

So many guys get their identity from what they do for a living. I've never been good at playing corporate politics, but that's never been that important to me. I think a more accurate measure of a man is reflected in his family. And I'm a good dad. —Carl McGillivray, Ohio

We fit in the book work on weekends and evenings sometimes because my shifts change and my husband is finishing nursing school. It's no problem; my daughter rolls with it because it's natural to our way of doing things. Without homeschooling she'd hardly see both her parents. I wouldn't have it any other way. —Tisha, Maryland

---

I did not plan to stay home with Jeffrey. As a licensed occupational therapist, I'd been eager to get back to work in a hospital setting. But when we put him in school he did very poorly. They slapped three labels on him before he turned six. We put him in private school. That was worse. We could see school wasn't an option for him. So Matt and I reassessed. Now I have a part-time practice at home. This is a much better situation for my stress level and my clients, too. Matt does more of the direct schooling with Jeffrey and I'm more the fun person. I think our family is closer as a result of this style of education, and Jeffrey has no evidence of the problems the school pointed to. I'm glad our son didn't adjust to school and we didn't accept their labels. —Linda, Ohio

---

Children understand there's a trade-off: a reduced income versus spending more time together. And the outcome is, again, positive. Children who have more time with their parents are actually happier. They would rather have family time than money or consumer goods. In a nationwide poll of American children ages nine to fourteen, commissioned by the Center for a New American Dream, 90 percent said they want more time with their friends and family rather than more material possessions. When asked if they could have one wish to change their parents' job, 63 percent said they would want their mom or dad to have a job that gave them more time to do enjoyable things together, while only 13 percent wished their parents made more money.

A few austerity measures put into place now are likely to benefit our children in the long term. How?

- They learn to conserve resources and generate their own fun, as a result naturally creating a more sustainable future.
- Children feel better about themselves when their self-image isn't reliant on what they own—a personal quality built in frugal households.
- Researchers have found that materialistic attitudes in children and teens are directly linked to low self-esteem. Directly.
- Living more simply teaches our children that everyone wants things they can't have right away, but noticing the desire doesn't require acting on it. This is a hallmark of maturity.
- Recall the long-term study of children who were able to delay the urge to eat a marshmallow at the age of four? It found that the children who were able to control their wants grew up to have more friends, more satisfying jobs, and a reduced risk of substance abuse.

Clearly, the ability to buy our children the best things in life doesn't benefit them nearly as much as learned willpower.

These young people already recognize and seek out the emotionally healthiest choice. It's a dilemma recognized by philosopher Erich Fromm. In his final book, *To Have or to Be?*, Fromm ascribed an increase in depression to the economic pressures inherent in our society. He argued that success in a consumer culture centers on selfish and acquisitive behaviors that alienate people from themselves and from each other. In contrast, joy stems from unselfish and cooperative attributes that connect people to each other and to nature. Current thinking links depression with biochemical changes in the body, yet doesn't discount the influence of negative circumstances, nor account for the way these circumstances alter body chemistry. The diagnosis of depression continues to be on the rise, particularly among young people. When we see that the simplest choice—togetherness with those we love—leads to the greater well-being, the importance of living more simply becomes clear.

Our daily lives are about simplicity. We homestead on 14 acres raising dairy goats, chickens and hogs. We maintain a big garden and are working toward getting off the grid. We believe that teaching our three children to be self-reliant is the best start in life. Our kids find satisfaction in the simplest things, like teaching the dog tricks or going fishing with Dad. There's no toy made that can match that. We are raising good kids with solid values. It fills my heart to homeschool this way.

—Tami B., Alabama

Living more simply relieves the strain on the planet as well as on our finances. It orients us toward gratitude rather than acquisition. The intensely personal decisions relating to work, finances and parenting roles are complex and often change as the years go by. But we do know that shared ordinary joys in our daily lives are one of the priceless benefits of homeschooling.

The Importance of Play

"Play is the only way the highest intelligence of humankind can unfold." —Joseph Chilton Pearce

Unstructured play, especially outdoor play, is much more rare than in years past. In fact, children have 25 percent less time for free play than they did a generation ago. Tight schedules, excessive schoolwork, even organized play such as sports deprive children of free play. Often the time they have left is used up on distractions like TV or video games. Is a simple thing like not enough play a problem?

Absolutely.

Children recognize early on that they are largely powerless in relation to the world of adults. Play, however, gives them a world of their own. Within this realm of imagination children can be and do anything. In fact, play is crucial to a child's well-being. Studies show that insufficient play hinders child development in areas such as emotional health, language, social skills, creativity, confidence, motivation and learning. Our children become more fully themselves as they grow and mature playfully. It's an essential function of childhood.

When children do have time to play, their access to open spaces and their freedom to innovate is often limited. Researchers have discovered that when children play in an unstructured setting such as a field or woods they engage in more creative games and devise more imaginative role-playing than when they have the options typically available in a playground. But excessive safety concerns have confined children to areas deemed appropriate, constrained by more adult scrutiny than ever before. Richard Louv, in *Last Child in the Woods: Saving Our Children from Nature-Deficit Disorder*, writes, "Nature—the sublime, the harsh, and the beautiful—offers something that the street or gated community or computer game cannot. Nature presents the young with something so much greater than they are; it offers an environment where they can easily contemplate infinity and eternity."

Children's play is inventive. Whether alone or with friends, they have the wonderful capacity to use whatever is at hand for make-believe or games of their own devising. Throughout most of history children were not provided specialized play instructions, let alone playthings. They created their own fun with minimal supervision. Adults often expected children to help with necessary tasks but considered play a child's domain. But according to historian Howard Chudacoff, the last two centuries in the United States have shown an ongoing struggle between independent play and well-meaning adults who have tried to manage and control play. In *Children at Play: An American History*, Chudacoff demonstrates that the way children play in our current era is severely impacted by commercialization. Play, he argues, has become more about objects than about the activity itself. Electronics and toys are heavily marketed to children, teaching them that these objects are necessary for play. But these objects essentially coopt imagination with predetermined activities.

The child who longs for plastic gadgets based on the latest movie is unlikely to enjoy them for long. If instead he builds a hideout with branches in the backyard or plays cops and robbers with his sisters, he has the satisfaction of generating fun. Sadly, innovating one's own play isn't as accepted as owning the newest items.

Only a few generations ago, children did not own many toys nor expect to receive them year-round. Gifts were confined to birthdays, with a present or two at holidays as well. But advertising and even the prizes in fast-food meals led children to expect a regular supply of new playthings. Parents obliged. Interestingly, the image persists of a young child preferring the box instead of the toy inside. And a cardboard box is exactly the sort of free-form object that encourages imaginative play.

When Skye was younger I noticed that her play was highly inventive in comparison to other little girls, who watched a lot of television and videos. Many times Skye's friends wanted to act out their favorite movies instead of their own make-believe. Skye would play along but when she suggested a riff on the story the girls protested that it didn't happen that way in the movie. To me they weren't pretending so much as reenacting. I only let Skye watch educational programming or high-quality movies, but even then I think these shows diminished her ability to play expressively for a few hours afterwards. —Mari, Oregon

---

Experience shows that children who have too little opportunity for unstructured play tend to resist it, as if they have lost the ability to create their own fun. When encouraged to play, these children whine, complain of boredom, get into disputes, or look to others for direction. If that sounds like your child, it isn't too late. It's a cue to slow down the child's schedule, reduce media exposure, and leave more time for simple pleasures.

Restoring a child's ease in generating his or her own play may take some time. Studies show that children who watch more than two hours of television a day in early childhood have shorter attention spans and show less interest in sustaining their own amusement when they grow older, as if their brains are cued toward distraction. But we also know that childhood is a highly malleable stage. Play can be fostered with a gentle approach. Spending more time in nature helps, in part because being outdoors tends to remove electronic distractions and promotes concentration and awareness.

You may also want to broaden your children's exposure to new experiences. A trip to a dairy farm, a tour through a historical fortress, or an afternoon theatrical performance can become something bigger and more meaningful to children when afterwards they've made it their own through their play.

Although children are quite capable of playing on their own, getting together with friends makes play delightfully expansive. Homeschoolers tend to meet up with peers in different groups so they are able to draw on potential friendships across many boundaries, providing a wealth of playmates. Some youth adopt a scornful attitude at an early age, already dismissive of what they deem to be incorrect or unpopular. Homeschoolers are not immune to the sorry cultural trend of the jaded eight-year-old, but experience shows that this is somewhat less common.

In the final analysis, it is not an adult's responsibility to create fun for a child. Trying to keep our children amused is part of the problem. At the very core, play is a child's own creation. When children play, ordinary moments are transformed with imagination and movement. Those who keep the spirit of play alive as they mature can maintain the sort of creativity and fresh thinking required to adapt in a quickly changing world.

When children complain of boredom, there's no need to provide them with endless distractions. Distraction is the problem. Constant activity and entertainment provided by someone other than the child isn't normal. It may be common today, but it doesn't rouse the growing mind, body and spirit to develop the depth found beyond distraction.

At the heart of boredom is a kind of discomfort, often with oneself. An itchy, icky, *I don't want to feel this way another second* sort of feeling. Boredom can be seen as a boundary, a line of demarcation between what is comfortable and what is unknown. The feeling of discomfort is an inner signal to pay attention. Children who rarely experience boredom know this boundary line. They recognize the tingle of possibility that lies here. This is where imagination lives. Some children think quietly, some ask questions, others run around. They are letting ideas rush in. Then play or introspection or art begins.

We can encourage children to stay with discomfort when they complain of boredom. We can explain that it's a signal to cross over into imagination. A personal signal and therefore no one else's responsibility to solve. The way to that other side is to welcome the feeling of discomfort, stay with it, and do nothing at all. Not long after they've accepted that they're bored forever, an idea will appear, likely more than one idea.

Distractions short-circuit this process, but we all use them. Distractions are easy. They keep us from accessing our inner lives. Most of us spend several thousand hours a year watching television, a few thousand hours more on the computer. Learning at a young age that one doesn't have to resort immediately to distraction adds dimension and depth to a child's character that can sustain imagination for life.

Kids of all ages in our homeschool group get along with each other so well that sometimes it brings tears to my eyes. Here's an example. Years ago some of them made up a game they call Fud. For each game they form teams based on something random so every team has a similar number of big and little kids, from toddlers to teenagers. Every player brings a large plastic bat and the object is to hit a playground ball so it hits the other team's goal. They play Fud almost every time we get together, so we all carry Fud equipment in our cars. Some of the fun parts of the game are how fast these kids will run and how quickly they'll turn to avoid mashing into a smaller player. These unintentional interferences are what make the game more challenging and exciting. If a team seems unbalanced, sometimes they'll change players in the middle. They have so much fun! I wish I had some of their games on film. The fair play and kindness I've seen during Fud shows how well kids of all ages and abilities can get along. Did I mention some of the kids have physical disabilities? They play Fud too. —Lauren, Minnesota

I find slack time and boredom to be essential to the growth of my children. Down time is the "antidote" to the instant gratification running rampant today. I believe that boredom breeds creativity. I have learned that if I can force myself to "let my kids be," even when they complain of boredom, they ALWAYS find something to do. That something usually turns into an hours-long game or story of their own creation. —L.C., Ohio

Technology and Learning

"We become what we behold. We shape our tools and then our tools shape us."—Marshall McLuhan

Integrating technology into our homeschooled lives can be creative and invigorating, as long as it doesn't supplant diverse ways of learning. A televised close-up of an insect can't replace the experience of walking through a field teeming with life. No video game can generate the insight that comes from traveling or volunteering. It's important that we adults provide an example to our children of a life fully lived, including but not consumed by technology.

We learn best by doing. We learn at the highest levels when we use what we've learned. This means hands-on manipulation of materials and direct interaction with others in ways that technology doesn't always permit. Video games are multifaceted but not as richly rewarding as experiences that offer sensory information along with the opportunity to innovate and test. The child who uses sticks to make a tiny bridge across a rain-soaked ditch, only to build it again when structural flaws make it collapse, garners valuable real-world experience. A group of teens writing and performing a humorous skit together create something that has a lasting impact in their personal growth.

Yes we tend to think we're getting more done as we IM, check websites, listen to music and talk on the phone but our minds are not keeping up. Studies show that multitaskers are less able to sustain attention, ignore irrelevancies, concentrate or remember than people who attend to one task at a time. Technology not only affects the way we function, taken to an extreme it may also diminish learning itself. In Japan, those who constantly click away at keypads are called *oyayubizoku,* or "thumb tribe." Reseachers at Hokkaido University School of Medicine studied these people whose lives are consumed by electronic organizers, cell phones and laptops. They discovered that 10 percent of them had diminished brain capacity to learn and store information. One neurobiologist commented that they'd "lost the ability to remember new things, to pull out old data or to distinguish between important and unimportant information."

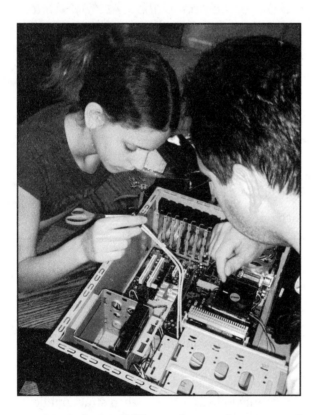

An analysis of fifty studies on learning and technology by UCLA professor Patricia Greenfield led her to conclude that learners have changed due to exposure to technology. Visual skills may have improved, but critical thinking and analysis have diminished.

That's why balance is so essential.

This doesn't imply that children aren't benefiting from digital technology; far from it. Multiple studies on video games have found that users develop skills such as rapid decision making, intense focus, risk assessment, logic and a variety of visual-spatial abilities. The games are not easy. They work by keeping the player right at the edge of his or her competence level, exactly the place where learning takes place.

Steven Johnson points out in *Everything Bad Is Good for You: How Today's Popular Culture Is Actually Making Us Smarter* that today's technologies enhance our capabilities. They offer intellectual challenges, complexity, and personal involvement to a degree never before seen. In that way, movies, television, video games and the Internet have made us think more sharply. Johnson writes, "The kids are forced to think like grownups: analyzing complex social networks, managing resources, tracking subtle narrative intertwinings, recognizing long-term patterns. The grownups, in turn, get to learn from the kids: decoding each new technological wave, parsing the interfaces, and discovering the intellectual rewards of play. Parents should see this as an opportunity, not a crisis. Smart culture is no longer something you force your kids to ingest, like green vegetables. It's something you share."

Digital technology is alluring precisely because it is so engaging. The best sorts of learning technologies are open-ended, allowing children to explore, create and play while providing them the option of collaborating with others.

Our children speed down new digital highways with ever accelerating proficiency. As Google computer engineer Kevin Marks said in a presentation at a LIFT conference, "My generation draws the Internet as a cloud that connects everyone. The younger generation experiences it as oxygen that supports their digital lives."

It isn't just the Internet, but a range of technology that shapes the lives of young people. Education expert Marc Prensky calls those who have grown up using information technology "digital natives." They are accused of having short attention spans, but actually they have a different way of attending to information. They learn by going deep, going sideways and going quickly, with little patience for dross. Theirs is a hypertext world where an expert across the world can be found in a fraction of the time it takes to read an outdated textbook entry. They prefer to communicate in quick bursts and get right to the point. They connect easily across barriers, often finding highly diverse touch points drawn from pop culture and current events. They self-educate. They pursue their interests with intense focus and are drawn to interactive sources of information.

Schools and curricula simply haven't caught up with them.

John Seely Brown, retired chief scientist at Xerox Corporation, writes in the online article "Learning in the Digital Age" that education doesn't grasp the current generation's mode of communication.

It's an ever-evolving language of interpretation and expression, an interactive approach to learning, creating, and responding to information through a complex montage of images, sound, and communication. Students are pushing learning into a new dimension; it's a mistake to continue to try to teach them in timeworn ways. Their choices of communication need to be diversified to include, for example, visual interpretations of texts and historical figures or soundtracks for poetry. Students can take advantage of the enormous resources of the Web, transforming what they find there by using digital technologies to create something new and expressive.

Today's youth are well ahead of most digital curricula designed by adults. Teens use cell phones and online spaces to constantly expand their interests while developing wider contexts for social interaction. Learning is a collateral effect as they discover, share and discuss music, movies, photos and other images, video clips, games, news and opinion. Many young people, completely on their own, become proficient in programming languages. They set up social networks and develop websites using online tools with ease. This comfort with digital media is proving an important avenue to success for innovative entrepreneurs who launched careers at an early age: Darren Herman's IGA Worldwide places advertising within video games; Ashley Qualls runs Whateverlife, offering MySpace backgrounds; and, of course, Mark Zuckerberg and his college friends created Facebook.

I figure out more different stuff and talk to more people in an hour online than my Gramps does in a week, no, maybe a month. —Corey, 15

Technology gives us more choices than previous generations could have imagined. These choices change our daily lives. We are linked to many more people, aware of more information, and able to accomplish more. But as a side effect, we're likely to face incessant interruption. We can use technology or minimize its impact to the extent we choose. It helps to consider the ramifications. What are the consequences of foregoing a rake for a power leaf blower? How could some of the time spent playing World of Warcraft be used otherwise? What is changed when accepting each new device in our lives?

There's usually a downside. Less eye contact, no reason to take a walk to the post office, or the way a parent's workload more easily intrudes on family time. Become more aware of technology's impact on your life by discussing it with family members and friends. You may choose to enforce guidelines, such as specific times when there can be no intrusion by phones, TVs or laptops. Mealtime and bedtime rituals are particularly vital parts of the day to keep communication on a simple human level, free of any devices that take us away from eye-to-eye interaction.

Of more importance, science and technology advance faster than our recognition of their ethical implications. Examples of this abound. Farmers use genetically modified crops, long-lasting pesticides, and radio-frequency livestock tags. Military personnel deploy cluster bombs and depleted uranium weapons. Because we *can* doesn't mean we *should*.

We need to have ongoing conversations about new technologies, particularly about potential moral quandaries. In a perfect circle of reasoning, some forms of technology, such as cheaper means of accessing the Internet and wider cell phone access, assist us in reaching out to people across the world whose experiences and ideas help us understand the impact of recent innovations. In this way technology grants us access to wisdom when used mindfully. As parents, we need to teach our children to continue asking questions and seeking out even difficult answers. A sustainable future relies on it.

Empathy and Cooperation

"Kindness can become its own motive. We are made kind by being kind."—Eric Hoffer

---

Empathy happens when we "feel" another person's grief, pain, happiness, anticipation or despair. We tend to react with compassion. By the age of two, most children already demonstrate empathy. This is a cornerstone of ethical development.

For decades science has told us that we act compassionately for somewhat selfish reasons. Such theories say altruism has more to do with promoting a cause important to us, advancing our own moral standing, or simply making us feel good about ourselves. Those factors may come into play. But people generate kindness from a level much deeper than self-interest. Researchers are discovering what poets and theologians have long surmised: we are by nature caring beings.

Experiments and brain imaging technology show that acting charitably stimulates parts of the brain associated not with personal reward but related to perceiving the needs of others. In other words, we are stirred to act selflessly when we recognize our shared humanity, not by any conscious or unconscious desire to feel good about it. Other studies show that acts of generosity activate an older part of the brain, suggesting that altruism is so basic to who we are that we are likely to react this way even without thinking about it. It may be that much of the strife and unhappiness we see in the world today has to do with suppressing this very natural part of ourselves.

As mentioned earlier, mirror neurons in our brains respond as we observe other people, causing us to feel before we think. These mirror neurons are part of our biological hardware for compassion.

The evidence that we are empathetic by nature also goes to the heart of who we are. It turns out that our emotional and thought processes are directly linked to the rhythmic thumping in the center of our chests. Research by the Institute of HeartMath reveals that the heart has its own intelligence. Our hearts have forty thousand neurons, as many as in our brains, making them truly organs of perception and expression. Heartbeats are a language affecting the way we perceive and react to the world around us. It's known that strong negative emotion can cause heart rhythms to become irregular and disordered, disordering other body systems as well. In contrast, positive feelings of love, gratitude and compassion create coherent heart rhythms. These coherent heartbeats put the body in sync. As a result, the two branches of the nervous system coordinate with enhanced efficiency, immune responses are boosted, protective and regenerative hormones are released, even brain function improves in alignment with the heart. It's no wonder that positive emotions summon a full-body sense of well-being. We are biologically predisposed toward feelings such as compassion and appreciation, since our bodies function most effectively in this state.

Our heart provides even more evidence that we are empathic beings. That's because our loving hearts affect others, even without words. The strongest electromagnetic field produced by the body comes from the heart. It's about five times stronger than the field produced by the brain. The heart's field radiates through every cell in the body, extending well beyond the skin. Using a sensitive detector called a magnetometer, this field can be measured up to eight or ten feet away. In other words, we broadcast the electromagnetic signal of our own hearts. As HeartMath has shown, the most powerfully coherent heartbeat is that of the caring heart. Love and compassion are not only emotional experiences, they are sent outward like signals that can calm the heart rates of people nearby. Reaching for your child's hand on a crowded subway may give you a feeling of gratitude, and your loving heart may affect your child as well as the stranger next to you—both blessed by your harmonious heart.

The most profound effect is found in touch. Research shows that caring touch can have an extraordinarily positive effect on health, mental state, even longevity. Touch is as vital as any nutrient. Infants raised in foundling homes in the early 1900s were fed and kept clean, but employees had no extra time to cuddle them. These babies developed what was called *marasmus*, meaning they literally wasted away. The majority died. Those who survived were often severely impaired. Your hand on a child's shoulder and your hug before bed conveys much more than words can say.

Positive emotions such as compassion, happiness and gratitude are a unique form of intelligence, directing us toward more authentic behaviors. It's only natural that we use this inner guidance system rather than rely on intellect alone.

Homeschooling lets us raise a tender-hearted child ... —Tisha, Maryland

---

Creating a more heart-centered lifestyle may be second nature for some of us. This has to do with being attuned to one's feelings and intuitions while remaining sensitive to and respectful of other people. When children are brought up in this atmosphere, the best in themselves is called forth. They are empowered to develop strong values and trust their own perceptions. They can learn to solve problems without extensive adult intervention. And they don't have to hide their tenderness, warmth, enthusiasm and optimism.

Many people continue to assert that children do best when raised with more punitive, heavy-handed methods. After all, they say, our violent history proves that it's human nature to be selfish and out of control.

That's shortsighted. While a cursory look at history shows a swath of bloodshed across the centuries, this is hardly a balanced perspective. Tales of conquest and destruction never mention the real underpinning of civilization. Cooperation.

Every minute of every day people take care of one another and uphold one another's interests, as they have throughout time. Without careful tending, the sick would not heal, babies would not grow, and humanity would not flourish. Infinite acts of kindness and generosity have brought us to this moment in time.

Let's remember that history doesn't provide the barest glimpse of human nature. History consists of details recorded from our earliest civilizations until now. The unwritten span of prehistory makes up 99 percent of our time on earth. Most anthropologists affirm that cooperation was pivotal for survival during this stage of nomadic hunter-gatherer bands. A lone human would not last long. No claws, fangs or heavy fur protected them. Interdependence was the key. Our forebears

lived in small groups where together they developed language, healing arts, and methods of procuring and storing food. Their cooperative efforts in child rearing, protection from predators, and shelter from the elements gave them a survival edge. Those who lived long enough to reproduce passed on the traits of cooperation to their descendants. This stage of our development was characterized by generally peaceable human interactions. No convincing evidence of warfare exists in this long span of prehistory. Planned aggression against others apparently began around the start of agriculture.

Violence, but not against other humans, was a factor in our prehistory, according to Barbara Ehrenreich in her book, *Blood Rites*. She says the "original trauma" shaping the human psyche was the terror of being preyed on by large carnivores. Rooted deep in our human makeup are "the powerful emotions, associated with courage and altruism, that were required for group defense." Dangerous predators were numerous, and escape was not always an option. Survival of the group required that some, most often young males, fight so that the others might live. Traditions sprang up to celebrate these men who suffered for the lives of their people. This blood and limb sacrifice played out until the technology of defensive weaponry began to turn the advantage to humans. A quick response to alarm and a willingness to align with one's group are encoded in our genes.

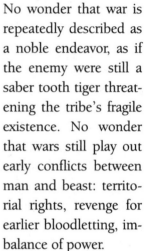

No wonder that war is repeatedly described as a noble endeavor, as if the enemy were still a saber tooth tiger threatening the tribe's fragile existence. No wonder that wars still play out early conflicts between man and beast: territorial rights, revenge for earlier bloodletting, imbalance of power.

From the larger perspective of time, we are barely out of prehistory, just beginning to adjust to the complexities of civilization. But as anthropologist Douglas P. Fry notes in *Beyond War: The Human Potential for Peace*, this does not mean that humans are intrinsically violent. Instead, cooperation and empathy, along with the willingness to sacrifice for a greater cause, are characteristics that more accurately represent humankind. Fry says that awareness of our interdependence helps individuals as well as leaders replace violence with cooperation.

When children lash out, it does not reflect humanity's tendency toward violence or cruelty so much as reflect influences in their own lives. Newborns are remarkably similar whether they are raised in an American suburb, a Swedish farm or a Chinese city. In fact, researchers tell us that the youngest among us tend to be innately helpful and cooperative. But cultural differences in behavior become noticeable as these children grow. Jean Liedloff, author of *The Continuum Concept*, describes what she observed while living among tribal families in a South American rainforest. The children were responsible, yet playful. They spent their days together happily, unsupervised and without antagonism. Older children carried babies, toddlers explored freely. Adults didn't undermine children by cautioning them. As a consequence, the children spent their days safely and independently, continuing to develop competence. Liedloff says, "We are paying a terrible price when we do not trust our human nature, which works beautifully when we do. When we don't trust it, our expectations are inappropriate for ourselves and our children."

I believe that children who are raised in a free range environment enjoy the natural benefit of love and nurturing that every child deserves. In turn, they learn to trust themselves because of the confidence their parents have in them and their abilities ... Because they have lived in an environment of unconditional acceptance, it seems only natural that they are often very accepting and sensitive to others as well. As my children have gone out into the world, they have found great joy in helping friends, family and neighbors.

I think you can help nurture this in many ways. The most obvious is practicing empathy, but I think it also helps to go out into the community and meet others who do and don't practice empathy. Both prove to be very good examples. Not being confined to school nine months out of the year, my boys were free to spend quality time with their friends of all ages, grandparents, aunts, uncles and older neighbors. We share a duplex with my parents and

handicapped sister, so they have had the opportunity to help them daily. On the other side of that coin, they have received so much from them as well. Between them and our many neighbors whom they often volunteered to help with yard work or other chores, the boys got glimpses into their lives and experienced even more hands-on examples of the goodness that others in our community have to share.

—Mary Nix, Ohio

Interestingly, versions of the Golden Rule, *Treat others as you would have others treat you*, are found in all major religions. This benchmark of empathic reasoning teaches us to understand others by reflecting on our own feelings. This hints at how our heart rhythms, our minds and emotions, teach us to care, from the inside out.

The built-in empathic response is only part of our moral development as humans. People in children's lives help them attach ideas to these feelings. They learn what is acceptable and unacceptable in the context of family, community, and often a religious upbringing, providing an intricate web of value-rich relationships that shape decision making well into adulthood.

All of us who nurture children are their elders. It is our role to provide loving guidance and accept each child for who he or she is. This begins at a baby's birth and continues throughout the growing years. It is the elders' task to enforce standards gently but consistently, express affection, and build on positive behavior. We do ordinary caring things each day—things that are unexceptional and require no acclaim—yet these are exactly the things that demonstrate compassion. When our homeschooling lives center on empathy and cooperation, our children are provided with the tools to build a promising future—tools handed down from their earliest ancestors.

CHAPTER FOUR

Connecting with Others

Synergy

"The meeting of two personalities is like the contact of two chemical substances: if there is any reaction, both are transformed."
—Carl Jung

Our children are free to learn in the wider community, so the possibilities for personal growth are multiplied. One perk is that their friendships open up beyond standard parameters like similar ages and shared interests. Often in our society children are confined to contacts with people very much like themselves. But at any age, it's when we confront the dilemmas posed by differences between us that we learn more about each other, and ultimately about ourselves. Sometimes this is uncomfortable. We encounter people who make us doubt or disagree, who stretch our minds and emotions. This is invaluable. Character develops through such challenges.

Children make crucial strides in personality and social development through their relationships. Interacting with all sorts of people can enliven their lives. In fact a rich variety of friends and mentors is a characteristic often shared by the world's leading thinkers and innovators. You will find that sharing field trips and activities with homeschoolers is convenient, but by all means don't limit yourself only to friendships with other homeschoolers. Be open to connecting with people of different ages, ethnicities, talents and persuasions.

The most important thing about education is always people, I think. I do believe that homeschooling helped expose me to a wider variety of people than I might otherwise have met. —Melissa Barton, Colorado

I'm not sure what regular society means when they say that homeschoolers will not be exposed to others with different ideas. Honestly, if it weren't for the freedoms of homeschooling, I never would have had the opportunity to be exposed to others who are very, very different. You can't tell me it isn't challenging to be in the same room with a conservative Catholic family, an atheist family and a family who practices Wicca ... and not only do you get along, but you laugh, find common ground, and even dare I say learn something new? In public school, I never would have even been allowed to hear about these religious differences and how these people live their daily lives—that would have been forbidden, not considered politically correct, and would not have fit in the model of giving everyone the same opportunity (in other words making everyone the same). Homeschooling and exposing myself and my kids to those who are different is a mental, spiritual, emotional and educational exercise. —L.C., Ohio

The ability to communicate well with one another is crucial. Our children need to learn early on the value of listening and empathizing with others. They also need to take part in meaningful conversations rather than typically rote adult-child dialogue consisting of questions and commands. Discussion, compassionate problem solving and active collaboration are essential skills in our increasingly complex world.

Friendships

"Each friend represents a world in us, a world possibly not born until they arrive, and it's only by this meeting that a new world is born." —Anais Nin

The relationships in our children's lives can make a world of difference. While family influence has the greatest impact, as children grow they naturally seek out models for themselves beyond the sphere of home. They need to bounce self-perceptions off other people as much as they need the playful dynamic found in friendship. Many parents recognize that the happiest homeschoolers are those who have good friends.

Sometimes the friendships providing the most pivotal turning points in our lives come about by sheer synchronicity. A homeschooler from a large family rebels against his parents' strictness. His parents react with punishments. One of those punishments is to help the church janitor clean the basement in preparation for an upcoming event. It turns out that the church janitor is a young Sudanese man with a limited command of English. The janitor is living in a small room in the church as part of a refugee resettlement program. This young man spent much of his childhood on the run from a civil war that wiped out his family and village before he found a refugee camp. The homeschooled youth tells his family that he'll continue volunteering at church in order to spend more time with his new friend. The Sudanese man has endured starvation, disease and the attacks of wild animals, but he needs help navigating a new language and culture. The homeschooled youth finds greater strengths in himself through his friendship with someone who is stronger than anyone he's ever met. Both the homeschooled teen and the Sudanese man remain friends, supporting one another across what others might perceive as a cultural divide, as they work toward their own goals.

Many times, friendships jump-start an interest with surprising vigor. One preteen attended a game session at a nearby hobby store, planning to play a favorite card game with a friend. When his friend didn't arrive he played a board game with others gathered there instead. The game was fast paced and people cheered him on. He started attending each weekly session to play the game. It turned out that the game was a prototype designed by a college physics class. The boy was learning about principles of physics while honing the higher math skills required to make moves on the board. The encouragement of his fellow players launched him into a whole new field of inquiry. At the age of twelve he now enjoys modifying and designing games of his own, spends at least two evenings a week with his game-playing friends and is considering physics as a career.

> Homeschooled children are more likely to ignore distinctions like grade level and ability when making friends. In part this is an outgrowth of the homeschooling community where events are typically multi-aged. It's also due to differences among the children since they develop skills on more individual timelines and experience less peer pressure to "fit in."

Explore a variety of activities. You'll be providing your children with priceless opportunities to make friends. These may not be of the sort depicted in popular culture— typically two children of the same age and gender. You may need to look through a different lens at the relationships your child enjoys to notice their significance.

Our children have always had friends of all ages. They are comfortable carrying on an in-depth conversation with people their grandparents' ages as equally as their own peers ... We deliver Meals on Wheels once a week and several of our recipients share some of their life experiences with my children—and they often speak of these people throughout their week.

We have neighbors of varying ages and varying backgrounds. A gentleman down the street, whose lawn my son mows, shares his rich knowledge of fishing with my 12-year-old son. Josh is now up-to-date on which are the "good" lures!

We just met an unschooling family from Israel. They are in our area for 3 years. In just a short week we have learned SO much from them and I know there is much more to learn. We've learned that there is much that is different, but MANY things are universal to life no matter where you live! I know that when they return to Israel, we will remain in contact with them. It brings the Middle East conflict into our living room and gives us faces and real lives to the stories we hear on the news and in the papers.　　　—Angie Beck, Kansas

My son was 7 years old when he claimed Ray as his best friend. We often had Ray over for dinner, and he regularly joined James and my husband at our local arena football games. Ray is a 65-year-old nuclear physicist! He was working with my husband on temporary assignment from another state and spent six months of the year here for several years. His work here has ended, and I have no idea what James may have learned from him, but Ray did smoke a pipe and wear suspenders—both things James had never seen before! And he could recite the alphabet backwards, which always enthralled the kids.   —Susan, Alabama

When Cassidy was thirteen, he started a part-time job at the home of a woman who made necklaces of semi-precious stones. He was her helper and apprentice. The work was creative but somewhat repetitive, offering them time for much conversation. A friendship developed and the woman became an influence about going to college. She even paid for Cass to consult with a guidance counselor and that led him to find just the college he wanted and all the necessary information in order to apply and become admitted. He was a highly successful student in college—had his own apartment off campus; dean's list every semester; pres of film society; graduated Magna Cum Laude.   —Ned Vare, Connecticut

Because our children are not confined to a classroom, they are able to, and expect to be able to make friends from any culture of which they are exposed. They are not tied down with homework in the evening, so they are able to get out of the house to play, visit the parks and playgroups, attend the churches of their choice, and so on. This freedom has exposed them to many different people of many different backgrounds, and different ranges in age. They do not feel that they have to play only with children of their own ages, and they do not seem to carry around many of the prejudices that their public schooling counterparts develop in the form of clicks and gangs. To them, the more playmates, the merrier, and they are not swayed by race, religion or background.

—Laurel Santiago, Texas

Elders

"The truly human society is a learning society, where grandparents, parents, and children are students together." —Eric Hoffer

Younger age groups in our society are largely deprived of meaningful contact with their elders. Judging by the media exposure or hiring practices of the business world, seniors are simply irrelevant. Yet throughout history, older people have always provided teaching and guidance based on their experience. Elders were expected to balance the headstrong tendencies of young people with reason and knowledge borne of greater understanding. Elders provided continuity with their memories, their regard for ritual, their respect for stories and the link to ancestry their advanced age represented. Communities that marginalized the wisdom of their elders did not flourish. We have dismissed the contributions of seniors for so many generations that, in many cases, they may not wish to or be able to rise to the challenge of acting as our cultural wisdom keepers. But expecting our elders to amuse themselves in retirement is dismissive if they have real contributions they wish to make.

Homeschoolers are in a unique position to welcome a spectrum of ages into their educational experience. We don't have institutional rules to work around; instead, we can work around the schedules of seniors who are available to share time with us.

When Arden was 11 he wanted to learn to play the accordion. He saw one in a second-hand store ... and that's all he wanted for his birthday. I asked around to find him a teacher and by the grace of God found a retired military man who has been playing the accordion his whole life. I drove Arden for lessons every week and he got in the van afterwards each

time and told me stories about military honor, about family values, about history, and as he got older, some bawdy stories too.

The colonel is in a polka band and many times Arden appeared as a special guest even though he didn't like polka music too much. The colonel taught him to play all kinds of music and how to transpose Coldplay and White Stripes music for the accordion.

Arden is 17 now. He doesn't need lessons any more but he drives over to visit his old teacher a few times a month. I asked him what they do when he visits because it's hard for me to imagine a kid and a guy in his 70's being friends. Arden looks surprised like there's something wrong with me for not having older friends. Arden's friendship with the colonel has been a blessing. I know he listened to him when he wouldn't listen to his father or me. I can't imagine what these teen years would have been like without the colonel in Ardens's life.

—Cathy Lynne

My daughter, Kylia, spent several years working at a local cafe which attracts a very diverse group of people. Every morning, about seven or eight retired gentlemen meet for coffee and conversation. Kylia was immediately drawn to them, and always says that they were one of her favorite groups. They brought her vegetables from their gardens, told her about interesting things they had done in their lives, shared their thoughts on problems she was facing, and overall, became very close friends of hers.

—Ruth Radney, Ohio

My family consists of two girls, ages 6 and 10, my significant other who is a software programmer for a large consulting firm in Seattle, and myself, a graduate student of clinical psychology working towards a doctorate. We use a classical homeschool model with lots of reading, writing, memorization, Latin, etc. All hard work!

But I have classes and I work 20 hours a week at an internship site to meet supervision requirements for my degree. So for two days a week, my girls stay with their grandmother and grandfather. This last year, the days I needed childcare rested on the days my parents would go to the Senior Center in Black Diamond. So for over 10 months my two girls would go with them.

Slowly, my mom got the little one used to seeing older adults who in some cases were missing limbs, eyes and control of their face. My youngest daughter began the sweetest and most wonderful friendship with a man named Jack (and still loves him!) who has had a stroke and cannot move half of his face and is missing an eye. He can barely walk.

The girls have learned to be helpful. They have learned to respectfully listen and use an inside voice. They have learned to wait up for those who can't walk as fast when the senior center would go on field trips ... My mom told me that all the seniors are jealous because some of them don't get to see their grandchildren more than once a year! And here she gets to be with these beautiful children every week. They are the light of the senior center. Everyone looks forward to seeing them.

The girls will sometimes sit quietly and catch up on their workbooks if there is not much going on or their grandfather is busy playing pool with friends at the center. Every week there is a raffle drawing. The girls often win, and they regularly give their winnings to the seniors who did not perhaps win anything that week. My 10-year-old will help them look up Scrabble words in the dictionary if they have trouble seeing, and have even been known to fix Jack's coffee just the way he likes it before carefully bringing it to him at his table.

I don't think there are words to really describe how these experiences have influenced their development as human beings! I think the benefits may still be yet to come as they grow and mature and we get to see how this last year will shape them into the young ladies they will become. My girls ... have learned that they can socialize with all ages. They are just as wonderful and gentle with younger children and babies. They can play a mean game of chess with any 35-year-old and they can take turns playing Italian lawn bowling with players ages 3 to 72!

—Nicole Laurent, Washington

The most natural way to connect with elders who have skills and interests to share with your family and/or homeschool group is by establishing relationships through your own networks, such as your extended family, neighborhood, church and organizations to which you belong. Check out special interest groups (a lapidary club, quilter's guild, historical society), the local senior center, veterans associations and other community groups. You can request volunteer educators and mentors through Senior Corps www.seniorcorps.org (202) 606-5000 and the RSVP program www.seniorcorps.org/about/programs/rsvp.asp

Homeschool Groups

"Great things are done by a series of small things brought together." —Vincent Van Gogh

The popularity of homeschooling makes it likely that there are plenty of other self-educators in your area. Chances are you'll notice other families with children out and about during school hours. Stepping up to make these acquaintances can lead to wonderful friendships.

I've never been a joiner. That's probably one reason I want to make my kids' education more personal. We share homeschooling fun with two other families. The Watsons we met by chance. Our kids started playing at Waterbury Park and next thing I knew Charmaine and I were talking about ways to make math more fun. We have been getting together at least once a week ever since. Our friends the Freemans started homeschooling sort of at our instigation. Sometimes we all go on outings together. Often it seems like we are going through the same things. It helps to share ideas. My kids at 4, 7 and 9 have fun playing with their cousins and neighbors but they love time spent with their homeschooling friends.

—Angel, New Jersey

There are well-established homeschool groups nearly everywhere. Tapping into local support networks and learning co-ops shouldn't be difficult. You can find them by word of mouth, local library community listings and church bulletins. Or you can try database searches such as the *Home Education Magazine* support group listings, which also provide information on starting or running a support group. www.homeedmag.com/wlcm_groups.html

It wasn't until ... we were able to attend kids' meetings, roller skating days, field trips and enrichment classes that I began to feel less isolated, more validated almost. I was able to connect with moms who homeschooled for years. They had so much to share, so much real experience. I was able to vent my frustrations and concerns and yet still feel accepted even when my family was still at odds with our decision to homeschool. I sincerely doubt I would be enjoying this adventure as much as I am, and therefore my children enjoying it as well, without the support of like-minded women. Having a group of people that I can feel very comfortable with, to share ups and downs, joys and fears has been absolutely invaluable in this journey.

—Michele, Ohio

When people think of support groups, they often think of a great resource for their children. That's certainly true. I can't name the amount of field trips, enrichment classes, contests and competitions my children have done with other children within different support groups we've belonged to.

But, as a stay-at-home mom who happens to homeschool, I've found that the support groups have a way of becoming MY support as well. I get to know the moms of my children's friends and am amazed at how many have turned into wonderful friendships. We share each other's joys and sorrows. We sometimes share vacations and we share rants. While these moms help support our homeschooling efforts, they seem to help support our every day lives as well.

Not only do I feel that support groups have enriched our learning experience, but the parents in the trenches have also blessed us with friendship for a lifetime.
—Beth Whitson, Ohio

Some parents choose a homeschool group limited to a particular religious orientation or one tied to a specific educational outlook. Others will only consider joining an inclusive group, preferring that no one be excluded.

A homeschool group I started was very loose and fun. It grew by leaps and bounds, suddenly we had 150 people with us at the zoo. I was organizing all the field trips. Then it became exclusive, requiring a statement of faith. I felt at the time like I was the only one this was happening to. A board meeting decided that

I and another woman, a Muslim, could not be on the board. It was very hurtful, relying on their support, then all of a sudden being excluded ... I thought that people who were homeschooling were doing so for the reasons we were, to find out about the world. But they were homeschooling to keep them from it.

I'm grateful it didn't work out. That experience sent us farther afield where the field trips were more interesting and the energy was better. Most people in our old homeschool group I know to this day and speak to on a regular basis. It's an amazing bond to help each other find our way and follow our intuition. It validates you. People should not close the circle to others.   *—Lynn Reed, Georgia*

We are Christian homeschoolers with three very active boys. I am grateful for all the opportunities they have to learn how to become good Christian men through our church, like Awana. When they were younger I strongly preferred that their friends have the same religious foundation as we do. But in our church there are kids I don't want them to associate with due to bad behavior and poor morals, and on the other hand

in our secular homeschool group there are wonderful kids who have been great role models even though they don't attend church.

When we started homeschooling I almost joined the large homeschool group in town. Every member had to sign a statement of faith. The statement reflected my beliefs so I had no problem with it but when I thought about it that meant that my neighbor in a mixed religion marriage couldn't join if she started homeschooling, my sister who became a Mormon couldn't join if she moved closer to us, probably a lot of people would be left out. So I joined the secular group instead and I haven't been sorry. I was surprised how many Christians are in the secular group for the same reasons I am, they objected to a statement of faith that left other people out. My friend Sandy said it best. She said, "How are we supposed to teach our children that we're all God's children if we exclude His people?"

—Callie Palinki, Texas

Although homeschoolers often have strongly held opinions on religion, types of instruction and parenting styles, with minimal effort we can still find common ground with one another. Despite the cross-currents of different political and corporate agendas that influence our growing demographic, we are simply families dedicated to what we believe is best for our children. Treating each other with respect is basic human decency. This also demonstrates to our children a trait necessary to create a more livable society.

Whenever possible, share information about learning opportunities with all homeschoolers in your area. When you are involved in developing programs, collaborate with other support groups to make these programs meet as many needs as possible. Networking with each other across so-called boundary lines of lifestyle or learning choice helps us create stronger support groups and better options for enrichment in our communities for all families.

I've set up homeschool theater discounts for several years now through Broadway Across America ... I also set up Dallas theater discounts on Broadway shows with a different company that was running similar shows ...

Also, this will be my fifth season with setting up Houston Rockets Homeschool Days. I run a statewide TX homeschool website and mailing list (Taffie), so that helps with networking other groups. When the final Lord of the Rings movie was released in 2003, I set up a private homeschool showing for 600. We also do select shows at Toyota Center in downtown Houston. Texas has lots of homeschoolers, so businesses are willing to work with us for the most part. In Houston alone, there are over 80 support groups, some have over 300 families. —Susan Frederick, Texas
www.jsoft.com/archive/taffie

I began Take Off! Field Tripping when my older daughter was about 5 years old. I wanted Take Off! to be totally inclusive and user-friendly for all homeschoolers, so I left out what I personally found to be unnecessary, including monthly meetings, and focused on field trips. [Two years later]... I set up a website and turned the snail mail list into an email list. I listed Take Off! on a few home school resource pages, and sat back to watch what would happen. It was pretty incredible! I had 6 families on my list before I went online in April, and by September, the same year, I was congratulating my 100th family for joining! It "took off" like a rocket! ... By the end of that year, Take Off! was nearing 500 families.

... I have been surprised by the kindness and appreciation I receive on a daily basis from list members. Many people are truly just too happy to find that Take Off! exists and that all they have to do is sign up and join us for trips. I get quite a few friendly notes of gratitude and people are just as wonderful in person.

—Jen Lake, Ohio

Our group has a great time together. We've found that what works for our group as it gets bigger is having a general structure with flexibility within the structure. We meet as a group the first week of the month with a speaker or workshop for the kids, the second and fourth weeks for learning co-op classes and the third week for indoor and outdoor games. Plus field trips and whatever else we can do. We have new members all the time. A book we've been using for ideas to get everyone involved at meetings is Team Challenges: 170+ Group Activities to Build Cooperation, Communication, and Creativity by Kris Bordessa. It's very important to me to invite everyone. —Lauren, Minnesota

---

Homeschoolers aren't limited to support group meetings and newsletters. Connecting with others has never been easier.

- Search for or generate forums easily using services such as Yahoo! Groups http://groups.yahoo.com or Google Groups http://groups.google.com to set up calendars, share files, post information and develop plans.
- Use social network sites such as facebook.com, ning.com and 360.yahoo.com to facilitate lively interactions.
- Share experiences and generate interest in activities by blogging.
- Combine efforts to provide educational tours, trips and other events through field trip co-ops.
- Coordinate your own activities with friends, neighbors and family.

Regardless of the method used, it's simple to create groups of any size devoted to exploring the wide range of options available to families looking for enrichment.

Interest-based Groups

"The people who get on in this world are the people who get up and look for the circumstances they want, and, if they can't find them, make them." —George Bernard Shaw

Many homeschoolers develop small, interest-based groups either as informal arrangements between friends or as offshoots of a larger organization. These get-togethers can be loosely or carefully structured.

Some examples include:

- stop motion movie-makers with individual projects and team movies, hosting regular screenings of their short films (youngest member five years old)
- cooking club for preteens, meeting at members' homes to make (and eat) themed foods and plan recipes for next club event
- nature sketching and journaling group of parents and youth, scheduling hikes in different wilderness areas to write, draw and share their work
- boys' bookgroup with activities based on a sci-fi and adventure books
- rock climbers, practicing at indoor climbing walls as well as outdoor locations
- young children's hands-on science club
- fiberworks group with projects, farm trips and events with adult spinning/ weaving guilds
- families joining to make costumes, chain mail and armor for re-enactments
- beachcombers group where young children play along the waterside while adults and older children monitor ecological conditions for a non-profit organization

- debate and elocution society (members' aspirations include acting, politics, law)
- cartoonists meeting, members working on graphic novels, cartoon strips, cards.

The benefits can be extraordinary. Children (and often their parents) relish delving into a favorite topic or activity with fellow enthusiasts. And enthusiasm is a powerful motivator. These interest-based groups provide flexibility. While some groups are parent-led, many times the children progress toward planning and running the sessions on their own. Some of these gatherings have continued for years, others stay active for a short time or move ahead with new goals. The camaraderie in these groups is often as reinforcing as the activities themselves.

Learning Communities

"If we value independence, if we are disturbed by the growing conformity of knowledge, of values, of attitudes, which our present system induces, then we may wish to set up conditions of learning which make for uniqueness, for self-direction, and for self-initiated learning." —Carl Rogers

Homeschool learning communities form in many ways and range in size from a few families to hundreds of members. Many of them are organized with limited hierarchy. These groups tend to share the work as equally as possible and remain open to change. Homeschoolers meet in homes, libraries, churches, town halls, recreation centers—wherever there's space. They call their gatherings all sorts of names: Cottage School, Friday Club, Learning Co-op, Enrichment Sessions. Many members wouldn't term their organization a learning community. The variety of names is a testament to the local flavor and freely chosen subject matter. There, youth participate in classes or workshops, art and theater experiences, open playtime and any other options collectively made available. The content varies as the interests and needs of the group change. Most often parents facilitate these sessions, but it isn't unusual to find older youths or members of the community at large providing guidance.

Enrichment Days have been one of those things my children just can't seem to live without while we've homeschooled. While field trips are fun, oftentimes children don't get to interact as much with the other children. With Enrichment Days, children get to see each other often enough to make friendships and encourage each other with projects they are working on together—Those are the friendships that have lasted for years—for both moms and children. How exciting to watch children grow from elementary aged kids to successful college students.

Some sessions that we've had at our Enrichment Days were a little more academic like government, speech and poetry. Some were less academic, but just as valuable like Living History and Mousetrap Inventions. My children always seemed to enjoy the classes that had some structure to them, but allowed them free rein in the creative department. Imagine being given certain materials and an objective of what something must do by the end of class and then having to come up with a finished project with team members in an hour! Not only did children have to learn how things worked (and what didn't), but they had to make their voices and ideas heard and become part of a cooperative team to try and compete against others doing the same thing.

—Beth Whitson, Ohio

Co-op classes have been the most structured part of our homeschool experience. The kids pick and choose what they want to do. Sometimes what they learn in co-op is a springboard for ongoing interests like photography.

—Debbie

Many cooperative learning communities have found their programs increasingly in demand. Then the need to organize along more formal lines becomes apparent. Some learning communities rent or own their own meeting space and are open several days a week to meet the demand for high quality, hands-on learning opportunities with flexible and shared resources.

The details of how to start and maintain a learning community aren't within the scope of this book. Excellent information can be found at www.pathsoflearning.net and in the book *Creating Learning Communities* by Ron Miller. Other ways to engage your community in learning can be found at lauragraceweldon.com/category/community

Youth Organizations

"A ship is safe in a harbor, but that's not what a ship is for." —Admiral Grace Hopper

Youth organizations are a traditional way to gather children for learning and recreation. Join an existing group or start your own. If forming a new group consider your options. Some families prefer to organize an all-homeschool group while others appreciate the chance to include area youth whether or not they homeschool. The choices will affect meeting and activity times.

There are many youth organizations to choose from, each with different approaches to serving children. From the links listed below check out specific options. Most links have local resources with additional information and all will refer you to groups in your area.

I've been a 4-H member for a long time and probably done about every project there is. My favorites were woodworking and model rockets, I placed at state level with both of those. I'm on the youth board. We help at the fair and have fun meetings. I use a hand held radio at the fair to direct the supplies. It's the best time of year.
—Joshua, 14

I was really glad to find Earth Scouts. It's a nature-based, open-minded alternative that fits my fairie daughter better than a more regimented group might.
—Kelly

Resources

- 4-H offers hands-on projects, educational programs and summer camps. A 4-H Club can be as small as two children. The focus is on leadership, citizenship and life skills for youth ages 8 to 18. (301)-961-2800 www.4-h.org
- **Boy Scouts** is committed to building character, physical fitness and responsible citizenship through Boy Scouts, Exploring and Venturing programs. Boys from ages 7 to 20 can participate in a variety of challenging programs. www.scouting.org World Scouts www. scouting.org/International
- **Camp Fire USA** emphasizes leadership, self-reliance and environmental education for youth ages 3 to 21. They provide summer camps, teen action campaigns and community

service. Leaders can form a multi-age club to meet the needs of homeschooling families. (816)-285-2010 www.campfireusa.org

- **Earth Scouts** is a national organization for boys and girls ages 3 to 13. Groups can include one family or many young people. They foster understanding and responsibility for planetary health and cooperation. (813)-254-8454 www.earthscouts.org
- **Exploring and Venturing** are scout oriented programs for youths up to age 20. Exploring (972)-580-2420 www.learning-for-life.org/exploring/index.html, Venturing www.scouting.org/scoutsource/Venturing.aspx
- **Girl Scouts of America** focuses on helping girls develop strong values and the skills to become successful. Starting at age five they offer active options for girls. (800)-478-7248 www.girlscouts.org
- **World Assoc. of Girl Guides and Girl Scouts** +44 (0)20 7794 1181 www.wagggsworld.org
- **Interact** is a service club for teens 14 to 18 sponsored by Rotary International providing youth with the opportunity to identify a problem and work together on the solution. (847)-866-3000. www.rotary.org click on 'students and youth' tab.
- **Kiwanis International** offers clubs for youth, all emphasizing community service and leadership skills. Kiwanis Kids for elementary ages, Builders Club for middle school grades and Key Club for high schoolers. Homeschooled students are welcome to form their own clubs with an advisor. (800)-549-2647 www.kiwanis.org
- **Leo Clubs** are the youth branch of Lions Club International. They provide young people with the opportunity to serve their communities and develop leadership skills. (630)-571-5466 www.lionsclubs.org/EN/content/youth_leo_clubs.shtml
- **Roots and Shoots** is an organization started by primatologist Jane Goodall, empowering youth to connect with one another and work for positive change. From preschool to young adult this global program promotes learning and problem solving. (800)-592-JANE www.rootsandshoots.org
- **SpiralScouts International** is designed to be more child-led than most youth organizations. These Earth-based groups emphasize outdoor activities, mythology and interpersonal skills for those ages 8 and up. (248)-703-4750 www.spiralscouts.org
- **YMCA Adventure Guides** offers a flexible program geared to the parent-child connection for ages 5 through 9. Most activities involve a core group with some larger events such as campouts. (800)-872-9622 www.ymca.net/adventureguides

My granddaughters belonged to a 4H dance group for 7 years that performed English, Irish and Scottish folk dancing. After the group broke up, they continue to perform and my older granddaughter has, on her own, advertised to start a Morris Dancing 4H performance group that she is willing to lead. 4H has also been a wonderful experience, with opportunities to meet people, travel and learn new things.

—Karen Pennebaker, West Virginia

Also check with your religious denomination. Many have very active local and national youth organizations offering conferences and camps as well as local fellowship, recreation and charitable opportunities.

Our son was involved in a group called Young Judaea at about eight or nine years old. He kind of grew up in that program. It was wonderful because we are in such a small Jewish community that it allowed him to find a larger world out there. He went to Israel for his first year of college with that group after many years of going to summer camp and other leadership training. He made friends worldwide and his best friend is now in Africa with the Peace Corps.

—Lynn Reed, Georgia

Hosting

"What is there more kindly than the feeling between host and guest?"—Aeschylus

---

Consider expanding your "neighborhood" by hosting a person from abroad. This typically means offering room and board in your home to an exchange student. Your family gets to know a young person from another country for the summer or school year. You see your culture from his or her perspective. It's an excellent way to bring the world closer and the result is often a lasting friendship.

- **American Field Service** www.afs.org (212) 352-9810

- **Rotary Youth Exchange** www.rotary.org/en/studentsandyouth/youthprograms/rotaryyouthexchange

- **Youth For Understanding** www.yfu-usa.org (240)-235-2100

- **World Exchange** www.worldexchange.org (800) 444-3924

Contact the Council on Standards for International Educational Travel for more information www.csiet.org (703)-739-9050.

We have a new exchange student who just came from Poland on Friday ... Last night we had corn on the cob, he thought it was odd, we thought it was fun to show him ...

We've had exchange students 10 years—from Greenland, Costa Rica, Germany, Brazil, Sweden and now Poland. We love it. We love having other teenagers in our household. We love finding out about their cultures and showing them ours. There are a lot more similarities than differences. We've gotten all our kids through Rotary. We've noticed the kids are really ready for the experience. If you're going to leave home at 16 you're going to be an outgoing person. It helps to have younger kids in the house. The younger kids are a good distraction, more playful, and that helps a lot.

We include them in everything the family does. It's been a really positive thing. We've been back to visit them too.

We've traveled with their families, gone on vacation together. It gives you connections all over the world.

You learn things from them that you wouldn't know unless you knew a native ... It's a totally different perspective. Their vision of America is the media, tourists and what the government does, but here they hopefully get a real view. They become part of your family. It's really been a great experience.

—Jeanne Freeman, Ohio

You may also choose to host adult visitors. Check out groups you are affiliated with such as a religious institution, charity or political club. Oftentimes such organizations need short term lodging for a speaker or visiting dignitary. Also check with AFS Intercultural Programs www.afs.org and National Council for International Visitors www.nciv.org to find out about similar hosting opportunities.

Another option? Join Servas, the oldest of the international homestay programs. Approved hosts and travelers share the goals of building goodwill and understanding. Hosts who cannot offer overnight shelter may register as Day Hosts to provide conversation, a tour or a meal together. This non-profit organization has an application fee and interview. http://joomla.servas.org/

Other families open their homes to visitors in less formal ways. They invite friends they've made through conferences, forums or other long-distance connections. Each time we expand the circle of friendship beyond the usual boundaries we develop a greater awareness of our commonality with others as well as a deeper respect for the diversity of the human family.

My mom is a surgical nurse. She volunteered to let a kid from Turkey stay in our guest room. Nourhan needed a couple surgeries for a bad birth defect. Her mom came too. My brothers and I weren't too sure we wanted to do this. But she was cool. She hardly ever complained no matter what they did. She learned a lot of English considering she's a little kid. We could make her laugh at anything. Her mom made us lots of food we hadn't tasted. They stayed for about two months. Now we miss them alot. I think we might go visit some day. I am interested in the news about their country and try to picture their family there.

—Joshua, 14

Finding a Mentor

"Children have never been very good at listening to their elders, but they have never failed to imitate them." —James Baldwin

We hear a lot about the importance of having a mentor. When youth admire and choose to emulate someone it can change their lives. This sort of relationship is a time-honored way to grow into adulthood. Ideally our children are informally mentored by many people as they mature. But often a more specific mentoring relationship is sought to help a young person gain experience and knowledge in an area of interest.

Sometimes fate and opportunity collide, providing the right mentor. This isn't unusual. When a young person has an abiding interest in a certain area, whether forensics or vintage auto restoration, they get involved in the field in their own way. They read magazines and books on the topic, join special interest organizations, contribute to online forums, attend public workshops or lectures, do projects that require them to seek out advice. Many of these activities put them in touch with adults who are experts in the field.

But sometimes fate and opportunity need a little prompting. There are keys to finding an adult who will be a good match. These keys include making the effort to find resource people, showing appreciation, continuing to maintain contact, and asking how you might gain experience in the field.

I'm getting to the point where I trust that you put it out there to the universe and things happen. There's desire and passion and, you recognize later, gratefully, that the right things fell into place.

My daughter was interested in birds and got a cockatiel for her birthday. My son wasn't so happy that his sister had the coolest pet ever and wanted one too … We went to the breeder's house to get him a bird because the pet store was going out of business … We were enthralled. Hand feeding these little birds was the closest thing to nursing. It's such a nurturing thing to do. We went from bird to bird to feed them. We found a bird for Forrest, but really what we were amazed by were all these baby birds that looked like little featherless aliens.

My daughter asked if anyone ever helped clean the cages. They said yes.

FIND A MENTOR

1. Identify and connect
• **Identify resource people via active participation.** Take part in competitions, summer camp programs, museum classes and workshops. Read articles in your field of interest and attend lectures. People you encounter have already shown a willingness to be involved in educating the public when they judge competitions, speak at programs and lead classes. Even if you were only briefly acquainted with these professionals as a competition participant or lecture attendee, each time you are, send these men and women a letter or email of appreciation and mention your interest in the same field.

- **Identify resource people via organizations**. Chances are good that there are professional or networking associations in your area of interest. Consult such groups for information including outreach programs. Read newsletters and research put out by the organization. Identify members who have been involved in area projects. Ask if there are local people you might interview for your own research. Again, if you take part in an outreach program, conduct an interview, or read an article by a professional, send a letter or email of appreciation and mention your interest in the same field.
- **Identify resource people via academia**. Look up faculty listings at nearby universities or research institutions. Check for names of those who have written books or articles, contributed to blogs or websites, or been recently interviewed. Do an Internet search to check out their bios, paying attention to scholarly articles they have recently authored. Look those articles up. You may need to go through a subscription database offered by your library system. If, for example, you are hoping to assist a scientist in the lab, check out current articles to determine if this is the sort of research you would be interested in doing. To establish contact, write a note of appreciation about either an article they have written or a lecture you have attended.

2. Extend the connection

Continue your own learning. As you progress, establish questions you are unable to resolve on your own. These are questions to ask a resource person you have previously contacted. Ask a question or two by mail or email that you have been unable to answer through your own reading and investigation. Intelligent, well-written questions from young people are likely to spark a response. Why? For several reasons. First, these professionals are often excited about their own field and enjoy talking about it. Second, they are likely to be impressed by a motivated young person who independently seeks greater expertise. And third, it's a time-honored tradition to pass along knowledge to young people. That's how humanity progresses. If you don't get an answer, try another of your resource people. If you do get an answer, respond right away with your thanks. Stay in touch, letting this person know how his or her answer helped you continue with your learning.

3. Ask

Finally, ask how you can gain more experience. This step may not be necessary. Connections made in the first two steps often naturally lead to helpful and interesting relationships. If not, it's time to plead your case. Write a short but carefully constructed letter identifying yourself, your educational background, your study in this field and your specific interest in this person's field. Add that you are looking for experience. Then ask about several options: Ask if you might shadow them at work. Ask if they would consider taking you on as a volunteer for a few hours a week. Ask if you might assist them with research. Ask if they would consider being a mentor. You may also ask them to share your request with others if they are unable to consider your request at this time. Remember, as a homeschooler you are available a wider range of hours, while other teens are ordinarily available only during the summer months or a few hours after school. Make sure you can coordinate with a busy person's schedule. And of course, remember to be respectful and appreciative.

Working with a mentor is an excellent way to explore your interests, even if the situation is not what you expected. The research may be dull, the project may not give you any responsibility, the professional may not give your much time but you are certainly learning as you head in your own direction.

I started taking her for a couple of hours and Sue, the owner, said our daughter was amazing for her age at 12 or 13. She was dependable, self-directed, resourceful. They didn't have to check up on her. Brook worked for them for six years and fostered friendships with that family which changed her life. They really liked Brook and she became part of the family. She ended up traveling extensively with them. They had ten children. One of the daughters is a NASA pilot who flew the Space Shuttle two times. They were mentors in many different ways, always supportive and encouraging. The father of the family is a doctor. Now Brook is in nursing school.

—Lynn Reed, Georgia

Resources

- **Big Brothers, Big Sisters** offers supportive mentorships backed by ongoing professional support. www.bbbs.org (215)-567-7000
- **Get in Their Shoes** is a campaign action by business leaders, athletes, entertainers and politicians to rally youth toward greater achievement by proactively interviewing successful professionals within their own communities. www.getintheirshoes.imno.org
- **International Mentoring Network Organization** is an open source solution to mentoring. IMNO members interview successful professionals within their own communities. Members can record and post the interviews to develop their own careers and help others learn from the professional's knowledge and experience. www.imno.org (801)-361-9942
- **MENTOR**/National Mentoring Partnership offers mentorship connections via zipcode search. www.mentoring.org (703)-224-2200
- **Mentor Youth** is a faith-based site linking young people with mentors. www.mentoryouth.com (858) 451-1111
- **National Apprenticeship System**, through the U.S. Department of Labor, helps industry and skilled trades register to find and train qualified young people. www.doleta.gov/oa/apprentices.cfm#content (202) 693-2796
- **Society for Amateur Scientists** operates a program called Labrats joining young people from ages 12 to 18 in groups under the guidance of a scientist. Their organization's site provides research material, reference information and archived newsletters. www.sas.org (401)-487-1462

Your local chamber of commerce, Rotary club and other business associations may provide referrals. Your library will also have reference guides such as the *Ferguson Career Resource Guide to Apprenticeship Programs* (Facts on File, 2006).

Reaching Out Through Technology

"It shouldn't be too much of a surprise that the Internet has evolved into a force strong enough to reflect the greatest hopes and fears of those who use it." —Denise Caruso

---

Internet users have the opportunity to collaborate with people anywhere. A child can gather information, exchange ideas and develop new concepts with speed and connectivity unknown in the past. He or she can work with other children on a science experiment, an art project or a musical composition and then share this creation with anyone who might be interested. In the world.

My older son has a passion for video and computer gaming— including online computer gaming. Over the past year he has made countless online friendships with others of all ages, from much younger than him to adults who all share his passion for gaming. While they will not ever meet or will likely never know their actual real names, other than their gaming screen names, they regularly play games together via the Internet, and while doing so communicate with each other and socialize. He meets others sharing his gaming passion from all over the world.

—Tamara Markwick, California

My kids have been online for about seven years now and they have had email, along with belonging to several message boards. Now they all have Myspace pages and Facebook pages. They have met and correspond with several people on the Internet. My kids are big into alternative Christian music and have been on "street teams" where they help to share

the knowledge of the groups/bands with others … The kids have also become friends with other fans of these groups whom they have met at the concerts and online communities … My kids have used, and continue to use the Internet to reach out and meet many new people all the time. (And yes! They know the dangers!) They have never had any trouble and have had a fun time making new friendships in this manner.

—Lori Smith, Ohio

There are legitimate concerns that young people may be victimized. Many parents protect children from inappropriate material and unsafe information exchange. Their approaches include installing parental control filters, restricting and/or adding parents to social networking sites, keeping the computer in an area where the monitor can be seen at all times, maintaining only one password for all children in the family and limiting the use of handheld web access devices.

Another concern is the way that technology can marginalize existing relationships. Although the electronic age links us unrelentingly, it can also keep our discourse more superficial. The real nitty gritty of what it takes to get along happens when we are together, face to face. Human interaction is mostly non-verbal. Experts have no exact figure but it is estimated that words themselves comprise less than ten percent of full communication. The remaining ninety percent is expressed in a subtle mix of gestures, tone of voice, posture, facial expression and gaze. These nuances are lost in email, text messaging and cell calls. Furthermore, when we are together with other people we build associations with one another through all our senses. A carefully constructed social network page filled with friends can't approach the depth of a relationship built on shared experiences.

However there's no doubt that the connections made online can have a pivotal impact in reaching across the so-called divides of race, class, nationality and religion. There is no more important goal than knowing how to co-exist with one another on this diverse planet, and the Internet has made possible an increasingly global conversation. When people gather online to discuss and share they find common ground transcending all boundaries. The resulting friendships, collaborations and partnerships create links of goodwill across the planet.

An astonishingly large amount of my learning has stemmed from seeking knowledge online. Asking questions on online forums has helped me learn, started great friendships and directed me towards even more new subjects.

The people I have met online I couldn't have met in the farming community where I live. I talked to a blind man about his perception of sight. I've discussed "Back to the Future" with a Libyan. I regularly talk to an Australian guy about that country's Internet policies. I argue about politics with a traditional conservative law student who lives in Tennessee. Through the Internet I'm able to learn new things, keep up with people and stay amused daily. —Kirby, 19

Technology is an undeniable stimulus to learn and do on a larger scale. Young people are comfortable using it creatively.

- A group of teens compose a rap-and-spoken-word tribute to their faith, practice it a few times, then capture the performance for streaming video through their church website.

- A child learns to create fractal art, expands her abilities via online tutorials and help from others on forums, then posts her work on virtual art galleries.

- Several teens leaving a movie hear of an act of violence suffered by an elderly homeless man. They search for more information on a smart phone, call a local advocacy organization to ask advice and let friends know via text messaging that they'll be standing with homemade signs of concern outside the homeless shelter at rush hour.

Technology can be essential when connecting with those of similar interests. After reading survival stories such as *My Side of the Mountain* (Puffin, 2004) by Jean Craighead George, a homeschooling family became interested in primitive camping. Their first attempt at the fire-plow method of starting a campfire were unsuccessful and left them suffering through a cold night in the woods. Soon after, they found a whole community of fellow enthusiasts on Internet forums. Now they share tips for tanning hides and making containers out of birch bark; forward articles on such topics as parenting and ecology; and plan physically challenging outdoor campouts for the group in remote areas. All online. Each time they travel to one of these primitive camping events they deepen their understanding of how their ancestors lived off the land while enjoying the company of new friends.

A mother and daughter who are involved in hand spinning and weaving link up with others via blogs and forums. They share photos of their work, mail packages of wool and dye to one another, discuss techniques and participate in round-robin art projects. When the daughter became ill with a blood disorder, the mother notified forums that she and her daughter would be out of touch for a while due to travel, as they sought treatment several states away. Within hours they had offers

David Dalrymple, a 15-year-old student at MIT's Center for Bits and Atoms, wrote an essay for World Question Center at www.edge.org from which this is excerpted with his permission.

Before I entered college, I had never been enrolled in a school. Some of my education was provided by books, magazines, museums and the like, but I feel the most useful was provided by technology.

I was in the first generation to grow up with the Web as a fact of life, and made use of online references and search engines every day to research topics in which I'd become interested. From early childhood, many of my questions were answered by a mix of university websites, ad-supported niche reference works, and charitable individuals sharing their own personal knowledge with the world …

When I was 7, I emailed a science consultant whenever I had a question that I couldn't find a ready answer for on the Web—questions such as "Why don't the passengers in the Concorde hear a sonic boom?" and "Where can I find the Bohr model of every chemical element?" In 1999, during the week of my 8th birthday, I used email to first contact the author of a book I really liked, When Things Start to Think, who happened to be Neil Gershenfeld, now my faculty advisor. I probably wouldn't have bothered to write a formal letter, so if email didn't exist, my educational trajectory would have been entirely different. I was also mentored from many miles away by Ray Kurzweil, in a series of conversations enabled by email; this was another major influence on my life.

Computing is also a creative tool: it can be used to write essays (like this one), produce works of art (I've sold fractal-based art at local festivals), and write computer programs. Programming fascinated me from a very early age, but it wouldn't have kept my interest long if I didn't have access to a computer. I think that my experiences in programming may have been the most influential in my intellectual development: problem-solving and critical thinking are rewarded, math skills are enforced, and I even wrote programs to help teach me things, like an arithmetic drill I wrote in LOGO at age 5. I was also greatly aided throughout my college education in computer science by my earlier self-guided learning of many of the same concepts. Whereas I was taught 8 programming languages in college, I've learned over twice as many others on my own, and those were some of my most valuable and (so far) useful learning experiences.

Seymour Papert's constructionist theory best explains my personal experience with education: "Constructionism is built on the assumption that children will do best by finding ('fishing') for themselves the specific knowledge they need. Organized or informal education can help most by making sure they are supported morally, psychologically, materially, and intellectually in their efforts."

… Media artist Toshio Iwai, who was Artist-in-Residence at San Francisco's Exploratorium and wrote the video game Electroplankton, told a story that his mother took away all his toys when he was a small child and told him that he could only play with toys he made himself. Iwai credits that moment as a turning point in his life: from passive to active, consumer to creator. I'm optimistic that in the future, education will not take place in centralized Houses of Learning, places where students listen to lectures and then answer questions about them; that education will take place at construction sites, in art studios, in computing centers: places where useful and creative things are done. I'm optimistic that it will be a more useful and creative education that will produce more useful and creative people that will contribute, in turn, to a more useful and creative society.

from people all along their route to stop by for meals and lodging plus a free place proffered for their stay near the medical center. Many others sent notes of support. Their community of on-line friends reached out to them, sheltered them through medical treatment and cheered when the daughter was pronounced free of lasting illness.

These kinds of connections are made every day, every minute, online. We find one another through our shared interests and concerns. The consequence can be envisioned as a "global heartening" with the power to change our planet for the better.

Resources

- **TakingITGlobal ICT Network** connects youth as they develop content, collaborate on projects and discuss the power of information technology. www.takingitglobal.org
- **Youth Ventures** assists young people working to create change in their own communities. It supplies templates for action based on working programs and forums to connect with others. www.genv.net

CHAPTER FIVE

Collaborating Benefits Everyone

Homeschooling Beyond Home

"The world is the true classroom." —Jack Hanna

We want our children to grow up to be caring, resourceful people. We want to help them explore their capabilities so they can pursue rewarding endeavors. And we want to preserve the curiosity and creativity they offer to the future. Now, what approach to take?

Whatever style of homeschooling we choose, a major benefit to this form of education is the freedom it can give our families. How will you and your children fill the day?

Sometimes it seems there's very little "home" to schooling. Some days homeschooling families leave early, arriving back just in time for dinner. We may be exploring a nature preserve, throwing pots or learning to speak Japanese. Other times we are home but there's less "schooling" than an observer might expect. The kids may be reading, daydreaming, working on their own projects or playing outside. This is all part of the ongoing process of finding the balance that best meets the needs of each family member.

Learning in our family is doing. Our kids learn valuable skills that they could never learn in public schools. They are immersed in their culture since both my husband and I are traditional artists as were our families before us. For generations our families have either been artists or farmers. So we make no real special effort for the kids to learn,

they just do. We go to museums and libraries. Two weeks ago we took them to the local extension service to find out about a plant growing in our yard. We all learn things by going places. It is better to experience something for real rather than imagining it from a textbook.
—Jessie Mato Toyela, Florida
http://blue-bear.onerednation.com/

Homeschooling can easily accommodate changing needs. It's a matter of finding what blend of structure and relaxation works for everyone in your family. A positive emotional state is a key component of learning, so finding that balance is essential.

Many parents begin homeschooling with the idea that they will have to provide for all aspects of their child's education, from sports to music, without recognizing that the community around them is filled with organizations dedicated to imparting skills and knowledge to the next generation. Oftentimes families don't know there are unique opportunities available to them until they've been homeschooling for years. Despite an increasingly connected world, it can be difficult to find out that the church around the corner has an active Scrabble club, that a local lapidary organization offers rock hunting days, or an arts center provides classes in puppetry.

You can educate your children using local resources without overwhelming your budget or your schedule. Keep in mind that activities are no longer fun for anyone if they deplete your energy.

You don't want to exhaust yourselves in a misguided effort to make learning fun. Learning itself is intrinsically rewarding.

I go by the "Velcro® philosophy" of homeschooling. I offer my kids all kinds of choices. Want to go on this field trip? Take that co-op class? Join that team? Volunteer with that group? I figure if I toss enough their way something will stick. Works for my kids.
—Craig, Indiana

The excitement that builds as we homeschool in collaboration with the wider world is the energy generated by authentic growth. We know a plant expands upward and outward while also deepening its roots. New experiences also stretch us in all directions, enriching us in ways that cannot be seen or fully understood at the time.

Building Knowledge Networks

"The best way to know life is to love many things." —Vincent Van Gogh

Homeschooling never needs to be about dry, dusty facts. Learning takes active exploration and inspiring examples. The possibilities are endless.

Homeschooling parents have many more resources than they might imagine. Not money, but people. Consider all the people who might share their knowledge and experience. Your sister-in-law's cake decorating business may give your children insight into entrepreneurship, the catering industry, the humorous side of overindulgent weddings and the art found in shaping sugar. Your former boss' penchant for explaining probabilities—whether about insurance or the numbers involved in betting on the horses—could provide new math insight. Your bird watching neighbor, your world traveler friend, your stepbrother with his tales of incarceration for larceny, your father who is teaching himself alternative building design—all these people can provide direct learning opportunities for your children. This potential knowledge network is available to your family and your homeschool group for the asking.

Asking friends and family to share what they know is actually a way of honoring them. From time immemorial adults have passed down skills and wisdom to the next generation. This is a tradition practically encoded in our genes, so it's likely your request will be taken seriously. Consider how you might incorporate the expertise of your knowledge network into your homeschool life. When you are ready to ask your "experts," make sure to express respect for their knowledge and experience. Explain that you regard their time as valuable and that you hope they'll find an opportunity to share what they know with your children or with the children in your homeschool group.

There's a good chance they will agree. That's when the synergy begins. They may bring stories and photos from their years in the military. They may invite your children to the kitchen where they make pierogi, the garage where they create stained glass windows or the university lab where they test polymers. This doesn't need to be a formal presentation. They can let children watch them work and ask questions. They can talk about how their skills or careers progressed. They can fill in background information. They might even bring along hands-on projects for each child.

Rather than offer a visit, some busy adults in your knowledge network may respond to your request by referring you to websites and books they have found helpful. They may agree to let your children correspond with them, interview them or answer questions.

Your knowledge network extends well beyond people you know. Not far from your home there are thousands of people with a wealth of experience and ideas to share. Children are fascinated by the working world. If given the chance, most children would leap at the opportunity to watch, question and possibly help adults as they go about their jobs. For too long there has been a disconnect between youth and adults. The real work that keeps the country fed, housed, safe and informed exists beyond the realm that most children can access. Yet they want to know first-hand. Give a child the choice to fill out worksheets about the economic system or to go to a warehouse to see how products are inventoried, ordered and shipped. Worksheets aren't likely to win.

Actually, young people's perspectives can make a real difference when adults take them seriously. A homeschool field trip to a municipal waste management system inspired one youth to ask a question about the process. Based on that teen's observation, an aspect of the system was changed to a more efficient method. That's an example of how a mutually beneficial result can occur when age groups are not separated.

Find out if your children or your homeschool group can observe or talk to someone working in a railroad yard, repair shop, fire station, chemist's lab, lumberyard, bank, farm, greenhouse, veterinarian's office, stable, fishing boat, auction, artist's studio, grain mill, any workplace in your community. Explain that parents will be there to supervise. If a visiting group or family are not acceptable due to company policy or insurance reasons, perhaps one interested older child can interview a worker or observe the workplace for a short time.

Homeschool groups often invite members of the community to speak at children's meetings. Contact a business person, hobbyist or other specialist and create the conditions for a successful meeting. Explain that your group is made up of mixed-age children who like to be involved with their learning, in other words they like to have something to do and something to figure out if possible. Offer several different meeting dates. Some groups have daytime as well as evening meetings, others regularly reserve meeting rooms at the local library or town hall for their programs. Put a description of the event on your site, in your newsletter and in the local newspaper. Arrive well ahead of time to set up tables and chairs, put out refreshments, and arrange quiet activities for preschoolers. When the event is over, make sure that children from your group write a thank-you note or two.

Building connections between youth and adults in the community is invaluable. It fosters understanding of the working world, perhaps stimulating interest in a wider array of careers. It also goes a long way toward rebalancing the age segregation in our culture.

Segregating children in schools is a relatively new experiment. Child development research shows unequivocally that young humans are designed to watch and imitate the actions of those around them. When children grow up around people of different ages who are engaged in all sorts of real-life activities they'll still choose other children as playmates but will model themselves after those with more advanced skills and intellectual maturity. This is how our species has thrived. This natural process is turned upside down when today's children are limited to others close to their own age in daycare, school and sports. In that case, most examples of reasoning, behavior and ability they witness are from children at a similar level of maturity. Rather than choosing role model options from their peers and media celebrities,our young people can learn from the talented, caring and motivated people of all ages right in their own communities.

Our homeschool group has tapped into a wealth of expertise. You can't believe how many people will come and talk at a homeschool meeting. For example, someone's neighbor was a retired geologist. He came to speak at one of our kids' meetings. He brought posters and hand-outs he made. He gave us parents lots of suggestions to educate our kids in geology. He even gave each kid a rock to take home. And he was a great speaker with funny stories.

This last year at our kids' meetings our speakers have included missionaries who have been to El Salvador who brought home movies of their work, a nutritionist, an air traffic controller who brought a whole bunch of technical material for the kids, a wildlife rehabilitator, a group of teens who perform music they write themselves, a meteorologist, a guy who demonstrated easy ways to draw cartoons and a candy store owner who did a candy making demonstration. Next week's meeting features a dentist. I hear he's bringing a giant jaw with removable teeth.

The kids love it but the speakers love it more. Just about every one of them rhapsodizes about how many smart questions our kids ask and how well behaved they are. I think the speakers get a real kick out of our eager learners.

—Kariann

We're starting to expand out and approach businesses to start up classes. We have a homeschool band, art classes, an aviation class and more in the works. *—Kim Railey, Washington*

There are many places and people offering services to children who are very happy to offer specific classes or sessions for homeschoolers. I have found that many have their days wide open as most children cannot attend classes until after school is out. Most are more than happy to offer a class to homeschoolers during the day while their usual customer base is in school. Locally here, myself and other homeschoolers have suggested and put in place classes for homeschoolers in engineering, science, art, gym, scouting and much more.

—Tamara Markwick, California

I had an approach I learned to take whenever we were ANYWHERE that had a "behind the scenes" aspect to it: "Ask for a tour." For example, we once got to a movie theater almost an hour early, having confused the starting times. The theater was empty, and they told us we

could wait there, which was all the invitation we needed. "We're homeschoolers," I told them, with three children in tow. "Do you think it would be possible to go up to the projection room so my kids could see what goes on behind the scenes?"

They were more than happy to give us a glimpse, and my kids went home with a reel for a trailer that they had stopped showing, a cool souvenir. We did this at a grocery store, the post office, and several other places. The only place I can remember that turned us down was our bank. Incidentally, all of those places showed us things I had wondered about personally, but would never have been bold enough to ask to see just for myself. "We're homeschoolers" was our magic password to all kinds of places.

—Kim O'Hara, Washington

Your knowledge network will grow as your children and children in your homeschool group get to know adults who share their expertise. These people are probably busy with careers, hobbies and families of their own. But when they are appreciated for their knowledge it adds a dimension to their lives as much as it enriches the lives of our children.

Wider Collaboration

"All real living is meeting." —Martin Buber

The communities we live in are the world we show our children. And children pay close attention. They see not only the kindness we demonstrate to neighbors and the respect we accord service people, but also the generosity of spirit we express for the well-being of our community as a whole. Where we live may not come close to the ideal. No one place can be. But there's power in noticing what works, what has its own charm, what means "home" where you live. This puts the focus on what is appreciated.

You may wish your community had more opportunities for recreation, or was working toward greater sustainability. Envisioning and talking about these improvements is the first step. Next comes working toward our ideals. Taking these steps shows our children how to improve the world around them.

When we get out of our homes and get involved, our communities become better places. Neighborhood meetings, babysitting co-ops and potluck dinners strengthen networks between people. Such activities build what's called "social capital." According to Robert Putnam, Lewis Feldstein and Don Cohen, authors of *Better Together: Restoring the American Community*, there are significant benefits that result from the bonds we establish with one another through clubs, churches, local restaurants, civic groups and neighborly relationships. Social networks build friendship and trust. And when people have established friendship and trust, they are not likely to limit their concerns to their own petty self-interests. Instead, they share information, cooperate and help one another in times of need. This widens the circle of reciprocity. Such networks make our communities places where citizens work together and react compassionately.

Many of us already take part in numerous activities, both small and large, that build social capital. It turns out that homeschoolers are excellent models of community involvement. Using data from the U.S. Department of Education that included private, parochial, public and homeschooled students, researchers noted that homeschoolers are hardly isolated. Instead, their families network well and are active in the community. Homeschoolers and private school families are the most civically engaged. Researchers Christian Smith and David Sikkink concluded, "Indeed, we have reason to believe that the organizations and practices involved in private and home schooling, in themselves, tend to foster public participation in civic affairs . . . the challenges, responsibilities, and practices that private schooling and home education normally entail for their participants may actually help reinvigorate America's civic culture and the participation of her citizens in the public square."

We get involved as a natural consequence of seeking out ways to enliven learning for our children. We discover new ways to collaborate with local organizations and businesses. As a result everyone benefits, not just homeschoolers.

Imagine your local bakery welcoming people as more than just customers. The possibilities might include making meeting space available for a kids' chess club, hosting "Invent a Cookie" contests, opening the kitchen for tours, offering apprenticeships to aspiring young pastry chefs, donating bread to hunger centers, partnering with culinary schools to teach parent-child classes, hanging children's art on the walls, inviting speakers to explain the science of yeast and flour. These and other innovative activities happen when local companies are tuned in to the needs of the surrounding neighborhood. Those same neighbors are likely to become loyal customers and share news about the establishment, helping to grow the business.

Businesses engaged with the community not only see their profits increase, their efforts enliven the community. If you hope to precipitate such a process, start small and build. Ask your independent coffee shop or locally owned restaurant for permission to meet there each week at a non-peak hour with a group of homeschoolers. The kids can sketch, play card games or learn Latin together. Over time you'll get to know the employees and owner. Chances are that conversations will ensue about ways that the business can meet the needs of families in the area. As families benefit, they will spread the word. More customers will patronize the business and its programs, encouraging the owner to increase efforts to collaborate.

An Ohio store called Underhill's Games (www.underhillsgames.com) started a regular event they call "Bored? Game Day!" On these days, customers can eat, play games and take part in demos all day long. This is popular with youth and attendance continues to increase. The owner, Lee McLain, is very accommodating to the interests of board gamers, whom he describes as highly intelligent and imaginative. In fact, a recent "Bored? Game Day!" didn't end until 3:30 A.M. the next morning to permit those who were intently involved to finish their games.

Non-profit organizations are an integral part of the community as well. These groups increase membership and make greater strides in reaching their goals when they react readily to the needs around them. More and more, partnerships are evolving between groups even when their needs seem contradictory. You can approach non-profits with an eye to getting this process started. Meet

with them to find out what interactions might be mutually beneficial. Perhaps you can offer to set up a program or two between homeschoolers and members. Sometimes these programs result from more casual beginnings.

One such successful program was called Girlfriend Circle. It began when several female members of a senior center commented to a volunteer that they had no hope for the future because children "nowadays" were rude. They went on to complain about what they considered inappropriate clothes and language. None of these ladies knew any children well, as their own grandchildren lived out of town or were already adults. The volunteer happened to be the mother of several young daughters. She asked these older women if they would like have a tea party with a group of girls, suggesting that the ladies could pass along tips on politeness as well as learn about what it was like being a girl these days. The elders were delighted. The event was set up with the center's activities director, who invited all interested older women, while the volunteer invited girls around her daughter's ages (eight to eleven).

During that first tea party the young guests were seated in-between their older hostesses. Before refreshments were served all guests had a lesson in napkin origami. Then they took part in a question and answer session designed to show the differences between growing up now compared to sixty and seventy years ago. After the first tea party the girls were eager to meet again. The Girlfriend Circle met bi-monthly for several years. The friendships were instructive as well as rewarding for both generations.

Government agencies also find that opening up to youth involvement leads to much greater civic engagement. When young people are given a genuine chance to contribute, their efforts can transform stagnant government policies and generate energetic ongoing programs

The progressive approach in Hampton, Virginia means that young people not only volunteer, they also create policy and help it turn into reality. They have many opportunities to take part in leadership roles (www.areyouinthegame.com). Youth leadership groups in each neighborhood advise the Parks and Recreation division on program planning. Teens make a visible difference to the community through activism, organizing, and service learning in an organization called Youth Achieving Change Together. And city administration includes a Youth Commission, with twenty-four youth commissioners, three paid youth planners, and one youth secretary—all high school age. These teens work on everything from policy to Youth Civic Engagement conferences. They also hold open forums to get input from the young people of Hampton. These focus groups led to the opening of a 42,000-square-foot Hampton Teen Center where youth serve as advisors and board members, and also provide operation and security services.

Sometimes more formal efforts are necessary to effect change in a city administration or large non-profit organization. You might want to form a coalition involving all segments of the community. During meetings, share ideas about problems and potential solutions, and perhaps most importantly envision positive outcomes together. Then act. Such coalitions have been formed as partnerships among homeschoolers, schools and neighborhood organizations to develop arts programs. They've also been successful as citywide efforts to restore civic engagement among much larger groups of people.

Resources

- *The Great Neighborhood Book: A Do-It-Yourself Guide to Placemaking* (New Society, 2007) by Jay Walljasper.
- *Superbia: 31 Ways to Create Sustainable Neighborhoods* (New Society, 2003) by Daniel D. Chiras.
- *Creating Community Anywhere: Finding Support and Connection in a Fragmented World* (CCC, 2005) by Carolyn R. Shaffer and Kristin Anundsen.
- *Works of Heart: Building Village Through the Arts* (New Village, 2006) Lynne Elizabeth, Suzanne Young, editors.
- *Beginner's Guide to Community-Based Arts* (New Village, 2005) by Keith Knight and Mat Schwarzman.

Respectful, caring conversations are essential to get collaborative efforts going, and ongoing conversations are essential to maintaining them. Unlike other species, we humans are able to let others see into our thoughts, memories and hopes through language. Conversation enables us to sort through one another's ideas, thereby advancing our own understanding. When we approach a conversation openly we find that everyone has something to contribute—a different viewpoint, a story, an emotional reaction. In discussion we find ways to act together for our mutual benefit. That's collaboration.

When searching for ways to collaborate
- converse with gentle regard for potential differences
- discuss the needs of your group and what your group has to offer
- discuss the needs of others and what they have to offer
- listen, brainstorm, find common goals
- build on these collective ideas
- agree to regular conversations so the process can be refined.

It's about sharing energy to create a more vibrant, enriching community. You'll find that such efforts have a way of improving things on a greater scale than you might imagine. A groundswell of enthusiasm and action can result from positive input by just a few people.

What ways would you would like to:
- Network with others?
- Create learning opportunities?
- Enrich your community?

Consider:
- **Senior Knowledge Bank:** Perhaps your neighborhood clock repair expert would like to pass on skills to the newest generation, and a world traveler is eager to share stories of adventures. Somewhere nearby are soldiers, dancers, astronomers and storytellers who can share their gifts with children in a situation of mutual respect. The definition of "senior" doesn't have to be age, just the maturity of an advanced perspective. Put together an application explaining your idea and requesting information from interested community members, then leave copies at senior centers, churches and libraries. Once you have a few applicants, start setting up programs for youth—apprenticeships, workshops or classes to best use the skills offered.
- **Street Play Day:** Why not seek a permit to close off your street for the afternoon? Put fliers in everyone's door (not just homes with children) and invite them to play. Plan ahead to have plenty of lemonade and supplies. Get folks involved who want to play old games like stickball, marbles and hopscotch. Bring out tables and chairs so neighbors can sit down for cards if they aren't up to active play. Innovate. Consider a huge chess game using live playing pieces, or a game of hot potato using actual potatoes.
- **Skills Clinics:** Although many communities offer adult education classes, there are hundreds of other skilled people who can teach what they know. Organize a regular day set aside for city-wide workshops. The lumber yard could offer mini-woodworking sessions, the auto repair shop could give troubleshooting pointers, the fitness center could set up an agility course. Best of all, regular individuals could have space available in community buildings to offer workshops and demonstrations. Try proposing the idea to the community affairs coordinator of your city.
- **Parking Lot Quilt:** Get permission (in writing) to decorate a parking lot with washable paint. It could be the lot used by your church, a nearby park or city hall. Have on hand plenty of paint—the powdered type you mix with water is often inexpensive. Ask participants to bring brushes and empty containers for smaller amounts of paint. Mark off the lot with sidewalk chalk into squares (or a crazy quilt of shapes) and assign each person (or team) a section to paint. It can be themed or free for all. If passersby stop to marvel invite them to join in! Afterwards celebrate the art project with group photos and refreshments.
- **Everyone's College:** Meet with the public relations department of a nearby college or university. These institutions of higher learning are eager to promote positive community interaction. Propose that they coordinate a learning co-op with homeschoolers during the day, enrichment classes during afterschool hours, or mixed-age classes that permit everyone from children to seniors to attend. The benefit to the college? You are not requesting busy professors' time, you are asking for college students to do the teaching. The college knows that their students will develop a broader knowledge base by teaching others. Professors could simply announce to their classes that they'd provide extra credit toward a grade if a student was willing to teach a session, workshop or hands-on demonstration at "Everyone's College."

Collaborating via Internet

"I have an almost religious zeal—not for technology per se, but for the Internet which is for me, the nervous system of mother Earth, which I see as a living creature, linking up."—Dan Millman

---

Minute by minute the possibilities found on the web expand, providing ever widening opportunities for homeschoolers to share resources, experience and insight in ways they choose.

Our children may spot an unusual tree fungus and make a sketch of it. While their enthusiasm is high we have many opportunities to use the Internet, not only for accessing data but for applying information and reaching out to others. We can look up three-dimensional illustrations of the fungal growth that will help us recognize it in other seasons, helping us sketch the full lifecycle. We can look up the Latin name and genus, map out where in the forest we spot it and even communicate with mycologists doing research. We can look at artistic depictions of fungi and perhaps contribute our child's drawing to an online gallery of children's art. We can delve into the role of fungi in myth, folktale and magic around the world; possibly posting a story our child has written. We can find dynamic demonstrations of the role fungi play in medicine, ecology and culinary arts. We can learn about the way this particular fungus interconnects with other life forms in the forest. We can look up recipes featuring mushrooms, then go to a farmer's market to stock up on interesting varieties. The Internet can lead our interests in nearly every direction.

Resources

Collaborative sites welcome continuous, everchanging input.

- **iEARN** is a non-profit network helping educators and youth in more than 120 countries collaborate through a global telecommunications network. Young people design projects that make a difference in the world. www.iearn.org/projects/projectbook.html
- **Instructables** is a diverse do-it-yourself site. www.instructables.com
- **LearningScience** offers real-time data collection, simulations, interactive web lessons, and imaging. This site is an open community for sharing science resources from around the world. http://learningscience.org
- **Online Education Database** offers open courseware collections, podcasts, videos and invisible web search. http://oedb.org/library/features/236-open-courseware-collections
- **Think Quest** provides resources created by and for students. www.thinkquest.org/library
- **Wolfram Demonstrations Project** is a collection of interactive demonstrations in science, music, math and more. http://demonstrations.wolfram.com

CHAPTER SIX

Homeschooling Changes Everything

Homeschooling as a Daily Exercise in Open Source Living

"Education is for improving the lives of others and for leaving your community and world better than you found it."
—Marian Wright Edelman

Most styles of homeschooling are intrinsically collaborative and open source. We are highly interactive with other homeschoolers, the community and the wider world. New ideas, or old ideas brought to our consciousness, are easily incorporated into the way we homeschool as we creatively shape what works best for our own families.

The first homeschooler I met was Marion. She had a houseful of kids including her own and foster children and I think a grandchild. Where I was anxious about doing everything right, she was relaxed and casual. Where I bought science kits and craft kits and textbooks she had raw learning materials in abundance in her home and yard. Marion invited me to every event she set up. Most of them were at her house. Informal plays by boys featuring lots of swordplay, a regular "messy arts day" and a book club that was mostly a read aloud for little kids followed by making up stories and drawing pictures. I didn't think much of Marion's homeschooling style at first but there's a method to what looks like happy chaos at her house. I'm still more structured but I'm working to let our homeschool become more like life at Marion's house. —Marcie, Vermont

---

Without the constraints found in the typical educational system we are free to make changes. We pay close attention: listening to conversations, noticing behavior, mulling our options over and adapting to our children's needs.

As we innovate we discuss our ideas with other homeschoolers. This cooperative and continuous improvement is shared freely for the widest good. We discuss the big picture as well as nuanced learning issues with one another all the time. We talk when our children get together, but also disseminate ideas at local meetings, on forums, through blogs, at conventions and in publications. We're eager to share our concerns and ideas because we tend to refine our approach through discussion. These ongoing conversations help us to make sense of what we are doing and why we are doing it.

This self-scrutiny often arises out of our exposure to differing viewpoints and very real forces on us that result from choosing to educate out of the mainstream. The dynamic tension causes us to remain continually aware of our choices. We wade right into the stream of information, opinions and fresh possibilities that come our way. We discuss. We reflect. And then we go a step beyond any open source model. We go to the heart of the matter, staying in touch with our intuitive sense as parents, throughout our homeschooling lives. Acting for the benefit of our families we are also adding to an open source of homeschooling wisdom that redefines and reshapes what education is becoming.

We live our lives in meaningful ways. That looks different each moment but includes, sharing life together, playing, reading, playing video games, playing lots of board games, cooking, cleaning, shopping, doing errands, building models, assembling Legos®, writing letters, coloring, doing art, taking walks, going swimming, playing with friends, laughing, loving, living.

—Tamara Marwick, California

Homeschooling as a Harbinger of Educational Change

"Only the fresh air from millions upon millions of freely made choices will create the educational climate we need to realize a better destiny."—John Taylor Gatto

The history of civilization shows that knowledge has always been a well-protected asset. It was used to benefit a limited circle of people or to gain greater holdings. Ordinary people had no access to the information held by chieftains, priests, kings or other members of the elite. When written language was devised very few could read, fewer still owned scrolls or books. Often the first acts of conquerors included burning books and killing those who had knowledge. Even in more recent revolutions, people suspected of being "intellectual" have been killed, and evidence of all but approved information banned. That's because knowledge is power in the grandest sense of the term. If you told anyone a generation ago that knowledge and resources, even information closely guarded by business, religion, science, would be freely exchanged—no one would have believed you.

Now we share information with generosity that has no precedent in recorded history. We have open source programs and freeware; extensive online texts, music and art; wikis; millions of blogs and forums oriented to every interest; trillions of webpages; ongoing research and more. On the web we expect an endless range of technological, intellectual and artistic creations to be available for all seekers. Of course the quality varies and it teems with advertising. But that doesn't diminish the fact that people seeking nothing more than the satisfaction of sharing knowledge, insight and personal support make remarkable content available. The technology has provided the means for global connection that has helped raise awareness across many divides. Strangers reach out

providing resources, sharing the results of their efforts and relating what they have learned from personal experience. Who could have imagined such generosity just a few decades ago?

Paul Hawken, author of *Blessed Unrest: How the Largest Movement in the World Came into Being and Why No One Saw It Coming,* brings attention to the astonishing efforts of people working for positive change in greater numbers than ever before. These are often small, unconnected groups working for human rights, ecological balance, justice, a whole slew of selfless causes. As a whole, Hawken sees these actions forming a critical mass. When any life form is threatened by serious illness the immune system reacts. Hawken calls on us to envision our Earth as a living organism and to see caring people working for change across the world as our planet's immune system.

Upcoming challenges are great but concerted efforts can surmount daunting obstacles. After all, the past one hundred years have seen enormous changes brought about by ordinary individuals. Environmental, civil rights and social justice movements across the globe have saved untold suffering. Who knows what monumental good can be wrought by the collective power of regular people stirring to a fuller use of their creative energies?

Homeschooling is surely part of this movement for beneficial change even if families forging their own way are not aware of the collective impact. Each of us who educates our children demonstrates what young people can accomplish without institutional intervention. We can share the wonders we have learned alongside our children with those who still believe young people need a remedy for youthful exuberance.

Someday, teachers may be liberated from static forms of education; free to inspire, facilitate and mentor rather than enforce. Competitive, test-based systems that manipulate students toward pre-determined objectives may transform into environments enabling young people to reach self-determined goals. Then education will center on cooperation and wholeness. In such an atmosphere the gifts and capabilities of each person can awaken more completely. Homeschoolers know this ideal can work because we live it.

Reaching out in mutual respect to educators across the globe welcomes wider possibilities for future generations. There are already innumerable educational forums with ideas and information shared between homeschoolers and professional educators. We can also form reciprocal relationships with local teachers. All of these connections help us work together to ensure that tomorrow's education is designed to uphold a child's awe and curiosity.

Differing viewpoints must be understood to create necessary changes in education. Starting from a position of mutual respect is a prerequisite.

───────────────

Arianna's father and I are both educators. I left full-time teaching to homeschool her after her second grade school year because the system had a very negative effect on her ... I feel guilty in a way because I have the privilege to provide this for my daughter. Thinking of the students I had in my nine years as a middle school science teacher, some thrived but others required closer attention to their needs and I couldn't give that to them ...

It's kind of funny how many teachers I know who are homeschooling their own kids. I fully intend to return to my career and I know a lot of them will be too. *We got into teaching because we love to be part of that learning process. Homeschooling gives us another perspective to bring with us that can help our future students.* —Krista, California

───────────────

I tell new homeschoolers to get a teacher any chance you can. In my experience they are chomping at the bit to really let loose with teaching ideas they aren't allowed to use. They couldn't be more thrilled to find eager students like homeschoolers.

We hired a math teacher from the high school to work with our son, Braden, when he was thirteen and already working towards trig and calculus. This guy was great. He came to the house every week and didn't charge much and best of all he was such an inspiration. He really loved math. He made it fun for Braden.

Last spring we set up an evening program with our homeschool co-op so he could present a session for everyone. He called it something like "Decoding Math Around You." He put a lot of work into it. He had the kids in the room raise their hands to take a poll, then showed them on an overhead how he could skew the numbers into different kinds of data to explain why people should be aware when reading statistics. He asked the kids to pick out their favorite meals from fast food restaurants and then compared prices different ways. Then he took the prices and showed them how much they would earn by investing by the time they were 25 and then 50 if they gave up a single fast food meal every week. He made it very relevant. Unfortunately not too many people showed up, probably because they had no idea someone could make math interesting.

Teachers get a bad rap but they are just as stuck as the school kids are in a system that doesn't give them room to be individuals. The kid next door said that this teacher is considered "boring" at school. —Ed, Michigan

---

My mother taught in a girl's school until she retired. Back then teachers were given freedom to develop their own lesson plans because they weren't judged by test scores like they are now. There were all kinds of great projects she made up. Like, she had the girls develop their own businesses. They girls had to write proposals and keep accounts and at the end of the school year determine if the businesses were workable. These were real businesses that the girls started, like printing stationery. I have gotten a lot of my homeschooling ideas from my mother. I know that teachers today want to educate but are stuck with too much teaching to the test. If teachers had real say over their lesson plans they would be happier and the students would learn more ... Now that we see how well homeschoolers do in college and jobs, it seems like this emphasis on test scores should diminish. —Katie, New Jersey

---

Over the years teachers have pioneered progressive and inspiring school options. In 1921, A. S. Neill founded Summerhill School with the principle, "freedom not license." Today Summerhill flourishes in England. Teachers and classes are available, but children have complete freedom of choice to attend lessons or take part in their own activities. Students as well as staff members have an equal voice since anyone can take their concerns to regular meetings for discussion and vote. Similar schools, often called Democratic schools, now operate in many countries. Such schools maintain an atmosphere of mutual respect that upholds the child's autonomy, allowing each child the integrity to learn in alignment with his or her optimum potential.

A resurgence of Waldkindergärten, or forest kindergartens, are beginning to appear in Denmark, Germany and other countries. They are modeled around the ideas of Friedrich Fröbel, a German educator who developed the first kindergarten over 150 years ago. These forest kindergartens take place entirely outdoors, relying on open-ended learning experiences found in nature. The children sing, hike and climb trees. Instead of early exposure to academics, they learn to whittle and identify animal tracks. Greater imagination, concentration and communication skills appear to be a result of a child's time in a forest kindergarten.

Around the world, there are remarkable schools incorporating ideals of educational visionaries such as Rudolf Steiner, Sri Aurobindo, Celestin Freinet, NFS Grundtvig, Loris Malaguzzi and others. There are many holistic educational settings that share an open search for truth within spiritual guidelines, such as schools in the Quaker tradition. In addition, new educational programs continue to form, shifting rigid paradigms to models incorporating wider ways of learning. One promising effort has resulted in two independent schools—Wondertree Learning Center and Virtual High in Vancouver, B.C., developed by Brent Cameron and Barbara Meyer. Education at these schools involves the whole mind and whole body. As Cameron and Meyer describe in *Self Design: Nurturing Genius Through Natural Learning*, "It is a model that has emerged from real children learning together in true freedom—freedom to be curious and enthusiastic and freedom to work together in community." At Wondertree, each student is encouraged to look within as they develop personal goals based, in part, on a mandala of human experience.

Public schools are also slowly evolving as innovative teachers, forward thinking administrators and dedicated parents drag the institutional model toward a freer future. Significant projects launched by individual public school systems and daily creative effort put forth by engaged teachers are particularly impressive in light of the restrictions under which they currently labor.

These are signposts on a pathway to a more vigorous, participatory involvement by educators, members of the community and students themselves. This movement has parallels in the learning communities that homeschoolers create when they choose to learn together.

Whether we consider the journey represented by an independent learner, a homeschooling family, a community learning center, an alternative school or progressive educational program in public schools, it's clear that they all have something in common. Those involved may not be trying to change the way society educates, but their efforts have a larger social effect. Each move away from rigid, authoritarian education is a transformative choice that contributes to the momentum for change. It takes a relatively small percentage of people to raise the awareness of those around them. As Malcolm Gladwell points out in *The Tipping Point: How Little Things Can Make a Big Difference*, there comes a threshold point at which change is inevitable. The reality of mainstream education, as we know it, can't help but be affected.

Stifling, limiting forms of education must do more than adapt. When we raise our children to think for themselves and to act compassionately toward others, they are unlikely to accept anything less than true change. The quiet revolution of self-determined learning going on today will create changes benefiting many more children in the coming generations. Education is gradually shifting toward the kind of inclusive, positive, interest-based learning that remains vital throughout a lifetime.

The accelerating rate of change doesn't mean that we shouldn't incorporate the best of ancient wisdom. As previously noted, most of humanity's time on earth took place during the hunter-gatherer era, before the advent of agriculture. Anthropologists affirm that cooperation, not aggression, was essential for the development of language, healing arts, food collection and safety. Our ancestors lived in small bands, maintaining close ties with the same people throughout life. Their children were given purposeful roles. Their lives were rich with story, ritual and song. Each person was inextricably connected to the seasons and forces of nature. While civilization has altered our lives, our bodies and temperament have not changed from this era. We have the same need for closeness, cooperation, connection to nature, story, song and meaning. We cannot forget to incorporate these important elements from deep in our collective history into our ever-unfolding future.

Homeschooling as a Right

"The highest result of education is tolerance." —Helen Keller

Homeschoolers are an educational minority, comprising a tiny fraction of all school-aged children. Our educational choices are widely misunderstood by the general public and often subject to a number of misconceptions. The word "prejudice" means to judge in advance, to make a decision or form an opinion (often adverse) before developing sufficient understanding. And homeschoolers do face prejudice. Our extended families and even our spouses may not understand or support homeschooling. Our friends and neighbors may regard our decision to homeschool as a critical reflection on their parenting or a disparaging judgment of the schools their children attend. Strangers may question our fitness to "teach" or they may regard our children as aberrations from the norm. People in a position of authority may impose ever-tightening standards even if the law doesn't require us to be "approved" as homeschoolers. These and less overt forms of prejudice can have an insidious effect.

The educational attainments of homeschooled children tend to be exaggerated while other aspects of the homeschooling movement tend to be simplified. News reports highlight the few homeschooled children who win national spelling bees or science contests. Television, movies and novels portray homeschooled children as brilliant, eccentric and friendless. It doesn't help that some of the "research" about homeschooling reported by various foundations and institutes is far from scientifically valid. Such claims have exaggerated the educational attainments of homeschoolers based on select samples of standardized test scores, implied that homeschooling parents want greater governmental assistance, and generalized about what "kind" of people choose to homeschool. When reports such as these are widely accepted, it can't help but affect the way homeschoolers are perceived.

Homeschooling families come from all income levels, religions, political orientations and backgrounds. We homeschool for complicated and heartfelt reasons that defy categorization. Our families may have only one thing in common—an abiding interest in preserving the right to homeschool. As parents, we can provide balance to the portrayals of homeschoolers in the media by pointing out the positives of homeschooling without hyperbole. We can resist the heavy-handed influence of organizations using homeschooling to promote a political or religious agenda. Our fully-lived lives provide the best example. No one should be subject to stereotyping. Whether good or bad, oversimplification negates who we are as individuals.

I am not interested in one more story about a mega achieving homeschooled child. My kids are normal average kids. We happen to learn on our own terms but that doesn't make us any different than anyone else. Some homeschoolers are disappointed when their kids don't turn out to be superheroes. My kids are happy and healthy and like to learn. What else could I wish for?

—Katie, New Jersey

I've learned to really take a close look at organizations that claim to protect homeschoolers rights. More often they whip up hysteria and cause trouble (and make money!) in the process. Stick with grassroots organizations run by homeschooling families. *—Sarah Brill, New York*

A significant threat to homeschooling rights is the way the word "homeschool" is being co-opted for profit. We base homeschooling on what works best for our families. Our daily life experiences help us to self-correct. We rely on our own values to guide us. In this way we live in relation to what has meaning for us. Each of us is centered in the ever-changing reality that is our unique homeschooling family. Our choices, freely made, give homeschooling credibility.

When government or corporate entities promote the word "homeschool" it tends to mean something entirely different. Increasingly, parents are offering "homeschool" options by their school districts as if their families have greater self-determination than ever before, but that is hardly the definition of liberty. Real freedom means determining what our options are in the first place. Tracing this route back to who profits and why they profit isn't in the scope of this discussion. Suffice to say that people are easily lured by the concept of choice even when careful examination demonstrates that the so-called options still take away the child's self-determination and the family's autonomy. In many states e-schools, cyber schools, voucher programs and charter schools are termed "homeschooling" yet students are required to follow a mandated curriculum under the supervision of a teacher. The school district or a private company receives reimbursement for providing these services. This is not homeschooling. We cannot permit entrepreneurs selling education as a product through our school districts to co-opt our hard won freedoms or use the term "homeschooling." We must continue to define homeschooling for ourselves.

No matter what changes are made to the educational systems in our wider culture, the right to homeschool must be protected. This is the oldest and most successful form of learning known to mankind. It's also the most natural form of learning. Children playing, learning and growing up with close family ties in a community where they gain experience among people of all ages—this is how nearly every one of our ancestors learned. This works. Learning does not have to be regulated and legislated. It does not have to be a for-profit venture. If we don't defend homeschooling, our right to define homeschooling for ourselves can be lost.

Homeschooling misconceptions have an effect on teachers. The existence of homeschooling can cause the public to question assumptions about education. After all, homeschooling families aren't "experts" and approach learning in a way that is not popularly understood, yet the overall results tend to be positive. Many teachers and administrators choose to homeschool their own children, but professional educators on the whole seem less than pleased with the homeschooling movement. The largest teacher's union in the U.S., the National Education Association, passed another in a series of anti-homeschooling resolutions. The 2007-2008 Resolution reads, in part:

> The National Education Association believes that home schooling programs based on parental choice cannot provide

the student with a comprehensive education experience. When home schooling occurs, students enrolled must meet all state curricular requirements, including the taking and passing of assessments to ensure adequate academic progress. Home schooling should be limited to the children of the immediate family, with all expenses being borne by the parents/guardians. Instruction should be by persons who are licensed by the appropriate state education licensure agency, and a curriculum approved by the state department of education should be used.

This resolution shows a profound disconnect between the homeschool and school perspective. We consciously choose to approach learning on our own terms. Many of us do not use curricula or if we do, we would not necessarily use the exact curriculum our state department of education might mandate for our use. Many of us carefully avoid introducing academic subjects before our children show readiness, since experience shows that children can master them in a short time when they are eager to learn. Many of us find that a lively, interest-based approach brings forth the fullness of our child's joyful learning ability. Even though we have chosen to take responsibility for the education of our children, in some states homeschoolingchildren must pass the same standardized tests their schooled peers face in order to continue homeschooling. As noted earlier, research shows that standardized tests are correlated with shallow thinking and are not a good predictor of future success. Teachers and state school boards surely believe they are protecting homeschooled children by advancing such recommendations, but they are undermining an entirely different approach to learning, one that has proven highly beneficial to the whole child. This method has a much longer history than any form of schooling.

Our homeschooling choices offer an adaptable, individualized and endlessly creative way of learning. These are positive options that we can freely share with professional educators in an open and mutually respectful exchange. Homeschoolers and teachers regularly discuss ideas on educational forums. We learn together from journals such as *Education Revolution Magazine* and *Encounter: Education for Meaning and Social Justice*. We need further ways to reduce the level of judgment and even hostility evident in the NEA resolution as well as in some of our own homeschooling commentaries.

The ongoing comparison between schooling and homeschooling is not only thrust upon us by society at large, it's also an examination we homeschooling parents take on ourselves. That's inevitable when we are such a small minority. Our daily choices exist in opposition to standardized education as it exists today. Oftentimes, parents whose children have been in school go through an intense period of comparing educational choices. Criticism of oneself and of the educational system can serve as an important tool. As we struggle to develop perspective, ongoing conversations and articles about homeschooling versus schooling are helpful. But we need to temper these explorations with the maturity born of understanding and compassion. All of us (parents, teachers, school administrators and members of the community) have a similar goal. We care about nurturing the child today and guiding the child toward his or her potential. That's a goal best met in a society where the adults as well as the youth can talk respectfully and knowledgeably with one another, without expecting anyone to convert to our point of view.

The effort to sway opinions may be a problem in some homeschool organizations just as it is in other educational circles. We go a long way toward increasing understanding, both within the homeschool community and in the larger population, when we focus on maintaining homeschooling freedoms, and do so in the most honest and aboveboard ways possible.

A common accusation leveled against homeschooling persists despite extraordinary evidence to the contrary. Homeschooling parents are regularly asked, "What about socialization?" For some reason it is assumed that collecting approximately twenty-five same-aged children under the paid instruction of a teacher for six hours a day is the best way for young humans to learn the standard values and behaviors of society, hence, to become "socialized." As discussed earlier, segregating children away from their families and the community at large is a condition that creates inherently unnatural socialization. In these situations, children often become intensely peer oriented. When peer culture becomes paramount, young people resist maturing influences such as parents and other adults. Unfortunately, peer culture can be cruel, exclusionary and unpredictable. This forces children to adopt cynical attitudes as self-protection even in the early grades.

What most people mean by "socialization" is simply socializing. And they regard children who are not in school as being deprived of this opportunity. However, studies show that homeschooled children participate in more activities than the average child. They have more free time for both planned and spontaneous play with friends of all ages. As noted previously, some studies have shown homeschooled youth to be more mature and cooperative among their peers than schooled children.

The perception that schooling is required for children to make friends highlights how little is understood about the lives of homeschooled youth. Yet this stereotype is so pervasive that new homeschooling parents often ask the standard "what about socialization" question. Until they get involved. Soon, they find their children have more opportunities for friendships than they'd imagined. And many times, parents are surprised to discover that our societal preoccupation with friendship is overemphasized. They find that their own children enjoy family time as much as time with friends. After all, where a young child cultivates his or her earliest and most enduring sense of self is within the bonds of family relationships.

Standing in line at the store, a man told me that school was good for kids because it toughened them up. He said, "If they don't get beat up a few times they'll be Mama's boys their whole lives." Then he winked at my twins who are five years old. —R.C., Texas

I shudder to think of Issa in the confines of a class or recess. Those circumstances encourage the development of cliques and over competitiveness. I notice that every one of Issa's friendships have a different quality that allow each child's character to shine through. —Kelly

I was asked yesterday how my kids are going to learn to handle ridicule or face bullying if they're home with people who are nice to them all the time. —Samantha, Kentucky

Our friends and neighbors may infer that our decision to homeschool passes judgment on the schools their children attend, or even on their parenting choices. They may accuse us of undermining education or refusing to pay taxes to support local schools. These are common assumptions, sometimes grounded in our own comments. Because we have chosen to educate differently does not reflect on the freely made choices of others. We pay taxes to support schools regardless of our child's attendance. We know it is in everyone's best interest that all children are well educated. That's what we're doing for our children, on our own terms. Admittedly, sometimes homeschoolers criticize the institutional methods used in today's schools. Critiques often help new home-schoolers define their standards and help to resolve the dilemmas some of us feel when taking back the responsibility for learning. But assuming a role as watchdogs for educational improvement is not helpful in conversation with parents whose children are in local schools. We need to be mindful of the ways in which our comments might undermine support for those who are making their own considered educational choices. Children are our collective future. Keeping current with local school policies, attending school plays and showing genuine interest in school activities are just a few ways we can show concern for all children. In this way we model the sort of acceptance and understanding that we, in turn, hope to receive.

Doncha just love labels? Because my kids are homeschooled, people assume I'll be some denim jumper, straight-laced mom with a dozen kids. I've met a few of those moms so the label exists for a reason;, and you know what, they're nice people and their kids are great. But I'm not one of them. I homeschool my teenage sons and work part time for the school system. Among other things, my boys and I compete in target shoot competitions, deliver Meals on Wheels, take pottery classes, and watch Comedy Channel in the evenings. My guys are growing up to be fine men. There are a lot of places I don't admit to homeschooling, like in certain social settings and especially at work. It just spares me from explaining or being labeled. In our last house we had neighbors who treated us like s*** because they figured we were renegades. One was a school board member who told me we were "undermining the social order." Even in my stomping boots I'm no threat to any social order. —Tammy

---

Some homeschoolers experience negativity from family members, neighbors and friends. These people care about our children. Unfortunately, they have decided that they know what is best for our children and are convinced that homeschooling, or our form of homeschooling, is in some way hurtful. They may deliberately undercut our chosen style of learning for years yet these same people often refuse to hear any positive information about homeschooling, preferring to retain their own misconceptions.

I try to avoid taking the boys (6 and 8) to my parent's house very often because my dad quizzes the boys on their math facts or history factoids. Every time they get something wrong he looks at me with complete satisfaction. He and my mother have told me that I'm 'destroying' my children's chances for a normal life by homeschooling. —Wendy

---

My sister may be embarrassed because my daughter reads better than her son, who is in private school, so she mocks homeschooling in front of my children every chance she gets. She acts like they're deprived if they don't get new school supplies and actually said that I probably don't want to spend quality time with them like she does helping her son do school projects! —Unsigned

---

Someone called Child Protective on me because my kids were riding their bikes during the school day. The social worker turned out to be nice but I can't begin to tell you how upsetting that was. My youngest is still afraid to go outside for fear that she'll be in trouble for playing. I don't know who called, but I'd like to show the vindictive person who called all the wonderful projects my kids have done this year. If they aren't working the exact hours school is in session that's nobody's business. —Unsigned

---

I run across people who find out they [my children] are homeschooled and they are inspired to ask them if their mother is a good teacher. I'm hardly going to explain our exploratory style of learning which doesn't put me in the teaching mode too often, yet this inquiry leaves my children confused because they don't think of me as a teacher. I'm the mom. Other people start asking my kids what grade they're in, what they learned today and how hard their work is. Our version of homeschooling is fundamentally different than school. That's why we do it. But it makes it hard for my children to face these inquisitions in the hardware store. Thankfully my children see these strangers as interested friends and start talking. —Toni Grundy

---

My husband still isn't convinced that homeschooling is a good idea. I prove it to him with the kids' test scores but I feel pressured to always talk it up. —Unsigned

---

Ollie told his Sunday School teacher about a science experiment we did at home. It was a really fun experiment that gave off a blast of smoke and fire, so we performed it outside. Since he liked it so much we did it a few more times. His teacher asked Ol if he was learning to be a terrorist. Then she spread rumors about our homeschooling methods around church. —Aimee, Tennessee

My parents pay for their other grandchildren's school fees, class trips, school photos and prom dresses. They know we have to buy any materials that we use to educate our children (their youngest grandchildren) as well as pay for every program or class our children attend. It's their way of punishing us for our educational choice. They make sure to mention every single expense they cover. It's a glaring inequality. — J.S.

When people treat us unfairly it presents a learning opportunity, since we can talk with our children about how opinions and judgments are formed. Some of us choose to defend our choices with well-reasoned explanations. Some dismiss or ignore negative comments. Some make an effort to welcome naysayers, asking them to take part in a homeschooling event or share their expertise with our children hoping to reverse prejudicial attitudes. Whatever our reaction, as we go about our daily lives we demonstrate that there is no one way to learn, no apt stereotype about homeschoolers, no reason to feel threatened by who we are. In general, most people don't react negatively or differently to us. They treat us exactly as they treat everyone else. That's only fair.

Misconceptions about homeschooling can actually interfere with our ability to educate our own children. In some cases parents have to fight for the right to homeschool. Oftentimes these are custody battles in which homeschooling is used as a weapon of contention. The parent who wishes to continue homeschooling is forced to defend this decision in front of attorneys and judges who are not always well informed about the relevant state laws, let alone knowledgeable about homeschooling.

In other cases, courts or school districts overreach state regulations. They impose unfair restrictions or oversight on homeschooling families. Because officials have the weight of authority, homeschoolers can feel threatened. Occasionally homeschoolers report receiving truancy notices,

educational neglect claims or other types of harassment. More commonly, forms they submit reporting their status as homeschoolers are rejected even when all required documents are in order. Many families are eager to comply with additional requirements in order to satisfy these officials. They assume that additional testing or further documents are necessary, even when requests exceed the reach of the law. However, this isn't helpful as it sets a precedent that other families may have to follow, therefore imposing further constraints on homeschooling freedoms.

According to homeschoolers, when officials overstep their authority the effect is nothing less than oppressive. For example, Cyndi Sherrill of Virginia homeschools on religious grounds. In her fifth year of homeschooling she was surprised to have her documentation questioned. She began receiving letters from officials, some with

Any time our right to homeschool is threatened by truant officers, school officials, court filings or other constraints our response needs to be careful and considered. Since we are a little understood minority it is best if we have established a firm foundation to support us.

- Remain apprised of state laws and comply to the best of your ability in a timely manner without exceeding the requirements.
- Consider composing a family homeschooling mission statement. Change it over time as your ideals and goals evolve. This exercise helps to clarify what you value, putting the emphasis on the bigger picture. It also exists as proof of your longstanding and ongoing shared family goals.
- Maintain good records for your own use. These records can include photos; brochures and fliers from places visited; lists of favorite books, movies, games and websites; samples of art, writing, math and other work; notations from a daybook or calendar about daily activities; your own observations.
- Use educational terms to describe your activities to those who are concerned. No matter your style of homeschooling, this provides assurance that you are following an educational plan and tracking your child's progress.
- Develop supportive relationships with other homeschoolers through groups, forums and activities. Learn from one another's experiences if problems arise.
- Join grassroots organizations. These are groups made up and run by unpaid homeschoolers making decisions together, working to maintain homeschool freedoms regardless of religious or political differences. Avoid groups promoting a legal agenda, as such efforts tend to backfire and cause increased government oversight and regulation.
- If you face a custody issue or other court-related challenge, make every effort to use mediation or other negotiated arrangement rather than resort to more adversarial litigation.

passages highlighted in yellow, making repeated demands. "It's extremely stressful," Sherrill says, "you live in a state of fear."

She shares a section of the form that she submitted to her local school district, with district questions in bold.

Please describe in your own words, what you consider to be the basic tenets or beliefs to which you adhere?

We believe that Cherokee children are best raised with the beliefs and values of the Cherokee Nation. We believe that Cherokee children learn and grow best at home, while preserving their heritage and culture. We teach by nurturing our children in body, mind, and spirit as part of the living world around them. We teach our children to preserve the heritage and ways of the First Nations and to promote harmony and balance in the natural world around us. Our children are taught daily observance of our spiritual beliefs through prayer and use of traditional Cherokee practices throughout the day. We encourage excellence while practicing humility, respect, and gratitude.

Please state specifically the elements of the ********** Public Schools curriculum and / or policies / procedures that conflict with the tenets and or beliefs of your religion.

The Policies and Procedures of the ********** school system do not allow for the freedom of spiritual expression that my children have come to know and excel with. My lesson plans allow me to provide information to my sons that would be denied or at best incorrectly taught in a public school.

Cherokee history and culture are strong influences in our daily lives. Our lessons are infused with the understanding that we are not just on this planet, we are part of the Earth and every breath is sacred and to be

given thanks for; every action has a consequence for which we are responsible.

We believe that children should be who they are, not what others say they are, as is the case in most textbooks. Our beliefs do not recognize labels or limitations as acknowledged by standardized testing. Each child is different and must be allowed to progress in the way that is best suited to their individual-style of learning. My children are taught at their pace not a group pace that would simply recycle them or place them in a remedial class for desiring to linger over topics of interest or difficulty. Nor do we recognize "accelerated or gifted" labels that promote unhealthy attitudes of superiority and segregate children.

My children are taught each day the proper use of traditional regalia, music and spiritual principle; none of these are part of any public curriculum that I am aware of. We encourage curiosity with lots of open discussion and as many questions as my children wish. My sons have been taught that their opinions are just as important as those of their father and mother and they are encouraged to express them openly and with respect.

We encourage our children to think independently without restraint; to touch real things and create their own impressions for themselves instead of sitting indoors and accepting as fact the words of others not familiar with our culture, traditions and deep spiritual connection to our world.

We encourage our children to be independent thinkers while maintaining our family's cultural values and developing an attitude of respect and compassion for the world around them. We discourage our children becoming "peer-dependent" and accepting as suitable the media influenced behavior and poor social conduct displayed and accepted in public school.

To this end we maintain that is not simply our right but our responsibility as good parents and members of a quickly disappearing culture to provide our children with an environment conducive to the development of strong traditional Cherokee beliefs and spiritual values.

Despite this document Sherrill says, "The school system was insistent that I have my 'minister' contact them to prove we are bona fide." It seemed to her as if no one had even read what she had written. Her family waited in legal limbo, since they were not officially in compliance with the state's homeschool regulations. Finally she received a notice stating, "It appears that you have the appropriate documentation," six months after she filed to homeschool for the year.

Cyndi Sherrill relied on firm foundations supporting her homeschooling journey. She spoke eloquently for her beliefs and values. She did not bend to unreasonable demands. Her sons continued homeschooling, perhaps learning more resolute lessons about independence and cultural meaning.

Homeschooling as Self-Correcting

"Let us put our minds together and see what life we will make for our children."
—Tatanka Iotanka (Sitting Bull)

Homeschooling is self-correcting. With basic attunement to the child's needs a family can adjust how and when they approach certain essentials of learning. Failure is unnecessary because the child doesn't have to approach the subject matter until he or she is ready. That readiness is highly individual, but when it is in place the child eagerly comprehends and wants to learn more. This eliminates the diminished self-image that inevitably tugs at any child who is less than a high achieving student in school.

In addition to readiness, homeschoolers can examine a topic from any direction on the way to mastery. Even the most perceptive teacher isn't able to make concepts relevant to each student's life. But it's easy for us to explain ratios while discussing baseball statistics or during a dispute over dessert portions—making the calculations instantly useful. When the moment is right and the topic is engaging, learning happens effortlessly. Teachers know this, but the classroom structure inhibits them from meeting this need.

This approach also eliminates boredom, anathema to learning. A child can access learning from his or her own particular angle of interest. In this way the inherent wonder and excitement in such disciplines as the arts, sciences, mathematics, literature and history stays alive, ready to be discovered anew exactly as it is most meaningful to the individual. If the topic becomes stultifying or beyond the child's capacity, no matter how well presented it may be, the child won't absorb it in any real way. Because we're on a one-to-one basis it's much easier for parents to rebalance the approach taken along our child's journey of exploration than it is for even the most dedicated teacher supervising a class of several dozen children.

Forcing a child to learn is like admonishing a child to eat when she is merely thirsty, or forcing him to have dessert on a full stomach. Children are remarkably resilient as they teach the adults around them to recognize that they learn best by self-regulating. Sometimes this takes years for parents to catch on. In some families the adults impose punishments, rewards or additional educational materials in an effort to teach. But usually the child's own nature is recognized and they are given freer rein to learn. Each family approaches homeschooling somewhat differently. But almost all come to recognize that the way each child learns is perfect for that child.

> Sometimes children gulp in learning and at other times they seem to be fasting, preparing for another step in their development. The child doesn't understand the process. The adults in the child's life don't either. Yet they do know a hunger must be fed. And by their loving attention they also help the child find balance, meaning and belonging.

A more perfect school may be able to nurture children individually but the dynamics of a closer relationship best allows the self to emerge, be known and nourished. You can force feed any student facts. Or you can empower a child to gather the necessary ingredients for learning any time the hunger is felt. That strength will last a lifetime.

In a recent interview with edutopia.org about his book *Revolutionary Wealth: How it will be created and how it will change our lives*, Alvin Toffler asserts that customized education is well overdue. He suggests that all instruction be individualized, explaining that some children may need to begin an education in preschool years and others not until they are seven or eight. He also suggests that subjects be approached via the child's interests. He says if students are interested in sports, then teachers should teach them about business, culture and history through sports.

"You need to find out what each student loves," Toffler says. "If you want kids to really learn, they've got to love something." He is describing exactly what many homeschoolers have been doing all along. We may not all do it, nor start out intending to do so, but we tend to

customize the learning process to each child. And we find that's what works. No child is exactly like another and therefore the learning process should be as unique as the child.

I just am very connected with my kids. I read their reactions. When they stop being interested in something, I either change my tactic, or change subjects, revisiting the subject later. —Margaret S., Texas

---

I'm nearly convinced that without my homeschooled upbringing, I wouldn't have truly found my seemingly ingrown sense of adventure when it comes to learning. —Kirby, 19

Homeschooling as Collective Intelligence

"You are held within the web of life, within flows of energy and intelligence far exceeding your own."
—Joanna Macy

We arrange ourselves into organizations, businesses and nations. Collectively these structures function with an intelligence based on what works. The aspects that continue to function effectively persist. Those that do not are constantly readjusted. Sometimes these structures become resistant to change or become unable to work intelligently. When that happens ordinary individuals making up these organizations, businesses and nations react. We resist, compete, struggle, debate, discuss, break away, reinvent and collaborate. This ongoing effort affects the way a society frames reality. Whether we intend to impact the larger civic good or not, the collective intelligence of our culture is continually refined as we seek out more conscious and life enhancing ways to live. It takes a small percentage of people to change our cultural mindset.

We see examples of this taking place around us right now. Systems that are unable or unwilling to change become more brittle, even domineering, as they try to hang on to outmoded methods. This can be seen in business, medicine, politics and finance. Many people within these same systems are opening up to new ways of doing what was done before. The concept of "power over" shifts to "power with." We see businesses choosing sustainability. We note medicine beginning to embrace holistic healing modalities. We find finance accepting transparency.

More and more we see ordinary individuals resisting the structure of institutional education in its current form. Their concerns are collective intelligence in action. They question the limiting concept of education as a pathway to material success. They ask whether learning might have something to do with character formation and independent thinking. And they object to the way education is packaged and sold.

We recognize that decisions are made for schoolchildren on a societal level. Legislators, think tanks and educators typically influence these choices. The choices are also steered by those who profit from schools (software and textbook manufacturers, school lunch program providers, etc.). Those taking a stand against public schools also affect educational choices, some influenced by private financial interests of school options (private schools, charter schools) as well those options that misleadingly co-opt our homeschool identity (e-schools, virtual schools). These influences are one of the reasons for the test-oriented educational system we have in place. Children, parents, teachers and local districts do not make the top-down educational decisions that profoundly affect today's students, although these people are often told that they are being given more choices. Not real choices.

Real choice exists when the people directly affected are the same people who create the options and have control over the decisions. Real choice gives parents, children, teachers and members of the community the freedom to do what best serves their unique needs. But in today's divisive educational climate, often the only choices left are between unsatisfactory options that result in the same oppressive educational climate.

Until people recognize the limitations of those options and react.

It usually takes a certain amount of irritation, unfairness or suffering before people look at the bigger picture. Suffering has a way of making us more fully aware and more authentically in charge of our lives. Public debate about education has gone on for years. The whole structure is at a critical juncture. Just as it seems schools are being taken over as corporate entities, concerned people are fighting back to maintain local integrity. Just as it seems that meaningless busywork, homework and testing will suffocate the joyous nature of childhood, research mounts to prove that these concepts have minimal educational value. Just as millions of children are medicated into compliance with narrow, stifling educational environments parents are fighting for freedom from negative labels and knee-jerk pharmaceutical intervention. These are ordinary individuals whose actions are changing the collective intelligence surrounding education.

Homeschooling is an example of collective intelligence at work. We homeschool for diverse reasons. Among the many "whys" parents discuss as they start homeschooling are the importance of adapting learning to the child's abilities, giving values and faith a wider role, preserving curiosity and enthusiasm, cherishing family time, providing closer guidance, and allowing education to become a natural part of a child's whole life. The rationale for homeschooling does not necessarily exist in opposition to anything. Admittedly many parents begin homeschooling their children to repudiate certain aspects of schooling or reinforce their choices by negative comparisons. Whatever our opinions about individuality and conformity, cooperation and competition, freedom and morality; our perceptions can form a more seamless whole when we see that there are many stories we tell ourselves as a society. It may be that we comprehend the genuine beauty of homeschooling better only after glimpsing a wider angle. No matter why we homeschool, the story becomes a positive choice about integrating education into our daily lives and into the larger community. By our choices we show the sort of fluid responsiveness that affects the larger intelligence behind education.

As homeschooled youth go forth into the world as confident, self-directed adults their experiences begin to shift the cultural mindset. It becomes ever more evident that learning is a natural process that does not require coercion or stratification. In this way homeschooling can improve the educational milieu for all children whether in school or not.

Often it seems that this kind of wider awareness can't come soon enough. Decades of groundbreaking work have gone into the effort. But as philosopher Arthur Schopenhauer observed, what is true is not initially accepted. He said, "All truth passes through three stages. First, it is ridiculed. Second, it is violently opposed. Third, it is accepted as being self-evident." The stages he names are evident in this as well as other cultural shifts. It seems that a certain percentage of people have to understand a concept before acceptance begins to spread. Once this critical number is reached, awareness achieves a social momentum that propels it easily into the collective mindset.

Homeschooling as Strengthening Families, Friendships and Communities

"We cannot live for ourselves alone. Our lives are connected by a thousand invisible threads, and along these sympathetic fibers our actions run as causes and return to us as results." —Herman Melville

What we do impacts our children right down to their biology. In *The Biology of Transcendence: A Blueprint for the Human Spirit* Joseph Chilton Pearce cites evidence that "…a mother who is emotionally mature, stable, loved, and feels secure gives birth to a child with advanced forebrain and…an infant protected and nurtured has a larger prefrontal growth after birth and maintains that growth during the toddler period if nurturing is unbroken." The prefrontal cortex is related to personality, intelligence, perhaps even conscience, meaning each child's highest potential may be inextricably linked back to love felt in the womb and cradle.

The connection doesn't end there. The science of epigenics shows that the choices we make today will resonate in the minds and bodies of our great grandchildren. Biochemical markers called epigenes signal our genes in response to such environmental input as nutrients, toxins and even behavior. As a result, gene expression is switched on or off. Studies have shown that early nurturance can turn off "dimmer switches" on genes related to stress, permanently shaping offspring to be calmer and better able to handle new situations. These epigenic changes persist well after the original stimulus for change is gone. Some of these changes pass on through generations like biologic memories of what our ancestors ate, breathed and felt. This also means that our personal choices today can become a living inheritance sent on to those we won't live to see.

❀

Who we are as people effectively creates a worldview for our young children. Carl Jung described the child as living within the unconscious and often the unlived life of the parent. Our cynicism can sadden a young spirit. Our fussiness with instructing and managing can hinder his self-confidence. Our blame or fearfulness can staunch her curiosity and limit her trust. Without intending to harm we affect our children with our own limitations. That is, unless we actively recognize that each child is a full person just as he or she is at the moment, making nurturance a conscious process.

> Few things can tweak a person's self-awareness like parenthood. Raising children takes us beyond physical, emotional and spiritual comfort zones. Just when we feel we have adjusted to a phase the child is going through, a new stage begins. It's a continual process of adjustment for parent and child. Family life involves sacrifice and energy that we could not imagine before these small people entered our lives. And until we became parents, we could not conceive of what we, as individuals, would mean to our children. To a very young child, a parent is the definition of what it means to be person. No matter how old that child becomes, the expression of humanity witnessed in the earliest years continues to resonate in his or her life.

The affection between parent and child is the strongest bond known to humankind. The tenderness and protectiveness that characterize this relationship are even exhibited in the parent's body. Expectant parents, both mothers and fathers, show elevated levels of hormones including cortisol and prolactin, which promote responsiveness to the new baby. New parents also show increased connectivity in areas of the brain related to planning, memory and relational bonding. The infant's secure attachment to a caring, attentive parent teaches him to recognize his own worth. It also gives him a reason to trust in others. This is the foundation on which he learns to build future relationships. The love the infant experiences in the arms of his parents forms the basis for the love he will express for many other people in his life.

Adjustment to parenthood isn't necessarily smooth. The personalities of parent and child are not always an easy fit. Ideally they have years to strengthen this uniquely precious relationship without lengthy separations. Parents and children have, along with extended families, lived in close proximity throughout time. This provided more than safety, it allowed for the transmission of family and cultural identity. The essential elements found in a nurturing family also contributed to a stable community.

Sometimes social norms work against families. At various points in history popular opinion dictated that children would benefit from restricted affection, warmth, sufficient food and physical contact while adults in their lives were expected to mete out harsh punishments, sometimes in advance of any wrongdoing. There is a direct correlation between child rearing styles and the resultant society.

James W. Prescott, former administrator at the National Institute of Child Health and Human Development, explains that particular sensory experiences during the early years set in place a neuropsychological predisposition for either violence-seeking or pleasure-seeking behaviors later on. We know if infants are deprived of vital sensory information such as sound or sight for a significant period of time they will suffer from abnormalities in hearing or vision. We also know if children are not permitted to play and explore that their ability to learn will be stunted. But they need more than sight, sound and play. "Somatosensors" refers to the bodily sensor systems including touch, movement and balance. Research by Prescott and others established that the development of these senses have a profound impact on later social abilities. Infants have a biological need to be held, carried and cared for tenderly. Abnormal brain changes leading to depression, impulse control disorders and violence can result when these needs are denied.

Prescott theorized that the deprivation of physical pleasure in the formative years is a root cause of violence. He went on to analyze data collected by cultural anthropologists using 20,000 statistically significant correlations from 400 cultural samples. The data included presence of physical punishment, freedom or repression of sexual practices, social status of women and degree of affection towards children in those cultures. The results confirmed many of the ideas Prescott advanced. His resounding conclusion? Societies based on affection were highly unlikely to be violent. In the article "Body Pleasure and the Origins of Violence" Prescott writes, "The reciprocal relationship between pleasure and violence is such that one inhibits the other; when physical pleasure is high, physical violence is low. When violence is high, pleasure is low. This basic premise of the somatosensory pleasure deprivation theory provides us with the tools necessary to fashion a world of peaceful, affectionate, cooperative individuals."

Today many cultural forces pull parents and children apart. This deprives children of crucial somatosensory experiences and inhibits deeper relationships. Some hospital policies still separate mothers and infants during the critical early hours of bonding. The majority of babies in the U.S. are not exclusively breastfed, if at all, through their sixth month of life. Infants and toddlers often spend many hours a day in car seats, carriers and other restraint devices. Then the bond is further strained, because parents are expected to hand young children over to the care of often-changing paid professionals in daycare, preschool and then school. Add lessons, organized sports, tutoring and other programs. Even while they are home or in the car together, children are kept busy with electronic distractions such as television, video games and computers. Currently many children enjoy little real time with their families. They live separate lives. Hours that would be typically devoted to conversation, shared work and play are spent apart. These are the years for establishing strong family ties and for learning the complex give and take that make up loving relationships.

When children are deprived of meaningful family time their basic needs for belonging, acceptance and purposefulness do not go away. Without close relationships children fill the void as best they can. Often that means seeking out more transitory gratification through materialism, celebrity worship, constant media distraction or other means. Such children tend to have fragile emotional lives. They hide their vulnerability. They are less able to acknowledge the sensitivities and interests that direct them to the true expression of their gifts. Young people separated too often and too early from the supportive network of a caring family are forced to rely more heavily on their peers to form their identity. That doesn't mean that friends are not a wondrous source of

fulfillment in a person's life. They are. But the sorts of peer relationships that form in age segregated settings are not a healthy replacement for a loving family. Children need to grow outward toward friendships and engagement with the wider community in gradual steps.

Although common stereotypes portray teens as eager to get away from their parents, young people recognize the need for family connections. They want more time with their parents throughout adolescence. A survey found that 84% of teens would rather eat meals with their families. Interestingly, when teens have infrequent family dinners (two or fewer per week) they are between two to six times more likely to use drugs and alcohol, depending on age, than teens who take part in family dinners five or more times per week.

The institutions pulling children away from their families cannot easily adjust to an individual child's temperament or needs despite the best efforts of caring professionals. Educational researcher Benjamin Bloom summed up data pointing to the possible deleterious effect of school on student's emotional health. He says, "... repeated failure in coping with the demands of the school appears to be a source of emotional difficulties and mental illness." He relates this to the judgments and marks of the teachers and the people in the lives of the students more than the tests taken by the youth. The tender growing spirits of our young people are not easily nurtured in institutions.

In a homeschool environment you are free to be who you are. You have the luxury of working through issues with children in an environment where they are loved instead of where they are just trying to keep order.

—Carl McGillivray, Ohio

We spent a lot of time together instead of just seeing each other at the end of a long stressful day. Instead of getting the kids up early and rushing around to get them on a school bus on cold winter days we would snuggle up and read a good book. We genuinely know each other, warts and all. I know we wouldn't be as close as a family if we had spent all that time apart.   —Lori Scelina

Common sense tells us close family connections are optimal for all age groups. The National Institute of Health is conducting a longitudinal study of 90,000 adolescents throughout the U.S. to identify factors that influence teen health choices from nutrition to risk taking. Some findings stand out. The teens least likely to make risky choices were those who said they felt "connected" to their parents and felt that their families cared. These youths reported that they shared activities with their parents and that there was a parent with them at key times of the day such as morning, dinner and bedtime.

Cultivating strong family bonds is a natural side effect of homeschooling as we pursue our interests, share chores and simply enjoy one another's company. Our children are freer to relax and allow their natural enthusiasms to shine through. They aren't forced to spend most of their waking hours in controlled settings so they are under less pressure. Because they are not prematurely forced to separate, children can develop a strong sense

of self. With that strength our children are able to form lasting relationships with friends and come to know themselves as whole people.

I would not be the person I am today if I had stayed in school. School crushes the individuality and the wonderful weirdness out of you. You reject your own little quirks and odd interests and enjoyments because you are afraid of being ostracized and rejected. I know because I did that to myself, even though I was only in school from kindergarten through 6th grade. You don't have the time to pursue your own interests in school and you can't let yourself appear to be enthusiastic or interested in something outside of what is 'cool' or 'normal' because you will be made fun of. I would have never, ever done the things I did as a homeschooler and that I love now if I had been schooled—no study of muskrat decomposition, no dissections, no reading about forensics or getting a cow or culturing bacteria and fungi from between my toes. I would have been afraid to let myself enjoy these things.

And because I was free to be the strange human I am (and that, actually, pretty much everyone is) I wouldn't be the sort of person who came back from a rainy, cold day at work spent slogging around for hours in waist deep mud, stinking and exhausted, feeling like it was one of the most awesome experiences I've had in a while. There was an interesting contrast during that day, too, as we had a high school student shadowing us for the day and he was miserable much of the time, in large part, I think, because he was worried about looking silly or uncool. And there I was, falling down on my butt and having to scrabble

on my hands and knees to escape the worse spots and laughing the entire day. I would have been that miserable, awkward kid if I had been in school, too.
—Claire, 22

Rebellion and angst are considered de rigueur for adolescents. Young adults in movies and TV series are portrayed as disgusted with their parents, moving as far away as possible and avoiding family members except for obligatory holiday gatherings. This says something about our society as a whole. It is contrary what has worked best for humankind throughout the ages. And it is not an accurate picture of the complex, fulfilling relationships between parents and their adult offspring, schooled or homeschooled. Despite the prevailing stereotypes, youth raised in cooperative and loving homes tend to mature into adults who maintain warm, supportive relationships with their parents and siblings. This starts early on. We work together and rely on one another. We come to value one another's strengths. In such homes it may be easier to accept doubts, disagreements and personal quirks.

We benefit from a certain amount of freedom because as homeschoolers we live somewhat outside of the mainstream. As parents we don't have to enforce the rules of external institutions nor permit our children to be evaluated, judged and tested by others. That removes a great deal of pressure. The approach we take honors our family's needs and values, and that lets us focus more on celebrating who we are than correcting who we aren't.

Oftentimes the boundaries of age are not as relevant for homeschoolers. Some teens begin working, traveling or attending college much younger than 18. Others may not be ready to rush into life changing decisions until later. There's no reason to enforce arbitrary standards of dependence and independence. We're free to operate on timetables that work for us. Homeschooling teaches

us that the cooperative approach works. When we emphasize interdependence in our families we put into place ways of relating to one another that are similar to those of our earliest ancestors. This means we emphasize each person's strengths and uphold the highest good for our family unit. As our children grow they naturally become full participants in the functioning of the family. This helps them to go on to take their rightful place as active members of the larger community.

My kids love each other. They live together now at college. Our daughter bought a house at college and our son helps her make her mortgage payment. Putting them away in an institution all the time is unnatural. Institutions teach us to have these 'times' to be with our families and 'times' where we are separated. I remember the first time my daughter crawled away from me, and she crawled back to touch me and then crawled away. It's a natural process. We interrupt that process by forcing them to do things they aren't ready to do. I remember the librarian telling us when she was three that she had to go to the 'by herself' group separate from her brother. I asked why, and was told so she could get ready for school. That's just one example of experts making decisions for us. I think when my daughter was born I began to be suspect of people telling me what to do …

I don't have any recollections of my kids being annoyed with each other. They palled around. Homeschooling allows that relationship to happen naturally. If we lived in a tribal community or little village, with close family nearby and kids running from hut to hut, I would have loved that. I think it would have been a lot more sane. We try to do everything and I don't think we're all meant to do everything. We're supposed to be doing what brings us joy, what we have an affinity for like weaving or cooking. But we sold that out a long time ago.

—Lynn Reed, Georgia

I always tell people that we live a "Perpetual Summer" existence. I sometimes get perplexed looks on this one! I tell them we live life like they do when their kids are on summer break. I tell them that we live like adults live: we live life, experience things via hands on, visual, interactive, and immersion method. The kids watch some educational TV (PBS, we do not have cable by choice), write to pen-pals, maintain their Internet sites, have real jobs, babysit, do crafts, read, write, experiment (they love to do experiments when they come across them!), make movies, watch movies, scrapbook, bake, cook, visit museums, go to science events, go to the mall, attend the local theater, join in the teen library programs, go to youth group at church, and whatever opportunity comes their way.

They are always finding their own things to do, just like adults. And like adults, they continue to learn through real-life interactive living. Occasionally there will be times when one of the kids will want to work on math or history, then I help, if asked. Mainly, I am their mentor, teacher, and guide in life, just as all parents are. This way of learning and living has produced independent thinkers, independent learners, and most of all, independent people who are sure of who they are and what they want. They may not know what they want to do in life (isn't this always changing as we change?), but in the here and now, they know what they want to be doing.

I have always tried to prepare my kids to grow up and be ready for the adult world by handing them the reins in small amounts as they could handle them. Many parents shield their kids, make their decisions and try to keep them 'kids' as long as they can, then wonder why, when these same kids turn 18, that they can't make decisions, choices or grow up. Growing up is a process that begins when the kids are young. I still allow them to be kids, but with the knowledge they need to know as they age. They take on more responsibility (laundry, housework, cooking) and they become prepared to be on their own … It works. Having two kids who have now 'graduated' from our homeschool, I have seen the wonderful young people they have become. —Lori Smith, Ohio

Homeschooling as Re-envisioning Success

"To me success means effectiveness in the world, that I am able to carry my ideas and values into the world—that I am able to change it in positive ways." —Maxine Hong Kingston

Among today's homeschoolers are children who wonder aloud any time of day and whose questions are answered. Children who stay up late to stargaze, who eagerly practice the violin and study Latin, who slosh in the edges of a pond to see tadpoles, who design their own video games, who read books till noon in their pajamas. These children are empowered to be free range learners. As their interests take them on journeys of discovery we provide encouragement along the way. These children grow up to think for themselves and care passionately about the world around them.

Homeschooling is part of a wave of positive change sweeping our planet. The first homeschooled generation of our era is in adulthood. Research shows that they are more than just capable. They are wonderfully self-directed, flexible, independent, civic-minded and oriented to lifelong learning. They are living demonstrations that there are other ways to nurture our young people. They prove that the emphasis on rigid curricula and testing is not the direction for the brightest future.

As homeschoolers we reject the concept that narrow channels of pre-determined experiences are necessary for education. Some of us follow our own carefully chosen path, others make it up as we go along. These choices are a mark of freedom. They allow our children to learn in conditions that fit their interests, temperaments and needs. They make learning relevant to people and places in the child's life. They allow diversity and self-determination to make up a central part of the homeschool experience. As John Kao says in *Innovation Nation,* "Diversity of perspective has long been recognized as a spur to creativity... Diversity also directly influences the power and richness of open innovation. The greater the variety, the wider the range of issues considered and the fundamentally more innovative the process. Diversity will also increase the likelihood that a process will deal meaningfully with the kind of wicked problems the world now faces."

> The freedom to fill our days meaningfully and in the direction of our interests stimulates expertise. Research continues to indicate that practice is a greater factor in achievement than talent. The highest levels of mastery in fields such as athletics, computer science and the arts are reached when individuals have put in 10,000 hours of practice, performance and play. These hours are nearly impossible for today's schoolchild, while a motivated homeschooler can easily spend a few hours each day at golf, physics or dance. Their time may result in conventional success in those fields, or the kind of self-discipline and satisfaction that simply cannot be measured by society's limited definition of success.

There's a lot of pressure in any society to fit in. As homeschoolers we don't always fit in nor do we necessarily see this as a goal. After all, "average" hardly encompasses the range of real human experience. Maybe the kind of suffering that people endure in order to be "themselves" is the proving ground for what later emerges in them—wisdom, clarity, creativity, strength of spirit.

Young people encouraged to be themselves are freer of the constraints forcing them into roles they haven't chosen. They can grow up into responsible, engaged citizens while living out their own definition of success. What might our world be if people manifested their gifts, lived out their best selves and saw beyond divisions to the wider perspective?

There would be more successful people because they'd have more faith in their abilities. —Benjamin, 26

I'm hoping that success will be achieving goals they set for themselves, not ones set by society or their peers. —Jenny

I think [defining success individually] will make our culture more free-thinking and adaptable. —Tamara Markwick, California

We redefine success every day by raising children with closely held values. That puts the emphasis on what is good, not what feels good for the moment. —Unsigned

My girls all are outspoken and not afraid to voice their opinions. I have tried to raise them to know that they are the masters of their own education, that God gave each one of them innate gifts, talents and abilities, and that they can do whatever they set their minds to do …I already know that my girls define their own success based on what they are doing, and not on some subjective view by some arbitrary societal standard. I believe my girls will succeed in whatever they do because they believe in themselves. —Lori Smith, Ohio

I hope that my children will define success as doing something they are passionate about —whether that is raising a family, writing, acting, knitting, engineering, volunteering, or a combination of their favorites. I hope that they continue to respect themselves and others with an open mind and a love of learning. What would happen to our culture if we cared about each other and worked in areas we loved? —Margaret S., Texas

As shown in earlier chapters, success isn't linked to test scores or careful adherence to an academic track. As a society, we may be limiting success itself in a foolhardy quest for measurable outcomes. A rigid educational model doesn't prepare our children to find personal meaning in ideas, handle feelings, think for themselves, develop fulfilling relationships, create positive solutions out of difficult circumstances, or embed values in their words and actions.

We parents may be vested in the choices our children make, whether we are advancing a traditional or untraditional view of success. But sometimes homeschooled youth have a clearer vision of what works for them. They are redefining success on their own terms.

My husband and I made the conventional choices. Basically that meant we were tied to heavy academic loads, then kids and a mortgage. It took forever to pay off our grad school loans. That put us on the track to success but made us miserable. We were robbed of important time with our kids. Our bodies and emotions were telling us this was wrong but we kept pushing because we had been trained all our lives to be overachievers.

It started to dawn on us when our son Darrin developed chronic headaches in daycare and was diagnosed with migraines at three years old. My husband and I added up all the health problems our family had and how much money we spent trying to recover from stress. We talked about all the purchases we'd made in hopes that we'd feel happier. It was funny, because we were driving to a car dealership while we had this talk. We were going to look at a van that had a feature we wanted—separate screens and separate DVD players so each kid could watch what they wanted. This would help us take a trip we dreaded, seeing my in-laws who had shoehorned my husband into a branch of law he didn't enjoy. The irony dawned on us that we

had a little boy with migraines from an academically oriented, very expensive daycare aimed at making him a success in prep school and here we were complaining about driving to see people who pushed their version of success on us. They did it because they loved their son, we were doing it because we loved our son. When would it stop?

I won't say we changed everything in one day. But we started putting our relationships and health first. We started homeschooling 11 years ago. I still expected each of my kids to go to college to ensure their own success. I admit I also wanted to prove our detractors wrong. I know I pushed the issue with my kids. As always, my kids taught me a lot. They've learned to think for themselves after all these years of homeschooling.

Our older son is 19 and working at a local restaurant. He composes music and plays in a band he's formed. He's saving up to start an animal sanctuary with a group of friends. He says college isn't in his plans. Our younger son is in the process of applying to colleges. I'm tempted to brag about his SAT results but I don't dare. When we congratulated him on an outstanding score he told us the number is just a tool to use. 'That can't measure anything important. They can't test how much anyone cares about anyone else.' he said. Obviously both of them are ahead of their parents at that age. —Jess, Vermont

---

Although we live in a typical midwest suburb we've made anything but typical choices for this area. I homebirthed four of my five babies, shared a family bed, avoid allopathic medicine, maintain a whole foods diet and unschool

the children. What I observe around me confirms that my choices have been exactly what my family needed to be healthy and happy … Thank goodness we have fantastic friends, otherwise we would have felt like aliens around here.

I have to admit that there's no other way to put it but say that I think there's an element of brainwashing involving in raising a child. School is structured to turn out better workers for a corporate driven society and think that's right. I know that I "propagandize" to my children on behalf of all sorts of causes from preserving nature to speaking up for your opinions and think that's right too. Maybe we just get a little rigid in our attitudes. I see it around me everywhere. We tend to associate with people who think like us, visit websites and read magazines that confirm our beliefs, and get threatened when our opinions are challenged.

Now that my children span a spectrum of ages from 5 to 19 I am beginning to think differently. This is all thanks to the children themselves … They are much freer of the baggage I have from my schooling. My older daughters like to put it right in my face and challenge me to think for myself as much as I preach it. A good example is college. As they got closer to college age I started talking up the alternatives to them just like my unschooling friends did; work on a co-op farm, or travel the world, or volunteer full time for awhile, you know, expand their horizons. My oldest daughter wanted nothing to do with the choices I laid in front of her. She got a job at the mall and is taking courses at the local community college in marketing. It was hard for me to accept that she immerses herself in popular culture until I saw

that she is able to do so without buying in to the painful aspects of judging herself by those standards. Or maybe she is strengthening herself by exposing herself fully to these standards. My second daughter is in college in hopes of gaining a medical degree. It's sort of funny in a way that we avoided doctors and now she wants to learn the profession. Someone like her would be able to bring all sorts of healing arts back into the practice.

What has been interesting is the reaction of my unschooling friends. They really judge my daughters for 'copping out.' These parents are putting their baggage on a whole new generation. I rejected the institutional track for my children when they were young and it was my turn to make choices for them. But now the choices are all theirs. It's my job to encourage them and care about them as I always have. Friends who judge my children for making conventional choices are actually being narrow and unfair. Some of their children are searching for their place in the world in ways they approve and some of them are not … For a formerly unschooled child it's exciting and challenging to explore conventional institutions. Who knows how structures like retail, medicine, education and science will change when enough unschooled minds are involved?

—Esme Stein, Pennsylvania

We discover for ourselves that success isn't necessarily what popular culture preaches. It's about making choices coherent with one's own inner voice. That leads us to craft a life based our passions, our integrity, the unique vision we bring to the world. At times these decisions seem to go in the direction of difficulty or hardship, but these experiences may provide valuable accelerated learning in the long run. As parents it's painful if our children make such decisions. But the journey is theirs to make.

As we homeschool we encourage each child to walk the path of his or her own possibilities. The guiding light on that path is unique to each individual. It's illuminated by elements found in imagination, talent, intellect and the strongest aspirations of the heart. Living in harmony with those aspirations allows each person be at peace with who they are. A world made up of people directed by meaning, purpose and integrity would indeed be a better place. In such a world, limiting definitions of success would become irrelevant.

PART TWO

CHAPTER SEVEN

Adventure Homeschooling

Travel Homeschooling

"Travel and change of place impart new vigor to the mind." —Seneca

Travel is a perfect stimulus for learning. Since few trips go as planned, we have to be flexible in order to deal with unexpected circumstances. Traveling takes us beyond our comfortable boundaries, exposing us to fresh vistas and new ways of doing things. Even if we haven't gone far from home we have the opportunity to step out of our daily lives and get to know different people. When we are open to new perspectives, our travels have a way of bringing a dynamic element to learning that can't be found any other way. The people and places we encounter on our adventures not only broaden our horizons, they truly invigorate our lives.

One homeschooling mother is a fiber artist. She brings her daughters to arts fairs. As they drive, they play games or listen to stories. At fairs the girls help her make sales or demonstrate techniques for passers-by. Certain festivals are their favorites, where they enjoy visiting old friends; others inspire them to get acquainted with new people. They try to take different routes home to see new things. Their travel photos include many funny or strange signs. The girls laugh about their mother's willingness to pull off the road to photograph an odd sign for their collection.

"Travel learners" is the name another homeschooling family have given themselves. When the children are interested in a subject they use that as an excuse to get packing. Sometimes they head off on day trips, other times they stow the van with tent and gear to spend part of a week exploring. They say anticipation is half the fun. This family likes to go over maps and information together, beforehand, as they strategize where they'll go and what they'll do. They explain that reading about geology can't compare to seeing rock formations first hand.

Homeschooling families are uniquely suited to travel. We aren't locked into the same school schedules so we are free to take off whenever it suits work and home life considerations.

My children have had the benefit of being able to travel a lot at any given time. They have had the opportunity to meet different people from all over the world. My oldest son River, age 9, has been to Mexico twice, my daughter Makasha, age 4, has been once. When my children meet someone new they are always very excited. They do not limit themselves and have not been limited to people in their age groups. In fact they prefer older people because they tend to be more on their level of understanding. We are a traditional Native American family and travel around to a lot of powwows. Recently this past year my son River has made friends with a powwow dancer named Bobby who is 14. My son and Bobby get along well and play together at every powwow we meet at. Bobby has made a good impression on my son who now wants to be a grass dancer like him.

—Jessie Mato Toyela, Florida

Inveterate expats, we haven't lived long term in the U.S. for years. My husband's postings have given us the opportunity

to make a home in different countries for six months to two years at a time. Getting acquainted with new customs and foods is a great experience for the whole family. Homeschooling provides us with continuity from place to place.

We've noticed that many other families in our situation prefer to socialize with other ex-pats. They act as if they are deprived of what they could have or do in the U.S. rather than enjoying where they are. That extends to schooling. The parents make every effort to keep their children up with U.S. standards and administer academic tests. They worry that their child's scope and sequence won't match up once they return. We have a different attitude. Homeschooling lets us learn best within the environment and community where we live, no matter where it is. —Rachel, Cambodia

---

Some homeschoolers make a commitment to long-term travel. The journey itself forms the backbone of the learning process. Becoming acquainted with unfamiliar places and people fleshes out a fully engaged education. Many nomadic families share their experiences online. The traveling life gives them a unique perspective on what other people consider "normal" life.

Mark and Denise Tyson began journeying a few years ago. While traveling they pay close attention to learning opportunities for their son Vance, as well as for themselves. All three of them are guided by their curiosity. While on the road they may listen to a lecture they've downloaded, or stop by a historical site for a reenactment. "We're not unschoolers," Mark says. "We do sit down for several hours each morning and work on core subjects but the real opportunity is never turning the learning off."

Sometimes the Tysons aren't sure if they'll head right or left at the next juncture. It's a big change for Mark, who once longed to spend more time with his son than the few hours his corporate career allowed. Although they live at home for half the year, he says he's ready to make life on the road a full time adventure. He keeps track of their experiences at www.haveschoolwilltravel.com

Mark wants his son to gain an understanding of the bigger picture, like the diversity of the country and lessons of history. He believes that intangible qualities such as confidence are more valuable than society's measurements of success.

One day the family was hiking in a canyon outside of Amarillo, Texas. They started downhill with Vance walking ahead. Suddenly Vance halted. Calmly he held a hand up to stop his parents. In front of him was a rattlesnake. Mark says, "I don't think I was ever prouder of him than that moment. It was a validation of what we're trying to do. At a young age he did exactly what he needed to do, instinctively. Inside I was going yes yes yes, it's working!"

Other families make travel a full time choice. They backpack. They live on a sailboat, RV or houseboat. They go by bike, train or other conveyance. They get by frugally, adapt to changing conditions and live in much closer proximity than most families are accustomed to doing. Their education takes place everywhere they go.

The Goza family has been on the road for over fifteen years as traveling performers. Dennis and Kimberly began touring nationally when their son Zephyr was a toddler. Together the three of them develop stories, songs and comedy to entertain others, sustaining themselves with the same creativity they bring to the bigger choices in life. They make the circuit of the U.S. about once a year, but have also been to Mexico, Canada and Japan. Each day is distinct.

The Gozas find that homeschooling fits perfectly with their lifestyle. "Travel is an education," Dennis says. "It gives you an opportunity to see the world you only imagined … Our son has been on a constant field trip."

Zephyr says, "A lot of stay-at-home families see things on TV, like the Grand Canyon, but never go there. Sometimes they even live nearby and never go there. We get out and actually see things other families miss."

Zephyr not only helps develop material and performs as an integral member of his family's troupe, Act!vated Storytellers, he also has done radio and TV commercials, written two books, is a member of a band and has time for hobbies. He says, "It wouldn't occur to a lot of people that they could pursue an interest or hobby on the road, but you can gain more experience than in your local area. You get a more complete picture. It can be done to great success."

The family website, www.activated-storytellers.com, details a full life. As Zephyr says, he doesn't know what "ordinary day" means.

The White family formerly lived what conventional thinkers would describe as the American Dream. Greg White's job with a start-up company called Dell turned into a position of responsibility and increasing wealth. He and Jenn had the big home, stock options, cars and other possessions that are supposed to bring happiness. What they didn't have was enough time to be a family. So they sold it all to live on the road. Greg and Jenn White have traveled through forty states with their three children—Kesley, Sunny and Austin. They call themselves the BareNaked Family because they stripped themselves bare of every possession except the essentials in order to play, learn and work together. As Jenn White says, they found much more than they left behind. Their children easily make friends with people from around the world. Each time they look out the windows of their RV they find that they have an ever-changing view of the real America. And perhaps most importantly, they are together in the here and now. They share their story on www.barenakedfamily.com with photos and updates. The White family lives full blast like the rock music they love, caring with the kind of intensity no lyrics could ever fully express.

Resources

There are many innovative and inexpensive ways for homeschoolers to immerse themselves in the worldwide possibilities of travel: swap homes, teach English overseas, work as a camp counselor in exchange for your family's free room and board, take a bicycle trip and stay in hostels, take a temporary job in another country.

Online

- **Couchsurfing** lets you network with people around the world, stay in their homes (perhaps on a couch) and offer your own home to travelers. www.couchsurfing.com
- **Escape Artist** provides reports on living abroad, with profiles of countries and job listings. www.escapeartist.com
- **Home Swapping** organizations provide a screened database of exchange participants around the world. Most of these services require a registration fee although the exchange is free. Use "home swap" as your search term.
- **World's Cheapest Destinations** offers a wealth of frugal resources. www.worldscheapestdestinations.com/id2.html

Books

- *Adventuring With Children: An Inspirational Guide to World Travel and the Outdoors* (Avalon, 1995) by Nan Jeffrey.
- *Educational Travel on a Shoestring: Frugal Family Fun and Learning Away from Home* (Shaw, 2002) by Judith Waite Allee and Melissa L. Morgan.
- *The New Global Student: Skip the SAT, Save Thousands on Tuition, and Get a Truly International Education* (Three Rivers, 2009) by Maya Frost.

Service Travel

"If you have come to help me, you are wasting your time. But if you have come because your liberation is bound up with mine then let us work together." —Aboriginal activist group, Queensland 1970s

Traveling to provide service in partnership with others is the most direct way to reach out, relate and understand. You have the benefit of seeing your time and energy make a tangible difference. Check with service organizations and your house of worship for upcoming service trips. Some are costly, but the impact is invaluable.

Resources

Agencies
- Idealist.org International Volunteerism Resource Center 212-695-7243, www.idealist.org
- International Volunteer Program Association 646-505-8209, www.volunteerinternational.org

Books
- *Volunteer Vacations Across America: Immersion Travel USA* (Countryman, 2009) by Sheryl Kayne.
- *Volunteer Vacations: Short-Term Adventures That Will Benefit You and Others* (Chicago Review, 2009) by Bill McMillon, Doug Cutchins and Anne Geissinger.
- *Wildlife & Conservation Volunteering: The Complete Guide* (Bradt, 2009) by Peter Lynch.

CHAPTER EIGHT

Field Tripping

Field Trip Tips

"We live in a wonderful world that is full of beauty, charm and adventure. There is no end to the adventures that we can have if only we seek them with our eyes open." —Jawaharlal Nehru

Field trips are smaller versions of travel. On a field trip young people may see how tires are manufactured, try sheep shearing, listen to a jazz band or explore an underground cavern. Afterwards, they'll remember the sights, sounds and smells that accompany understanding. They will also be blessed with an extra bit of wonder at the way the world works.

A child's mind develops as his or her experiences expand. The human brain is amazingly capable of making connections between disparate subjects and moving on to higher level thinking. A curriculum isn't necessary for field trips and activities, although some advance preparation may be helpful. What makes the difference is openness to what the child is thinking and feeling.

Before a Field Trip

- You need not over prepare, but it's helpful if your children can anticipate what they may encounter on the field trip. Curiosity is a highly receptive state of learning. If you are visiting a business you might find out something about the company's product or service in advance. If you are going to a living history event you might read a story about people who lived in that era. If you are going to a concert you might check out information about the composer, the instruments or the style of music you'll be hearing. Older children can be encouraged to take in more extensive information. Typically they'll be motivated to find out more after their interest has been piqued by an experience.

- On the way there you and your children may want to come up with a few open-ended questions you hope the event will answer. If you are touring an apiary, they may want to know how the beekeeper gets the honey from the hive to the jars. If you are going to a hot air balloon festival, they may wonder if balloonists can steer. Ask yourselves, "What do we want to find out?"
- Keep a bag or pack prepared with healthy snacks, water, camera, small notebook and writing utensils. The bag is also useful for materials gathered during the event.
- Inform your children about expected behavior on the field trip and how long the event will last. Adults often assume that children will recognize what behavior is expected by their surroundings, but that isn't always the case. After all, children must act differently when touring a stained glass studio, participating in an athletic field day or volunteering to weed invasive plant species in a wildlife area. Letting them know privately honors a child's dignity.
- Remember that the emotional atmosphere of a situation affects a child's learning so it's important to wait until a child is mature enough to enjoy an event. Taking a small child to the symphony when he or she may not be old enough to remain quiet throughout the performance will likely result in too much shushing and glaring, building negative associations with the experience. Not the outcome you'd anticipated nor a pleasant experience for other concert-goers. Instead of hurrying your child, don't sign up until he or she is ready to truly enjoy an event.

During a Field Trip

- Let enjoyment be the top priority. Children don't appreciate intrusive questions designed to test if they are paying attention to what adults think is important. They are attending in their own way. Your own pleasure

and appreciation will help fuel their interest in the event.
- Remember that learning is not simply a matter for the brain. It is a process of perception based on attitude, awareness and even the state of health at the moment. The child connects information with his or her own experiences, making what is learned unique to each person.
- Remove a child from the situation if he or she has a significant behavior problem. Rejoin the group once the child is restored to self-control. Mirror in your attitude the calm you want your children to display. If behavior problems are a common occurrence on certain field trips, recognize that this type of activity is clearly too stultifying or overwhelming for your child's current developmental stage.
- Consider expanding the way your children remember the event. Bring sketchbooks so they can draw details, scenes and artifacts. Let them use electronic devices such as a camera, audio recorder or the video options on a cell phone if regulations permit. Children may also like to gather ephemera to create scrapbook pages afterwards.
- Before the field trip is over you might want to find out if your children's questions were answered. Ask them. Or allow those questions to remain open to experimentation, reading, research and other inquiry in the coming weeks.

After a Field Trip

- Make sure your group expresses appreciation and cleans up any mess.
- Listen as your children discuss the experience on the way home. Their conversation will tell you what was important to them. If not, ask them a few questions such as what they found most surprising, what they'll remember the best, if they'd like to visit someplace similar. Share your impressions. Encourage inquisitiveness with a casually accepting approach.
- Send a thank-you note to the organization or business from your children or homeschool group.
- Encourage the youth who attended the event to contribute photos, drawings, journal entries, poems and other work stimulated by the field trip to your homeschool group's website, e-zine or newsletter.
- Notice the ways your child's curiosity has been piqued by the event. Questions and conversations afterwards typically indicate interest. You may want to look for related activities, library materials, web sites and hands-on projects. When your child's interest has waned, you'll know the subject has run its course, for now.

I am a huge fan of the field trip and feel like almost anything can be a learning experience and therefore a worthwhile field trip. From a field trip to the grocery store or the bank or something more adventurous we enjoy field tripping often. We are blessed to live in a suburb of a large city and near the ocean, the mountains and several micro climates and communities. So we have hundreds of things worthy of turning into a field trip.

—Tamara Markwick, California

My sister and I like to go for day trips. Our whole family piles in the car. We spend the day together going to far away places. We take photos, collect things like ticket stubs and funny advertisements and then afterwards we make mini scrapbooks about it for a homeschool report.

—Jillian, Ohio

I organize events for homeschooling families here. There are usually four a month, sometimes more. We've done School on Trains through Amtrak, Mad Science, plays, etc. I've even set it up for a weatherman from Channel 2 news to come out and do a weather school

— Kim Railey, Washington

Every year our list of field trips fills several pages—I am a field trip queen! (And yet with all these trips we are still able to enjoy many hours on end of unscheduled time at home). Field trips are one of my favorite aspects of homeschooling. I especially enjoy our ability to visit places when they are not crowded. My children groan if they see a school bus parked outside, knowing there will be a big crowd of noisy kids rushing through the exhibits. If that happens, we just wait a few minutes and let them get ahead. These groups almost always move very quickly; at one exhibit we heard a lone teenage voice ring out, "Don't we even get to look at it?!" The voice was ignored and the school group moved on. The teacher had just told the group to take their time, read the signs, and look around the Medieval and Byzantine art exhibit. But in less than one minute (not an exaggeration) she told them they had to move on. We are able to take our time and linger over the things that interest us, skip those that don't. At that exhibit my children had the time to admire the stones in a Visigoth cloak pin; to marvel that the painting of Hagia Sophia looked so much like Queen Amidala's palace (in Star Wars); and to note that a reliquary in the exhibit was made to hold relics like the hand of St. James, which we had just learned about in a book on Empress Matilda.

We always get the audio tours when they are available at museums, and my kids have even more patience than I do in listening to these; now they push the buttons for the extra information too! We visit art museums, science museums, history museums, historic sites, industrial sites, reenactments, historical replicas (such as Columbus's ship the Niña, UMR's Stonehenge, and Birmingham's Statue of Liberty), and much more.

In learning about world religions we have toured a local synagogue, an Amish community, a Hindu temple, and the St. Louis Basilica; watched a performance of Sacred Music Sacred Dance for World Healing by the Tibetan Monks of Drepung Loseling Monastary; attended festivals such as a Japanese Festival, a Hispanic Heritage Festival, and a Cherokee Pow Wow; and explored museum exhibits such as From the Dead Sea Scrolls to the Forbidden Book and Desire and Devotion: Art from India, Nepal, and Tibet.

While learning about the Civil War we have visited numerous battlefields, attended skirmish reenactments, toured coastal forts, Lincoln's birth site, The National Underground Railroad Freedom Center in Cincinnati, The First Whitehouse of the Confederacy in Montgomery, Ulysses S. Grant's home in St. Louis, the Mary Todd Lincoln House in Kentucky, and even The Battle for Chattanooga Electric Map and Museum in Tennessee. When we were studying Lewis & Clark we saw Meriwether Lewis's grave on the Natchez Trace; William Clark's grave at Bellefontaine Cemetery in St. Louis; Cahokia Mounds State Historic Site in Illinois; the confluence of the Missouri and Mississippi Rivers; the Lewis and Clark Center in St. Charles, Missouri; the National Expansion Monument (the St. Louis Arch); and the Lewis & Clark Interpretative Center at "Camp River Dubois" Illinois. In learning our local history we have toured "living history" museums, library exhibits, historic churches, a Masonic lodge, 1920's-era downtown buildings, the train depot, the mayor's office, and the city council chambers. We have gone on many historic homes pilgrimages and historic district walking tours. We have watched our history reenacted at the Maple Hill Cemetery Stroll and in a history play based on actual court transcripts: The Trial of Frank James in Huntsville, Alabama. I could go on and on with this list.

We have repeated this pattern many times for many subjects of historic, scientific, and/or artistic interest. Often these studies have stretched out over years. We are never "finished" studying a particular subject so we don't pass up opportunities to visit sites even if they relate to something we are not actively studying at the moment.

Our field trips also include industrial tours which are some of our favorite trips: the Corvette Manufacturing Plant Tour in Kentucky, St. Nicholas Boat Line Sponge Diving Exhibition in Florida, Sloss Furnaces National Historic Site in Birmingham, Wright Dairy in Anniston, Golden Flake Factory in Birmingham (the kids' all time favorite), Jack Daniel's Distillery in Tennessee, CNN Studio Tour in Atlanta, Coors Memphis Brewery, Living Marine Adventure Cruise (shrimping in the Mississippi Sound), Koetter Rough Mill plant tour in Indiana, radio and TV station tours, G&N Berry Farm and Apiary, the National Weather Forecast Office in Huntsville, a recyclery, and Huntsville's Waste-to-Energy Facility (steam plant).

Other field trips have included caves, aquariums, dams, air shows, zoos, robotics competitions, farms, a solar car race, botanic gardens, oceanariums, covered bridges, courthouses, lighthouses, the "Fountain of Youth" in St. Augustine, alligator preserves, incline railways, Renaissance Faires, historic jails, Frank Lloyd Wright-designed homes and buildings, a rodeo, cat shows, planetariums, a Mardi Gras museum, a quilt museum, a toy museum, a circus museum, and a sponge museum (Sponge-O-Rama— who could pass up a museum with a name like that?!).

We have attended a wide variety of music, theater, and dance performances; explored many natural sites (waterfalls, canyons, gorges, springs, deserts, beaches, mountains, swamps, and rivers); ridden on historic trains, WWII amphibious vehicles, and 4-seater airplanes; and overall have had a fabulous time learning! —Susan, Alabama

CHAPTER NINE

Full Spectrum Learning

Finding Your Own Way

"How are you going to spend this one odd and precious life you have been issued? Whether you're going to spend it trying to look good and creating the illusion that you have power over people and circumstances, or whether you are going to taste it, enjoy it and find out the truth about who you are." —Anne Lamott

How homeschooling proceeds day by day is different for each family. Therein lies the beauty. And also the quandary. We have to find our own way.

There are myriad styles of homeschooling: Charlotte Mason, Waldorf, unschooling, classical, Enki, unit studies and many more. Some of us adhere carefully to one form of homeschooling but experience shows that many families mix and match from different approaches according to what best suits their needs. Even those who start out firmly in the mindset of completing six hours a day in the school-at-home mode tend to soften their approach to learning. They quickly discover that a child can finish "schoolwork" in a short time, leaving the rest of the day for more enlivening activities.

Those who invest the most money in curricula and educational materials, or who most loudly espouse a particular style of homeschooling to the exclusion of others, seem the least likely to change their approach. This may be due to what economists call the "irrational escalation of commitment." It's a common reaction. We make a careful decision, then persist in that course of action in order to justify it even when evidence suggests that the outcome isn't what we'd hoped. If one or more of your children are struggling, resistant or unhappy, or if you feel burned out or frustrated, it is time to take a break from your chosen style of homeschooling. Have fun. Pay more attention to the present moment. Look at learning and family life from a wider angle. After all, used curricula can be sold. Other approaches can be tried. The process of finding what works for your family isn't static. It changes as your children grow, interests shift and your trust in the homeschooling process evolves.

It helps to pay attention to how much children learn as they simply take part in the normal activities of daily living. As our children play, work and converse with family and friends they live out a daily example of the same qualities that characterizes responsible adulthood.

You'll find it helpful to record what you see your children learning. Take photos, make notes, scrawl a few words in a datebook—these things help you recognize what is under the surface of your days together. You'll notice how natural learning covers a whole range of subjects that are normally separated in the average curriculum.

Sometimes we need to have our minds expanded regarding what each subject entails. I think if more homeschooling parents understood how the activities they do come under the different subject headings, they'd feel more comfortable that their daily lives are educational. When I started out, I gathered checklists of preschool skills from several resources and kept track occasionally of what my son mastered. Primarily I learned that he mastered the skills whether or not I was intentionally working on them …

Grade level checklists can be helpful if you don't take them too seriously. Using several different sources, instead of relying on just one, shows how no one really agrees on what topics should be covered when. There will be plenty of pleasant surprises when you refer

back to the checklists and see that the field trip or cooking dinner or whatever you did yesterday covered skills in five or six different subject areas. Then the checklists don't become a cage in which your family is trapped but can become a guide that helps you relax into the process of learning together.

—Karen, Texas

My sister, thinking that she was being supportive of our homeschooling lifestyle, gave us a holiday gift of those books with titles like What Your Second Grader Needs To Know. *I spent some time with those books feeling terrifically diminished before my friends helped me recognize that we aren't homeschooling in order to churn out kids who can pass a test about the Civil War or make a poster about air pollution. My two homeschoolers are learning about whatever they are exposed to. There's no coercion here. No grading. No one is threatened with a loss of recess. They ask to have me or their dad read to them all the time, they love to go on field trips, they plunk out tunes on the piano and act out scenes from stories. I can tell by their questions how much they are really pondering big things. They aren't distracted by stupid rules about what they "have" to learn, so they go ahead and learn. This week I watched my daughter try milking a goat on a field trip, I saw my son answer questions at an astronomy program, I heard my kids speculating about world population before dinner and on their own (ages 7 and 9) they already knew enough to go look it up for a conclusive answer. I don't give tests a lot of credence, but our state requires them. My second and third grader both tested in the 90th percentile in the Iowa tests, so I guess our method of helping the kids learn is as effective as forcing them to learn what some book says they are supposed to know.*

I don't remember a thing about my second grade year in school, by the way!
—R. Wayans

As child-led, life learners, we consider all moments "learning." Cooking involves tons of math and science. Listening to NPR while driving promotes a discussion on politics, science, history or almost any other subject! Playing games can reinforce math, spelling, as well as socialization! Playing an on-line game teaches real life lessons when an item is purchased for one amount, but then when you no longer need it and want to resell it—surprise—you don't get nearly as much as you paid for it! Allowances, or odd jobs, reinforce math, and essential life skills such as creating a bank account, balancing your account each month, learning about interest and the importance of saving for your future. Playing the stock market (whether with real or fake dollars) is great practice for understanding how it works!
—Angie Beck, Kansas

The struggles facing homeschooling families are similar to those facing all families, except that homeschoolers typically spend much more time with one another. In every relationship, interpersonal issues crop up from time to time. When we confront problems in order to heal them, and do so with compassion and strength of spirit, we demonstrate to our children a model for handling such issues throughout life.

I had children after my retirement. This gives me the chance to be involved in home education. I am very ambitious and goal-oriented, my wife is artistic and feelings-oriented and our two children bring entirely different temperaments into the mix. The learning environment here was a significant push and pull over everything from time management to expectations. That caused a lot a problems resulting in arguments and temper tantrums, and that was just my behavior!

I learned to relinquish control by making home education a matter of family choice. That doesn't mean I care less by any means. It certainly doesn't mean we don't have rules or standards. It means I've gotten my ego out of the way. I have learned to respect each member of my family exactly as they are. I'm just as involved but that means watching, listening and responding more than controlling. I can honestly say that my expectations got in the way of learning.
—Tom Chan

We didn't pull Emery out of school until he was 14 and failing in every subject but math. His attitude at home was horrible. We went into family therapy but our first counselor was not a good fit. My husband and I reacted with a lot of anger at Emery because of his attitude and had no idea how to instruct him at home. We found a better counselor and did a lot of reading up on homeschooling. A year later we moved and found a great homeschool support group where Emery has made good friends. I'm proud to say that everyone tells me how sweet Emery is and how they hope their kids are such great teens. His schoolwork has turned around too. He is taking early college courses through MWCC and so far he has made straight A's. —M.B.

I work every day at parenting my kids in a kinder and more aware manner. My own childhood wasn't harsh or abusive but a lot of unkind things were said to me and some really unthoughtful things were done or left undone that still hurt today. That's probably true for l of us. I know that if I don't make an effort to watch what I say and do I'll fall right back into my parent's patterns of behavior with my kids. I have a little girl with some physical disabilities and a stepson in his teens. It isn't always easy to parent them. But who ever equated easy with good? This is hard stuff. The process of helping them be well-rounded, caring people is the most important thing I've ever done. —Mary Ann, Pennsylvania

Homeschooling is by no means a cure-all. If you are dealing with family problems, there are remedies even if resolving the problems may take longer than you expect. Bring issues out in the open and discuss solutions. Hold regular family meetings. Keep track of mutual goals, restructuring them as needed. In the meantime accentuate the positive. Write caring notes to your partner and children. Spend time in enjoyable activities, building up a reserve of good feelings. Leave time for yourself. Let every member in the family know what qualities you admire in them. Breathe deeply. Read supportive parenting books such as *Raising Our Children, Raising Ourselves: Transforming Parent-child Relationships from Reaction And Struggle to Freedom, Power And Joy* by Naomi Aldort, Ph.D. and *Raising Self-Reliant Children in a Self-Indulgent World: Seven Building Blocks for Developing Capable Young People* by Stephen H. Glenn and Jane Nelsen. Close each day by recounting what went well, not dwelling on what did not. And remember that sometimes our limiting perceptions are lifted through problems we encounter and the growth that follows. In that way, difficulties are some of our most important lessons. By working on these concerns together you are empowering your children to be proactive problem solvers.

Many times a child's development doesn't correspond to a parent's expectations. While this volume cannot address such issues in detail, a parent's concerns are reason enough to investigate a problem further. Seek out information and support for your unique circumstances. Start out with a broad range of people who understand children. Talk to friends, neighbors and relatives you trust. Consult professional advisors such as physicians, counselors and naturopaths. Check out support groups and non-profit organizations, but make sure that you understand that some are funded by pharmaceutical or other interests and may be promoting a specific agenda. Read a wide variety of materials to get a broad perspective. It is always a relief to find resources to help with your situation.

We have been dealing with my 9-year-old son's diagnosis of high-functioning autism since he was three years old. I quickly realized that this challenge is a life challenge, rather than strictly an educational challenge. We did the "school thing" from preschool through kindergarten. Let me tell you, that in and of itself was a challenge! This is our third year of homeschooling, and I can honestly say that the challenges brought on by adapting a child with autism to the public school system was much more stressful than any challenges brought on by dealing with my son's autism in the homeschool setting. We will have our challenges, no matter the educational setting.

With that said, homeschooling became the way for us to deal with this challenge. Specifically, I am able to handle my son's learning and sensory issues in more adaptive and meaningful ways at home. In school, though well-meaning, the professionals tried to make my son into someone different than his core being. At home, I can nurture my son's core being and help him adapt to the world in small, less overwhelming steps. We use breaks whenever we need breaks. We sleep in if we need to sleep in. We have snacks and lunch when we are hungry. We get out into nature on a regular basis, both for exercise and peace of mind. By homeschooling, we live a much more natural life, in tune to our personal rhythms and needs. Stress is reduced and my son is better able to cope with issues brought on by autism. This way of life also benefits my 7-year-old "typical" daughter. —L.C., Ohio

There's no recipe for the ingredients that go into our homeschooling lives. We build our days around what works for us, what our families value, what opportunities are available. This tends to be exactly what our children need.

It's particularly helpful to hear from young people who have been homeschooled. When they share their experiences it gives us a wider perspective.

We began ... homeschooling ... when I was 7, after first grade. My parents put the choice to me, and I leapt at it—I was academically bored and socially ostracized (partly for the same reasons) in school.

For the most part, my parents gave me a library card (three, actually), a microscope, and free rein ... I took some classes through a local extracurricular class organization (science, writing, art) and art classes from the rec center, and I went to art and science camps in summer. These were definitely really great experiences—my parents aren't really inclined towards fine arts, and we didn't have all the science resources other places could offer. I learned all sorts of things with the aid of my library card; I learned to cook and sew from my mom, and some weaving from my grandmother. I spent hours exploring a local wetlands and looking at things I found with my microscope. I loved all things science, particularly geology, as well as arts and crafts. I had a writing tutor for a while, which was a reasonable idea but not entirely successful in terms of what I got out of the experience. I learned from other homeschoolers and their parents. I was on great terms with my local librarians ... The only really organized thing we did was for my mom to work me through Algebra I. It took two years, and I didn't like it much, but I think it was important.

Socially, homeschooling was better for me than school, although in retrospect I didn't have a particularly good social life. I think a lot of that has to do with the general social climate. I found adults much more interesting than kids my age.

I'd say my most memorable experiences were the various summer camps and programs I participated in. In particular, I participated in the Green City Data Project in Vancouver, WA, a scientific research program run by a friend of my mom's. We did a lot of wetlands monitoring. The science camps I participated in through the Oregon Museum of Science and Industry were also really important. I did one three-week camp when I was 14 where we worked with National Park Service paleontologists. That's pretty much directly responsible for me being where I am today—working for the National Park Service and pursuing an M.S. in Museum Studies, as well as for

my specific research interests. I also really loved having the time to be creative—writing and drawing and making things. I miss that today, as I try to balance my work with more artistic hobbies.

I think unschooling fundamentally confirmed my approach to learning as something fun and self-guided ... I think the best thing homeschooling did for me was to keep me interested and curious and committed to owning my own learning rather than passively accepting what people give me. We're all born curious about the world around us, but too many people lose that.
            —Melissa Barton, Colorado

Taking the approach of finding out what you need to know helps you advance in any career you choose. When you have the interest you can be self-taught and get ahead of anyone else. It beats conventional training. Schools teach you to learn one way. You have to do it their way and nothing else. They discourage thinking on your own.   —Benjamin, 26

Every time I attend a class at college, I wonder how we all manage it, after all, we all learn differently. Which is why home-education worked so well for me, allowing me to learn in the way that best suited me. Learning, for me, is best facilitated by hands-on experience and integration into every day life. Reading and learning math from a book just isn't the same as figuring out how to budget at the store!   —Kate Steven, 19

I'm the oldest of five. My mom has gotten more casual with the younger ones but I'm glad that I had a more rigorous start.

The only untraditional part was that I always decided what I would study. That's why I spent a lot of time on Constitutional Law, aviation science and math.

I am a youth leader at church. I also attained the rank of Eagle Scout. I'm a senior and will be attending the United States Air Force Academy in a few months. Because of homeschooling I'm very determined and able to learn anything I set my mind to.   —Joshua, 18

My mom used to complain my homeschooling was too haphazard. I'd go for weeks without doing math and then do a lot. I read, sketched and practiced music all the time. She was a single parent. Sometimes she was out of work because her field was copyediting. I spent a lot of time with my grandparents and that was awesome. My grandfather was on early retirement … He had a big garden and liked to cook. He was a ham radio operator and we talked to hams all over. My grandma did dispatch for a trucking company. She took me to work with her sometimes. I'd hang out with her in the office for awhile. Then the mechanics let me help and when they got tired of me I would talk to guys on the loading dock. Being around both my grandparents was amazingly educational.

My mom was big on reading and art. We spent a lot of time doing things together after she was done working because we didn't have a TV. I think we were the first people I knew to get a computer, one of the early Tandy models, back when I was about 6. We had a computer but no TV for years.

Growing up for me was all about feeling more powerful. That sounds superhero-ish, but for a boy it's really important. I wanted the power that comes from knowing how to do things. Almost everything I did as a homeschooled kid helped me that way. I got curious about school when I was 14 and talked my mom into letting me start high school.

I thought it was great the first couple of days but I couldn't figure out why the other kids were so turned off. Then I realized that the place took away the power in learning. I didn't go back.

I got asked not too long ago about "how I got this way." Maybe because things are going really well. I have an import/export business. I travel when I want and work the hours I choose. I got into this work by connecting with friends online. This summer I'm getting married to an amazing woman I met in Belgium. I may not have gone to college but I read more books and go to more lectures than any college grad I know. I still think ideas have power.

—Sebastian, 27

Nothing is Really Separate

"When we try to pick out anything by itself, we find it hitched to everything else in the Universe."
—John Muir

Learning takes place across a spectrum. History, arithmetic, music, science, art, literature, philosophy and athletics don't neatly divide into "subjects." They're interrelated. A child notices one bare sliver of a topic, and intrigued, follows it. That pursuit lights up a totally new subject until a dazzling array of possibilities opens, each refracting new angles. The thrill of exploring is inseparable from a love of learning.

A nine-year-old boy is enthusiastic about all things automotive. He makes realistic gear shifting and brake shrieking noises as if he wants to know what it feels like to be a car himself. He memorizes car models and years in an impressive display of mental discipline, although his family doesn't enjoy being quizzed about passing cars. He learns how engines work. That leads to inquiries about types of fuels and manufacturing processes. He asks questions about the history of the assembly line and the start of unions. Books and documentaries have made him familiar with figures such as Nikolaus Otto and Karl Benz. He enjoys trips to auto museums, car shows and races. Although he says a visit to a demolition derby didn't upset him he's been talking ever since about ways to save cars from junkyards. Currently he's excited about the potential for energy efficient vehicles. Notice how this fascination leads him eagerly through business, history, science, math, literature and design?

Most of the time children learn unobtrusively. It may seem they go through their days unaffected by the influences that pour in all around them. Yet gradually their comprehension deepens. This is a mysterious process, an ongoing improvisation incorporating knowledge, experience and insight. But then, our children are changed by what they've come to understand in ways none of us will know.

Once children are immersed in one thing they suddenly find interrelated aspects fascinating. They branch out from one query to many. As they comprehend, they make connections extending in all directions.

Sometimes they take a full-bore approach, incorporating everything they encounter as they learn. Parents may be amazed by how relentless their children can be in the pursuit of topics related to an interest. Children ask questions, explore, imagine and experiment as they map out the world around them.

Esther hasn't narrowed down to any certain interests. She's curious about nearly everything. Maybe because we answer her questions and treat her intelligently she approaches whatever she's exposed to with enthusiasm. People like grocers, cab drivers, store clerks and museum guards ask me about her all the time because they are surprised how smart she is. I tell them she's eight and she likes to find things out. I'm glad we homeschool. —Rena, New York

One daughter loves cooking and will hang around the kitchen watching me as I am cooking. She now is searching for recipes herself, making shopping lists, buying them in the supermarket herself and then creating them! (She just turned 6 years old.) This cooking has helped her comprehension grow in

measuring, estimating, reading recipes, Organizing the ingredients, hygiene and safety, cooking and baking techniques, textures, tastes, ingredients combining differently, well really the list is endless.
—Maaike Johnston, Australia

My son Danny isn't one of those brilliant homeschooled kids you hear so much about. He's an average kid. I couldn't be less motivated to have him win a spelling bee. He likes to play video games and go to the dog park with our St. Bernard, Sasha. If I had to give an overall I'd say he reads well and isn't so great in math. We use a Waldorf-inspired curriculum although not all the parts of it because he gets tired of some of the arts and crafts. He's everything I could hope for in that he's a nice person to be around. Plus he's funny and caring and I think that's maybe his real strength. He's a lot more compassionate than most kids his age.

When we went to a play in the city last week a homeless man asked us for money. Danny hasn't stopped asking about that encounter. Every topic that comes up, like the difference between homelessness now compared to the Great Depression, just starts off another one. I'd say he's thought more about ethics, religion, history, social policy, health, business and our responsibility to one another in this week than he ever has in his short life.
—E. Williams, New Jersey

Learning across a spectrum is enhanced by a variety of activities. People and places nearby are rich resources for real-world learning that engages the mind, body and spirit.

Children become familiar with how their communities work as they go behind-the-scenes in such places as banks, courtrooms, municipal waste systems, artists' studios, fire stations, truck depots and software firms. People there share skills and knowledge through tours, field trips, mentoring programs, and workshops. Engineers, potters, historians, biologists, musicians and others demonstrate to children what it means to thrive in a chosen career. These experiences form a framework for the child to understand what he or she wants to make of adulthood.

Young people have the opportunity to be useful and engaged in the lives of those around them. They may volunteer at a food bank or take part in the library's youth board. As they interact with people and organizations in the wider community they gain direct understanding of the meaning embedded in citizenry. They begin to see that the rights of the individual are always in a tenuous balance with the responsibilities of living together in society.

Young people also form a kinship with the natural world around them. They relate to their surroundings and develop a sense of rootedness to the places that have meaning for them. They may meet for regular homeschool days at a nearby park, playing through the seasons among the same tree-lined fields. They may travel to the same canyon each month to hike and take photographs. That park, that canyon become an integral part of who they are and leave a lasting mosaic of childhood memories.

Children gain a sense of proportion from the ethical and practical complexities encountered in the community around them. What roots them to a distinct experience of place and time will form a deep wellspring of knowledge and meaning they will refer to the rest of their lives.

A couple of years ago I was beginning to worry because my middle daughter, at nine-years-old, wanted to stay home all the time and seemed to have no interests besides Pokemon cards and Nancy Drew books. Then we watched the 2006 Winter Olympics. All three kids enjoyed watching the figure skating, so I volunteered to take them to our local ice rink for the first time. I figured they would be frustrated after about 15 minutes and that would be the end of it, but that was not the case.

Elizabeth, the girl who did not like to leave home, actually wanted to sign up for weekly lessons. After a few months of group lessons, she (and her younger brother) were also working with a private coach and began competing at successively higher levels. She was getting out on the ice, all by herself, and competing in front of audiences—something I never expected to see from this very reserved child. She got additional practice once or twice a week when we all skated at the morning public session. During the school year this meant we shared the rink with only two or three other skaters—adults who got to know Elizabeth and enjoyed giving her pointers and encouragement. One of the women is from Germany and another is from Japan. This gave Elizabeth a chance to test out some Japanese words she had learned, and later she decided she would like to learn German. She also took a ballet class for skaters, read every skater's biography she could get her hands on, subscribed to skating magazines, and made a notebook filled with photos and her own writing about champion skaters of the past and present.

After a year and a half, as she and her brother continued to advance, the sport required more and more of their time. They both made the decision to

quit recently, but it was a wonderful experience for both of them, and Elizabeth continues to read and write about figure skaters. And, while I was concerned about the need for her to expand her horizons, she actually expanded mine— I now own my own pair of good skates and overcame my fear of the ice enough to be able to perform a few tricks that she taught me.   —Susan, Alabama

My husband and I are Indian but we've been influenced by Arab foods, Italian foods, Thai etc. So I end up making all kinds of foods and Raghu is right along making adjustments to my recipe. He will sometimes concoct his own variations on a traditional recipe. Through cooking time we have touched upon math (dividing portions, adding up raisins etc), talked about stories related to food, talked about why we are vegetarian, which animals are herbivores / carnivores / omnivores, nutritive value, holistic choices, composting, back and forth the questions flow and are answered. And of *course then retelling to a grandparent how the dish turned out and describing how it tasted over the phone.*

—Hema A. Bharadwaj, Singapore

Some children become so absorbed in a single subject that it seems their entire personalities are wrapped up in that passion. Their bemused families can't help but stoke the fire of that interest. Activities and discussions with the child take on a distinct hue, colored anew by relevance to the topic of choice. Indeed, most members of the family find themselves changed by close association with someone who loves the world in such a focused manner. When we take an open-minded approach to learning, we readily find the interconnections that exist everywhere.

My children loved drawing maps. These were usually sparked by a story they had heard, or a movie, or a game they were playing. Sometimes they simply drew maps because it was fun and they were obviously interested in drawing maps. Maybe it was because whenever we heard about a new place we'd look it up in the atlas or try to find it on the globe.

It's hard to separate learning associated with using maps into the different curriculum subjects. Maths is covered— scale, distance, compass direction, degrees of latitude and longitude. History often comes into it because maps change over time. Our globe was ancient and showed the Soviet Union whereas our atlas was much younger. One of our atlases even showed Commonwealth countries displayed as pink, which then lead to a discussion on the downfall of the British Empire.

Conventional education separates learning into hundreds of rubrics or objectives. What can be measured, graded and therefore proven becomes the purpose of the lesson. A parallel can be found comparing an orange to a pill. A fresh orange has phytonutrients, fiber, minerals and vitamins. When a person regularly consumes oranges it's thought these are the essential ingredients that help promote health. Researchers have isolated a nutritious flavanone from oranges called the hesperidin molecule. These days it is extracted and offered it as a supplement to prevent diseases. Other components provided by the fruit, such as vitamin C and fiber, can be purchased in separate doses as well. That overlooks the bigger picture. These isolated compounds don't work as effectively as the whole fruit. The expense of taking a supplement is prohibitive compared to consuming fruit. And besides, where is the sensation of eating an orange bursting with juice? Lost. Divided into a fraction of the experience in order to have what has been deemed more valuable, measurable and effective by some authority somewhere. Our intuition and our bodies themselves tell us otherwise if we listen.

We can emphasize mindful rather than mindless learning. Show children the way things interconnect. Answer questions and raise a few more. This is how we create a meaningful education, by welcoming complexities. After all, life itself is infinitely complex. An orange gleaming in our hands reminds us of the untold numbers of people involved in growing it, picking it, transporting it, and selling it. The bigger picture. A whole orange leads us back to the orange tree, which links us to the perfect intersection of sunlight, water, minerals and microbial life. Considering that perfection connects us to yet greater meaning.

Although drawing maps didn't result in an enormous amount of writing, writing skills and knowledge were developed. Finding destinations on maps when travelling either to the next town or on holiday was a favourite past time. It's a good way to begin a discussion on the early exploration of Australia, or about the first Australians—places are usually given Aboriginal names or names of early settlers or explorers. It's easy to learn history and geography this way.

The little writing my children did when drawing maps, coupled with the lists they often wrote, was usually enough for me to check their developing spelling skills. Titles, legends, names of rivers and towns—often made up of course.

Map drawing probably only lasted a few years: I can't remember them drawing maps into their teen years, except a really comprehensive one for ... an elaborate game they created and refined over a four year period which included a great deal of writing.

I learned to translate almost everything my children did into educational jargon to satisfy myself that no matter what they were always learning. It didn't look anything like school, but once I got the hang of doing this it was really easy to reassure myself that they were learning just as much as their school mates, just in a different way.

—Beverley Paine, Australia

CHAPTER TEN

Science & Nature

Science

"The beginning of knowledge is the discovery of something we do not understand." —Frank Herbert

Children are compelled to figure things out. That makes them natural scientists. The world of science interconnects with every realm of interest, offering lifelong fascination. How we approach science makes a difference.

- Scientific concepts, the very basis of understanding the physical world, are more understandable when approached hands-on. Scientists gain knowledge through experimentation, study and observation. This is the best way for children to develop scientific literacy as well.

- Research shows that when children are given the opportunity to take an active role in science they are much more likely to retain what is learned. Involvement and exploration help them assimilate the information and relate it to other areas.

- When children are actually engaged in the process of science they must rely on evidence, thinking for themselves as they analyze possible conclusions. This enhances critical thinking skills at the same time as it teaches the topics under consideration.

- Fifteen years of research has shown that hands-on science makes a dramatic difference in many areas. When children engage in active science exploration rather than textbook-based instruction the result is improved language skills, logic development, mathematics, creativity and positive attitudes.

- Activity-based science is fun. Children not only increase science proficiency and become more independent problem-solvers when presented with factual dilemmas, they are also more motivated to pursue scientific learning.

Some homeschooling parents become concerned that their children will fall behind in demanding fields such as the sciences. They hear media reports about high school students doing important lab work or winning competitions and feel anxious that their own teens may be shortchanged. The truth is that pupils in school rarely have the opportunities afforded homeschoolers. Self-directed youth, accustomed to following individual interests, are in the best position to advance in scientific understanding. Study after study has identified errors in textbooks and a serious lack of true experimentation in typical school lab settings. It takes a few library books, basic equipment and the desire to find out. A homeschooler can hone in on his or her own investigations, or better yet, get together with other youths and work through a subject area of interest to all of them. As homeschoolers they have advantages:

- Homeschooled teens can study any branch of science they find intriguing, and through this focus learn a great deal about science as a whole.

- They can spend significantly more time than the typical class session scrutinizing in depth what intrigues them.

- They can go back and forth between reading, experimentation, field trips and other investigations in order to make sense of what they're learning.

- They can seek out adults who are willing to answer their questions, permit them to observe science in action and serve as mentors. Doctors, veterinarians, dentists, chemists, botanists, research scientists, farmers, professors and teachers, ecologists, astronomers and others live in our communities. Time spent in the company of a knowledgeable and enthusiastic person has transformative power.

Although the emphasis in science curricula is often on the history of ideas and the formalized rules that have resulted, real science is an ongoing work of wonderfully adventurous speculation. It's risky, intense and full of mistakes that sometimes lead in new directions. To "do" science one needs to observe, wonder, hypothesize, test out ideas, figure out why those ideas did or did not work, and then do it all over again. Some of the greatest learning comes from refining one's understanding in that "do it all over again" stage.

Science isn't a dead thing consigned to books. Science is an ongoing process. It takes place in the lab and in the field. It's theoretical. A postulate is commonly accepted until proof is found that another one is better. Science isn't static. Amateur scientists throughout history have made profound discoveries, many times confounding the erudite and knowledge-bound of their day. Interestingly, many of those same scientists did not develop that competence in school.

Conventional science education teaches across a broad swath, trying to cover a vast expanse of many fields in a few short years. That's an impossible task to do well. Often it leads to little more than a superficial grasp of the concepts. The way homeschoolers approach science differs from family to family. Some of us employ textbooks or other science curricula to give a solid grounding in the disciplines, some of us enjoy science as it comes up in everyday life. Most of us incorporate a rich mix of materials and experiences. We take part in field trips, workshops and projects. We read a range of books from lighthearted to more formal science texts. We watch documentaries, encourage our children to experiment, use the Internet, subscribe to science periodicals and talk about the science behind topics in the news. And when our children latch on to something that excites them we help fuel that momentum.

My husband is an amateur astronomer and we own two large telescopes. Our children have been exposed to astronomy all their lives but never showed a particular interest in it—not until about a year ago when Caroline tried out some astronomy software (Starry Night desktop planetarium). She loves using it to explore the universe. Being a voracious reader, she was soon reading all about astronomy, including reading straight through her dad's copy of the Peterson Field Guide to Stars and Planets. *Being a homeschooling mom, I was soon ordering more books and magazine subscriptions and letting her know about opportunities such as lectures at our nearby planetarium/observatory. We quickly became members of the Von Braun Astronomical Society and have been going to the planetarium about twice a month ever since. Who would have thought a 12-year-old would voluntarily (happily!) sit through lectures on topics such as spectroscopy, stellar life cycles, and the sun's electric/magnetic effect on the earth? These lectures are given by experts in a variety of fields: an astronomer from NASA's Space Environments Group; the Chief Meteorologist of a local TV station; a solar astronomer from the National Space Science and Technology Center; an optical engineer from the U.S. Army Missile Command; a physicist from NASA's Space Plasma Physics Group, etc. Caroline has learned how to use our telescopes and also looks through the scopes at the observatory. She is enjoying watching a college-level Teaching Company astronomy course on DVD; reading articles in the science section of the newspaper; reading* Sky & Telescope *and* Astronomy *magazine; listening to Dava Sobel's* The Planets *audio book; reading on-line space science newsletters; and watching many astronomy related shows on the Discovery Channel and National Geographic. If I had set out to teach her astronomy I am sure I would not have gone into the depth she*

has done on her own. (When I took astronomy in high school we never even got to see a telescope, much less go to an observatory or hear from anyone who worked in the field.)

—Susan, Alabama

Being left to my own devices and allowed to throw myself completely into researching and devouring every aspect of some (often very strange) subjects that interested me led to my becoming a biologist. If I had been forced to follow a curriculum or do certain subjects on a schedule I doubt I would have ever had the time or inspiration to pursue all the topics that caught my eye. Having the freedom to truly enjoy learning (vs. being forced to learn some subject because it was deemed "necessary" at some arbitrary point in my education) gave me a passion for researching and learning new things—something I noticed was basically destroyed in my fellow students in college who had just come out of 12 years of formal schooling. I love researching and expanding my knowledge on both random topics and things that are relevant for school or work alike. Being homeschooled taught me to be open to the possibility that a subject that on first glance seemed boring or not something I was interested in can actually end up being fascinating if given the chance.   —Claire, 22

Science often has an intense focus. A mycologist may spend a lifetime studying fungus, working to discover exactly how mycelial mats break down pollutants in the soil. Children are also perfectly suited to focus on a compelling endeavor. They want to be competent, to really know how the world works. They aren't afraid to ask questions. Too often adults are not willing to admit their ignorance in order to learn more. They've gotten used to having little comprehension of how satellites communicate or viruses mutate. As Carl Sagan said, "We live in a society exquisitely dependent on science and technology, in which hardly anyone knows anything about science and technology." However, children who have been encouraged to persist with eager questions and explorations are likely to continue the pursuit of greater understanding.

We can also recognize how much young people learn even through ordinary activities. Training the dog can result in understanding incentive, reinforcement and other behavioral psychology principles. Fixing a computer can lead to a greater comprehension of electronics and technology. Adjusting ingredients in a recipe in order to make healthier cookies for a diabetic grandfather can lead to understanding chemistry and nutrition. These are experiences with built-in motivation and unknown results. Real science.

We may never fully ascertain how the knowledge and experience our children have gained affect their scientific understanding. But we do know that this can't be fully measured or quantified. When they can think for themselves, make connections between disparate bits of information, observe with interest, ask their own questions and unashamedly follow an interest in any direction, they are in league with some of the greatest scientists in history. The British chemist Michael Faraday was the son of a blacksmith and treated throughout his early years as a lower class citizen. He was responsible for discovering the magneto-optical effect, electro-magnetic induction, electro-magnetic rotations, diamagnetism, field theory and more. Some regard Faraday as the most outstanding experimentalist in history. The Austrian geneticist Gregor Mendel, son of peasant farmers, twice failed the qualifying examination to become a teacher. He went on to make groundbreaking discoveries about heredity and is considered the father of genetics. These scientists

had the drive to understand that transcended standard thinking. That same kind of drive is essential today. As Nobel Prize winning physiologist Albert Szent-Gyorgyi said, "Discovery consists of seeing what everybody has seen and thinking what nobody has thought." That approach can't be taught. It has to be experienced.

Starting Places

- **Enjoy junkbox science.** Collect boxes, cardboard tubes, wire, mousetraps, string, pulleys, rubber bands, marbles, corks, straws, cups and other materials. Challenge your children to use these to construct working models. They can attempt to make a moving toy car, a gumball sorting "machine," catapult that flings corks, a bridge to hold weight, and so on. Some homeschool co-ops or science clubs set up junkbox science competitions. Check out Discovery Education's Junkyard Wars http://school.discoveryeducation.com/networks/junkyardwars

- **Learn about the lives of scientists, explorers and inventors.** When we understand an individual's struggles and accomplishments it puts science in a personal context. Read biographies, watch movies, attend plays and visit historical presentations to help your children feel the impact these men and women made. Their discoveries and inventions changed the culture around them and continue to affect the way we live now.

- **Take a shine to metallurgy.** The science of metallic elements connects with history, industry, art, engineering and more. At a history museum, notice exhibits from Bronze Age to Iron Age and onward. Contact a blacksmith, metalworking artist or welder and ask if you can observe from a safe distance. Borrow a metal detector for your next visit to the park or beach to see what you can dig up. Check out: Go Metal Detecting http://gometaldetecting.com

- **Develop an attraction to magnets.** Make a magnetic toy. Use a compass. Make an electromagnet. Challenge yourself to understand some of the applications of magnets such as credit cards, computer monitors, electric motors and particle accelerators.

- **Sign up for First Competitions.** Youth form teams to work on challenges in science, math and technology. The competitions include Robotics Competition, Lego® League and Tech Challenge. www.usfirst.org

---

We've been heavily involved with robotics and run a regional Robofest tournament in TX. For the last 6 years, we've been running a national robotics list and website ... Homeschoolers usually do quite well at competitions, even though they only represent a fraction of the participants. —Susan, Texas

---

- **Make use of science museums.** Most museums offer much more than exhibits. They have workshops, activity days and competitions. Older youth are often permitted to volunteer as docents, apprentice with researchers and to take part in community relations boards.

- **Learn about simple machines** like the lever, pulley and wedge. Create your own Rube Goldberg Invention, which is any device that expends the maximum amount of effort for minimal results. You might want to have a Rube Goldberg Fair to display these marvels. Check out *Rube Goldberg: Inventions!* (Simon & Schuster, 2000) by Maynard Frank Wolfe, or use Rube Goldberg as a search term on YouTube.com for inspiration.

- **Start or join a swapbox group.** They are also called "geography exchange boxes." Find them on Yahoo! Groups or other sites. A swapbook group links you with others to promote learning about geography, regional science and more. Each group has specific suggestions, but in general you exchange addresses with other families and send each other a standard sized postal box. The box contains a letter of introduction with information about hobbies, favorite learning activities, newest experiments, and so on. It also might contain maps, sketches of the area, natural objects such as stones, brochures of local attractions and more.

- **Learn via postcards.** Collect postcards on your travels. Create your own postcards, perhaps to commemorate an interesting field trip. You can put homemade art or cut-outs on one side and facts or notes about the area on the other. Join a postcard exchange group, found online, to learn about other regions.

- **Discover animals.** Our fellow creatures add important dimensions to the understanding of behavior, health, physiology and ecology. Even if your family has pets, consider having regular contact with other animals. Visit small family farms, help out at an animal sanctuary, spend time in nature observing creatures and keep binoculars near a window to grab at a moment's notice. Check out Animaland—Animaland.org—for tips on animal issues, careers involving animals, games and more.

Our family cats have been a springboard for Lisa. Because she loves the cats she has spoken up at the vet's office to ask questions. I think it has helped her coordination when she makes little toys for them. She can tell you anything about cats in history or odd cat facts since she has nearly memorized the library's stock of books on the subject. It sure gives her physical therapist a topic to talk about when their sessions aren't going well. A while ago when we couldn't find one of the cats hiding in the house Lisa said it always hid after her brother's trumpet lesson. We never made that correlation. That led to a good discussion about animal sensitivities.

—Mary Ann, Pennsylvania

- **Keep a science notebook or journal.** Make notes on ideas to explore. Keep track of charts, drawings, procedures and other information. Store labeled photos. Speculate. Ask unanswerable questions. Write sideways, upside down and in code. Some of the greatest scientists in history kept notebooks filled with their ideas, observations and drawings.

- **Uncover the science of magic tricks.** Some principles of physics, chemistry and biology seem to confound logic. That's what makes them appear magical. Look up the science of magic tricks. Practice old style magic done with simple objects rather than expensive gadgets.

- **Learn about electronics and wireless communication** through amateur radio. Amateur radio operators participate in public service, advance scientific literacy and seek to involve the newest generation. Check out the resources at National Association for Amateur Radio www.arrl.org and www.hello-radio.org

We do science labs that get pretty intense. We are in the middle of a cotton unit that has us going to the cotton fields, learning about cotton from the inception to the finished product. It's complete with a ride on the combine while the cotton is being picked, and a visit to our nearest cotton gin. It's been a blast so far.

—M. Holman, Texas

- **Go along on a virtual exploration.** The Jason Project www.jason.org links children with explorers and great events. Global Online Adventure Learning www.goals.com connects them with today's active explorers. Either site allows you to connect a child's interest to a real time exploration, to stay updated with the progress and to ask questions—bringing science as it happens to your home.

- **Investigate the science underlying specific interests.** Find out about the physics of a curve ball or a martial arts move. Improve as a sailor while learning about meteorology, navigation and relative velocity. Let interests open directly into science.

- **Make science toys.** Interesting instructions can be found at http://scitoys.com/ or try the projects in *Gizmos & Gadgets: Creating Science Contraptions That Work (& Knowing Why)* (Williamson, 1999) by Jill Frankel Hauser.

My 10 year old son and I have spent many happy times making "toys" from junk that illustrate scientific principles. If and when he reads or hears about the principles, he will have already experienced them. —Urmila, India

- **Get inventive.** Discover inventions that played a part in your favorite recreations.

Encourage your children to look at problems with an eye to inventing solutions. Check out *Kids Inventing! A Handbook for Young Inventors* (Jossey-Bass, 2005) by Susan Casey. Allow young people to use real tools and supplies, under supervision.

- **Organize an inventor's fair.** At a traditional inventor's fair each participant sets up a display about an inventor and what was invented. At a more challenging inventor's fair, each participant brings his or her own invention with a display that explains about it. Many times children take part in workshops or form their own invention clubs beforehand, helping them get from idea to invention.

- **If you can imagine it, you can make it.** Technology, physics, chemistry and more are accessible to those who enjoy tinkering. Look into books explaining the science behind compellingly unusual projects, such as *Vacuum Bazookas, Electric Rainbow Jelly, and 27 Other Saturday Science Projects* (Princeton University, 2001) by Neil A. Downie. *MAKE* magazine and companion site www.makezine. com are filled with hands-on ideas ranging from easy to extraordinarily challenging.

- **Play with geography.** Use a world map or globe for games. With eyes closed, pick a spot somewhere in the world and name five things you'd need to survive if dropped in that climate and terrain. How many ways could you describe this place (longitude/latitude, type of vegetation, language spoken, etc)? Let children frost a sheet cake to resemble a map. Look through the information provided by different atlases at the library. If you had to move, where would you go and why? Consider competing in the Geography Bee www. nationalgeographic.com/geographybee

- **Discover your area.** Learn about the natural advantages that led to the settlement of your area. Are those advantages still relevant today? Make a map of your neighborhood including landmarks and topographical features. Try locating a specific spot using your map compared to using written instructions. MapMachine http://plasma.nationalgeographic.com/ mapmachine offers a variety of searches plus a cartography tutorial. Google Earth http:// earth.google.com provides satellite imagery, maps, 3D imagery and research tools.

- **Get forceful.** Go beyond vinegar and baking soda to projects that really take off. The science behind propulsion is best learned under the guidance of adults. Check out *Backyard Ballistics: Build Potato Cannons, Paper Match Rockets, Cincinnati Fire Kites, Tennis Ball Mortars, and More Dynamite Devices* (Chicago Review, 2001) by William Gurstelle.

- **Subscribe to science magazines.** This provides a regular infusion of ideas and inspiration. Magazines are great to bring along on trips, to leave around the house for children to "find" and to clip ideas for later use. Among the many wonderful science magazines for younger children are *Odyssey* www.odyssey-magazine.com, *National Geographic Explorer* http://magma.nationalgeographic.com/ngex-plorer, *Kids Discover* www.kidsdiscover.com and *Muse* www.musemag.com. For teens and up, depending on their interests consider *New Scientist* www.newscientist.com, *Natural History* www.naturalhistorymag.com or any science magazines steered to the layperson.

- **Find out the story that rocks have to tell.** Learn how to tell the difference between the three basic types of rocks and the sequence of the rock cycle. Discover the uses of minerals. Start a rock collection. Join a local lapidary club.

- **Try kitchen science.** Understand chemistry by creating emulsions, suspensions, temperature reactions, manipulating acids and bases, using the gas laws—all while cooking. Enjoy *Science Experiments You Can Eat: Revised Edition* (HarperCollins, 1984) by Vicki Cobb.

- **Start a traveling journal.** Contact people through forums or interest groups who live in other parts of the country or world. If you are circulating a geology journal, have each participant fill in details about local rock formations, fossil finds, topographical drawings, favorite hikes, etc. A botany journal might include pressed plants, drawings, timetables of growth, information about local species, etc. Each time the journal is sent on to another family, a postcard or blog is posted, letting all participants know that the journal is on its way. Younger children might also enjoy sending a small traveling toy on the journey.

Resources

Online

- ActionBioscience is the education resource for the American Institute of Biological Sciences offering research, lessons and information. www.actionbioscience.org
- BBC Science and Nature offers updates, in-depth articles, games, quizzes and links. www.bbc.co.uk/sn
- BioInteractive provides details on such topics as immunology and DNA. Virtual labs let the user act as the pathologist. There are also animations, lessons and videos available. www.hhmi.org/biointeractive
- Biology Place features upper level interactives on such topics as cell respiration and genetics. www.phschool.com/science/biology_place
- Eureka Alert Science for Kids is a project of AAAS (Advancing Science, Serving Society) providing child and teen-friendly information from research organizations. www.eurekalert.org/kidsnews
- How Stuff Works has clear, dynamic images showing how such things as NASDAQ, solar cells or the brain works. www.howstuffworks.com
- Mad Scientist Network provides answers to your questions. www.madsci.org
- Human Anatomy Online offers animations and thousands of descriptive links. www.innerbody.com

- Ian Reed's Science Wizards Homepage provides demonstrations and simple experiments. www.science-wizards.com
- National Geographic Kids www.nationalgeographic.com/kids and www.mywonderfulworld.org are packed with activities, games, crafts, videos and stories. National Geographic World www.nationalgeographic.com offers world music, searchable videos and updates.
- National Science Foundation classroom resources are actually links, organized by subject, to project-based science education programs. www.nsf.gov/news/classroom
- Science News For Kids provides news and interactives. www.sciencenewsforkids.org
- Windows to the Universe covers earth and space science. Gather data for citizen science projects, view interactive multimedia files, check out science history and play games. www.windows.ucar.edu

Books

- *Caveman Chemistry: 28 Projects, from the Creation of Fire to the Production of Plastics* (Universal, 20030 by Kevin M. Dunn.
- Larry Gonick's many cartoon books are wonderful resources for teens. They include *The Cartoon Guide to Physics* (HarperPerennial, 1991), *The Cartoon Guide to Genetics* (Collins, 1991), *The Cartoon Guide to the Environment* (Collins, 1996), *The Cartoon Guide to Chemistry* (Collins, 2005) and *The Cartoon Guide to Statistics* (Collins, 1993).
- *Illustrated Guide to Astronomical Wonders: From Novice to Master Observer* (O'Reilly, 2007) by Robert Thompson and Barbara Fritchman Thompson.
- *Illustrated Guide to Home Chemistry Experiments: All Lab, No Lecture* (O'Reilly, 2008) by Robert Thompson.
- Janice VanCleave has authored dozens of engaging science-related books, all filled with proven projects and experiments.

- *There Are No Electrons: Electronics for Earthlings* (Clearwater, 1991) by Kenn Amdahl.

- *The Mystery of the Periodic Table* (Bethlehem, 2003) by Benjamin Wiker and Jeanne Bendick.

Nature

"Man's heart, away from nature, becomes hard."—Luther Standing Bear

In a natural setting young children can't help but explore. They climb on fallen logs, leap over tiny streams and wander through tall grasses. Their imaginations are as activated as their senses. These kinds of experiences open new worlds to them.

In *Sharing Nature with Children,* Joseph Cornell writes, "It is very helpful—almost essential— for people at first to have startling, captivating experiences in nature. This kind of first contact extinguishes for a moment the self-enclosing preoccupations and worries that keep us from feeling our identity with other expressions of life. From that release into expanded awareness and concern, love naturally follows. And memories of moments of love and expansion act as reminders of, and incentives to, a more sensitive way of living."

Cornell suggests expanding on a child's outdoor experience. For example, he describes a unique game of hide and seek. Hiders try to blend in with natural objects to "feel that they are a natural part of the objects around them, and the searchers can try to sense a foreign presence among the rocks and leaves."

Although time spent in unspoiled areas is vitally important, children can experience nature in their own way and on their own terms every day, even in the smallest city apartment, as they pay attention to the weather, observe insects, grow plants from seed, use binoculars to watch birds, and more. Children notice seasonal changes around them in the constellations, nearby trees and the changing patterns of light falling on surrounding buildings. We are creatures of the ecosystems enfolding us. The youngest children are receptive to lessons generously available to them in every aspect of nature.

One homeschooling family lived near a large park system. The children grew up appreciating the healthy streams and woodlands. Throughout the seasons, year after year, they had climbed the same boulders, listened for nesting hawks, watched saplings grow and seen fallen trees slowly return to humus. One girl had notebooks filled with drawings of salamanders, fish, dragonflies, frogs and birds. The oldest son spent much less time outdoors as he entered his teen years although his connection to the land was evident. When a large housing development was being built along the park border, the children were appalled as bulldozers and other heavy equipment encroached on the streams, shoving waste materials over the banks. When this son contacted the state natural resources division, he was told that the department wouldn't be able to send out a biologist. The staffer was only able to send a letter with state guidelines. The teen began documenting the health of the at-risk waterway with photographs. He contacted a college professor who explained how to test water samples and take photographs there as well as elsewhere in the park for comparison. The teen read books on riparian ecosystems and studied state ordinances. Together with local environmental groups they mounted a public relations challenge to the housing developer, forcing a change in the heedless construction techniques and halting further damage.

I think the important thing is for us, as adults, to retain our love of learning, our enthusiasm, awe, and wonder of the world around us, and to model learning all the time as the norm. I have always been a bit fanciful in the way I view the world, so I have tried to pass this on to my kids. I have gotten the "Oh mom, you are sooo weird!!!" looks and answers, but then I see my kids get so excited about something new or cool that they read or do, and it is so much fun to see them continue to experience this excitement as they age. If you are pragmatic about everything all the time and never get excited, how will your kids learn to keep and use their own innate excitement? I believe many things are learned behavior and we can turn this natural trait off by not allowing it to be expressed.

I also believe that kids need to know it is okay to get excited about the small things in life. This past spring, my daughter went out her second story window to sit on the roof. She had paper, pen, binoculars, and a bird field guide with her. She stayed up there for almost two hours ... and then she very excitedly came downstairs to tell me about the birds at the feeder, the squirrel building his nest, and all the things she had observed. She had a lot of enthusiasm, and so I stopped what I was doing and we discussed all she had seen and experienced, learned and witnessed. And I was able to share some of the things I had seen before. It was an exciting time for my 15-year-old daughter. She had the wonder, awe, and enthusiasm that is often lost in kids her age.

—Lori Smith, Ohio

Our sons are grown. The wife and I are interested to hear them talk about what they remember of home education as that shows what had an impact on their development. They chat up the friendships and laugh at how it seemed there was always food at every event. I see their memories are warm ones centered around convivial times.

I never had realized, though, how important their little camp-outs were to them. On and off for years the boys dragged tents or tarps out back of our property and set up camp. Sometimes they made a fuss of it setting up snares to get a rabbit to roast or hiked off with nothing but sharp sticks and flint. Mostly they unburdened the house of blankets and pots and made themselves quite comfortable. As I hear them talk over these camp outs I see how much they gained. They learned to see themselves as visitors to the land, privy to a few secrets about the ways of nature. The few times they stayed out in a storm, their fire gone out, they felt themselves quite brave like grown men. They got dirty and argued, fought a few times as well. These chats we've had now that they are grown help me understand the importance of that time. —Rob, Ireland

Starting Places

- **Appoint a child as the hike navigator** when setting off on a nature walk. For safety's sake note the trail taken and the way back, but encourage your child to pay attention along the way so that he or she can guide your return. If the child is confused, assist by pointing out signs found in nature such as the position of the sun and direction of nearby water flow. Note signpost items like rock outcroppings, elevations and unusually formed trees.

- **Build specific memories** that encourage children to identify with nature. Go back to the same wilderness area year after year to check out a certain stream where you saw a beaver dam. Remember to notice the growth of a sapling in a nearby park as it matures into a young tree. Casually name places something unique to your family, such as "shoe-tying rock" or "Dad's-go-no-further bend in the trail." And let your children find their own special places in your backyard, in the park and while on a campout. Remembering natural areas helps them become your child's and your family's, not in the sense of ownership but because you care about them. They remain distinctly in the memory even if the places themselves may eventually no longer exist.

- **Allow time for solitude in nature.** A child's time alone, even though a parent may be within hearing, helps them feel grounded and whole as beings in a world teeming with less meaningful distractions. Given enough time, they will see and hear the natural world with more complexity than from a typically quick observation.

- **Get involved in bird science.** Audubon Society www.audubon.org has local chapters that host bird walks, advocacy campaigns, nature outings, and educational programs. Participate in the annual Great Backyard Bird Count www.birdsource.org to help track bird populations www.birdsource.org Also log your bird sightings at ebird.org.

- **Participate in citizen science.** Add your efforts to help today's scientists. Projects are constantly taking place including learning how canines play, measuring weathering rates of marble with images of gravestones, recording soundscapes from different areas, and mapping firefly appearances. Use the term "citizen science" to find projects for your family.

- **Encourage micro and macro viewpoints.** Go on micro level explorations. Intently watch what goes on in a small area of a tide pool. Observe sand, rocks and water. Look for invertebrates, fish, crustaceans. What actions are they taking? Why? Cover a carton with clear plastic over the bottom in order to see more easily. Or sit on the ground and observe the same tiny section for fifteen minutes or so. Notice plants, rocks and soil. Check the effect of wind. Listen to nearby sounds. Watch for insects. Use a magnifying glass.

- **Try the macro viewpoint.** Go from the close-up to farther away. Step from the tide pool to a pier or hill. Get up off the grass and climb a tree. Observe from that vantage point. What conditions might affect the soil, water and creatures you were watching so intently? Go to a more distant mindset, to a view of the larger ecosystem.

- **Get involved as a family** in pursuits upholding the importance of natural systems. Volunteer with an active ecology group to restore a wetlands area or to pull invasive plant species. In your own backyard make sure to leave wild areas so native pollinators, birds and other creatures have a diversity of materials for forage and nesting. When pursuing outdoor recreation remember to treat nature with respect. Check out Leave No Trace www.lnt.org for more information on ethical enjoyment of natural places.

- **Draw attention to the sky.** Take time to look up each time you go outdoors. Consider sending your favorite cloud photos to The Cloud Appreciation Society www.cloudappreciationsociety.org Whenever possible, lie on the ground and look at the sky from that perspective. Some children like to lie still, watching the sky long enough to claim they can feel the earth's rotation.

  Build family traditions around the sky. Make a habit of taking a walk at dusk. See who can be first to notice the first faint sliver of a new moon. Point out constellations to one another. Look for shooting stars. When there's a particularly beautiful sunset go outside to enjoy it. Notice how the sunset and sunrise change on the horizon as the seasons change.

- **Garden together.** Absorb lessons about photosynthesis, microbiology and botany. Growing their own foods has been found to inspire children to be more adventurous eaters. Check out *Gardening with Children (Brooklyn Botanic, 2007)* by Monika Hanneman, Patricia Hulse, Brian Johnson, Barbara Kurland and Tracey Patterson.

  Don't forget to garden indoors too. Start plants using sprouted potatoes, garlic or yams. Try planting an avocado pit or pineapple top. Enjoy a tasty windowsill herb garden. Grow sprouts for salads, stir fries and sandwiches. Create a terrarium in any sort of glass container with small, moisture-loving plants. Keep a houseplant or two in each bedroom, letting children care for their own if desired.

To teach ourselves how to garden, we've raised carrots, a watermelon, tomatoes, beans, etc … using pots on our patio but I hope to soon make a full fledged garden. The kids have helped me with preparing the soil, planting, tending, and harvesting. We've talked a lot about what living things need in order to thrive which tied back into our study of the food groups. My son is particularly excited about the store-bought pineapples that we cut the tops off of and planted. He proudly explains to visitors that we'll have real pineapples in about two years!

—Karen, Texas

- **Focus on local foods.** Challenge your family to see what percentage of your meals can be made with locally grown foods. Food travels an average of 1,500 miles before reaching the consumer's fork. Combination foods travel even farther. One study found that the sugar, yogurt and strawberries in fruit yogurt traveled over 2,200 miles. It isn't hard to buy local yogurt, honey and fruit to mix up a homemade snack. This also cuts down on global warming gasses, making the end product more sustainable. In fact, the World Watch Institute reports that a typical North American meal uses up to seventeen times more fossil fuel than a locally sourced meal. Search out local farms, CSA's (community supported agriculture) and farmer's markets with Local Harvest www.localharvest.org Become familiar with harvest times of favorite foods and eat them in season. Teens may enjoy *Animal, Vegetable, Miracle: A Year of Food Life* (Harper, 2008) by Barbara Kingsolver, Camille Kingsolver and Steven L. Hopp

- **Learn about current agricultural issues.** Whether your family has an interest in farming or not, no doubt they're interested in eating. Check out Acres U.S.A. www.acresu-sa.com

- **Take hikes or nature walks regularly.** You may want to note findings, make a sketch or write a description. Field guides to trees, birds or insects are handy if you'd like to confirm your sightings. Or simply enjoy the experience.
- **Cook with the sun.** Find out how to make your own solar oven and cook at home or on campouts using nature's free energy supply. www.solarcooking.org/plans
- **Understand habitats.** Discover the science behind conservation of invertebrate habitat through Xerces Society www.xerces.org. Create wildlife habitat with tips from the National Wildlife Federation www.nwf.org/backyard or check out *National Wildlife Federation Attracting Birds, Butterflies & Backyard Wildlife* (Creative Homeowner, 2004) by David Mizejewski.
- **Pay attention to complexity.** Look behind a promotional campaign or news story to discover more about the situation. How do efforts to control or "help" nature overlook interdependent natural systems? A good illustration of well-intentioned efforts gone wrong are found in *There's a Hair in My Dirt! A Worm's Story* (Harper, 1999) by Gary Larson.
- **Understand recycling.** Buying easily recyclable items aids the process of reclamation, but of course buying less in the first place leads to fewer items requiring disposal. Find out what happens to recyclables. Visit an artist who relies on used materials. Call your local recycling, solid waste or public works department for information, tours or speakers. If there are items you cannot easily recycle (furniture, batteries, paint) locate organizations that will take them from the resources in www.earth911.org To recycle electronics check out the organizations listed in www.techsoup.org

Enjoy recyclables too. Toys from Trash www.arvindguptatoys.com/toys.html provides instructions for making a variety of playthings from recycled items.

- **Take along useful information.** Maintain a clipboard or folder to store take-along science ideas. Instructions to measure a slope using a string and jar of water, the methods of testing for rock hardness, charts of constellations are all great to have on hand when the timing is right.
- **Brainstorm** signs of the season, indications of animal life or other areas of interest, then set out with this list and check off what can be found.

- Emphasize optimism. When choosing resources, focus on those which help young people become informed and active in positive ways. Try Meet the Greens www.meetthegreens.org, a site with animated adventures and projects.

Enjoy using the tips found in *The New 50 Simple Things Kids Can Do to Save the Earth* (Andrews McMeel, 2009) by Sophie Javna and EarthWorks Group.

- **Emphasize hands-on fun.** Use guides such as Let's Go Outside!: Outdoor Activities and Projects to Get You and Your Kids Closer to Nature (Trumpeter, 2009) by Jennifer Ward. *The Everything Kids' Nature Book: Create Clouds, Make Waves, Defy Gravity and Much More!* (Adams, 2002) by Kathiann M. Kowalski, and *Nature's Playground: Activities, Crafts and Games to Encourage Your Children to Enjoy the Great Outdoors* (Chicago Review, 2007) by Fiona Danks and Jo Schofield.

- **Focus on one thing over time.** Pick out a tree or stream. Describe it fully to yourself, perhaps writing about it in a journal. Spend time nearby each day or week.

- Notice changes in different seasons. Pay attention to everything that's beautiful, distressing and hard to understand. As questions arise, look for the answers.

Resources

Online

- Earth & Sky offers podcasts, updates, lessons and Ask the Scientist. www.earthsky.org
- President's Environmental Youth Awards (PEYA) recognizes youth for environmental projects. www.epa.gov/enviroed/peya

Books

- *A Drop Around the World* (Dawn, 1998) by Barbara McKinney.
- *My Nature Journal: A Personal Nature Guide for Young People* (Pajaro, 1999) by Adrienne Olmstead.
- *Fun With Nature* (NorthWord, 1998) by Mel Boring.
- *Nature Ranger* (Dorling Kindersley, 2006) by David Burnie and Richard Walker.
- *Insectigations: 40 Hands-on Activities to Explore the Insect World* (Chicago Review, 2005) by Cindy Blobaum.
- *Tree of Life: The Incredible Biodiversity of Life on Earth* (Kids Can, 2004) by Rochelle Strauss.
- *Weather!* (Storey, 2003) by Rebecca Rupp.
- Any of Jane Kirkland's books in the Take A Walk series (Stillwater).

CHAPTER ELEVEN

Math, Business & Critical Thinking

Math

"Go down deep enough into anything and you will find mathematics."
—Dean Schlicter

Equations, patterns and probabilities surround us. Math is everywhere. Sometimes it takes a wider way of thinking about math to celebrate the beauty and perfection it represents. Notice nature's examples of Fibonacci sequences in pinecones and sunflowers. Pay attention to mathematical precision and cultural symbolism found in medieval "girih"-patterned Islamic tiles, or fractals woven into Fulani wedding blankets. Recognize arithmetic represented in a bridge stretching across the water or a new building under construction. Get reacquainted with mathematical constants such as pi. Understand current issues by checking out statistics used by both sides to support their claims. Master logic.

Mathematical readiness varies widely from child to child. Some are eager to do mental math, memorize math tricks and take on increasingly complex calculations. Others need a significantly greater amount of time before they are able to tackle these same tasks. As previously discussed, readiness is one of the key factors in learning. When readiness is paired with self-motivation, there's no limit to what a child can accomplish.

An experience at Sudbury Valley School (Framingham, Massachusetts) provides an excellent example. Sudbury Valley is a democratic school where students are free to spend their time as they choose, and are not evaluated by tests, grades or scores. So, when a group of students told teacher Daniel Greenberg that they wanted to learn arithmetic he tried to dissuade them, explaining that they'd need to meet twice a week for a half an hour each session, plus do homework. The students eagerly agreed. In the school library, Greenberg located a math book written in 1898 that was perfect in its simplicity. Memorization, exercises and quizzes were not ordinarily part of the school day for these students, but they arrived on time, did their homework and took part eagerly. Greenberg reflects, "In twenty weeks, after twenty contact hours, they had covered it all. Six years' worth. Every one of them knew the material cold." A week later he described what he regarded as a miracle to a friend, Alan White, who had worked as a math specialist in the public schools. White wasn't surprised. He said, "… everyone knows that the subject matter itself isn't that hard. What's hard, virtually impossible, is beating it into the heads of youngsters who hate every step. The only way we have a ghost of a chance is to hammer away at the stuff bit by bit every day for years. Even then it does not work. Most of the sixth graders are mathematical illiterates. Give me a kid who wants to learn the stuff—well, twenty hours or so makes sense."

The example of Sudbury Valley not only speaks to the importance of readiness and self-motivation, it also speaks to the underpinning of mathematical understanding those students brought to class. They had learned to reason and think for themselves through years of natural learning. This proved an excellent foundation for learning traditional math with such speed.

Benoit Mandelbrot is the Yale mathematics professor credited with identifying structures of self-similarity that he termed "fractal geometry." His work changed the way we see patterns in nature, economies and other systems. Mandelbrot doesn't believe that students should struggle with Euclidean mathematics. Instead, he says, "Learning mathematics should begin by learning the geometry of mountains, of humans. In a certain sense, the geometry of … well, of Mother Nature, and also of buildings, of great architecture." In other words, by focusing on inspiration found everywhere around them before turning to formal equations.

Learning math requires children to link language with images as they work through equations. It helps if they can easily picture the problem being solved before they move ahead into representational and abstract math. Normally a child who has spent plenty of time playing with manipulatives (water, sand, building blocks and countable objects) and who uses real world applications of math (cooking, carpentry, shopping) has a wealth of experience to fall back on. This child can call up mental images that are firmly connected to sensory memory, helping him understand more advanced concepts. Without being able to visualize the logic behind arithmetic, children can become frustrated. Even Albert Einstein relied on imagery, saying "If I can't picture it, I can't understand it."

Many people prefer increased emphasis on more rigorous instruction and testing. They dispute the value of learning math through concrete examples or real life applications. They point to declining test scores and the resulting low academic ranking of U.S. students compared to others worldwide. Some cite a study that showed students were more able to retain a mathematical concept when taught with an abstract rather than a concrete example. However, the students in that study weren't young children, they were college students who had already been exposed to twelve to fifteen years of mathematics instruction. The college students' familiarity with abstract principles has little relevance to the sort of learning that goes on in earlier years. More importantly, children in the current generation are much less likely than previous generations to learn through play, exploration and meaningful work. Concerns about the math abilities of the nation's children should instead turn to the ways that we have manipulated childhood; substituting tightly controlled environments and managed recreation for the very real, messy and highly stimulating experiences that are the building blocks for higher level thinking.

It's much more interesting to use math when we care about the outcome. And direct experience offers the greatest learning benefits because it provides unique context as well as multi-sensory impact. A teen given the job of landscaping his grandparent's backyard will plan the project on graph paper. He will estimate the materials required, measure distance and depth for planting, and probably compare the wisdom of an hourly rate of pay versus payment by the job. The mistakes he makes and the lessons he learns will form a broader understanding of applied math. And he will see the results of his work grow both in his bank account and from the earth.

When a math-based project arises from a child's own motivation, even complex calculations seem more do-able because there's a purpose that drives the child toward completion. Before a competition, a girl decides to make beaded armbands for her martial arts team. She estimates pricing as she figures out her supply list. She measures and multiplies in order to customize the instructions so that she can put each player's name on the bands, then works out new patterns by incorporating her team colors into the design. These are complicated mathematical tasks. She may struggle, seek out help repeatedly and find herself working well beyond her skill level, but she has her own reasons to continue. As a result she not only masters difficult mathematical concepts, she feels the satisfaction that comes from seeing those armbands worn by her teammates.

As often as possible math can be incorporated into naturally occurring parts of the day, into things children care about. This gives children a comfortable familiarity with math. Why is that so important?

- **Problem solving.** Learning math accentuates the skills necessary to solve problems in many areas of life. These skills include finding out variables, paying attention to detail, examining choices, planning strategies and testing potential solutions. Studies show that students with high ability in math don't have enhanced development in a specific mathematical area of the brain. Instead, these young people are actually better at using both hemispheres of the brain to process information and solve problems.
- **Logic.** Math is a logical discipline. It teaches clear, reasoned thinking built on proofs. This helps build critical thinking abilities.
- **Technology and innovation.** A solid background in math assists in understanding and using technology while providing a framework for innovation in a variety of areas. This goes both ways, because high familiarity with technology and openness to innovation also lend themselves to a greater interest in using math.
- **Daily living.** Enabling children to learn self-sufficiency means they need to be competent at everyday tasks such as cooking, personal

budgeting, making repairs, shopping, scheduling and following directions—all of which require math skills.

- **Math skills are cross-related to other forms of learning.** For example, dozens of studies show that spatial-temporal reasoning improves when children learn to play a musical instrument. That holds true for other forms of learning including chess, sports and computer programming.
- **Math links seamlessly with nearly every other subject.** It is used to analyze historical claims and to understand current events. It is essential to many art forms, from music to sculpture. It creates substance in literature, purpose in physical education and data in science. No matter where one's interests lie, math isn't far.

Starting Places

- **Revel in measurement.** Investigate joules, BTUs, calories, watts, gallons, degrees, fathoms, meters, hertz, attoseconds and more. Measure your everyday world. Calculate such things as the energy usage to get to grandma's house in the car compared to taking the train, what angle a paper plane can be thrown and still fly, how much wood it will take to build a shelf for the baby's toys, how many footsteps are required to walk to the corner. Figure out how to gather measurements and apply data.
- **Learn to dance.** The fox trot or the hokey pokey may be funny names to children, but they also describe specific patterned steps. Mastering simple dances are a way of transforming mathematical instruction into art. Choreographers use dance notation to symbolize exact movements. Over the years different methods of dance notation have been used including: track mapping, numerical systems, graphs, symbols, letter and word notations, even figures to represent moves. Choreograph using your own system of dance

notation. Draw chalk footprints on the floor to show where the dancer's feet move to a waltz. Try dance classes. Music and dance make math come alive.

- **Enjoy math songs.** Play them while traveling and sing them casually as you go about your day; you'll find your children are memorizing math facts effortlessly. There's something about a catchy tune that helps the mind retain concepts. There are many sources of math songs including www.science-groove. org/MASSIVE with a database containing information on 2,500 science and math songs.
- **Find the magic in pi.** Measure circles of all sizes such as bike tires and bathtub drains, then divide the circumference by the diameter to find pi. Younger children will enjoy *Sir Cumference and the Dragon of Pi: A Math Adventure* (Charlesbridge, 1999) by Cindy Neuschwander, teens may appreciate *The Joy of Pi* (Walker & Co., 1999) by David Blatner. Consider celebrating Pi Day on March 14th by eating pie, making a pi chain out of paper or beads that link colors to each digit of pi, or seeing how many digits of pi you can recite.
- **Learn big, bold numbers.** Figure out how many days, minutes and seconds each member of the family has been alive. Estimate the mass of the Earth, then look up the answer. Read *Can You Count to a Googol?* (Albert Whitman & Co., 2000) by Robert Wells. Stretch your mind to include Graham's Number. Talk about why big numbers are best expressed in scientific notation. Check out the Mega Penny Project www.kokogiak.com/megapenny
- **Play games.** Nearly every board game and card game includes arithmetic. Make time to play the games your children enjoy. Try new ones and make up your own. Many homeschoolers set up game days so their children can share games with their friends. Games make strategizing and calculating effortlessly fun. For the latest information on games, check in with the aficionados at www.boardgamegeek.com.

For educational game reviews, consult Games for Homeschooling blog http://homeschool-games.blogspot.com.

- **Learn chess.** This game is in a class all its own. Research shows that children who play chess have improved spatial and numerical abilities, increased memory and concentration, enhanced problem-solving skills as well as a greater awareness of these skills in action. Interestingly, chess also promotes improved reading ability and self-esteem.

Cody is really good with basic math, which is a direct result of playing games.
—Kim Railey, Washington

My kids make up all sorts of games with playing cards. They have their own complicated rules and use multiple decks and keep score with color-coded markers. I just think-writing! math! logic! Even when playing regular games they made them harder. I can't always keep track but I've noticed they'll do things like at every turn the player takes two cards from the pile and multiplies to see who wins the cards. These kids hate flash cards but they love games. The seven-year-old is great at multiplication. They'll probably be adding trig to their games just for the challenge.
—Renee, Kentucky

- **Investigate the early uses of geometry.** Learn about structures such as Stonehenge or the Great Pyramid of Khufu. Our forbearers used sophisticated methods of measurement, engineering and building to construct these and many other ancient marvels. One way to learn about such structures is to build models using clay, poster board or craft sticks.

An excellent introduction to ancestral geometry incorporates art projects teaching about square roots, proportional constants and irrational numbers found in the Native American geometry program at www.earth-measure.com.

- **Learn more about yourselves.** One homeschooling family hangs a new chart each week to gather data. One week they might mark off where the dog takes a nap, then figure the percentage at the end of the week (40 percent of the time she sleeps in the window seat, 5 percent of the time under the table, etc), another week they might pick a subject like hours of computer use per person. They are also keeping several year-long graphs. One tracks the weight of trash and recyclables they discard weekly and a second graphs the amount of the produce they harvest from the garden. Yet another tracks money they are saving. They notice that in busy weeks, such as holidays, they fall short of sustainability goals they've set for themselves.

- **Find out about the math in meteorology.** Learn about weather trends and predictions, measurement of precipitation and temperature conversion. Keep a weather log using instruments to measure wind speed, precipitation, temperature, barometric pressure and humidity: then graph the results to determine average, mean and median for your data.

- **Play with shapes.** Enjoy puzzles, tangrams and tessellations. Notice the way shapes work together in the world around you both in natural and constructed settings. Keep a scrapbook of appealing shapes and designs. Create a sculpture out of toothpicks and miniature marshmallows. Cut paper snowflakes. Make collages out of pictures and three-dimensional objects. Grout bits of tile or broken dishes into mosaic designs. Fold origami. Make mobiles. Cut food into shapes.

- **Pick up a musical instrument.** Math, like reading, is reinforced by learning to play an instrument. Sounds are represented by symbols and interpreting them results in music.

- **Learn about the golden ratio.** Also known as the "divine proportion" or the "golden mean" this mathematical constant is repeatedly encountered in nature and expressed in art and architecture. Teens might enjoy reading *The Golden Ratio: The Story of PHI, the World's Most Astonishing Number* (Broadway, 2003) by Mario Livio. Look for the golden ratio around you. You'll see it in the features on a loved one's face, in the arrangement of objects in a museum, in the spirals of a seashell.

- **Use wheels.** Plan and build a skateboarding ramp. Time relay races using tricycles (the bigger the kids the greater the fun). Estimate how many revolutions different sized bike wheels make to cover the same distance (then get outside to find the answer). Adjust a wheelbarrow load to carry the greatest amount of weight. Use mass transit to get where you are going after figuring out the route and time schedule.

- **Estimate, then find out how to determine an accurate answer.** Predict how much a tablespoon of popcorn will expand, then measure after it has been popped. Before digging into an order of French fries, estimate how many there are or how far their combined length will reach. See how the guess compares with the actual figure. Guessing, then finding out the answer enlivens many endeavors.

- **Get into statistics.** Children go through a phase when they want to find out about the fastest, heaviest, most outrageous. Once they're duly impressed with the facts in such books as *Guinness World Records* (Guinness, annually) it's a great time to pique their interest using almanacs and atlases.

Sports offer a fun way to use statistics. Player and team stats are used to calculate odds, make comparisons and determine positioning. Children may want to keep track of their favorite teams or of their own activities. The numbers can help them to see patterns, debate trends and make predictions.

Collect and interpret your own statistics. You might develop a survey. Or take measurements, weights and other information about specific data, and record and analyze the statistics using a graph, histogram or other instrument.

Data provided by WorldoMeters www.worldometers.info makes fascinating reading and may lead to further investigation, but recognize that statistics aren't a complete way to understand our complex world.

When I was in first or second grade, at a rummage sale, I found a pack of cards. Those were my first baseball cards. Now I have over 1,000 baseball cards. When I was learning averages and percentages those really helped ... I'd figure out how many home runs the players would average in a season. It made the learning fun. I'd do it on my own, write it on a piece of paper and check it on a calculator or check it on the card. If you want to learn something you think is hard, find something you enjoy and work it in.

— Josh, 12

- **Enjoy geometry** using paper. Print out paper designs that fold into clever toys and games from The Toy Maker www.thetoymaker.com/2Toys.html including thaumatropes and windboats. Check out instruction books such as *Paper, Scissors, Sculpt!: Creating Cut-and-Fold Animals* (Sterling, 2006) by Ben Gonzales or *Absolute Beginner's Origami* (Watson-Guptill, 2006) by Nick Robinson. Although these may seem to be for amusement sake, they teach important lessons in conceptualizing shapes and making inferences about spatial relations.

- **Retell family tales** featuring math, such as the time your grandfather calculated that he had just enough money to buy a newspaper to scan the help wanted ads and on the first day of his new job met the woman who would end up being grandma. How much did that paper cost compared to today's paper? What might their wages have been? Is it possible to figure the probability of that meeting?

- **Make calculation part of household rules.** If children are permitted no more than a certain number of television-viewing hours per week, let them be responsible for dividing their time amongst favorite shows. If children rotate chores or privileges, assist them to create a workable tracking system.

I set up a dry erase calendar on the kitchen wall. This provides us a place to keep a to-do list of chores that need to be done as well as a place to write our daily and monthly schedules. If it all sounds too organized, it isn't. We don't do it every day. We found a pattern that works well for our family most days and we generally stick to it: a checklist for getting ready in the morning, an open spot for doing activities out or at home, lunch, quiet time in our rooms, then another spot for activities, then dinner and a checklist for getting ready to bed. I involved the children in making their checklists so we'd have the attitude of "these are the things we do to get ready" versus "Mommy is making me do this." It may not sound like math but it's working on time management, sequence of events, and logic.

The calendar also teaches math in a more traditional way. When I aided in a first grade during my teacher training I was blown away with how many math skills could be subtly taught through the use of the calendar and a numbers chart. I have hundreds of numbers charts tucked away for reference in several rooms because you never know when you'll need one in conversation ... At home, we use the calendar to teach counting and learning the days of the week and the months of the year. When my son turned four we counted every day he was four years old using popsicle sticks and cups labeled 1's, 10's, and 100's to teach place value. Since we don't do it every day, it created some great math problems.

—Karen, Texas

- **Make time for calendars.** Check out the history of African, Babylonian, Roman and Egyptian calendars. Learn how our calendar system came into use. Would it make sense to change to 13 equal months of 28 days each, with one remaining "day out of time" set aside? What are the definitions of "mean solar time," "sidereal time" and "apparent solar time"? Make a homemade sundial to see how accurately you can tell time.

- **Expand the concept of time** as you learn. Find out about time zones. Make a wheel representing time differences around the world so you can tell at a glance what hour it is in Tokyo, Reykjavik or Cairo. Learn why a pendulum is good for telling time.

Experiment using different lengths and weights to find out how far the swing goes, how long the swing takes to complete, and what length makes 60 swings per minute.

- **Make math edible.** Cereal, pretzels, crackers, small pieces of fruit or vegetables, cubes of cheese, nuts and other bite-sized foods are excellent tools to demonstrate addition, subtraction, multiplication, division, fractions, percentages, measurement and more. Using food to make math functions visible is a tasty way to solve equations. Your children can calculate recipe changes such as doubling or halving while they learn other useful meal preparation skills at home. Learn about geometry as children construct graham cracker buildings. They can use royal frosting to "glue" the pieces together. They'll need to cut triangles to support the roof and other shapes if they choose to make doors and walkways. The house can be decorated with dry cereals and pretzels.

- **Make math a moving experience.** Instead of relying on flash cards, memorize equations by clapping or stomping to them, rhyming and dancing with them, kicking a ball or tossing a bean bag to them, making number lines on the sidewalk with chalk and running to answer them, or any other method that enlivens learning. *Games for Math* (Pantheon, 1988) by Peggy Kaye offers many moving math activities for children.

- **Use trial and error.** This is a fun process, especially when applied to brain teasers, puzzles and mazes; try making up your own. Other math-related ways to stretch your mind include optical illusions, magic tricks and drawing in perspective. These activities go well beyond solving equations to figuring out larger concepts.

- **Use math reinforcers.** Make or buy math posters, placemats, t-shirts and shower curtains. A numbers chart from 1 to 100 is a great way to help younger children see patterns found in counting by 2's, 5's and 10's. For older youth, seeing concepts displayed on a casual basis may help reinforce information such as geometric formulas, prime numbers or quadratic equations. Don't forget to use your fingers, especially once you've mastered the Korean finger calculation method called "chisanbop."

- **Devise your own codes** and use them to send messages to one another. Check out the history of codes and code breakers. Set up treasure hunts by hiding a tiny treat and leaving codes or equations to be solved that lead to the next set of hints.

- **Read stories incorporating math.** Try books such as *The Man Who Counted: A Collection of Mathematical Adventures* (W.W. Norton, 1993) by Malba Tahan, *40 Fabulous Math Mysteries Kids Can't Resist* (Teaching Resources, 2001) by Marcia Miller and Martin Lee, *The Adventures of Penrose the Mathematical Cat* (World Wide, 1997) by Theoni Pappas, or any of the Math Adventure series. Consult www.sci.ta-mucc.edu/~eyoung/literature.html for more math-related literature.

- **Start a math club.** Meet regularly with others who enjoy making the subject fun and intriguing. Include projects, games, snacks and field trips related to math. There are several books available with "family math" in the title providing excellent activity suggestions.

- **Compete.** Check out American Mathematics Competition www.amc.maa.org, Math Counts www.mathcounts.org and Math Olympiads www.moems.org.

- **Enjoy the intersection of math and art.** Muse over puzzling visual patterns, for example the work of M.C. Escher. Learn about rugmaking, sculpture, weaving, basketry and many other art forms to discover the calculation, patterning and measurement used to create objects of beauty.

- **Visualize.** Arithmetic lends itself well to the sort of visualizations and games that computers do well. Try Math Cats www.mathcats.com, National Library of Virtual Manipulatives http://nlvm.usu.edu, NRICH http://nrich.maths.org/public/index.php, and Murderous Maths www.murderousmaths.co.uk

---

I've found the biggest aid in comprehension is for me to sit with them when they do some of their more difficult work. Discussion of math concepts has been so much more fun than drills and worksheets. Discussion also leads to so much more—for example, when working on our Montessori type math we may branch off and read a chapter in Mathematicians are People Too, *do a play about Descartes, look in the atlas to see where he was from, read from* Story of the World *about that time period. Discussion of anything they are working on inevitably leads us deeper and also lets me know exactly where they may need help. No need for testing.*

—Margaret S., Texas

- **Delve into maps.** Look at maps of the world together. Find maps of your locality. As well as road maps, your child may be intrigued by topographical and relief maps, economic and political maps, navigational and aeronautical charts, weather maps or land ownership maps. Draw maps of your neighborhood, home, yard or bedroom—notice what details your child includes. Make imaginary maps, perhaps to accompany a story or to demonstrate what an eight-year-old would consider a perfect place. Consider mapping somewhere you know well, but from different time frames—how might this place have looked 100 years ago, now, in the distant future? Some children who are reluctant to keep diaries or sketchbooks will cheerfully keep records of places they've been

by drawing maps. Maps and mapping can teach measurement, spatial awareness and complex geographical concepts.

My daughter (age 6) especially loves maps. She loves to do the map section of the all-encompassing 2nd grade workbook we have. We always get through that so quickly that I have to find other map activities for her. —Jenny

---

- **Compare related things** like the weight of a puppy to a full grown dog, or the size of a pitcher compared to the number of glasses it can fill. While shopping have children help check prices as part of the process of learning which choice offers a better deal. Talk about what other factors come into play—durability, ecological impact, value, overall worth. If you need to make a bigger purchase like a refrigerator, have the children compare the special features and cost effectiveness of running the appliance.
- **Use math to explore political and social issues.** Look at issues and the numbers backing them up. Try to explore the data from both sides, for example the pros and cons of voting to approve a lottery system or gambling in your state.
- **Try travel math.** Traveling is a great time to use math. Children can figure out fuel usage, keep track of expenditures, consult maps, estimate time of arrival and more. Playing math games also provides excellent distraction during a long trip.
- **Talk about math** as if you are thinking out loud. "I wonder how many bricks it took to make this entire wall?" then "remember" there's a formula for figuring that out; or "If we don't buy ____ for a whole week do you think we'll have enough money leftover for a ____?"

- **Enjoy hands-on projects** requiring sequential instruction. These hone logic and spatial skills as well as patience. Model-building, quilting, making repairs, knitting, carpentry, origami, beading and Legos® are examples of such projects.
- **Learn how alternative languages relate to numbers.** Check out Morse code, semaphore, Braille and sign language.
- **Play pool.** The sport known as billiards has a lot to teach about angles, trajectory, speed and calculation. And it's fun.
- **Find ways around math limitations.** A disorder called "dyscalculia" www.dyscalculia.org has been identified to explain why some students struggle with math.

Adults with this problem find their own ways to cope. They use tricks to compensate for their difficulty memorizing math facts. They don't do mental math easily, but benefit from using calculators and keeping handy pocket guides such as *Merriam-Webster's Pocket Guide to Business and Everyday Math* (Merriam-Webster, 1996) by Brian Burrell or *Pocket Ref* (Sequoia, 2002) by Thomas J. Glover. To follow directions they use several methods simultaneously to orient themselves—landmarks, road names and looking at maps.

These strategies are valuable for anyone learning math. Provide graph paper to draw number lines, make charts and visualize equations. Look up math tricks. Draw pictures to understand problems. Use rhymes or songs to remember math facts. Allow as much time as necessary. Be supportive. And be open to the very real possibility that children who learn math without pressure will be much less likely to develop long-term problems. Many adults suffer from math anxiety due to a lack of confidence more than lack of ability. When we approach math from a wider perspective, showing our children why it works and how it works, they own mathematical processes for themselves.

Resources

Online

- **Ask Dr. Math** is a searchable archive of answers using responses from 300 "Dr. Math" volunteers. http://mathforum.org/dr.math
- **Homeschool Math** provides fresh ideas from a math happy homeschooling parent. www.homeschoolmath.net
- **Living Math** brings math alive through resources and methods of linking math to history, science and literature. www.livingmath.net
- **S.O.S. Mathematics** www.sosmath.com is a resource for review material from algebra to differential equations.

Books

- *Algebra Unplugged* (Clearwater, 1996) by Kenn Amdahl and Jim Loats.
- *All the Math You'll Ever Need: A Self-Teaching Guide* (Wiley, 1999) by Steve Slavin.
- *Calculus for Cats* (Clearwater, 2001) by Kenn Amdahl.
- *Secrets of Mental Math: The Mathemagician's Guide to Lightning Calculation and Amazing Math Tricks* (Three Rivers, 2006) by Arthur Benjamin and Michael Shermer.
- *Speed Math for Kids: The Fast, Fun Way To Do Basic Calculations* (Jossey-Bass, 2007) by Bill Handley.
- *The Universal Book of Mathematics: From Abracadabra to Zeno's Paradoxes* (Chartwell, 2009) by David Darling.

Business & Finance

"Money often costs too much."—Ralph Waldo Emerson

Our society seems preoccupied with money, but on the most superficial level. The meaning underlying monetary choices is rarely discussed. There are bigger issues in how we obtain and use money. Right now, when our children are young, is when we have the greatest impact on their attitudes about finances, careers and spending. It helps to take a close look at the wisdom behind the choices we demonstrate to them.

Do our spending decisions reflect our values?

Do our careers make the best of our abilities?

Who are our financial role models?

What does it mean to have enough?

Do we have ample time for our families, for activities we enjoy, for quiet reflection?

Are our priorities consistent with where our time and money is spent?

In *Your Money Or Your Life: Transforming Your Relationship With Money And Achieving Financial Independence* authors Joe Dominguez and Vicki Robin redefine a transaction we take for granted, working. They describe it as trading our life energy for money. That life energy is subtracted from the hours we have to live. Thus, making the work we do a pursuit of meaning and purpose is a way to use our life energy with the greatest personal integrity. The same goes for spending. If money represents hours of life energy expended, our use of money is an expression of how we choose to spend the product of our time. Not everyone would agree with the authors' valuation. But most of us recognize the peace that comes of living in harmony with our own priorities.

Listen to your child's aspirations. Seek out definitions of abundance from your spiritual path, from great thinkers, from stories. Think about expenditures, even small ones, before spending money unthinkingly. Look to people who love the work they do. Talk about the reasons behind your choices.

The kids help me deliver newspapers early every morning. In our family we make decisions together like what we spend and what we do. The kids know full well that money is time; their dad's time at work, my time doing pet grooming and everyone's time delivering papers. They see kids their age spend money on stupid stuff and don't get it. My sixth grade son has friends that think a fun afternoon is going to the movies, getting a bunch of junk food and throwing half of it away and hanging out at the mall where they buy electronics or sports gear. He likes these kids but he won't go do that stuff with them. I notice that my son is a lot less selfish than these kids. He was saving up his own money but sent a bunch of it to help people after Katrina.

—Debbie

I don't know who said, "Do what you love, the money will follow." We did the reverse and learned the hard way. My husband and I worked hard in careers we didn't much like. He got transferred twice into divisions that were worse. I got downsized. It makes no sense after awhile. We are raising our kids to do the work their hearts tell them to do!

—Cindy, Maryland

Children want to understand how and why adults do what they do. As they enter adulthood we ask them to make choices that resonate through the rest of their lives, yet rarely do they have direct evidence upon which to base those choices. Too often young people choose a career without knowing what a day in that profession is like or what it takes to enter the field. That's a set-up for failure.

Bill Milliken, author of *The Last Dropout: Stop the Epidemic!* points out that the current generation is not sufficiently prepared for the job market. Milliken's prescription includes involving the community in student life. He's right, children have been separated from the life of the community for too long. They have been deprived of meaningful involvement with adults who work in a variety of fields. Milliken's organization addresses this problem with measures designed to bring people into the schools.

But homeschoolers are already engaged in the real world around them. We don't remain segregated in school buildings waiting for programs to come our way. Homeschoolers find friendships, mentorships, apprenticeships and volunteer positions with adults who welcome them into the sorts of careers they want to explore. These collaborative efforts already model what is possible for every young person. After all, when a teen longs to be a forensic pathologist or organic farmer or chef, it's ridiculous to keep that young person from observing real work, from learning exactly what educational preparation is necessary for success and from partnering with a professional in the field. (Refer to Chapter Four for steps to take in finding a mentor.)

Starting Places

- **Have fun.** Turn lunch at home into a restaurant meal complete with menu listings, service and bill. Write up movie descriptions with viewing times and prices for family video night. Invent a new form of currency. Learn about bartering, then try it.
- **Seek out connections.** Find responsive businesses and career-related clubs willing to offer programs, workshops, classes and volunteer opportunities for area youth. Your librarian can guide you to organizations, clubs and programs. Ask your local Chamber of Commerce www.uschamber.com to recommend civic-minded companies and business people.
- **Tour local businesses.** Whether on a field trip at a stamping plant or television news station, ask employees how they prepared for their careers and what the work entails.
- **Seek direct learning relationships** with adults who have careers or skills of interest.

Our son is very interested in becoming a chef. He loves to cook and fixes meals for himself and the rest of the family on a regular basis. Currently his interest is in cake decorating … We were fortunate in finding a local homeschooling mom who used to be a pastry chef, specializing in fondant, who will be working with him in the upcoming weeks to help him bring his cake visions to reality!

—Angie Beck, Kansas

Angelique volunteers with an equestrian therapy program. The woman who runs the program has taught her so much. Angel is really good working with the kids who attend the therapy sessions. She is hoping to go into physical therapy or occupational therapy as a career.

—Mandy, Iowa

- **Host an entrepreneur fair.** Invite children to create a product to sell. This may be a craft, service, invention, edible item or work of art. Provide an area to promote and display their wares at a homeschool meeting or public venue. They should have sufficient supply of their product to meet demand, but as with any business the exact number is an educated guess. You may choose to have start-up meetings beforehand to discuss product development, displays and other details. Encourage each child to keep track of expenses so they can evaluate the business potential of their product afterwards. Promote the fair to the public, invite extended family and encourage your homeschool group to support the efforts of their youngest business people. Have a follow-up meeting with participants to talk about their earnings in relation to the time and expense of making their product.
- **Involve young people in a family business.** Whether a small-scale eBay business or a full time company, children can provide valuable assistance while learning what it takes to find customers, keep track of expenses, pay taxes and build a strong business.

We had a tie dye business which we took to arts and crafts shows so people could make their own professionally dyed tie dyed shirts. We still do that as a family. You learn a lot about money and investing that way ...

It was a natural process for my kids to learn about money coming in and out. The main thing to learn was that not all money was profit, money had to be reinvested in the business. Let them see that there's ebb and flow. There was nothing formal about sitting down to teach accounting but they learned how business functioned. They worked together, and that was neat. —Lynn Reed, Georgia

- **Recognize business lessons in computer games.** Some games provide familiarity with basis business principles like cash flow, inventory, supply and demand, management and more.
- **Start budgeting and personal finance early.** Some parents prefer to have all family members involved in the household economy. They draw up a budget, talk over expenses and pay bills together. This way, children come to know what terms like "interest," "finance charge" and "invest" mean from taking part in this family chore, even if at a young age they are only putting stamps on envelopes and discussing what charities to support. Children are also less likely to wheedle for purchases because they understand exactly what it takes to save for longer-term goals such as a family vacation. And they learn how personal decisions impact financial security.
- **Use real money.** Adding up purchase prices, figuring percentages off and calculating change make more sense using actual money. Practice at home, then empower children to

use these new skills at the bank, farmer's market and movie theater.

- **Take math to the store.** Allow young people to be responsible for tallying up costs, figuring values and discussing spending priorities.

Ensure that children make regular decisions about spending, saving and donating. As with other learning experiences they need the opportunity to think through their choices, make mistakes and try again.

You might choose to create three budget categories (long-term savings, short-term savings, donations) with your child. Between you, decide on a percentage of money for each category. If the child decides to change the percentage or the amount when his or her income fluctuates, recalculate.

1. Long-term savings. This can be for the child's distant future (college, trip to Brazil, first car) or significant expenditures in the next year or two (laptop, pet, summer camp). Look up charts showing how interest accumulates with different strategies including CDs, mutual funds and savings accounts. Then decide where to keep long-term savings.
2. Short-term savings. This is money the child wants available for purchases (movie tickets, toys, snacks).
3. Donations. Some families pool donation money and allow a different child each month to choose a charity. Other families encourage the child to save for a charity of particular personal meaning.

I take both math and geography learning to the grocery store with me...I have my older son, 9, round the prices off so that he can get that down, then estimate the total at the end of the shopping errand.

My younger son, 6, I have read where in the USA the goods are produced so that he can later identify it on the USA map we have at home. We learn which states produce what products in the process. The boys love to shop this way and do not even realize they are learning new skills. —R. Cline, California

---

- **Learn how you vote with your dollars.** Research products according to health value, corporate responsibility and other standards using Good Guide www.goodguide.com. Check out how those statistics are gathered and how ethical shopping choices can make an impact.
- **Invest.** Build a mock investment portfolio with your children. Have them list several companies they choose (perhaps related to their interests or favorite products). Help them locate ticker symbols and current stock prices. Every week, help them record the latest prices along with the date. Calculate the gains or losses. These are short-term fluctuations, so talk about longer term trends as well.
- **Form an investment club.** Using hypothetical funds, members research stocks and returns, competing for the best results. They may wish to use online stock market simulation sites or register for The Stock Market Game www.stockmarketgame.org which has fees and other requirements.
- **Encourage budding enterprises** before your children reach a typical hiring age. They might mow lawns, walk dogs, help parents with younger children, sell homemade goodies, help with yard-sales, assist with computer service, remove pet waste in yards, move garbage cans from house to street and back, rake leaves, be a child-minder during meetings, weed garden beds, set up/explain electronics, help with holiday decorations, watch pets, sell crafts.

My kids always held lemonade stands (at least two-three a week during the summer!), and they would have to divide the money up between everyone who had been working the stand. Their basic math skills were cemented by using real-life applications of math in these ways. I actually had a couple of girls who had difficulty doing math problems unless we pretended we were working with money! The kids were so used to dealing with money that this was how they viewed their math and how they related numbers was by nickels, dimes, and quarters. For instance, if you asked one of the girls how much 25 x 8 were they would draw a blank. Ask the same child how much 8 quarters made and they would fly $2.00 off of their tongue faster than you could believe. Then I would say, well then, how much is 25 x 8, and I would still sometimes draw a blank! I'd then say, if one quarter equals 25c, then how much is 25 x 8? You'd see the comprehension kick in and they'd shout out 200! It was sometimes frustrating for me that they could not understand the correlation between the numbers on a page and the numbers they did in their head, but the kids were so used to using money that this was how they related numbers. They had real-life experience with money, but numbers on a page were foreign to them. They now understand both, but it was odd to experience this phenomenon with my kids.

I had the exact opposite experience growing up. I was used to having to do pages of math facts for school, and it wasn't until I went to work as a cashier that I began to be able to count money and do mental math without a problem. Once I began to use money in a real life way, money (and numbers) made more sense. —Lori Smith, Ohio

---

- **Hold a garage sale or charity fund-raiser.** Involve children in all phases from planning to follow-up.
- **Seek out finance lessons.** Companies dealing in finance such as banking institutions, insurance companies and brokerage firms may be eager to offer a speaker for a homeschool meeting or materials for a class. As with any curricula offered by a business, be aware that there may be implied advertising for the company's services or tendency to advance the company viewpoint. It's often eye-opening to discuss this aspect with your children.
- **Look at the larger economic picture.** Pay attention to the news with an eye to the impact on business, economy and financial trends. Talk about differing theories on what factors create high prices, inflation, unemployment and more. Teens may enjoy *Economics for the Impatient* (Clearwater, 2002) by C.A. Turner.
- **Understand the Federal Reserve System (The Fed).** This privately run system has a major economic impact. The Fed provides educational information at www.federalreserveeducation.org/fred
- **Guess where income tax dollars are spent.** Draw a pie chart and allocate resources where you think they are spent, or where you think they should be spent. Then compare your chart to data based on actual government spending by clicking on "interactive tax chart" at the National Priorities Project. www.nationalpriorities.org
- **Talk to people who use math in their work.** Consider a carpenter, financial advisor, architect, engineer, pilot, accountant, bricklayer, air traffic controller, astronomer, coach, physicist, pharmacist, banker, roofer, doctor, mechanic or business owner.

Resources

Online

- **Institute of Consumer Financial Education** offers quizzes, tips and facts in the "Children and Money" section of the website. www.financial-education-icfe.org

- **Interactive Mathematics Money Math** lets young people find out what a $1,000 credit card debt looks like over time, how long it takes to double money based on the interest rate, and other personal finance calculations. www.intmath.com/Money-Math/Money-Maths.php

- **Jumpstart Coalition** offers Reality Check with an online quiz to help teens figure out how to live the lives they want, realistically. www.jumpstart.org/realitycheck.html

- **Junior Achievement** (JA) www.ja.org provides volunteers from the business community to present JA curriculum to groups of students. Junior Achievement Student Center http://studentcenter.ja.org is a teen-friendly site geared to help explore careers, learn how to start up a business and prepare for higher education.

- **National Endowment for Financial Education** offers a free youth financial literacy curriculum for high school ages. www.nefe.org

- **PBS Kids Don't Buy It** has a wealth of resources about advertising tricks, the effect of commercials on buying habits and how to determine what a product is really worth. http://pbskids.org/dontbuyit

- **Young America's Business Trust** www.myybiz.net is a non-profit established as an outreach effort of the Organization of American States.

Books

- *Beyond the Traditional Lemonade Stand: Creative Business Stand Plans for Children of All Ages* (Expressions of Perceptions, 2009) by Randi Lynn Millward.

- *Money Sense for Kids* (Barron's, 2005) by Hollis Page Harman.

- *The New Totally Awesome Money Book for Kids, Third Edition* (Newmarket, 2007) by Arthur Bochner.

- *The Kid's Guide to Money: Earning It, Saving It, Spending It, Growing It, Sharing It* (Scholastic, 1996) by Steven Otfinoski.

Critical Thinking

"It is the mark of an educated mind to be able to entertain a thought without accepting it." —Aristotle

How do we know what is true? On what do we base our decisions? It has a lot to do with thinking for ourselves. We believe we use logic but studies have shown that most people do not have good reasoning skills. Instead we dismiss contradictory information and pay attention to data that supports what we choose to believe. We are easily fooled by illogic or extreme examples, especially if it comes from someone we want to believe. Our emotions strongly influence our thinking. We don't really know how to interpret statistics and too often we accept what we are told based on the way it is told. In fact we often take on what we hear or read as our own opinion with little reflection. That leaves us highly vulnerable to many forms of persuasion. That's why advertising has such an effect, why public relations "spin" is believed and why political pundits have such an influence.

It's particularly vital that we remain aware of the potentially harmful messages our children take in from the media and other sources and help them analyze these messages. That's because youth have fewer defenses. Studies show that a network in the brain necessary for many introspective abilities—forming a self-image, understanding the ongoing story of one's own life and gaining insight into other people's behavior—is profoundly weaker in children compared to adults. Children's brains have limited connections in that network until they reach adulthood.

Our children are readily able to access just about any information they might need in today's digital world. What they may be missing are the tools to interpret it. Cultures throughout time have developed techniques to be more aware of the mind and to bring the mind under greater conscious control. These include disciplines such as yoga, meditation and martial arts. It has also long been believed that memorization and recitation of verse or prose, conquering advanced mathematics, learning foreign languages and mastering difficult physical abilities are excellent

Critical thinking is one of the most important abilities to master. It has to do with evaluating persuasion and determining how to persuade others. It's an invigorating process that can summon the best in us. Our grandparents may have called it "common sense" but it is actually a complex and highly developed group of skills. Foremost it demands reason and reflection. But many other factors are required which help us develop strength of mind and character. These include being fair-minded, honest, curious, slow to judge, comfortable with ambiguity, willing to change conclusions, logical, persistent, able to face and overcome personal biases, and able to extrapolate based on data.

We want our children to use critical thinking every day. It will help them to reason clearly in relation to science, history, literature, current events—a whole spectrum of subjects. They'll be well suited to rely on it when they are faced with risky decisions and to apply it throughout their adult lives. In fact, an association has been found between a person's reasoning skills and the quality of his or her personal choices. Low ability to think through hypothetical situations is correlated with poor personal decisions, such as serious debt or illegal behavior. Interestingly, good decision-making doesn't necessarily go along with intelligence. Smart people can have very poor critical thinking skills. However the skills can be developed.

ways to exercise the mind. Choosing a form of mental discipline, especially as they approach the teen years, can be highly valuable.

It also helps when children understand how their own minds work. All children can become more aware of their thinking processes. Consult books and websites about the brain. Go to lectures and exhibits. Talk about the way the mind filters experiences, develops biases and embraces known patterns. The field known as metacognition refers to being actively in charge of your own thinking so that you can best accomplish the task set before you. All of us use the techniques of metacognition every day as we plan, assess and redirect our efforts for the most effective results. The idea is to make those tactics more conscious.

Encourage questions. Questions are a natural medium for children. They ask them all the time and recognize that good questions often lead to better questions before an answer is found. Questions can help get to the core of a matter. They sharpen our rational abilities. Try asking questions about any of the hundreds of assertions that are put in front of your child every day through advertising, news reports or opinion pieces. "Kids who play video games are more violent" or "Immigration is bad for the economy" or "Everyone wants whiter brighter teeth!"

- How else could you explain that information?
- What does this really mean?
- Does this remind you of something similar?
- Is the first-hand knowledge (direct experience, eyewitness, research) or second-hand?
- What is the source of the information?
- Why is this being said? Why is this important?
- Would that source have any motivation to distort the information?
- Is there other evidence?
- How is that evidence gathered? Who paid for or had an interest in that evidence?
- Do you think this is true? What else would you have to know to be sure?

Dissent is an essential component of critical thinking. Particularly in the teen years young people tend to hold expectations and beliefs up to the light of newly expanded reasoning powers. Even parents who have raised a child within a strong religious, political or philosophical framework can recognize that doubts and dissent is natural. The process of searching for greater understanding includes learning disparate viewpoints. It also includes looking for holes in reasoning and analyzing them against one's own standards. Along the way there will be inevitable dispute. This is actually an excellent sign that a young person is developing a quality that goes beyond the mere accumulation of knowledge. It has to do with independent, clear-eyed thinking.

As our children learn to think critically they will be able to rely on their increasing ability to inquire and make decisions. Knowing themselves and the way their minds work, they will be better able to distinguish truth from fallacy. This goes a long way towards developing that crucial trait known as common sense.

Starting Places

- **Opinion polls can be fun** as well as a great stimulus for discussion. How are polls used in the media or commentators? Compare related polls in the same topic through such sites as www.pollingreport.com/issues.htm or www.gallup.com to contrast the similarities and differences. What are the questions and how are they asked? Who were the people asked and how were they selected? Does the design of the poll affect the outcome? How do politicians and the media use the results?
- **Consider limited perspectives.** Can one view provide an accurate picture of a person or situation? Could a ten-minute observation of your family give a stranger the tools to make a clear assessment of the personalities involved? In general, the complexities of any situation go well beyond any single assessment tool. That's why multiple viewpoints are valuable.

It's important to remember that the perspective of those who are directly involved in any situation have more bearing than the input of outsiders.

- **Employ the rules of logic in arguments.** Youth may find themselves thinking more than disagreeing as they fit their points into classic forms using deductive reasoning. Use "logical fallacies" as an online search term to learn about terms such as ad homineum (attacking the personal instead of the issue), nirvana fallacy (comparing actual things with idealized alternatives), and horse laugh fallacy (presenting the opponent's argument in the extreme to make it seem ridiculous). Logic adds to critical thinking skills and cuts down on pointless arguments.

  Print out online explanations of logical fallacies to see how these are used on political talk shows, opinion blogs and other commentaries. Confine personal disagreements to rules of logic. FactCheckEd www.annenbergclassroom.org is a site for teens offering data to illustrate deductive and inductive reasoning, facts and fallacies, emotionally loaded language and more.

- **Pay attention to the process.** Critical thinking evolves slowly and requires maturity. Time for reflection is required. Studies have found that children who regularly eat meals with their parents and have plenty of conversation time develop higher-level reasoning skills.

Discussing our interests has been the most beneficial. Rabbit trails often deliver amazing insights. Even though we're home together, sometimes I don't make enough time to just be with them, listen to their thoughts, and answer their questions. I'm learning to answer their questions with more questions to help them come up with their own observations.

Also when we're discussing or reading something, I'm learning to pause when I recognize that look on their faces which mean they are thinking deeply. They often need more time to process than I allow them. Rushing is one of the worst impediments to learning.

—Karen, Texas

- **Enjoy critical thinking challenges.** Destination Imagination www.idodi.org is a team approach to creativity and problem solving. Participants solve challenges, advancing to global finals.

  Odyssey of the Mind www.odysseyofthemind.com is an international competition providing creative problem-solving opportunities for students from kindergarten through college.

- **Brainstorm.** That means welcoming any ideas, no matter how silly or unrelated to the problem they may seem at the time. Only afterwards are those ideas evaluated to see how they might fit as possible solutions. Brainstorming is used in business, the arts, science and many other fields. It can be a game on long car rides or while waiting in line. For example, think up all the possible uses for an object like a single piece of paper. Children may contribute ideas that require the paper to be rolled, folded, torn, cut, expanded to a size that could shade the city, shrunk to print an edition of a mouse newspaper, waterproofed, burned, etc. Although their ideas seem to go in all directions, they are engaging in the mind-expanding creativity of what Dr. Edward de Bono called "lateral thinking." This sort of thinking allows for greater awareness of the thought process. Excellent brainstorming prompts can be found online by using the search term "Odyssey of the Mind spontaneous problems" or "spontaneous problems."

Resources

Online

- **Media Literacy Clearinghouse** offers links, lessons, articles and updates on media literacy issues for adults and young people. www.frankwbaker.com
- **Media Literacy.com** is designed to increase awareness of the need for media literacy, providing a wealth of links to additional resources. www.medialiteracy.com
- **Understand Media** www.understandmedia.com offers articles, comics, lessons, podcasts, videos and more.

Books

- *A Rulebook for Arguments* (Hackett, 2008) by Anthony Weston.
- *Becoming a Critical Thinker: A User Friendly Manual* (Prentice Hall, 2008) by Sherry Diestler.
- *Becoming Logical: A Guide to Good Thinking* (Random House, 2005) by D.Q. McInerny.

(See more critical thinking resources in Chapter 15, Current Events.)

CHAPTER TWELVE

Physical Education & Health

Physical Education

"Whenever you trace the origin of a skill or practices which played a crucial role in the ascent of man, we usually reach the realm of play."
—Eric Hoffer

We know that being physically active is essential for building strength and maintaining health. When we incorporate fitness into our daily lives it's more likely our children will make this a lifelong habit. Research confirms that the benefits are not limited to the body. There are many reasons to encourage aerobic exercise, sports programs and vigorous play.

- **Increased motivation and accomplishment.** Regular exercise has been shown to improve creative thinking, completion of written tasks and memory. As with other effects, this may be due to the way exercise changes the brain. The mind is more calm and focused after vigorous activity.
- **Confidence.** The boost from achieving physical goals extends to other areas. Fit youth are more self-assured.
- **Stress reduction.** Inactive children tend to deal with stress more poorly than those who are active. Exercise provides a buffering effect by stimulating the release of positive neurotransmitters in the brain.
- **Self-esteem.** As youth reach their teen years, they report lower self-esteem. But those involved in team sports, martial arts and disciplines such as yoga retain a stronger self-image.
- **Greater self-control and improved emotional health.** Children with ADHD, learning disabilities and behavioral handicaps are better able to control their behavior when they participate in vigorous exercise. In fact, a regular running program has been found

to provide results similar to medications for hyperactivity and can reduce the need for psychotropic drugs to treat emotional disorders. Exercise can even alleviate depression.

- **Improved academic achievement.** Numerous studies show that higher levels of fitness are correlated with greater scholastic achievement. Regular exercise helps nerve cells form connections that make the brain operate more efficiently. Previously thought impossible, researchers have found that a program of vigorous exercise can stimulate the brain to grow new nerve cells in the area known to control learning.

Homeschoolers have the freedom to incorporate physical activity into all kinds of learning. Take math. You can incorporate calculation into relay races, learn spatial relations while checking maps on an architectural walk or understand hands-on geometry while your family volunteers for Habitat for Humanity. In fact, movement can be woven into every topic, from history to language, with a little creativity. Ask your children for their ideas. Chances are they'll be glad to make learning more active. When children have freedom of movement they don't become frustrated as quickly. The physical nature of childhood leans toward touching, laughing and running. Not sitting still.

Homeschoolers have another advantage. We can schedule activities during times when recreation facilities are unused and when parks, playgrounds and nature preserves are least crowded—during the school day. Skating rinks, yoga schools, fitness facilities, bowling alleys, martial arts schools and recreation centers seek out homeschoolers. Let the managers know what you and other homeschoolers need. If these facilities only offer tightly structured classes for specific age groups, they might be willing to try open-ended programs with looser age ranges. Another fresh approach to suggest is family-oriented sessions allowing parents, children and grandparents to enjoy recreation together rather than in age-segregated groups. When homeschoolers partner with people who manage community resources, we need to follow through by publicizing the classes and programs in our newsletters and forums. Programs such as daytime bowling leagues and rock climbing programs won't continue without sufficient attendance.

In addition to arranging special daytime programs, check nearby community recreation centers and YMCAs for their regular listings of summer and after-school programs, individual and team sports, and classes.

Accentuate the fun by exposing your children to activities of all kinds. More unusual pastimes, such as live action role-playing games or build-a-boat events, might appeal to teens. And you might be surprised how many sports are Olympic events—including billiards, volleyball, table tennis, rowing and snowboarding. In the final analysis, in sports and in life, it's not what we play but the way we play that reveals what kind of people we are.

Starting Places
- **Play is a child's realm.** It's a natural part of child development when children modify rules, make up games, pretend, argue and negotiate with one another as they play. Children often reach a stalemate only to end up playing again with renewed appreciation for one another. As long as no one is physically hurt or verbally abused, a bit of high drama is part of the fun. Children should manage their own play as much as possible.
- **Recognize the intrinsic need to test oneself.** As youth get older they long to measure their physical strength or ability. Other than hard work, athletics are a great way to channel this energy. Some young people compete, others

prefer continually improving individual performance. Denying the very natural urge to face physical challenges can be counterproductive, forcing young people to take the wrong kinds of risks.

- **Set up a regular park day.** This is a tradition with homeschoolers everywhere. These are casual gatherings where children get plenty of outdoor play. Parents have time to talk, set up other events and join in the games if they choose. It's a constant that children can count on.
- **Maximize time spent in green space.** Check out the national park system at www.nps.gov or *Frommer's National Parks with Kids* (Frommers, 2008) by Kurt Repanshek. Regularly visit state parks, nature preserves and parks near your home.
- **Orient birthday and holidays gifts toward activity.** Give passes to be used for horseback trail rides, a paintball range or local ski slopes. Wrap up a compass, a rubber-band-powered airplane kit or rollerblades. Consider making family celebrations more active with a hike and picnic or a day at the beach rather than a big dinner.
- **Introduce sidewalk games to the newest generation.** Using little more than chalk, rope or a few stones these games provide a great workout while encouraging memorization and strategy.
- **Exercise with animal friends.** Take the dog for a daily walk, or offer to take the neighbor's dog. Get involved in dog agility training programs and competitions. There are several organizations involved in canine agility: The United States Dog Agility Association www.usdaa.com 972-487-2200, the North American Dog Agility Council www.nadac.com and the American Kennel Club www.akc.org/events/agility 919-233-9767. Take part in the real effort of caring for pets or outdoor livestock. Enjoy the unique challenge and pleasure of horsemanship.

Both my 7 year old and 10 year old love their horseback riding lessons which they can do on a weekday early in the morning while the weather is cool rather than squeeze in between many children on the weekend. The horses are more relaxed and the stable feels peaceful.
—Margaret S., Texas

- **Sign up for the President's Challenge** at www.presidentschallenge.org 800-258-8146 to track progress toward personal fitness goals and earn awards. Both individuals and organizations can take part.
- **Make hiking a regular event.** Walk in natural settings as well as around town. Consider taking along a camera to capture the scenery, keeping track of the miles with a pedometer, posting hike notations on a blog, or keeping a hiking journal. One family tries to see how long they can hike in silence in order to listen more carefully to the sounds around them. The American Hiking Society www.american-hiking.org 800-972-8606 offers links to local hiking organizations, information, volunteer days and youth outreach.
- **Try volksmarching.** Volksmarching, or non-competitive walking, is a popular pastime in Europe. Now hundreds of volkssports clubs in the U.S. host regular walking events. These walks are chosen in historic or scenic areas and are open to the public. Contact American Volkssports Association www.ava.org 210-659-2112.
- **Encourage children to set up temporary obstacle courses.** A rainy day indoor course might consist of a few chairs to wriggle under, a rope to hop over, three somersaults through the hall and a quick climb up the bunk bed ladder. Outdoors, try a more energetic course.

- **Head for the water.** Swimming, diving, canoeing, sailing, surfing, water skiing and scuba diving all promote fitness, skill and pleasure.
- **Go by bike.** Encourage children to ride for fun, but also emphasize the use of bikes as an eco-conscious way to travel together to the store and library. Don't forget the allure of bike trails. There are many guidebooks showing trails by state and region.

  The League of American Bicyclists www.bikeleague.org offers Bike Education programs and links to local clubs. For those who enjoy competing, check out USA Cycling www.usacycling.org 719-866-4581. For fun, read *Go Fly a Bike! The Ultimate Book of Bicycle Fun, Freedom, and Science* (Dutton, 2004) by Bill Haduch.
- **Stretch.** Yoga is a natural for children, especially when instruction is as flexible as the postures (*asanas*). At younger ages children may enjoy pretending each asana is a different animal.
- **Golf.** Local courses often have reduced green fees and lessons for young people. Call a local course for information or check out the American Junior Golf Association www.ajga.org 877-373-2542.
- **Encourage outdoor adventuring.** Inspiring ideas abound in guides such as *The Field and Forest Handy Book: New Ideas for Out of Doors* (BN, 2009) by Daniel Carter Beard and David R. Godine, *The Daring Book for Girls* (William Morrow, 2007) by Andrea J. Buchanan and Miriam Peskowitz, *The Curious Boy's Book of Adventure* (Razorbill, 2007) by Sam Martin and *The Outdoor Book for Adventurous Boys: Over 200 Essential Skills and Activities For Boys of All Ages* (Lyons, 2008) by Adrian Besley.

Bronson started a weekly meeting of yo-yo fans at our homeschool support group meeting. For awhile they were really into practicing new tricks to show off but lately the kids who bring their yo-

yo's have been having fun making videos of their tricks, setting them to music or coordinating them to dialogue. They also are really patient teaching yo-yo to younger kids. —Mandy, Iowa

---

- **Enjoy the historic sport of fencing.** The United States Fencing Association www.usfencing.org 719-866-4511, offers youth programs, competitions and official information.
- **Look into challenge courses.** These are found in outdoor education centers and park programs. Participants gain the personal benefits of risk-taking experiences under professional guidance. Such programs go by a variety of names including: challenge course, ropes course or outdoor challenge. Many offer easier options for children and reduced rates for educational or non-profit groups.
- **Get oriented.** Orienteering offers an intellectual and physical challenge by combining navigation, map reading and decision-making. Participants walk, run, bike or ski using a map and compass to choose the best route, on or off the trail. Programs for very young children are available, and competitions for older youth are encouraged. Links to specialized orienteering—such as canoeing and horseback—are at U.S. Orienteering Federation www.us.orienteering.org

- **Try foam fighting.** This is enjoyed in live action role-playing games. For greater formality check out the chivalrous combat employed by the Society for Creative Anachronism www.sca.org

- **Go fly a kite.** There are many types of kites, each with distinct features to engage the wind. The American Kitefliers Association www.aka.kite.org 800-252-2550 sponsors competitions and festivals.

- **Become proficient at footbag,** more commonly known by the commercial name Hacky Sack®. There are official footbag sports, described by the International Footbag Players Association www.footbag.org, which provides rules and local club contacts. The sports include footbag net played on a Badminton court, freestyle footbag where players do tricks while passing the footbag around and advanced freestyling with choreographed routines to music.

- **Develop flexibility, strength and balance with gymnastics.** Community recreation centers and independent training programs offer gymnastic classes for all ages. Check out USA Gymnastics www.usa-gymnastics.org 317-237-5050 for information on training and qualifying meets.

- **Encourage games.** Games solidify friendships among those who have known one another their whole lives and help them make fast friends with new acquaintances. Keep a manual on hand for new ideas such as *Everyone Wins!: Cooperative Games and Activities* (New Society, 2007) by Josette Luvmour and Sambhava Luvmour or *The Adventurous Book of Outdoor Games: Classic Fun for Daring Boys and Girls* Sourcebooks, 2008) by Scott Strother.

- **Look into Letterboxing.** This pursuit combines walking, navigation and solving riddles. Clues help seekers find "letterboxes" hidden outdoors. The seekers use a rubber stamp found in this box to mark their own logbooks, mark the box logbook with their own personal stamp, then leave the box for the next seeker. This hobby is an interesting way to learn local history, encourage problem solving, explore new areas and leave creative clues or stamps. For more information and links to regional clues, check with Letterboxing North America www.letterboxing.org, Atlas Quest www.atlasquest.com or *It's a Treasure Hunt! Geocaching & Letterboxing* (CQ; G & R Publishing, 2007).

- **Recognize the allure of technology.** Geocaching is a modern-day treasure hunt made possible with a global positioning system (GPS). Caches are hidden, typically in a weatherproof box containing small trinkets. The GPS location and clues are posted on websites. The finder takes the "treasure," leaving something of similar value for the next seeker. Search for caches near you through Geocaching www.geocaching.com or Navicache http://navicache.com.

- **Check out technology requiring detailed know-how** with Amateur Radio Direction Finding (ARDF) www.ardf-r2.org/en. Amateur Radio operators hike to find radio transmitters using receivers, map and compass. They encourage young people to take part.

- **Learn wilderness survival skills.** It's satisfying to know how to start a fire, follow a trail, forage for edible plants and find shelter. Consult *Willy Whitefeather's Outdoor Survival Handbook for Kids* (Roberts Rinehart, 1997) by Willy Whitefeather

    There are excellent organizations dedicated to teaching these nearly lost skills as well as many books on the topic. Before setting off on any adventure make sure to have safety gear and a backup plan. Always inform others of your whereabouts.

- **Enjoy the snow.** The temporary nature of the white stuff in most areas tempts kids to get outdoors. Build snow sculptures and snow forts, engage in rousing snowball fights, go snowshoeing. Sledding is a time-honored pastime requiring little more than a rudimentary slope. There are also commercially run toboggan chutes, often with discounts available to groups. To build lifelong skills, learn how to ski. The Ski and Snowboard Association www.ussa.org 435-649-9090 coordinates nationwide programs in skiing and snowboarding for youth.

- **Toss a boomerang.** United States Boomerang Association www.usba.org promotes the science and sport of boomerangs through festivals, tournaments and informal games.
- **Develop active family traditions.** Set up a volleyball net when the cousins come over, collect litter along the beach every Labor Day, play croquet when grandma visits, take evening walks each month during the full moon.
- **Try disc golf.** Sometimes mistakenly called Frisbee golf, the game involves tossing discs and is set up on with rules similar to golf. But it's usually free to play since most courses are located in public parks. For a listing of courses by zipcode and other details, contact the Professional Disc Golf Association www.pdga.com 706-261-6342.
- **Go bowling.** Fit in a few games during open bowl sessions. If the interest is there, form leagues. The United States Bowling Congress www.bowl.com 800-514-BOWL sponsors leagues and tournaments.
- **Consider unique sports** such as spelunking, dog sledding, water polo, horse acrobatics, kayaking or synchronized swimming.
- **Enjoy the ice.** Skating rinks offer lessons and open sessions. Sports take the skill farther. Check out U.S. Speedskating www.usspeedskating.org, U.S. Figure Skating www.usfigureskating.org, or USA Hockey wwa.usahockey.com. Look into lesser-known ice sports. United States Curling Association www.usacurl.org organizes the game played by moving granite discs on ice and USA

Broomball www.usabroomball.com officiates a sport similar to hockey but played on ice without skates.

- **Try table games.** Pocket billiards, commonly known as pool, brings all ages together and teaches strategy and physics. Check out the Billiard Congress of America http://home.bca-pool.com or www.generationpool.com. Try the lively game of ping pong, known formally as table tennis, governed by U.S.A. Table Tennis www.usatt.org.
- **Climb the walls.** Climbing gyms train people of all ages in the skills they need to climb safely. USA Climbing http://usaclimbing.net 888-944-4244 promotes sport and speed climbing.

My daughter is one of those kids who can't sit still. When she was very young there was no way I could take her to a homeschool meeting unless I found ways to let her move her body. Many times I ended up being the "play lady" with all the younger kids. I would pile the coats over chairs or move a table on its side and let the kids pretend all sorts of things. Sometimes they were animals and they had burrows under there (I encouraged them to avoid assuming large carnivore identities due to the inevitable snarling). Or I helped them make up games that involved hand signals instead of yelling. There's no point having a homeschool meeting and expecting the kids to have no fun.

When she and I go on homeschool outings we try to choose only the active ones. Sometimes we are stuck with a guide who stands and lectures for a long time before letting us tour the cave or watch the demonstration we came to see. I taught my daughter some techniques to help her. She flexes her muscles while sitting or standing (tightens her abdominals, curls her toes, etc). This provides her with a way to release tension and gives her a sense of movement even though she is still "behaving."

We have never permitted her to be labeled as hyperactive. We help her channel her need for movement appropriately and try to look at her energy as a positive quality. Now that she is ten years old she has been learning rock climbing with her uncle and his girlfriend. That gives her a lot of confidence and this translates into an ability to be physically tolerant of sitting still when necessary.

—Nora, New Hampshire

- **Value the physical benefits of work.** Fitness isn't all fun and games. Beyond the meaning and satisfaction of helping out, there are enormous physical benefits in active chores.
- **Consider the wealth of team sports available.** Rugby, rowing, lacrosse, soccer, baseball, softball, field hockey, volleyball and more.

Resources

Online

- **Amateur Athletic Union** (AAU) promotes sports such as wrestling, cross country, gymnastics and soccer, including church and club teams. AAU teams go up to the national level including the Junior Olympic Games. http://aausports.org 800-AAU-4USA
- **Homeschool SportsNet** helps homeschoolers network to form teams. www.hspn.net 540-636-3713
- **National Christian School Athletic Association** provides homeschool groups and/or families benefits including team participation through a liaison service, and reduced rates to camps and tournaments. www.ncsaa.org 724-846-2764

Books

- *Camp Out!: The Ultimate Kids' Guide* (Workman, 2007) by Lynn Burnelle.
- *The Everything Fishing Book: Grab Your Tackle Box and Get Hooked on America's Favorite Outdoor Sport* (Adams, 2003) by Ronnie Garrison.
- *365 Activities for Fitness, Food, and Fun for the Whole Family* (McGraw-Hill, 2001) by Julia Sweet.

Health & Safety

"He who has health has hope; and he who has hope has everything."—Arabic proverb

Daily choices lead to a healthy lifestyle. But the messy, loud and often wildly unpredictable process of raising children doesn't lend itself to doing things "right" all the time, especially because there is no one right way. What is nourishing to one child is toxic to another. We can simply aim for greater awareness in our choices. What activities enliven your family? What foods bring energy or relaxed focus? What daily patterns of rest and motion best suit your household? What interactions build emotional resilience in your children?

Starting Places

- **Use creative conflict resolution.** Even very young children can be taught to set aside a disputed toy and discuss possible solutions to the problem. As children get older they can learn to recognize and defuse situations before they escalate. They can also understand that it's possible to channel strong emotion and conflict into positive problem solving. Different parts of our brain control the actions we perform. Aggression is

---

Food Choices Linked To Behavior and Learning

Every cell in our bodies is made up of what we eat and drink. Heavily processed products contain a number of ingredients that have more to do with the chemistry of shelf life and consumer appeal than they do with the sort of true nutritional value found in food. Even whole foods may not supply what we need. According to USDA data, random samples of fruits and vegetables now show 26 percent less calcium, 36 percent less iron and 29 percent less vitamin C compared to 1975. This is linked to conventional farming methods that deplete the soil. In contrast, organic farming methods result in improved nutrient levels. And children eating organic diets show significantly lower pesticide residue in their bodies. This is directly related to health, behavior and learning.

- Pesticide residues found in blood samples are six times higher in children eating conventional food compared to those eating organic food.
- According to the National Academy of Sciences, chemicals are up to ten times more toxic to children than adults relative to body weight, since children have developing brains and are less able to detoxify their bodies.
- Fifty-percent of a child's lifetime cancer risk is accumulated in the first two years of life according to the EPA.
- The FDA reports that half of all conventional produce contains measurable pesticide residue and the U.S. Centers for Disease Control acknowledges that a main source of a child's pesticide exposure is food.
- Half of all insecticide used in the U.S. is organophosphate pesticides (OP). Now, 95 percent of all Americans tested have OP residue in their blood according to the U.S. Department of Health and Human Services. The levels of OP found in blood samples are twice as high in children as adults. OP is linked to developmental delays, hyperactivity, learning disabilities, behavior disorders and motor dysfunction.

Media Choices Related to Self-Perception

Young people can't help but be influenced by media of all kinds. Wealth, leisure and extreme attractiveness is presented as the norm in popular culture. This distorts reality, often causing youth to make negative assumptions about themselves. That can lead to damaging behavior. For example, studies show that the more often teen-aged girls read beauty and fashion magazines the more likely they are to engage in dangerous forms of dieting. Over half of all teenage girls regularly read such magazines. Boys too find that the powerful, muscle-bound men portrayed in movies, magazines and video games negatively affect their body image and self-worth. From the earliest years we can help our children by making wise media choices. And we can teach them to apply critical thinking (see Chapter Eleven), enabling them to balance the messages of popular culture with realistic perceptions.

controlled by the lower, or reptilian brain. So, when we respond aggressively, this lower brain is triggered. When we respond with self-control we are using higher ordered thinking, calling on greater thought and humanity. Share books such as *We Can Work It Out: Conflict Resolution for Children* (Tricycle, 2004) by Barbara Kay Polland and *The Kids' Guide to Working Out Conflicts: How to Keep Cool, Stay Safe, and Get Along* (Free Spirit, 2004) by Naomi Drew.

- **Check out the local Red Cross** for CPR classes, babysitting certification and emergency preparedness sessions. Young people can form Red Cross clubs or volunteer for the Youth Services programs. www.redcross.org
- **Pay attention to safety**. Brainstorm a list of household rules together, talk about why they are necessary and post them. Ask a police officer to be a speaker at your next home-school meeting. Visit the local fire station to learn about fire safety and prevention. Make an exit plan for your home in case of emergency which includes a location where everyone should meet after leaving the house.. If young children show interest in fire, explain that they can learn about fire only with a parent. Then look up some experiments to do together in order to satisfy this curiosity in a safe manner.
- **Honor intuition.** When children are aware of and act on their intuition they are using an "inner knowing" which informs them before they can consciously access the information. A key component in intuition is paying attention to one's own body and the feelings associated with the bodily sensations. This is reinforced by adults around them.
- **Research favorite foods** and the nutrients found in those foods. Look into the nutritional and environmental science underlying mainstream diets as well as raw food diets, vegetarian and vegan diets, macrobiotic diets, Weston Price diet and other whole-foods approaches to eating.
- **Cook together.** Children can provide invaluable assistance getting dinner on the table as they learn to peel, chop and blend. Enjoy children's cookbooks such as *Kids' Fun and Healthy Cookbook* (DK Children, 2007) by Nicola Graimes or *Simply in Season Children's Cookbook* (Herald Pr, 2006) by Mark Beach and Julie Kauffman.
- **Make multicultural meals.** Teach your children to make family favorites as well as dishes from other cultural traditions. Younger children may enjoy the recipes highlighted in *Let's Eat: What Children Eat Around the World* (Henry Holt, 2004) by Beatrice Hollyer while older youth can make treats from *The International Cookbook for Kids* (Marshall Cavendish, 2004) by Matthew Locricchio.

- **Garden together.** Nothing encourages a child's interest in eating freshly harvested fruits, veggies and herbs more than being involved in the process of growing them. If you don't have the space for your own garden, plant in containers in a sunny window, sign up for a plot with a nearby community garden or petition your city to create community gardens in vacant lots. Find more information through the American Community Gardening Association www.communitygarden.org Donate overabundant harvests to your local food bank.
- **Make food choices a family matter.** Involve children in planning meals and selecting foods. Casually offer unfamiliar foods, recognizing that a child may not try them or like the taste until after repeated exposure. Studies show that children are more receptive to healthy foods and new tastes when they have background knowledge about the food, and are involved in the selection and preparation.
- **Calculate differences between processed and whole foods.** Compare the price and nutritional difference between a bag of potatoes and a bag of potato chips. Or homemade whole oats versus boxed cereals. Or a whole chicken versus lunchmeat.

Our health lessons started over meals. Kids are naturally curious about the things they do regularly. We talked about food groups, nutrition and digestion while we ate, which then lead to trips to the library and exploration of other body systems. I bought a body systems book that has a model of the human body in it and we've pulled in episodes of the Magic School Bus too. The biggest impact it's made on my life is that when my children ask for a particular snack I can say, "Sorry. You just ate something from the grains group an hour ago. Why don't you pick something from a different food group?" and they do.   —Karen, Texas

---

- **Demonstrate the science behind healthy habits.** For example, conduct experiments to learn about mold, viruses and bacteria in order to better understand the purpose of hand washing.
- **Use descriptive words for feelings.** "Happy" and "mad" don't express the full range of feeling. The more words our children know, the more able they are to identify, understand and deal with emotions. Describe emotions in your conversations. Use words like frustrated, relieved, surprised, lonely, jealous, excited, frightened, embarrassed, discouraged, confident, annoyed, satisfied, worried, anxious and optimistic.
- **Understand emotions through acting.** Take turns calling out different emotions and trying to display them through facial expression and body language. Or the reverse, act them out and try to guess what the nonverbal cues mean. Encourage your children to use puppets, stuffed animals and other toys to play-act scenarios.
- **Discuss feelings as well as ideas.** Talk about the emotions and motivations of characters in movies, television and books. "Why do you think she wouldn't answer?" "How could you tell he was jealous?" "What would make someone do that?"
- **Enjoy learning about oneself.** Take some tests in *Psychology for Kids: 40 Fun Tests That Help You Learn About Yourself* (Free Spirit, 2008) by Jonni Kincher, Julie S. Bach and Pamela Espeland. Keep a journal or notebook to write down feelings, keep track of favorite moments, draw self-portraits. A journal that supplies prompts is helpful. Younger children may like to use *All About Me, Revised Edition: A Keepsake Journal for Kids* (Rising Moon,

2004) by Linda Kranz and teens might like *List Your Self* (Andrews McMeel, 2008) by Ilene Segalove and Paul Bob Velick.

- **Embrace individuality.** Every year make an "All About Me" book using stapled together pages, a scrapbook or photo album. Include a drawn self-portrait and photo, information about family activities, favorite foods and places, and answers to prompts like "What I'm afraid of" and "What makes me happy." Don't show surprise or dismay over a child's answers, just help with writing or spelling if necessary. Such books help your child come to know him- or herself better. Over the years a collection of these homemade books will become an invaluable record of your child's growing self-awareness.

- Remain open. Listen, answer questions honestly and talk about problems in a shared search for understanding. In this atmosphere of trust, young people can freely discuss big issues such as sex, drug use, mental health, relationship violence, lifestyle choices, etc. Your preteens and teens can find suggestions for improving communication and taking responsibility in *Bringing Up Parents: The Teenager's Handbook* (ReadHowYouWant, 2009) by Alex J. Packer and *The How Rude! Handbook of Family Manners for Teens: Avoiding Strife in Family Life* (Free Spirit, 2004) by Alex J. Packer

---

My daughter and I don't like the same clothes or TV shows or music. But we like to read a lot of the same things. She really likes Oprah's magazine. The articles talk a lot about being who you are and making the best of things. Anything that keeps two-way communication going with a teenager is good in my book.
—Molly Renebeck

- **Promote positive self-talk.** Our internal dialog not only reflects our emotional state, it reinforces it. Many of us still struggle with negative self-talk we learned in our own childhoods, such as "I'll never be good enough." Positive self-talk can motivate us to maintain healthy behaviors, respect ourselves and others, remain calm in stressful situations, and more. We promote a child's positive self-talk by enforcing behavioral guidelines but not diminishing our acceptance of the child. We also do so by avoiding overgeneralizations, emphasizing solutions rather than problems, and affirming the importance of mistakes as learning tools. Try reading *Incredible You! 10 Ways to Let Your Greatness Shine Through* (Hay House, 2005) by Wayne W. Dyer.

Resources

Online

- **Girls Inc.** focuses on healthy approaches to self-awareness, emotions, body image and choices. www.girlsinc-online.org
- **Neuroscience for Kids** offers experiments, games, Q & A and extensive links. http://faculty.washington.edu/chudler/neurok.html
- **PBS Teachers** supplies a rich array of educational resources including health and fitness. www.pbs.org/teachers
- **World's Healthiest Foods** provides nutritional content and recipes. www.whfoods.com/foodstoc.php

Books

- *Have You Filled a Bucket Today: A Guide to Daily Happiness for Kids* (Ferne, 2006) by Carol McCloud.
- *What to Do When You Grumble Too Much: A Kid's Guide to Overcoming Negativity* (Magination, 2006) by Dawn Huebner.
- *What to Do When Your Temper Flares: A Kid's Guide to Overcoming Problems With Anger* (Magination, 2007) by Dawn Huebner.
- *What to Do When You Worry Too Much: A Kid's Guide to Overcoming Anxiety* (Magination, 2005) by Dawn Huebner.

CHAPTER THIRTEEN

The Arts

Creative Expression

"There is a vitality, a life-force, an energy, a quickening that is translated through you into action and because there is only one of you in all of time, this expression is unique. And if you block it, it will never exist through any other medium and be lost. The world will not have it. It is not your business to determine how good it is nor how valuable nor how it compares with other expressions. It is your business to keep it yours clearly and directly, to keep the channel open."
—Martha Graham

Cave painting, drumming, chanting and dance are thought to be among the earliest forms of art. Individually or collectively, art helped people shape ordinary reality into something that held larger meaning. It still does today.

Artistic expression is second nature for young children. They draw and paint eagerly, sing unselfconsciously, choreograph their own dances and act out dramas using whatever is nearby as props. Art is accessible long before children are able to interpret or master it.

There are as many reasons to get involved in the arts as there are individual artists. Here are just a few.

- Art is an expression of the human condition. Through art the child begins to understand our shared humanity; recognizing that others confront grief, love, injustice, suffering, joy and humor.
- Art teaches about the way reality is perceived by the artist, mirrored in the culture and responded to by the viewer.
- Sustained involvement in such arts as music or theater is correlated with success in math and reading, but more importantly, the arts promote achievement across the spectrum of academic and personal development.

- Art asks for a personal response rather than a right or wrong answer. Highly individual, art engages on many levels. Both experiencing and making art prompt a child to go deeper.
- Many works of art expose a child to cultural icons and standards known across other disciplines.
- Young people who study a musical instrument show improvement in wider areas such
- as verbal ability and visual pattern ability.
- Project-based art promotes high-level learning: active discovery, hands-on application of what is being learned, generativity, skilled guidance and critical analysis.
- Beauty and meaning are human necessities.

There are endless ways to keep the arts alive in our children's lives. Many of these have to do with the attitude we cultivate in our homes and beyond. Do we listen to music from other eras, other parts of the world, from new artists? Are we in the audience for local theater and dance performances? Do we opine on art before we see it and feel it? Do we express our own creativity?

I am a former mechanical engineer who never took a single art class in all my years of schooling (through a master's degree), and I have no artistic talent whatsoever. From her toddler days, my firstborn has demonstrated her love of making art – daily.

What was I to do? I gave her all kinds of supplies and an area (the kitchen table) where she could work whenever she wanted; we continue to just scoot her things out of the way at meal times.

I introduced her to more than just drawing and painting by getting kits for soapstone carving, calligraphy, wheel-thrown pottery, origami, and more, but drawing and painting have remained her favorites.

I have taken her to see artists (sculptors, painters, wood carvers, glass blowers) at work in their studios and at art fairs. I have taken her to many galleries and museums where she has been exposed to art from a variety of time periods, cultures, styles, and media, and from relatively unknown local artists to the masters. Sometimes these works of art have inspired her to try something new at home (such as when she saw her first pointillism painting), but more often her ideas seemed to spring from her own imagination.

I have let her know about every art class I can find, and she has taken advantage of many of them at our local art museum, a private studio, and even at the local children's theater. Although she always enjoyed all of her art classes, most of the children's classes were very structured (everyone made the same thing, the same way), and they were often more craft than art. This did not deter her, and she continued to create constantly at home. Pablo Picasso famously said, "All children are artists. The problem is how to remain an artist once he grows up."

Caroline is growing up, but as an adolescent she has not lost her strong drive to create art. She became interested in Anime and Manga, Japanese-style drawing, which led her to read numerous "how-to" art books in this area, and she was able to take an Anime drawing class with an artist who owns a comic book store. Last year she took a drawing class at the art museum that was geared toward older children and it provided much more technical instruction than she had received in earlier classes there. Recently our branch library had an Anime art contest for teenagers (which included 12-year-olds) and Caroline's painting of a dragon won the Viewer's Choice award. This was very inspiring to her and she soon began reading "how-to" painting books and asked me to find a painting class for her.

I found what she now calls her "favorite class of all time!" It is a weekly "independent study" painting class with a local artist. It meets during the school day at a craft store. The students are mostly older women and one other teenage homeschooler. Caroline loves the quiet atmosphere! She started out with watercolors, is now working in acrylics, and plans to try oils next. She tells the teacher what medium she wants to use, decides what she wants to paint, and the teacher gives her all the necessary information about supplies and tools, helps her with techniques, etc. Her younger sister has watched and learned, and now she is painting with watercolors and acrylics too. Caroline is now painting many pictures at home and is always anxious to show them to her teacher at the next class session. I do not foresee any end to Caroline's enjoyment of art. —Susan, Alabama

Arts opportunities can be surprisingly cost effective. Nearly every organization providing discounts or free admission to schools or students will offer those same perks to homeschoolers. In some cases families find that joining a group or network of other homeschoolers helps them to qualify for certain programs.

There are many ways to stay informed about upcoming programs and find out about discounted admission to cultural events. Subscribe to regional publications and e-zines, become a public radio member, join area arts organizations. In this way you are more likely to have access to cut-rate pricing, preferred seating and member's only events. Most museums have reciprocal membership arrangements providing benefits at sister institutions. Many metropolitan regions offer information on reduced priced admission to arts through cultural foundations or visitor's bureaus. Sometimes you'll be notified of "last minute" (usually a few days' notice) ticket price reductions, open seats for workshops listed as sold out and other surprising values. When the arts do seem expensive, remember the value of what you are supporting.

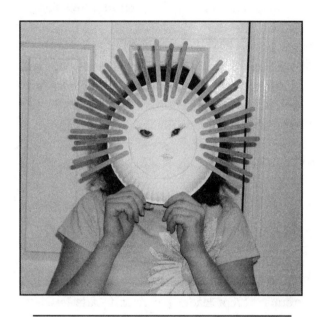

I homeschooled my kids practically for free in NYC. One cost to me each year was subway passes that let us go everywhere together. The other thing I spent money on was a membership in one of the major museums. That gave us access to all sorts of partnered arts institutions and the hundreds of children's programs they offered. We made use of the incredible library resources by ordering any materials we wanted and took advantage of sessions teaching things like book binding and sitar playing. I remember the kids taking free fencing lessons taught by Olympians, performing

in plays that they helped write, dancing on the grass during concerts at the park, that sort of thing. My father the skeptic visited us for a week in one of our early years of homeschooling and came away a convert. He realized that choice was such an important element in education and where do you have more choices than homeschooling in a big city? My kids come back to visit all the time. NYC is full of excellent memories and wonderful friends for them.

—Jude, New York

Chances are you can find arts classes and workshops for youth of all ages. Community arts centers, nearby colleges and local theaters are good starting places. Some homeschool groups arrange their own programs by relying on the expertise of parents, others hire professionals in the field. Increasingly, collaborative efforts in the arts are taking place. Homeschoolers work on murals along with senior citizens, participate in open invitation drumming circles, build mosaic planters with garden club members, act in plays with experienced thespians, join established musical groups, accept leadership roles in arts festivals, and more. Learning about culture takes place best in the midst of culture.

If you want those involved in the arts to share their work directly with your homeschool group, contact them. Describe your hopes of connecting children to the arts. Offer a stipend whenever possible. This offer acknowledges that these professionals are taking time from their own schedules, plus bringing supplies for demonstration or participation purposes. You can also offer perks. Offer promotions in your newsletter or website, as well as ongoing opportunities to find private students. Homeschoolers regularly find artists who are willing take part in workshops, classes and demonstrations. Many times they've also developed highly fruitful relationships with these artists resulting in community art projects, internships and lasting friendships.

My 10 year old loves her homeschool theater class where she gets to spend three hours a week working on a Shakespeare play. It's a small group so everyone gets at least one big part — compared to having to share parts with 30 kids in a classroom for one play done per year (as she did in school).

—Margaret S., Texas

We met every other week in the Unitarian Fellowship Hall for years. We found amazing people to share their work with us. I remember a dairy farmer, stamp collector, retired air traffic controller, newspaper editor, electrician, so many others. I arranged for speakers who were more on the artsy side since I'm a watercolorist. A potter brought in a heavy foot-pedal wheel and enough clay for everyone to try. That was a memorable mess. I think I can still see some of the dried clay on the ceiling. One time the kids carded wool and learned to make yarn on drop spindles. Another time they learned some kind of ethnic sword dance. If either of my kids were home right now they would probably remember what country it originated from but I forgot. Also the whole group of us learned from a mime (a group miming together is hysterically funny), and painted tattoo designs on our jeans and made Calder style mobiles. Over the years the kids were exposed to so many role models of people following their dreams. That's a lesson in itself.

—Jackie Milner-Foster

Smaller towns and rural areas have cultural richness to offer too. Homeschoolers simply need to work harder to find a diverse array of choices. Check with the area arts council. Consult librarians for information about local organizations. Ask people involved in music, theater, dance and other cultural disciplines for their suggestions. Pay attention to newspapers, radio and local blogs. Somewhere not far from you there are plays in rehearsal, sculptures forming, videographers filming, musicians practicing, quilts taking shape and dancers longing for an audience. Art is alive even in the most remote communities, although sometimes it takes people interested in energizing cultural affairs to get others involved. You may be one of those people.

A few years ago some people set out to transform our little Arts Week into something better than the crafts fair and high school performance that it had been. I joined up with the committee. I won't even sign this because I don't want to take any credit but I do want to brag about what we now call All Arts Week. This showcase fills every meeting space in our town including churches, schools and clubs. It kicks off with an art parade to which we invite every single child to participate. The whole week has performances, exhibits and dinners hosted by many organizations. What we're fostering the last few years are months of preparatory engagement so that groups of people work together to make All Arts Week a series of events that get more people involved. I can see the civic pride as well as the artistic sensibilities that All Arts Week has given my children.

—Unsigned

Our son Alex took some classes at the Apple store that really advanced his skills in making movies. When he was younger he liked to make stop-action animation and got really good at it. The last year or so he's been collecting videos of people playing music and talking about music. It started out sort of on a lark to see how many different kinds of music he could get but now it's a quest. He's really into it. We are digging deep to help him find people who play unusual instruments or sing in foreign languages. Alex has digital footage including German folks singers, gamelan players, a barbershop quartet and little kids singing their favorite songs. The best parts are Alex's interviews with the musicians. No matter what he does with the material, he's created something unique. It all started because he wanted to use more Mac applications. Alex doesn't play an instrument or sing at all!

—Tom and Alicia Moore

Of course we also enjoy homeschooled artists who share their talents with us. They play bagpipes, photograph graffiti, dance the zapateado, carve soapstone. They transform imagination into art, and as we know, that changes everything.

Starting Places

- **Keep art supplies available** and take them along on outings. One's perceptions are awakened by new places. Try different materials such as pastels, watercolor pencils and charcoal. Use them on different papers, on tree bark, on stone. Notice how texture, form and color abound in the natural world.

- **Carry a sketchbook** to ensure it's available for inspiration. Consider asking others to contribute a sketch. One artist enjoyed asking people she met to add a quick drawing of an imaginary creature to her sketchbook. She has been collecting these sketches for years, keeping them between the pages of her own drawings. They provide a glimpse into the fantastical realm of friends as well as strangers, inspire her art and help her family recognize that people of all ages continue to imagine.

- **Encourage studies of the same area** over a period of months. Lie on the living room rug or sit on a park bench. Look at this place from many angles, in different light, and then express that viewpoint in pencil, clay, collage or other media. The study can be expanded. Draw the scene as it might have looked thousands of years ago, or to a creature that sees only temperature, or from a worm's eye view.
- **Gather musicians together regularly.** Combine instruments, however unlikely, for improvisation and fun. Consider forming a homeschoolers' jam session, choir or band. Or open the ensemble to youth and adults of all ages. Whatever the style—bluegrass, chamber music, reggae, blues—it will lead your children deeper into the mysteries of music itself.
- **Combine music and movement.** Local classes for young children can be found through these organizations:

    American Orff-Schulwerk Association www.aosa.org 440-543-5366
    Kindermusik www.kindermusik.com 800-628-5687
    Music for Young Children www.myc. com 800-561-1692

- **Respect a child's aesthetic sense.** Your child may prefer unusual clothing ensembles or the juxtaposition of odd items displayed on a bookcase. Why not? Each of us forms a relationship with beauty and meaning. A child's choices are reflections of his or her taste.
- **Make photography a family endeavor.** Pass the camera around to get each family member's perspective of an event. Frame your child's photos, post them on a family blog, encourage your child to mash music with photos and video, talk about photos seen in magazines and galleries, get books about photography out of the library.
- **Talk about art, music, dance, theater** with the same interest level that you might use for conversations about sports or what to eat for dinner. Make it a pleasure.
- **Create art that makes a statement.** Sculpt your opinion, sing your feelings, dance your beliefs.
- **Organize a homeschool art fair.** Arrange an exhibition at a local coffee shop, church, shopping mall or recreation center. As with showings of adult works, request that homeschool artists submit several works although only one may be selected for display. Before it is shown have the work framed or at least mounted on a mat. Three-dimensional pieces such as ceramics and sculpture can be hung securely or placed on shelving. Show the title and artist's name on tags near the work. Make sure to recognize all submissions with a certificate. It isn't helpful to award "best of show" or make comparisons.
- **Involve everyone.** When setting up any cultural arts event, from puppet show to choral performance, recognize that everyone has talent and energy to offer. A special event put on by a few for the enjoyment of many is not as successful as a participatory event with the creative efforts of people working together.
- **Sing.** Singing is wonderful for the mood as well as the body. When parents sing unselfconsciously, children are empowered to make singing a more natural part of their lives. Sing silly songs about your daily activities, make up lyrics together, perform an original ditty as a gift.
- **Enjoy music that sparks learning** in a variety of subjects. Musicians United for Songs in the Classroom shares songs as teaching tools to engage the learner. www.learningfromlyrics.org

- **Use the brain-building tool of compare and contrast**. Casually use it every now and then. Compare favorite TV shows to plays, puppet shows and dance performances. Contrast an ethnic festival where one is exposed to the games, food, dances and music of a culture to the presentation of that culture in the media. When discussing any aspect of the arts it can be valuable to look at it from other viewpoints.
- **Take in live music** whenever possible. If you live near a college town or urban area your choices will be larger. Often you can find free or low cost performances at festivals, ethnic fairs, period music celebrations, student and faculty recitals, and brown bag lunch concerts. It may help younger children if you talk beforehand about what to watch for and listen for in order to enhance the child's attention span. Children may enjoy a concert more if they are allowed to bring along a small stuffed animal or toy that can dance on their laps to the music, or perhaps draw their impressions of the performance on a small sketchpad.
- **Attend plays.** Children tend to enjoy a play more if, beforehand, you read a synopsis or a picture book based on the play. Encourage your children to take theater workshop classes. Attend friends' plays and other performances, not only as a show of support but also to help your children understand the effort that goes into a production.
- **Check out community schools of art** near you. To find community schools of art check with area arts centers, theatres, and art museums for programs. Also ask people involved in the arts if they have considered taking individual students.

I've been involved in Hungarian folk dancing since the age of 12. What started out as a few classes turned into

joining a performing company, performing in several states, and eventually traveling to Hungary to dance after my senior year of homeschooling. It has been an all-around amazing experience for me—stage experience, learning the language and about Hungarian culture, and also discovering other cultures at the many diversity events that I danced at.

—Kate Steven, 19

I like learning interesting stuff. I'm taking woodcarving lessons. My teacher is a really nice lady. At her studio you have to be a minimum age to do it. I wasn't the age to do it, so you've got to take some private lessons so she knows you aren't going to start attacking people with the carving knife. The first lesson you make an otter letter opener … You carve it with the knife, then you get out the power tools, sand it down, then you hand sand it, then you put tung oil which makes it shiny, but it's flammable. It's very fun. I've got a lot of ideas that I want to do for my next project ... My next goal I'm making a dachshund, it's hard to do but it's really rewarding when you finish it.   —Josh, 12

- **Check into apprenticeships and mentoring** experiences with musicians, artists, actors, costumers, stagehands, dancers, vocalists and others in the arts field.

- **Sew.** Make useful, creative projects together using such guides as *Sewing Fun for Kids: Patchwork, Gifts and More!* (C&T, 2006) by Lynda Milligan and Nancy Smith, or *Handmade Home: Simple Ways to Repurpose Old Materials into New Family Treasures* (Trumpeter, 2009) by Amanda Blake Soule.

- **Make art a helpful diversion.** Keep different art resources reserved for travel or waiting at the dentist's office. The *Anti-Coloring Book* series (Holt) by Susan Striker and Edward Kimmel serve this purpose well.

- **Share art secretly.** Make a tiny house or staircase out of found objects such as sticks, pebbles and pinecones to place near trees in the park. Write poems or messages on shells and hide them on the beach for others to find. Wrap a small handmade gift with a card reading "for the next person to find" and leave in a crowded place. For more ideas check out *The Guerilla Art Kit* (Princeton Architectural, 2007) by Keri Smith.

- **Incorporate music into all areas of learning.** Talk about the meaning of song lyrics, notice how musical style historically reflects the culture from which it emerged, look for the links between music and math.

- **Share talents** with others. Perform with your water glass choir at a community concert, make a felted wall hanging with members of a nearby sheltered workshop, contribute a work of art to a benefit show.

- **Enjoy puppets.** Books and websites offer great suggestions for creating homemade puppets. Try *Make Your Own Puppets & Puppet Theaters* (Williamson, 2005) by Carolyn Carreiro. Check out Puppeteers of America www.puppeteers.org

- **Make gifts.** Give creativity away. Compose a song in Grandma's honor, invent a cookie recipe for Dad, paint a portrait of a friend. For more ideas, consult project guides such as *D.I.Y.: Kids* (Princeton Architectural, 2007) by Ellen Lupton and Julia Lupton, *Toymaking With Children* (Floris, 2003) by Freya Jaffke, *The Art of Feltmaking: Basic Techniques for Making Jewelry, Miniatures, Dolls, Buttons, Wearables, Puppets, Masks and Fine Art Pieces* (Watson-Guptill, 1997) by Anne Vickrey, *Kids Knitting: Projects for Kids of all Ages* (Artisan, 2003) by Melanie Falick.

- **Enjoy natural materials.** Create designs by adhering dry beans and seeds to cardboard or wood, build mazes outdoors with rocks and sticks, weave with fibers and found objects. For more ideas consult *Nature's Art Box: From T-Shirts to Twig Baskets, 65 Cool Projects for Crafty Kids to Make with Natural Materials You Can Find Anywhere* (Storey, 2003) by Laura C. Martin.

- **Take art walks.** Identify a theme of interest. An architecture walk may focus on particular structures such as houses of worship and the meaning reflected in different styles of buildings you encounter. A sculpture walk may follow a map of the city's historical district, but pay attention to unexpected things your children identify as sculpture. Try a "found art" walk with a camera or sketchbook, capturing what each person on the walk finds interesting. Or take a collage walk, where you and your children pick up objects to use later in an assemblage. If you are going with a group on an art walk you may want to find an expert to lead the walk.

- **Make museums fun.** These institutions are repositories of knowledge and creativity, meant to be enjoyed. Rather than make a museum trip an ordeal, stop by often to take in a new exhibit and don't stay long. Let your children guide the way according to what piques their interest. Fitting museums and art galleries into our lives makes the collections more accessible and allows our children to feel comfortable there. For teens, museum visits are more enjoyable when friends are along, or if they choose to go for their own reasons, perhaps to sketch a particular work or to volunteer as museum docents.

Resources

Online

- **Artcyclopedia:** The Guide to Great Art on the Internet enables searches by artist, medium, subject or nationality. www.artcyclopedia. com
- **Artslynx International** offers theater, dance and visual arts resources. www.artistsresourceguide.org
- Incredible Art provides podcasts, student art galleries, webrings, art activities, blogs, art zines, news and more. www.incredibleart.org
- **Inside Art** www.eduweb.com/insideart/ provides an Art History game taking the user into the story of how works of art are created. Also check the EduWeb offerings in performing arts www.eduweb.com/portfolio/performingarts.php and other visual arts www. eduweb.com/portfolio/visualarts.php
- **Last.FM** www.last.fm or Pandora of the Music Genome Project http://pandora.com assists users in finding music they might otherwise have missed. Type in a preferred artist and the site will play other, lesser-known artists who have related musical styles.

- **Music Teachers National Association** database lets you locate music teachers by instrument and zipcode. www.mtna.org
- **National Association of Teachers of Singing** helps you find a professional voice instructor in your area. www.nats.org
- **Sound Junction** enables creating and discovering all kinds of music. www.soundjunction. org
- **Youth and Music International** is a network providing greater access to young people as performers and listeners. It links youth in over eighty countries and is one of the oldest and largest cultural youth organizations in the world. www.jmi.net

Books

- *Drawing with Children* (Tarcher, rev, 1996) by Mona Brookes.
- *Drawing for Older Children & Teens* (Tarcher/ Perigee, 1991) by Mona Brookes.
- *Make Your Own Playdough, Paint, and Other Craft Materials: Easy Recipes to Use with Young Children* (Redleaf, 2007) by Patricia Caskey.
- *The Creative Family: How to Encourage and Nurture Family Connections* (Trumpeter, 2008) by Amanda Blake Soule.

CHAPTER FOURTEEN

Language Arts & Foreign Languages

Language Arts

"Language exerts hidden power, like a moon on the tides."
—Rita Mae Brown

We make sense of our lives through the stories we are told and those we tell ourselves. We are drawn to and remember these tales. The tradition of telling stories has a much longer history than the written word. Richly distinctive cultures all over the world were informed and inspired by stories. They gave people a reason to gather together, to cherish their shared history, to transmit wisdom, to laugh and ponder, to awaken to possibilities. The Homeric epic poems, *Iliad* and the *Odyssey,* are collected works passed down in this manner. The ancient Celtic poem *Amergin's Song* is thought to have been told aloud for millenia. African storytellers were keepers of cultural heritage as well as skilled musicians and entertainers. The most unchanged are the sacred Vedic mantras, memorized and recited, sometimes backwards as well as forward. This oral tradition, still kept alive today in many parts of the world, resonates in the way humanity relates to stories.

When listening to a storyteller, the audience often knew the stories well. They participated by calling out phrases, singing or dancing to accompany the story. The tale came alive in a way that it cannot do in any other form of presentation. Even today some young children can't help but get involved when listening to a story. They may instinctively call out a repeating phrase or yell a warning to a main character. They may tap their knees in excitement, hum a tune or otherwise accompany the tale's progress. Some children can barely stop themselves from crawling, jumping or at least fidgeting. They feel the story. They become the story.

Although we read to our children regularly we can go beyond the printed page. We can make storytelling a family tradition. Children enjoy hearing true tales, especially about themselves. Tell them about the day they joined your family—the weather, their appearance and behavior that first day, the comments of siblings and the months of anticipation. Tell them stories of their earliest years—the way he used to cry at the sight of dogs until he finally worked up the courage to pet one and fell in love with all things canine; the time she made friends with another three year old at the airport and the fathers got to talking only to discover they had grown up on the same street. Tell them stories about family members, especially those who have passed away. Help children imagine these people clearly by focusing on acts that were courageous, foolhardy, eccentric or otherwise out of the ordinary.

Children also enjoy tales spun for their enjoyment. Tell an ongoing yarn that features heroic young people, with names similar to theirs, who live in a make-believe world while undergoing a quest to reach a goal. Plot twists and turns can stretch the tale into months of bedtime stories. Your children may want to participate, add their own versions, insist on retellings or tell you stories as well.

Gathering together to tell tales is a tradition nearly as old as clustering around a fire for warmth. Beyond the value of the stories is the ritual itself—that of telling, listening and enjoying together. This has meaning that goes well beyond the story. It's something that no commercial product can ever duplicate.

In today's interconnected world, proficiency in the use of language has never been more important. Linguists predict that it won't be long before a third of the world's population will be able to communicate in English. How do reading, writing and speaking affect our lives?

- When we talk and listen, read and write we make sense of our experiences. We create, generate ideas and find meaning.

- Our communications connect us to one another. Through the artful use of words we can let another person share our perceptions and understand our feelings.

- Literature and poetry take us to the depths of understanding. They lead us to a world that has value well beyond any material wealth.

- Language allows us to transmit stories and ideas across centuries.

- The more words we understand and use, the greater the ability to articulate ideas with precision. The power of the right word to express a feeling or to convey information is invaluable because it says exactly what we mean.

- People form impressions about us based on our words and actions. If our use of language reflects badly on our ability to express ourselves—through poorly written communication or inarticulate speaking—others may make incorrect assumptions about our intentions, intelligence or beliefs.

- The strength of one's vocabulary may relate to the ability to think in more complex ways. It is clearly linked to career success. Psychometrician Johnson O'Connor researched the factors leading to career achievement. His studies took into account age, level of education and other variables, but O'Connor found the same results each time he analyzed the data: the better a person's vocabulary, the greater the correlation with success. Interestingly, he determined that a good vocabulary isn't the result of achievement, it's acquired in advance.

Reading remains a strong pastime. Hours spent reading material on the Internet is booming, but perhaps more surprisingly, the number of people who are reading books remains high. Recent Gallup Poll responses indicated that nearly half of the Americans surveyed were currently reading a book, while fifty years ago less than a quarter of adults gave the same answer. The surge in reading literary books is largest among eighteen to twenty-four year olds. Their rate of increase is three times the growth of all adult readers from 2002 to 2008 according to a survey by the National Endowment for the Arts.

Writing is also on the increase. A new blog is created every second. Reading and writing, however, are only part of what it means to be literate in today's world. We have to be able to find the truth in information that may seem insubstantial or difficult to verify, and to make sense of that information in context. That's because the digital information world requires us to read, write and comprehend in expanded formats. Our children may enjoy the simplicity of writing in a nature journal in the park. They may also like the challenge of expressing themselves by combining text, video, audio, graphics and animation. The concept of language arts is now wide open and more exciting than ever before.

I see by the number of views and positive ratings that my sons have developed a following on YouTube. They post videos that are pretty complicated affairs involving a mash-up of downloaded effects that I don't understand. They run a couple of different websites, some more active than others. I can't begin to explain their conversations about html and flash animation. I do know that Quinn (14) writes a storyline to accompany an animation he produces and that Avery (12) regularly posts long involved tutorials about video games. They meld art and technical writing and have fun. I stand back in awe of what they've taught themselves. At 37 there's no way I could compete with the speed that they learn.
—Steven Johnson, Arizona

For humanity, the capacity to speak and understand language is inborn. It emerges naturally in early childhood as it has throughout time. Unless there are significant problems, all children speak clearly by the time they are in their third year of life. However, representing words on the page with symbols that must be decoded back into silent or spoken speech is much newer to humanity and does not unfold as naturally. It takes a great deal of exposure to the written word and something even more intangible—a combination of readiness, optimal brain maturation and motivation that develops differently in each child. We can't generalize about when a child should be able to read and write in the same way that we tend to do about a toddler's speech. Yet it is assumed that "normal" children should begin to master these highly complex abilities within a short time after their fifth or sixth birthday. In some parts of the world the children are not taught to read until they are around eight years old so that a greater percentage of them will be ready, maximizing success. As homeschoolers we have the privilege of waiting until we see signs of readiness, then feeding that readiness helpfully and in doses lovingly calibrated to the child's eagerness.

Many homeschooling families carefully choose from a mix of materials to help beginning readers, such as enticing read-aloud books and educational games. Most parents adjust their use of these materials to the child. Even a few minutes a day may be too much for a child who is easily frustrated, signaling a lack of readiness or inappropriate materials. Other children may be excited and work through them eagerly to get to greater challenges. Children quite often want to get to the real business of reading what they want to read, *when* they want to read. They let the adults around them know when they want to figure out what a sign in the store means, or ask how to spell a word as they label their own drawings—these are the moments when their learning leaps ahead. This is a lesson in patience that may teach the parent more than the child.

A study conducted in the 1930s followed children who received formal reading instruction at different ages. Initially the early readers had an advantage when tested, although that disappeared by fourth grade. By their teens a more significant difference emerged. The children who were taught to read later were more spontaneous and enthusiastic readers than those taught earlier. Recent research echoes these results. Three studies by New Zealand researcher Sebastian Suggate found that students taught to read when they are five years old have no greater advantage than those who learn to read a few years later. "Because later starters at reading are still learning through play, language, and interactions with adults, their long-term learning is not disadvantaged. Instead, these activities prepare the soil well for later development of reading," Dr. Suggate says.

This also true for homeschoolers. A pilot study of child-led learning among homeschoolers focused on when and how reading ability was attained. Similar methods among parents interviewed for the study were noted. Their overriding goal was to foster a love of reading, so parents followed the child's signs of readiness and any instruction was provided with careful attention to the child's response. Parents also read aloud to their children every day, often for hours. The study's authors, Karen Keys and William Crain found that many children received little or no systematic teaching yet read at or above age level by eight years old. Those who were not reading at age level by eight years old tended to catch up by age eleven. Keys and Crain reported, "almost all the children in our samples—whether they were reading below, at, or above grade levels—seemed to be fulfilling their parents' main goal with respect to reading: they enjoyed reading very much."

Will didn't read until he was about ten years old. I was pretty worried. I didn't show my concern. I expected him to write regular things around here as he got older, like he had to write out the family shopping list and schedule our activities by transferring information to the calendar. Many times he'd yell out to me to spell a word and I'd yell back from wherever I was in the apartment.

Then he started in on reading on his own. It was slow the first few months. He was embarrassed if any of us made a fuss so we ignored him. I swear he read everything in the house. He even read the owner's manual in the car when we were driving. I wonder if this process is more natural. A great deal of creativity has been stored up waiting for more mature transmission to finished product. He is almost done with a screenplay. It's complete with dialogue for many actors, camera direction and plotting elements. It is more complex than anything I could do and yet he has "only" been reading for a few years. —Unsigned

Seven-year-old Sophia's favourite activity for now is reading. She's able to read for five hours a day if I don't stop her.

Sara, age five, reads a lot too. She also likes to make booklets for the unborn baby, write love notes, cut up her own puzzles. In fact they are both "creating" something or other the whole day—including forming clubs!

Hence our only problem is reading! The kids read too much on their own. They refuse to be read to and find my read-alouds too slow. I've a problem keeping up with their reading. We use Sonlight's Readers *and* Read-Alouds.

They can read all the recommended books in half the recommended time. They find my questioning or asking them to narrate back a waste of time. They just want to absorb all the books in a day! We borrow 20 books from the library each time and it's all read within four to five days. I have to release the books in batches.

Reading helps in all areas —comprehension, math, science, writing, imaginative play, socialization. In fact, they do very well for all the language arts activities and find them too easy. Hence, it makes homeschooling the girls a breeze for me. They do not like me to explain new concepts more than once.

—Linda Goh, Singapore

In one homeschooling family the mother believed that school nearly destroyed her love of reading and writing. As a result she vowed she would never teach grammar, assign books to read, or "autopsy" a book for literary allusions. Her daughter loved to listen to books read aloud and memorized picture books so she could pretend to read to her younger brother. The little girl began to recognize words by the age of five and read easily at age seven. She aspired to be a writer but was frustrated by her inability to write as well as her favorite authors. Instead she copied passages into spiral notebooks, mostly choosing to write down what she called "tummy grabbers." Her mother noticed this copying, but didn't intervene or suggest that she do her own work. By the time the girl was a preteen she began writing her own essays and poems. The time spent copying seemed to have done more than help her spelling and handwriting, it gave her a sense of the power of language. She says that she learned to revise rather than revile her work. Now at the age of seventeen she has had articles published online. Despite her mother's distaste for grammar,

this teen enjoys weekly grammar podcasts. And despite her family's assumption that she might make writing her life's work, she has other plans. Those "tummy grabber" sections by her favorite authors captivated more than the writer in her. She hopes to become a minister some day and share that search for meaning with a congregation through the sermons she writes and the words she offers in times of need.

In that same family the younger brother also enjoyed listening to books and liked to act out adventure tales with homemade swords and costumes. He showed no interest in learning to read. The only thing he wrote were the thank-you notes that his mother insisted he produce after receiving gifts. Even then his mother said letter-writing was "drawn out agony." When he was nine years old he played a new board game with friends and was unable to read the instructions on a card. Although his friends knew he didn't really read, he put the card down and refused to finish playing. He came home, and, as naturally as his sister sitting down to practice the piano, he grabbed a book on the couch and tried to read. When a family member walked through the room he asked them to explain the words that caused him trouble. "This is exhausting," he told his mother after a half hour. But the next day he started again, not with easy picture books, but with what he called "real" books. By the age of ten he enthusiastically read stacks of books and magazines. Writing was another matter. He still complained about thank you notes. Yet another peer group moves him past that block. Now at twelve his interest in building ship models evolves into a desire to build a full-sized canoe. He joins several online forums related to canoe building. Through these lists he becomes immersed in a new world of people who help one another with advice. He quickly gets over any reluctance to write as he interacts with these colleagues. To conform to list expectations for readable posts, he is careful to pay attention to capitalization, punctuation and sentence structure. His online friends call him "Professor" due to his careful grammar. He is saving money in hopes of building a serviceable canoe some day.

These siblings were raised in a word rich environment. Their parents shared an enjoyment of reading, took them to plays and library programs, engaged the family in lively discussions and demonstrated through their own actions that the written word was important. Yet the parents never assigned reading or writing, and never intervened in the direction their children took towards literacy. They trusted that their children would adopt these essential tools because they were modeled in the home. The brother and sister developed language arts skills through situations of value to them on personal timetables, with built-in problems to resolve.

While many homeschooling families find success using more conventional forms of reading and writing instruction, others find that their children learn in a highly individual manner. Some children read before age of five, others do not read until they are ten years old or older. In the case of children who read "late" by current cultural standards, adults need to avoid making the child feel impaired or diminished as this will block learning. Under duress the brain simply does not perform well. Most research on reading delays and difficulties are based on the school model, but that information doesn't translate well to homeschooling. In school, "late" readers suffer multiple wounds of scrutiny, humiliation and failure. This adds layers of painful emotion on the process of learning to read, convincing children that they detest anything to do with reading. A parent who is truly concerned that dyslexia or other functional disorder is present should seek help. But remember, readiness is one key. The other key is letting reading have unique meaning and purpose to children so the skills are fully their own.

We are Waldorf learners. That method doesn't prescribe reading until the child is seven. My daughter wasn't ready then either. She was "ready" all of a sudden at eight-and-a-half and what's funny is she didn't start reading at her grade level, she rapidly went right to much harder books. At ten she reads book after book eagerly. —Mandy Clark

---

As an infant, my son Bradley ... was diagnosed with atopic dermatitis also known as eczema ... a skin condition that causes a rash and incessant itching that can lead to infection... When Bradley was nearly bed bound, there were only so many books we could read and so many TV programs we could watch before we were bored. My son taught himself how to play video games when he was very young and it was a blessing...

As he got older he started encountering games he really wanted to play but that had a lot of text ... The story and text were important to the game play. He would often ask me to come in and sit with him while he played his games and

to read the screens of text to him as he played ... [and] when I could not sit for an hour reading his game to him ... I would notice him studying the words on the screen.

Bradley would start asking questions about various road signs. "Mom what does that sign say?" "Mom is that the letter S?" Within days he was figuring out the connection between letters, sounds and how they make words. [And] ... Within days he was reading the text on his own. He was incredibly proud of himself ... And with that motivation he learned to read proficiently.

To help him improve on his reading skills I went online and found online walkthroughs for his favorite video games ... often over 200 pages for each game ... He was very excited ... and immediately started spending hours reading. At first it took him a long time to read through one page but in almost no time at all he was flying through the pages ... Within a couple of months he was able to read anything ...

To this day he is an avid reader ... I had no idea that what we were doing by trusting our own instincts was unschooling because I had never heard of it.

[However, at first] he wasn't good at spelling. I trusted that he would learn to spell correctly when he found it necessary ... But Bradley was still having trouble communicating properly with the others on the games because many had trouble understanding what he was saying due to the misspellings of words. Through observation, he saw how others spelled certain words and he made a mental note to spell the same way. Within several weeks, he was typing fast with the correct spelling. He was able to do this because he had a reason

to learn these skills because they were suddenly practical and useful to his life.
    —Tamara Markwick, California

Starting Places

- **Make finding alphabet letters a game.** Young children may enjoy finding "letter of the day" in picture books, road signs and cloud shapes, as well as forming it with clay or bread dough. Seeing the letter in different contexts, slightly different shapes and paired with other letters will help her prepare for reading. If it is a letter with differing sounds, such as "C," occasionally point out that it looks the same but sounds different in words such as "cat" and "city."

- **When a child tells a story, offer to transcribe it.** Or if the child draws a picture and tells about it, offer to write the description down. When reading it back to him, run your finger under the words and keep these pages to read and re-read. It's a testament to the power of written language when a child's momentary thoughts are documented and read back to him.

- **Make books with your child.** Use photos of family, pets and neighborhood. Write stories or captions underneath the photos, using the child's name liberally throughout. When the child's dictated stories and pictures are longer than a page or two, make those into books as well, with front and back covers. If the child has memorized these books and "reads" them back to you he is well on his way to reading.

- **Send postcards.** When you are on a trip, even a day trip, help your child write a line or two on a postcard she has chosen and pop it in the mail right back to your home address. This helps keep track of your adventures, allows the child to get mail and reinforces writing for pleasure.

- **Encourage children to speak for themselves.** Rather than chiming in to answer for them, let them handle their own communications. Encourage them to look up phone numbers and make calls, request materials from librarians and ask questions of store clerks when they need to find an item.

- **Tell round robin stories.** One person starts out with an improbable situation and after telling a few lines passes the responsibility for continuing the story on to the next person, who adds a few more lines and stops at a crucial moment to pass the story on to the next person, around and around. If the children are too young, the parent can craft an ongoing story but regularly stop to ask children to add dramatic elements, such as "And then what jumped out of the tree?" "And then what did the bird say to the little girl?"

- **Prompt make-believe tales.** Ask your child to tell you what he imagines would happen if a flower started talking, a space craft landed nearby, an elf knocked on the door. Ask "Why does the wind sing?" or "How did the giraffe get so tall?"

- **Make daily reading a pleasurable activity.** Some children are impatient with one long read-aloud session, or want to hear different books than their siblings want. Pay attention to the needs they express and make read-aloud time relaxed and enjoyable. Many families read to their children separately at bedtime and together at some other point during the day, or vice versa. This allows a parent to read a chapter book to an older child and a stack of picture books to a younger child.

I make sure reading is front and center in our family. We take books everywhere. We keep books in backpacks ready to go when we are. We keep books in the van. Sometimes we read after hiking by the reservoir and sometimes we go out for lunch and read there afterwards. My littlest one Dishaun does best when we read together like this. At home there's too much that takes my attention from him and his attention from reading but when we're out places we make time. One of the twins looked up from a book about Arctic exploration while we were at the beach, and she said that she'd been feeling cold even out in the sun.

—LaVette, Florida

- **Use photos.** Let your children write humorous captions, make dialogue bubbles or create a story with the photos.

- **Assist cheerfully.** Some experts estimate that a child will need to see a word between twenty and thirty times before it is instantly recognized. As your child is building a repertoire of words it's helpful to respond right away when asked. Sound the word out together or simply provide the word readily.

- **Create a playwrights group** to extend the joy children feel when telling stories. The youngest children can dictate their stories to an adult or older child, then illustrate the story. Some children prefer to draw first, then dictate the story. Older children will be able to visualize their stories without illustrations. Members of the playwrights group may choose to bring stories readymade or do this process as a group. Then the fun really begins. The stories are read aloud. Children play various roles. These roles may include taking on the character of an animal, a storm or a plant depending on the story. Children can get creative as they costume and choreograph the play. They may incorporate leaves and sticks as props, make a park bench into a pirate ship, add a scarf for a queen's robe. After some rehearsal time they perform, mostly for their own enjoyment.

As they get older, children may choose to modify their playwrights group, bringing stories to life by building sets, making costumes and practicing the same play over a period of weeks rather than performing impromptu. Or by writing stories and acting them out in miniature with dioramas. Or by putting on puppet shows. Or making radio broadcasts, videos, animations or other productions of their work. The possibilities are unlimited.

- **Enjoy the magic of storytelling.** Visit a storyteller at a festival or fair. Encourage your children to practice the art of storytelling. They'll find useful suggestions in books such as *Storytelling for the Fun of It: A Handbook for Children* (Storycraft, 1999) by Vivian Dubrovin or *Tradin' Tales with Grandpa: A Kid's Guide for Intergenerational Storytelling* (Storycraft, 2000) by Vivian Dubrovin. They may want to form a storytelling club, perhaps performing at youth storytelling slams. Check out *Raising Voices: Youth Storytelling Groups and Troupes* (Libraries Unlimited, 2003) by Kevin Cordi and Judy Sima.

Story Arts provides additional information on the joys of storytelling. www.storyarts.org

- **Develop a book club.** Homeschool book clubs meet at members' homes, coffee shops, library meeting rooms or parks. Since homeschoolers tend to do things with multiple age-groups, some book clubs have an adult read a book to the youngest children and do activities with them, while older children get together with an adult for their book club, and the teens run their own book club. Oftentimes, members take turns planning and hosting sessions. Typically those who have planned the session discuss key points in the book with the children and have them take part in related activities. Another way to run a book club while incorporating all ages is to let each child read a different book and come prepared to share something about it. Or, a theme is given and children choose a book within a theme (i.e., fiction about dogs, Australian autobiography) and then make a brief presentation to the group about the book or show the group a project they've done related to it.

- **Mix sound with narration.** Bring along a recording device to make any outdoor walk into a "found-sound"-gathering expedition. Use snippets of conversation, footfalls, music from passing cars, barking dogs, a distant train whistle to build an audio track.

- **Take advantage of library programs.** Librarians develop creative and challenging programs for youth. Get to know the staff at your local library and let them know of your family and homeschool group's needs.

- **Write a family newsletter, blog or e-zine.** This encourages writing while, over time, also provides family memorabilia. Make sure everyone contributes something to each issue. Fill it with updates, inside jokes, photos, family-related trivia and memorable moments.

I never used to like writing much until I got to set up my own blog. Now I put on my pictures and reviews of movies and stuff I like. I can't wait to write in it most days. —Nyla, 12

- **Use microblog services** like Twitter or Jaiku not only to communicate, but to hone writing down to the essentials.

- **Create an imaginary planet.** Encourage your children to make up a place entirely of their own imagination. They may want to describe the inhabitants, what they eat, wear and do. They may choose to make maps, write up laws, draw pictures of the landscape, list unique holidays and the ways they are celebrated, build models of dwellings, write about the customs and technology, create art or newspapers for the planet, write about or demonstrate inventions from the planet, etc.
- **Memorize** literary passages, quotes, poems, dramatic roles. Committing even brief works to memory is a wonderful mental exercise with lasting value.
- **Practice the art of public speaking.** Find opportunities to build confident speakers. Set up a public speaking event for your group or join a competition.
- **Talk about stories.** Discuss different impressions of a character's motivations or focus on separate elements of the plot. Imagine a sequel or prequel for the book. If the story is set in another time or place, talk about how the characters would react to your present day lives. Or how you would react to suddenly appearing in the book's setting. Ask how the outcome would be different if the main character were a different gender or age, lived in a different country or time period, faced a different challenge. If there are upsetting parts to the book discuss the feelings these evoked and why the author chose to put in such difficult passages. Compare the story to other books, movies and plays. Talk about how you would transform the plot into a movie. Book lovers enjoy casual conversations on such topics because they open up new ways of thinking, and not only about the book itself.
- **Make reading one highlight of the day.** Do a dramatic reading with children taking on parts or adding sound effects. Let a favorite quote from the book become part of your family vernacular. Try a food, craft or experiment mentioned in the book. Read in different places—sitting in the kiddie pool on a hot day, next to a tree in the park, in a fort made of couch cushions. Try reading a scary story aloud in the closet with a flashlight. Count on reading time together at a certain time each day.

I have one child who will spend so much time reading that she will lose track of time and even of her own discomforts. This was particularly evident when she was reading the Harry Potter series of books. I even had to force her to stop reading at times so that she could eat and even go to bed.
—Laurel Santiago, Texas

- **Focus on the pleasures of writing.** Neat handwriting and correct spelling, although tempting to emphasize for many parents, are not top priorities. The child's pleasure in reading and writing are. Many children find that their dexterity isn't up to maintaining legible handwriting for long, and do better typing or dictating what they have to say. The effort to spell each word correctly also severely inhibits their work, particularly when writing eagerly.
- **Make writing worthwhile.** As much as possible, let writing be about what the child wants to express. This is one of the best ways to make it an ongoing practice.
- **Learn to craft well-reasoned points.** Consider asking children for written proposals regarding large purchases, vacation ideas and upgraded privileges. To settle common arguments, ask children to write down three good reasons before making a decision.

Our life is full of real opportunities for the kids to do their own writing, even if it's just their names. They like to send e-mails, thank you notes, and cards. We're going to write stories of trips we've taken to make memory books, but since I don't want the mechanics of writing to frustrate them, I'll let them dictate to me. Journaling their prayers and ideas is another way to get them interested in being able to write. There is so much more to writing than just forming the letters.

The whole language approach to reading and writing is often contrasted with the phonics approach. In reality teachers and parents use both. I would argue that "whole language" should include both large picture and small picture (phonics) instruction — otherwise we're not teaching the whole of language. Our primary goal is really generating a love for language and expression without neglecting the specifics of learning to read and write. What good is having perfect reading comprehension or lettering, or even memorizing math or science facts, if we kill the desire to use them in the process?   *—Karen, Texas*

- **Find reasons to write.** Let your children see you use writing often. Send letters to friends, make lists, write emails, keep a schedule or planner. Write notes to your children. Find an unexpected spot in the house or yard to serve as a hidden mailbox, then exchange secret notes or coded cards to one another.

  Teach children to write thank you notes for gifts and favors. Other letters that young people can write are even more reinforcing—to the editor, to companies with complaints or praise about a product (often getting samples or coupons in return), to a favorite author or celebrity. Check out *Families Writing, second edition* (Boynton/Cook, 1998) by Peter Stillman.

- **Have fun with words.** Tell jokes, puns and riddles. Play with words, such as thinking of every possible word to describe your bad mood. Make up rhyming songs to go with familiar tunes, customizing them to your family or your situation. Enjoy Mad Libs®. Speak in made-up accents using "big" words.

- **Correspond with a pen pal.** Write regularly to a far off cousin, a great aunt or a former neighbor. Sign up with an organization that matches children to an overseas pen pal. Form a postcard exchange, join an established postcard exchange (try searching Yahoo! Groups) or register with the international organization Postcrossing www.postcrossing.com

  One educational program called Trucker Buddy www.truckerbuddy.com links groups of children (12 or more) to a working truck driver. The driver shares news about his or her travels and the children send correspondence back.

- **Enjoy games.** Young children will enjoy the activities in *Games for Writing: Playful Ways to Help Your Child Learn to Write* (Farrar, Straus and Giroux, 1995) by Peggy Kaye and *Games for Reading: Playful Ways to Help Your Child Read* (Pantheon, 1984) by Peggy Kaye. Board games invariably require reading, including rules, special cards and the board itself. Make up your own board game by designing it together with your child, check online for helpful hints.

  Play the dictionary game Blackbird. Ask a question, such as "Why is my hair so curly?" Then open the dictionary at random, and without looking, put your finger on the page. Try to make the chosen word "fit" as an answer before passing it to the next person. Merriam-Webster's Word Central www.wordcentral.com offers children's word games and a daily buzzword.

Consult the National Scrabble Association to find or start a scrabble club. Homeschool groups can sign up for the school scrabble program to receive benefits such as supplies and regional competitions for children. www2.scrabble-assoc.com

---

Right now I'm doing something with Cody for writing and reading comprehension ... I take an article from one of his magazines. Recently it was one from Rolling Stone. I rewrite it on my compose page, leaving out all punctuation marks and capitals. I email this to him. He then needs to fix it and email it back. We do this back and forth until the article is right. Then I ask him reading comprehension type questions. He really likes this because it's short and simple.
—Kim Railey, Washington

- **Alter your dimensional outlook.** A boy named Stanley, in the book *Flat Stanley* by Jeff Brown, is squashed flat by a bulletin board. He takes advantage of his flattened state gleefully, even mails himself in a letter. You can join Flat Stanley projects or start up your own by checking for them on Yahoo! Groups, or registering at the Official Flat Stanley Project www.flatstanley.com. Mail your own version of Stanley to others, ask them to take a photo of Stanley, add information about their area and mail him to someone in another state. Other Flat Stanley projects might include making a diorama, racetrack or wardrobe for your Stanley character.
- **Take in movies, plays, television, video games and websites together.** Talk about them. Note how different forms of media change the experience. Compare them to books, personal experiences and dreams.

After my daughter and a few of her friends attended a workshop through the Lake Tahoe Shakespeare Festival they really got swept up in Shakespeare. They go around quoting the bard. Last week I picked them up after a movie and our car was cut off on the way out of the parking lot. The girls shouted out, "Lord, what fools these mortals be!" Then later at the pizza place when the server came over to cut their slices one of the girls said, "Is this a dagger I see before me?" My daughter likes to read a play first, then read the Cliff Notes *and then watch any movies made of the play. I think she gets a lot of pleasure out of memorizing quotes and using them in public too. It has become a game between the girls to quote from different plays.* —Linda

---

- **Learn to prove your point.** Try debating. It's a form of structured discussion where ideas are exchanged openly. Asking questions and weighing evidence takes place in an atmosphere of tolerance. Consult the International Debate Education Association for debate topics, expert advice and debate club ideas. www.idebate.org
- **Publish your writing.** A good resource, written by young people themselves, is *A Teen's Guide to Getting Published: Publishing for Profit, Recognition And Academic Success* (Prufrock, 2006) by Jessica Dunn and Danielle Dunn.
- **Write quickly.** Some writers swear by deadlines as motivators. Other writers find they do best when they time themselves, set word count goals or start out each day by journaling.

November is National Novel Writing Month www.nanowrimo.org with the challenge to write a full novel in thirty days. Well over 100,000 participate each year. Check out the Young Writer's Program at http://ywp.nanowrimo.org

Caroline has been composing stories since before she could write; as a toddler she dictated her stories and I typed them on the computer. Now, as a 12 year old, she always has several lengthy writing projects in work. Until recently, she had been learning creative writing techniques simply by reading lots of fiction and imitating what she read. Her favorite genre is fantasy fiction, and she read over 150 books in this genre during the past school year.

She decided she wanted to improve her skills and she began reading numerous non-fiction books about creative writing and writers. I offered her a book I had enjoyed, Eats, Shoots & Leaves: The Zero Tolerance Approach to Punctuation, *and she loved it. I helped her find other books such as* The Wand in the Word: Conversations with Writers of Fantasy, Writing Magic: Creating Stories That Fly, *and* Get Wise! Mastering Writing Skills*; and she asked me to purchase books she found such as* Shoujo Manga Techniques: Writing Stories and The Complete Handbook of Novel Writing.

I searched out other resources: we attended a lecture and book signing by children's book author/illustrator Jarrett Krosoczka at our local library and a lecture by science fiction author Travis Taylor at a library in a neighboring city. We watched a Standard Deviants DVD series on Fantasy Literature. I sought out writing classes, and Caroline participated in a 4-week Writer's Workshop with a local author during the summer. When that finished she asked me to find her another writing class. She said she likes to learn preferences, methods, and points of view from many different writers/teachers. Now she is in a 10-week Writer's Workshop held at a homeschooling bookstore. And, of course, I read her stories when she asks me; usually this means reading them aloud to the family without any request for critiquing them. She also enjoys writing poetry and, when she was younger, she used the book Writing Poetry with Children *to learn the formalities of different types of poems.*

One year, our library held a poetry contest and Caroline won third place in her age category. More recently, with her permission, I sent two of her poems to the editor of Live Free Learn Free *magazine and both were published in separate editions. She was surprised, overjoyed, and encouraged in her writing by this type of recognition (and she was not discouraged when she entered a couple of other local writing contests and did not receive any type of recognition). Her goal is to publish a book before she is 15 years old. So far, she has never completed one of her books, but she is always writing and whether or not she meets that particular goal she is enjoying herself and learning a lot.*

—Susan, Alabama

- **Compete.** The National Vocabulary Championship www.winwithwords.com is open to students ages thirteen to nineteen. The site also offers study tools, vocabulary games and podcasts. Scripps National Spelling Bee http://spellingbee.com has a fee to register. It offers study guides and other assistance.

There are also many essay and writing contests for young people. Steer away from those requiring entrance fees. One well-known youth poetry contest is River of Words (ROW) www.riverofwords.org in affiliation with the Library of Congress Center for the Book.

- **Find out about books you haven't read.** Whether you are a fan of sci-fi, graphic novels or a particular series, there are books you've never heard of that you'll love. Read book reviews, keep up with podcasts and blogs about books, talk with friends about books you've enjoyed. You might like to check in with Incredibooks http://incredibooks.com providing book reviews written by homeschooled youth.

- **Create opportunities for young writers to get together.** You may want to start a mystery writers' circle, a journalism club, a poetry gathering. Set up a regular open mike at a youth meeting. Organize a poetry slam. Write and read short plays as a group. Work together on a newsletter, e-zine, website or broadcast venture. Arrange to meet with established local authors, broadcasters, journalists and actors for a Q&A session. Coordinate literary events in cooperation with area groups.

- **Word origins can lead you to unexpected places and times.** Who knew the word "doom" reaches back to the year 825, but at that time meant "law" or "judgment"? Keep an etymology reference handy, or use an online site such as www.etymonline.com. Look up the etymology of your names. Dig into books such as *In a Word: 750 Words and Their Fascinating Stories and Origins* (Cricket, 2003) by Rosalie Baker.

- **Enjoy words in unusual places.** Use window markers to write messages to one another on patio doors or car windows. Use fabric markers to write vocabulary words on bedsheets to fill each other's dreams with sophisticated concepts. Leave silly notes taped on the shower curtain, inside cupboard doors or on the milk carton.

- **Stage a treasure hunt.** First hide a prize. Then place clues through the house or yard. You can write the clues in poems or riddles, each one leading to the next clue. Let the children create treasure hunts for each other. The prize doesn't need to be a toy or candy, since the hunt is more fun than the treasure itself. Announce that it's "hide a packed lunch day" and let everyone search. Those who find sustenance first need to help others so everyone can eat together.

- **Preserve your best work in hand-bound books.** Collect proofed pages of stories, essays, poems or other work. Book covers can be created from a range of materials. Search for "book binding how to" or "hand bound book instructions" online.

- **Writing about oneself is a favorite.** Until young people see it written out, they may not even recognize their own feelings or experiences quite so clearly. Diaries, journals and fill-in books make meaning of the growing up process. The youngest children will enjoy *My Book About Me* (Random House, 1969) by Dr. Seuss and Roy McKie, while older youth may appreciate *Through My Eyes: A Journal for Teens* (Rising Moon, 1998) by Linda Kranz.

I expect my kids to produce some writing each week. I want them to be comfortable with the process. What they produce is up to them. My younger daughter (8) likes to take a notebook with her. Sometime she writes when she's at the skating rink or riding in the car. She likes to do character sketches and describe people. My older daughter (11) likes to write letters. She writes to companies (hoping for samples), fan letters and really nice notes to pen pals in several different countries. My son (13) writes much longer pieces on things he wants to find out about. I recommend letting your kids write anything they want. My kids write well and get a lot of satisfaction from it. —Lily

---

- **Unblank a blank book together.** There are many ways to fill a blank book with imagination. First off, get inexpensive blank journals or decorate small composition notebooks. Usually the blank book owner starts off by filling in the first page or two explaining the project. Then the book is passed off to a friend, neighbor or someone in a group who has agreed to take part. By the time the book is complete it is a multi-author work, filled with unique contributions. A friendship book might ask each participant to draw a self-portrait, glue in favorite photos, fill in several pages responding to questions about him- or herself, and list questions for others to answer. An animal themed book might ask for stories and drawings of participant's pets. A group novel can start off with a few pages of a story in any genre—science fiction, mystery or adventure story—before being passed along. A blank book can also be used as a shared journal between two people, like best friends, or mother and daughter, who ask each other questions and leave comments.

- **Create word art.** Write a word in the middle of the page, such as "birds" and then encourage your child to really look at birds and write single words every which way on the page as they come to mind. Cut out shapes, pictures and words and hang them to make a mobile. Make collages of words and images cut from magazines. Inscribe words into clay and bake them to leave in a garden.

- **Write reviews.** Critiques of movies, video games and the local pizza place make writing fun and relevant.

- **Take poetry everywhere.** Read poems while sitting in a tree or on the subway. Compose poems while in a canoe, on the beach or at the coffee shop to see how your surroundings affect what you read and write. Use permanent markers to write poetry on t-shirts, book covers, beach towels, magnets and bicycle seats. Sleep on pillowcases decorated with poems. Take a walk or sit quietly to "catch" a poem in your notebook.

  Refer to ideas in *Pizza, Pigs, and Poetry: How to Write a Poem* (Greenwillow, 2008) by Jack Prelutsky and *Poetry Matters: Writing a Poem from the Inside Out* (HarperCollins, 2002) by Ralph Fletcher.

- **Use writing prompts.** Try incomplete sentences prompts such as "I used to think …" "This reminds me of …" "I dreamed that …" Buy a bag of dried lima beans and write a word on each bean with a fine point marker. Keep them in a box or bag, and when the mood hits pull out a handful of beans and write a poem, story or joke using the words on your beans.

  Scribble on paper and then try to make a story out of what you see in the scribble. Cut out or draw a picture, then write about it. Open a book to a random page, drop your finger on a spot and read what you selected. Use that word or sentence in the next thing you write.

  Use *Writing Down the Days: 365 Creative Journaling Ideas for Young People* (Free Spirit, 2000) by Lorraine M. Dahlstrom.

I read what I want to read and write about what I want to write about. I'm a surfer. I might read about wave dynamics or something from Daved Marsh's 200 Years of Surfing Literature: An Annotated Bibliography. *When I write a lot of times it's logging weather and ocean observations that I compare to what it's like on the board, my own amateur science. There's history, music, art, ecology and a lot of other stuff mixed together in surf culture.*

On the beach is where I do a lot of my reading. My stepdad and friends are usually out here with me. They respect where I'm coming from because I'm educating myself. Being out here by the water makes what I read and write part of the whole picture. —Corey, 15

- **Dialogue.** This is not a lost art, even in an era of sound bites and tweets. We foster the patience, mental organization and listening skills necessary for real conversations throughout our lives. Conversation is one of the primary ways that we understand one another. Important conversations are being facilitated by groups across the world. Check out topic suggestions and networking offered by Conversation Café http://conversationcafe.org or Wisdom Circles http://wisdomcircle.org.

- **Keep a journal.** Use it to record happenings, emotions and ideas. Write down your opinion of current events. Jot down favorite quotes and inspiring ideas. Write in your journal while listening to different music and in different moods. Try a park bench, basement steps, crowded room. Leonardo Da Vinci's notebooks contained sketches of interesting faces, shopping lists, ideas for art and inventions, thoughts on ethics and more.

Resources

Online

- **Artists for Literacy** shares a database of songs inspired by literature. Excellent writing inspires all forms of creativity. www.artistsforliteracy.org
- **Bartleby** www.bartleby.com offers an online library of classic works, verse, quotations, historical documents and more.
- **Children's Literature Web Guide** provides book lists, reviews and storytelling information. www.acs.ucalgary.ca/~dkbrown/
- **Easy Essay** helps organize ideas into a proven format through simple, automated steps. www.theeasyessay.com
- **Library of Congress** offers webcasts, digital collections, children's activities and literary events. www.loc.gov/index.html
- **National Film Board of Canada** has open archives including documentaries, animations and dramas. www.nfb.ca
- **Reading is Fundamental** promotes literacy with resources and games. www.rif.org

Books

- *Boy Writers: Reclaiming Their Voices* (Stenhouse, 2006) by Ralph Fletcher.
- *Seize the Story: A Handbook for Teens Who Like to Write* (Cottonwood, 2008) by Victoria Hanley .
- *The Kids' Book Club Book: Reading Ideas, Recipes, Activities, and Smart Tips for Organizing Terrific Kids' Book Clubs* (Tarcher, 2007) by Judy Gelman and Vicki Levy Krupp.

Audio Books—Free Sources

- **Kazoomzoom** www.kazoomzoom.com
- **LibriVox** http://librivox.org
- **OpenCulture** www.oculture.com

Foreign Languages

"The limits of your language are the limits of your world." —Ludwig Wittgenstein

Those who master a new language often describe an unexpected phenomenon. They find themselves thinking somewhat differently from one language to the other. They begin to see that language forms a frame of reference for understanding a culture from within, on its own terms. As our children learn a second or third language they can understand the world more broadly.

Of course there are many other benefits. It's also been found that as young people learn to speak another language, they can't help but grasp the nuances of their own language more completely. They find themselves thinking about the structure behind sentences, seeing similarities between languages and thinking about the meaning of what they're trying to express.

Learning a language isn't easy. It requires practice and ongoing dedication. Working hard at any one thing has a wonderfully positive effect. When children study a foreign language they are prone to improve in higher-order thinking skills, problem-solving, creativity, even mathematical ability. Clearly, learning another language is not a linguistic exercise, it expands the way we think.

Language exerts an influence that's hard to explain. But for those who are truly proficient, they find the results go deep. They even dream in more than one language.

Robert Wolff writes in *Original Wisdom: Stories of an Ancient Way of Knowing*, "As I learned two languages simultaneously, nobody told me that I must speak one language to my parents and another to other people. As all children do, I *knew* without having to be told. Children learn a language not from a book, or even from a teacher, but from their need to communicate ... It is quite unremarkable to me now to know that any language expresses a unique way of knowing."

Experts agree that there are enormous benefits to starting a second language when a child is young. Some recommend beginning at three years of age or younger. Children are able to achieve natural intonation and pronunciation in a new language as late as the onset of puberty. And the teen years remain a period of continued ability, although the "language center" in the brain is no longer in the formative stage.

Some families intentionally use a second language in the home soon after a baby is born. The little one isn't likely to speak quite as early as single language children, probably because his or her brain is sorting out two separate languages. This method leads to proficiency in both languages at an early age. Typically a parent, grandparent or other family member speaks exclusively in that language in the child's presence. This makes it easier for the child to understand the difference between two languages.

In one family a grandfather cares for his infant granddaughter several times a week. He speaks to her only in Danish. They play games he remembers from his childhood. As she gets older he continues to maintain communications with her in Danish, even as he has reason to speak to others in English. She switches from one language to another with casual ease even as a preschooler.

Learning a foreign language when the child is somewhat older is approached in several ways. Most often the child learns it as a distinct subject. Books, software and other materials are used to develop comprehension. In another approach, called "immersion," children spend at least part of the day with the language. They may speak the language exclusively all morning while working on division problems, eating lunch and playing cards.

Speaking in a new tongue is an excellent reason to revel in the flavors of another culture. Allow the language to lead you to new discoveries. Learn the dances, try new sports, read the poetry, study the terrain, taste unfamiliar fruits and vegetables, investigate the heroes and villains, celebrate the holidays and festivals, play the games, check up on the current news, find out about the history, and if possible, visit in person. As your children learn the words and customs of those in another part of the world they'll begin to understand the rich diversity of our planet.

Starting Places
- **Mix up learning methods.** One book, tape or program can't do it all. Make it a lively mix of conversation, play and activity. Whenever possible, interact with those who are proficient speakers of the language.
- **Involve others.** Invite friends and family to a cultural festival or feast. Teach them a few phrases you've learned, let them taste new foods, show them how to play games and otherwise share what you've learned about language and culture. You may end up with partners in your foreign language quest.
- **Choose a language based on wider interests.** Beyond the few foreign languages traditionally taught, consider learning a less common tongue. How about the language your great-grandparents spoke or the language of a country you hope to visit?
- **Make second language a family affair.** Expand your understanding together. One parent may choose to speak the second language exclusively at home as suggested in bilingual resources. Or everyone might devote part of each day to language immersion. Proceeding with daily activities like games, chores and meals in a new language places it more firmly in a child's memory.
- **Use resources targeted to native speakers.** Watch subtitled films, letting the dialogue become part of the pleasure of the movie.

Order foreign language magazines, books and music from the library to enjoy without expecting a masterful level of comprehension. Use items with foreign language words or symbols on them including placemats, t-shirts, posters, toys, greeting cards. Attend plays, concerts and other events for those who are primarily native speakers. Pay attention to news sources from the countries where the language is spoken, noting differences in the way stories are presented.

- **Keep it fun.** Even in the first few days of learning another language you can play familiar games such as Hide and Seek using just a few newly learned words. Find translations of picture books and comics. Use sticky notes or masking tape to label household objects. Put on puppet shows, make videos, draw your own cartoons with dialogue bubbles. Challenge yourselves to spend at least an hour a day speaking nothing but the language you are learning.
- **Make it musical.** Sing songs with foreign language lyrics. Have fun looking up music videos sung in Farsi, Dutch, Korean or

Hindi. Learn national anthems from around the world.

- **Connect with people who speak the language.** Consider setting up a foreign language playgroup or club. Contact a nearby ethnic center or exchange association for information. They may offer workshops in cultural arts as well. Find a pen pal and agree to write half of each letter in English and half in the second language. Seek out international students at a nearby college for language or cultural lessons.

My son has been learning Chinese from a college student who came from China about two years ago. She's teaching a couple of kids. They're learning to speak and form characters. They have also done a tea ceremony and made bean paste candies. She let them take home newspapers that she had her things wrapped in. We pay her $5 a lesson per child. We try to get her to take more but she won't take it. My son gets a lot more out of the sessions with her than he does from the Chinese language program we bought for him to learn from.

My daughter might be learning French from a family that moved here from the Quebec area. Right now we're working out plans to barter clarinet lessons in exchange. —Amy

---

- **Enjoy originals.** As your proficiency increases you'll notice that translations never truly duplicate the original intent or style. Unique elements are lost in each translation. Notice your growing ability to appreciate works such as poetry, music and theater in the original language.

- **Travel.** Take any reasonable opportunity to try out your language skills and participate more fully in a foreign culture. Even halting attempts to speak in the native tongue demonstrate that you are approaching communication with respect not often shown by travelers.

- **Study abroad.** Check out volunteer, academic and intensive language programs offered for a few weeks to most of the year. A trip abroad to visit friends or family, to sightsee or volunteer is also educationally rich. Check out IIE Passport www.iiepassport.org and Study Abroad www.studyabroaddirectory.com

Resources

Online
- **LiveMocha** is an online language community with self-study language lessons, live chat, progress tools and tutoring. www.livemocha.com
- **Multilingual Children's Association** offers articles, tips, forums and directories. www.multilingualchildren.org

Books
- *Raising a Bilingual Child* (Living Language, 2008) by Barbara Zurer Pearson.
- *The Bilingual Edge: Why, When, and How to Teach Your Child a Second Language* (Collins, 2007) by Kendall King and Alison Mackey.
- *The Bilingual Family: A Handbook for Parents* (Cambridge University, 2003) by Edith Harding-Esch and Philip Riley.

CHAPTER FIFTEEN

History & Current Events

History

"History is who we are and why we are the way we are."
—David C. McCullough

History is always relevant. It's the quiet reminder found in old buildings, tall trees and important decisions. It is present in the way we do things, although we rarely stop to realize that we do things a certain way because it was done that way in the past. When children ask "why" we often realize we don't know. Figuring out the answer invariably leads us to history.

The magnitude of history can't be confined to books. Travel is equally expansive. Beyond travel, there are engaging documentaries about all time periods, plus interactive websites on nearly any historical topic imaginable. There are also museum displays, preserved areas, living history presentations and historical fiction. History is embedded in the objects and words we use each day. Children become eager to learn about history when their imaginations are stimulated by creative and challenging experiences that awaken an interest in the past. As we begin to understand other cultures and eras we start to recognize how a broad stream of experiences contributes to different viewpoints, all of which make up our diverse world today.

We are the products of history. Our lives today are evidence that our ancestors survived unbelievable odds stretching back to prehistory. The ground we stand on and the flesh we are composed of is not new, each atom has history.

Our children can discover many fibers weaving them to the past. Each person is a member of many groups and subcultures. It's likely your family tree branches out into several regions or countries.

Explore your heritage together. If you are of Polish descent, who are the people who make up your cultural background? Chemist Marie Curie, astronomer Nicolaus Copernicus and composer Frederick Chopin are a few. If you are of Egyptian descent, who are your cultural forbearers? World's first doctor Imhotep, ruler Cleopatra and scholar Suyuti are three examples.

Your child is also linked to history by beliefs, attitudes and ideas. If she is a Christian, she may wish to learn about the way that religion spread across the world, or about changing interpretations of the Bible, the kinds of foods eaten by the prophets of old, the effect of Christianity on the political structure of various countries and earlier patterns of worship. If he is an adventurer at heart, he can learn how explorers, inventors, navigators and wanderers changed the course of history with the same intrepid desire to "find out" that he shares.

Your child is also inducted into subcultures by interests. Does she like to make her own cartoons? An entire history of those who used simple drawings for political commentary, social satire and storytelling shows them to be bold artists unafraid to advance ideas through deceptively simple sketches. Those earlier cartoonists made the medium what it is today.

There's always an historical angle to any interest. Whether your child has a passion for airplanes, stand-up comedy, glassblowing or skiing there's a backstory to be discovered. Taking an interest-based approach makes history suddenly relevant to who your child is today.

Exploring history is as relevant and essential as ever.

- Our individual lives are a direct result of the past. As we understand history more fully we can make decisions with greater awareness.
- History teaches us about ourselves. Looking back, we can't help but see a vast spectrum. Humankind has the ability to commit horrible acts of cruelty and justify those acts.

We also have the ability to rise to the best in ourselves by choosing wisdom and compassion to guide us. The future doesn't bode well for those who deny that they have the capacity for both good and evil, because the past shows us that the shadow of what is denied looms even larger. History, really, teaches us what it means to be human.

- History helps us learn from the actions of others. We can see the long term effects of mistakes and faulty reasoning. We can also see the results of highly ethical choices. A consideration of history helps develop good judgment.
- History inspires us. It gives us a choice of role models, people whose actions have demonstrated values we admire.
- History provides context and meaning for our lives.

I love history and so does my husband. It's rare when we talk about the news that one of us doesn't cite similarities from the past. Kennedy (7) and Allison (9) are beginning to ask questions which have really impressed us, and we're pretty sure that it's exposure to family conversation in addition to field trips.

We take an "everything" approach to history. Everything that comes our way and looks interesting, we do. If there are any questions about the time sequence keep a timeline or history atlas so you can clarify this for your children. Just this year alone the kids have gone on a narrated paddleboat excursion down the river; taken part in several different participatory living history programs; taken historical art classes teaching them how to do quilling, leather stitching and gourd crafts; helped construct a temporary trading post for a reenactment weekend; and visited countless museums and historical sites. We also use Story of The World *activity books and the* History Odyssey *books.*

—M.J., Missouri

I couldn't be more surprised that my children like history because I hated it when I was in school. I remember being loaded down with information. We were given lots of "relevant" assignments that added more homework time. My son in particular gets on a campaign. He asks questions that go from simple to post grad level in minutes. Then he and I go look up the answers. Gradually we are working through good books like Joy Hakim's work and Trisms texts. We find that the offshoots of our interests take us even farther into history. —Lily

---

Starting Places

- **Enjoy history brought to life.** Check out Living History offerings to witness life as it was in the past. Enter terms such as "open air museum," "folk museum," "living history" and "living farm museum" into a search engine to find listings. Such places provide immersion experiences, hands-on workshops and history theater.

  Don't forget historical reenactments. Reenactment organizations use meticulous care to replay pivotal events. And there are the ever popular Renaissance fairs filled with entertainment, jousting tournaments, art and foods.

- **Emphasize the importance of primary documents.** Rather than relying on the interpretations of others, discover what history has to say through letters, photos, deeds and more. Consider Eyewitness to History www.eyewitnesstohistory.com and American Memory Project http://memory.loc.gov. For information on

using primary documents go to The National Archives www.archives.gov/education.

- **Be aware of the past.** When facing an ordinary quandary, think back to how the same sort of problem was handled in the past. This is particularly effective on a personal level.

- **Dig into archeology.** This field connects history, anthropology, art, geography and more. History is underground awaiting discovery, just as our era will someday be a mystery to archeologists of the distant future. Children may be inspired to set up a backyard dig. They may want to wire bleached chicken bones back into a skeleton or excavate a garbage can for lifestyle "clues." Dig www.digonsite.com offers links, art and a state guide to educational events. For younger children, try *Archaeologists Dig for Clues* (Collins, 1996) by Kate Duke. For preteens, look into *Archaeology for Kids: Uncovering the Mysteries of Our Past, 25 Activities* (Chicago Review, 2001) by Richard Panchyk.

At this homeschool camp I go to we have debates. Lots of us like them because it's fun to argue and prove your point. Last year I picked the history category and the topic I pulled asked if the U.S. colonists needed to fight the British to gain independence. We have the whole week to prepare and then we debate the day before we go home.

Looking this stuff up was amazing because in my opinion there weren't really good reasons to go to war or at least go as soon as we did. The colonists didn't try very hard to negotiate. They could have gained independence in a few years with diplomatic efforts IMO. It looked to me like some of the stuff they did were just terrorist acts, except once the rebel side won then they were called patriots. It taught me to look at both sides. Like they say, history is written by the winners.

I lost the debate by the way. The way we do it at camp is the winners are decided by a show of hands, and kids voted against me. They got the issue mixed up with anti-war stuff in general. Some of the kids got mad at me. That's okay. We talked about it half the night ... Some of us are thinking about this stuff differently.

I'm reading about World War I right now and now I can't believe the reasons we had to get into that war either. It's not like I'm going to make history my career or anything but now I see it like a mystery story with clues that a lot of other people don't take the time to see.

—Ryan, 15

- **Notice qualities resonating with ancestral characterisitics.** Something clicks into place when discovering, at any age, that traits or abilities are a link, perhaps to a great great grandfather or a much loved aunt. You can't help but wonder what these relatives made of a life that now seems more similar to your own and to imagine how your own life will be remembered. A sense that one is carrying family traits onward gives any of us a sense of continuity with the past.

I'm a lot like my grandpa. I like to take things apart to figure them out and I'm good at drawing. My grandma saved some of his medals from the Vietnam war. My grandma told me that my grandpa would be proud of me if he was here now. She gave me his watch. —Tyler, 9

- **Maintain a special trunk, box or storage container** as a personal history cache for each child. Keep copies of photos, artwork, letters, special ticket stubs and programs, mementos such as a forgotten toddler toy, notes about the child's humorous sayings, a lock of hair, even a few baby teeth saved from the Tooth Fairy.

- **See history as a mystery.** The clues in letters, photographs and everyday items tell the story of people who can no longer speak for themselves. Books that children will enjoy are *The Mary Celeste: An Unsolved Mystery from History* (Simon & Schuster, 2002) and *Roanoke: The Lost Colony: An Unsolved Mystery from History* (Simon & Schuster, 2003) both by authors Jane Yolen and Heidi Elisabet Y Stemple. For older youth, enjoy *National Geographic Mysteries of History* (National Geographic, 2003) by Robert Stewart.

- **Indulge in biographies and autobiographies.** This is a great way to learn how the conditions of the time impacted individual lives. It also gives insight into the growing up years and factors affecting character formation. It's helpful to let your child choose who he or she would like to read about. Even if your child tends to prefer specific biographies, say only sports bios, he'll be learning about the forces shaping a person's life.

- **Gain perspective by playing historical games.** When children play long-forgotten games they recognize that people in earlier eras were also youngesters who longed to have fun. For example, nineteenth century immigrant children in crowded U.S. cities played games that fit on stoops, sidewalks or a section of the street. Pastimes like stickball, scully (bottle caps), marbles and hopscotch were challenging and inexpensive amusements for children even in the poorest families. Enjoy games from other cultures. Check out http://42explore.com/sidewlk.htm or the book *Kids Around the World Play!: The Best Fun and Games from Many Lands* (Wiley, 2002) by Arlette N. Braman.

- **Value stories from your own family history.** Tell your children stories of your childhood and what current events were going on at the time. Solicit stories from older members of the family. Encourage your children to record their elders answering questions such as, "What made your family come to this country?" and "What was your first job?" and "What was it like when you were my age?" Display photos of ancestors and mention what you knew of their history. This provides children with a sense of continuity. It also helps them recognize that those who came before them contributed to who they are now.

- **Record oral history.** Family members are a good way to start, but consider those in the community as well. Everyone has stories to tell, it's a matter of finding out what topics are the catalyst. Be prepared with questions but remember to avoid interrupting. Start out with comfortable topics and work toward any that may be more intense. Let the interviewee talk and the conversation go in unexpected directions.

   You may want to collect oral histories of a specific era, relevant to your ancestry or on a topic of interest. Augment this oral history with photographs, music and artwork. For more ideas, check out the oral history links found at www.42explore2.com/oralhst.htm.

- **Learn about time capsules.** Documents and artifacts are vital historical evidence. Sometimes such evidence is discovered hidden away in an attic, trunk or archeolgical dig, and this is a kind of unintentional time capsule. Many people create time capsules, either to be opened themselves a few decades later or to leave for future generations. Make a time capsule together, filling it with personally and historically relevant items.

   Learn about Golden Record included in both Voyager spacecraft launched in the late 1970s. Find out what it included and why. This message was sent along: "This is a present from a small, distant world, a token of our sounds, our science, our images, our music, our thoughts and our feelings. We are attempting to survive our time so we may live into yours." U.S. President Jimmy Carter.

- **Put yourself in history with books.** Good books, whether highlighting a fictional character's reaction to real events, or historical non-fiction, help young people imagine themselves in another place or era. Try an activity mentioned in the book such as darning a sock, shooting a slingshot or foretelling the future through dreams. A Book in Time http://abookintime.com offers a chronological list of children's books, plus crafts and other project ideas.

- **Explore the impact of culture.** Immerse yourself in a culture's art, music and stories. Learn about legends and beliefs. How do these aspects affect the way those people organized their societies and lived their lives? Who would you be in that society? How would your worldview change if that were your culture? Notice similarities and differences in current times.

My teens have been really involved in Society for Creative Anachronism (SCA) for the last few years. This organization is all about re-enacting the time of the knights. My kids have made up these elaborate personas. They make their own costumes and chain mail. They read Chaucer (and quote passages at me that I can't possibly understand!) and study medieval history with amazing passion. They have friends of all ages in SCA, all charmingly addicted to a time long before our own. Today my kids are looking up old Norse stuff like legends and quotes. —Sarah Brill, New York

- **Time travel**. Ask yourself "what if" questions to stimulate thinking about different outcomes. "What if the Black Plague never occurred?" or "What if the Allies had lost World War I?" Ask what event or decision in history you would most like to see altered, and why. Ask what person from the past you would most like to meet, and what you would ask him or her.

- **Let periodicals bring history to your door.** A freshly delivered magazine is enticing. There are wonderful historical and cultural magazines for children including *Calliope: World History for Kids*, *Cobblestone: American History for Kids* and *Faces: People, Places and Cultures*.

My oldest child is very interested in American history, particularly early American history. With no help from myself, she has researched this subject online, through library books, magazines, television programs and movies. Her interest also seems to be more focused on girls and women in early America, *because most of her research has centered upon that.*

—Laurel Santiago, Texas

- **Listen to the people who made an impact on history.** Hearing the actual voices of leaders, artists, scientists and others gives one an incomparable insight into the way their words made a difference. American Rhetoric offers free speeches online of 100 major speeches, many with video clips as well, at www.americanrhetoric.com. Older homeschoolers may enjoy interviews in the audiotape collection, *Voices of Our Time: Five Decades of Studs Terkel Interviews* (Highbridge Audio, 2005) by Studs Terkel.

- **Play marble games.** A bag of marbles left over from a grandparent's childhood may be valuable. Learn about them with a book such as *Marble Collectors Handbook* (Schiffer, 2005) by Robert S. Block. Afterwards, play marble games from generations ago. Check rules at www.kidsturncentral.com/topics/sports/marbles.htm

- **Make a gift of family history.** Give the tiny leather case with great grandma's reading glasses to your daughter, along with your memory of this lady who loved to write. This might mean a great deal to a teenager who harbors ambitions of becoming a novelist. The pocketknife from a great uncle who left to seek his fortune as a merchant marine, and who sent letters from ports all over the world may be a meaningful gift for your son who talks of setting off on his own travels.

- **Cook historically.** Try some of the characteristic foods and preparation techniques from the past. Cook stew over a fire, taste plantain, make hasty pudding, grind buckwheat. Ever wonder when people began eating certain foods or developing distinct recipes? The Food Timeline www.foodtimeline.org offers a look back, with each foodstuff clickable to an historical article.

- **Look at your life as an historian or anthropologist might.** What's called "folklife" is simply the everyday creativity surrounding us right now. Jump rope chants, ghost stories, jokes, the way your parents or grandparents warn you to behave, celebrations and daily rituals—these are folklife. The memories you are building right now are history in the making.

- **Hold a fair.** Some homeschool groups have a yearly fair oriented toward history or social studies. Consider a biography fair, genealogy fair, history fair or international fair. For example, at an international fair each young person sets up a display for the country or region they've chosen. They might have posters, projects, foods to sample, crafts and interactive activities. Each participant comes prepared to lead a game from the country they studied, making the fair a lively event. Some homeschool groups might also require each participant to provide a hand-out so that everyone leaves with information about all countries featured at the fair.

- **Imagine history.** Take a walk in a natural area while thinking about how earlier peoples used resources they encountered. What could be utilized to hold water, provide shelter and heat, to cut or pound foods, to heal, to defend? How would natural conditions affect the stories, celebrations and religion of the region? What evidence might be left behind by the earliest inhabitants?

  Take a walk in the city and ask children to imagine it as it was long ago. Notice buildings that were standing more than 100 years ago, talk about what sounds may have been heard then, ask what sort of businesses and transportation they would have seen.

- **Investigate the past in your backyard.** Stage an archeological dig before putting in a new garden or extending the patio. Learn about the people who lived in the area long before you by researching the settlement of the town, early explorers and original inhabitants. Discover what you can about the history of your home and previous owners. Check out *Discovering the History of Your House: And Your Neighborhood* (Santa Monica, 2002) by Betsy J. Green.

- **Develop a book of family lore.** Compile family recipes and any anecdotes that go with these foods. Add family sayings, funny stories and traditions.

- **Visit graveyards.** Cemeteries have stories to tell. Children can learn about family size, immigration and wartime. They can look for the most unusual names, notice the frequency of childhood death in different eras, write down interesting epitaphs. Discuss in advance the necessity for showing respect for gravesites and acting with decorum.

Resources

Online

- **BBC History** offers a wealth of information from ancient to recent history through in-depth articles, animations, games and videos. www.bbc.co.uk/history
- **History Matters** emphasizes the use of primary sources in text, image and audio. http://historymatters.gmu.edu
- **HyperHistory Online** presents world history through interactive timelines, maps, images and text files. www.hyperhistory.com/online_n2/History_n2/a.html
- **The Day I Was Born** has news, music and arts on the day of your birth. Record this data and share with others, play games, listen to audio clips and more. www.dayiwasborn.net
- **World Digital Library** offers multilingual primary materials to promote current and historical understanding. www.wdl.org/en

Books

- *Around the World Crafts: Great Activities for Kids Who Like History, Math, Art, Science and More!* (CreateSpace, 2008) by Kathy Ceceri.
- *A Street Through Time* (DK, 1998) by Anne Millard.
- *Constitution Translated for Kids* (Ovation, 2009) by Cathy Travis.
- *Turn of the Century: Eleven Centuries of Children and Change* (Charlesbridge, 2003) by Ellen Jackson.
- *We Were There, Too!: Young People in U.S. History* (Farrar, Straus and Girous, 2001) by Phillip Hoose.

Current Events

"Very few people really see things unless they've had someone in early life who made them look at things. And name them too. But the looking is primary, the focus."—Denise Levertov

Young people want to know what is going on around them. If they learn to engage in civil discourse they are on the way to understanding and discussing diverse viewpoints. If they can comfortably access details about current events from a variety of sources they are better equipped to think for themselves rather than rely on authority figures or be swayed by popular opinion. This is the path to active, involved citizenship.

We all read the newspaper, even the nine-year-old. None of us gets around to talking things over until we're together at dinner. Our dinnertable conversations might be the most educational part of the day. When we're eating together is when we have a chance to talk. We don't always agree. Most dinners there are a lot of opinions flying around! I think that's great. They're the most well informed kids I know. —M. Stein

Our world is increasingly interdependent. A greater familiarity with the politics, religious background and history of other countries is a richly satisfying endeavor that can lead to a wiser future.

We bought a globe and two large maps, one of the world and one of the U.S. on

which to plot our travels. I keep laminated poster sized reference maps upstairs and downstairs for whenever they are needed in conversation. We have friends from other cultures and sometimes share in their food, language, and festivities. I encourage Spanish a little at home and plan to attend Spanish/English story time at the library. We also have enrolled our oldest in a Chinese class with some of his homeschool friends.

Social studies includes more though than "odd" food and unfamiliar languages. We talk about conservation and why we recycle. I'm trying to teach my kids about social justice and serving others by sponsoring a kid from another country and helping out occasionally at a thrift store/food pantry. We talk about the way we should treat other people regardless of how they treat us. —Karen, Texas

---

Starting Places
- **Make a timeline of your life.** Link the months or years to what was happening in your area, country or the world. Continue your timeline on toward the future, speculating where you will live, what you will do and what will be happening in the world around you.
- **Play video games.** Socially responsible games are a newly emerging form of the craft. These games, some much more compelling than others, combine the allure of challenging obstacles with real life lessons about current situations. Check out the listings at Games for Change www.gamesforchange.org/play
- **Notice news reporting and commentary from other countries.** How is the same event seen in different cultures? Check out a variety of media to get a clearer idea of how the information is reported in other parts of the world.

PEARL World Youth News is an online international news service managed by students from around the world. Adhering to the highest journalistic standards, students select the issues they want to report on, and write, edit and publish their articles on the web-based news service. www.pearl.iearn.org/pearlnews

OneWorld is a global information network designed to link people who see and share the news. It provides access to video and in-depth commentary in the news supplied by people from around the world. http://us.oneworld.net

Southern Center for International Studies provides dozens of links to regional news sources around the world. www.southerncenter.org/info_links.html

- **What makes a topic newsworthy?** Discuss factors such as immediacy, relevance to local people, degree of seriousness, negative impact ("bad" sells better than good), celebrity connection and surprise factor. Why are some stories in the front of the newspaper or first on the show, others "hidden" farther on and still others never reported? How are the same stories handled by different kinds of media— radio, Internet, blog, newspaper, magazines, television, text message, Twitter? Find out how much of what we call news is actually material developed from press releases by think tanks, lobbying organizations and businesses.
- **Read a daily newspaper.** Discuss current events, find science news to pursue, locate nearby activities, discover new field trip ideas, debate editorials, find new words.
- **Analyze the news.** Take in news from a wider range of sources. Check out the same news story from different information outlets by checking a major television station, a major newspaper, an alternative newspaper or site, an international news source and a critical blog. What angles are reflected differently? What is missing from a single news source and why? Note the funding and impetus be-

hind the news story by checking with Source Watch www.sourcewatch.org which tracks the people and organizations shaping the public agenda and www.prwatch.org which exposes public relations spin and propaganda, both provided by The Center for Media and Democracy.

What effect do advertisers have on news content?

How can you find news and information that isn't favorable to advertisers?

Check out the changing statistics on media consolidation in the last thirty years. Do you think a few companies owning the media changes access to relevant information?

- **Good news.** Report your own news. Capture the sights and sounds of your family, neighborhood or travels. What is new to you, what makes a compelling photo, what interesting facts can be added? You might make this into a newspaper, blog or video. Get updates from organizations collecting positive news such as Daily Good www.dailygood.org or Good News Daily www.goodnewsdaily.com

- **Learn where candidates and politicians stand.** Then figure out if there's a reason why. Project Vote Smart www.vote-smart.org is run by thousands of citizens (conservative, moderate and liberal together) researching the backgrounds and records of political candidates and elected officials to discover their voting records, campaign contributions, public statements and biographical data. Every election, through the National Political Awareness Test (NPAT), these volunteers test each candidate's willingness to provide citizens with their positions on the issues they will most likely face if elected. The Project refuses financial assistance from all organizations and special interest groups that lobby or support or oppose any candidate or issue.

Open Secrets www.opensecrets.org provides information on political donations by lobbyists and industry, tracks "paybacks" on

selected legislation, and offers a list of "revolving door" jobs between politics and industry.

FactCheck www.factcheck.org is a nonpartisan organization devoted to truth in politics and public discussion, where facts in the public arena are answered and background is provided.

- **Take a fresh approach to current events.** Read two diametrically opposed news sources, such as conservative and liberal, then have fun highlighting the extremes between them. You may want to note how many times a logical fallacy is used (such as guilt by association, appeal to fear or red herring) or determine where the facts originate. Weigh the assertions made by leaders in politics or business against historical example. Watch popular Comedy Central shows "The Daily Show with Jon Stewart" or "The Colbert Report," then watch popular Fox News shows "Fox & Friends" or "The O'Reilly Factor" and talk over the topics covered. Film your own interviews about an issue and post them on your blog, uncritically.

- **Enjoy the world's greatness.** What do you think are the best aspects of your culture?

UNESCO maintains a list called Masterpieces of the Oral and Intangible Heritage of Humanity www.unesco.org/culture/en/masterpieces showcasing cultural traditions such as Georgian polyphonic singing, Lithuania oak cross crafting and Wayang puppetry in Indonesia. Make a life list of what you would like to experience.

- **Practice the art of dialogue.** When people who disagree can engage in conversations with respect and integrity, they're on the way to creating solutions. This is true in backyard squabbles, regional disputes and diplomatic negotiations. A key is finding common ground. That happens after every person involved has access to the same information and feels that their input is understood. This is a critical skill to practice. Make it a part of your daily life for smaller issues so you can more easily use it when harder issues arise. Notice it in use by individuals and groups around the world.

  Legacy International www.legacyintl.org brings youth together to learn about leadership, conflict resolution and dialogue.

- **Filter media input.** Consider the messages that come into our lives in an unrelenting stream from all sorts of media. The impact is overwhelming. The emphasis on celebrity worship, superficial attractiveness, material possessions and violent use of power is ubiquitous. There are excellent sources of information on media literacy for parents and young people. Many of these sources offer updated information, educational resources and research. Check out: Media Awareness Network www.media-awareness.ca, Center for Media Literacy www.medialit.org, Mind on the Media www.mindonthemedia.org, National Association for Media Literacy Education www.amlainfo.org and Campaign for a Commercial Free Childhood www.commercialexploitation.org Also check out such books as *Made You Look: How Advertising Works and Why You Should Know* (Annick, 2003) by Shari Graydon, *Can't Buy My Love: How Advertising Changes the Way We Think and Feel* (Free Press, 2000) by Jean Kilbourne.

- **Talk about the impact of marketing on daily decision-making.** Count product placements in movies, video games and television shows. Notice the way ads are targeted to specific markets—for example, the commercials during a football game differ from those shown during a wildlife documentary. Talk about the way beauty is portrayed and the effect on self-image. Research how marketing information is gathered on potential customers, from psychology tests to online tracking cookies.

- **Keep a laminated world map on your wall.** Keep track of where news happens, where friends travel and the locales mentioned in books. Whiteboard markers wipe off this surface, so it's easy to write directly on the continents.

- **Think globally.** Notice where your toys, clothing and other purchases are made, perhaps locating the country of origin on a map. Focus your interest on an area in the world, paying attention to the news, weather and celebrations taking place there. Get involved in iEarn youth forums and collaborative projects with students around the world. http://iearn.org Put into place suggestions found in *Growing Up Global: Raising Children to Be At Home in the World* (Ballantine, 2009) by Homa Sabet Tavangar.

Resources

Online

- **Cultural Survival** partners with indigenous peoples across the world to protect language, culture and rights. This site provides lessons, programs and action alerts. www.cs.org
- **Dropping Knowledge** links people globally who ask questions, exchange ideas and start

initiatives around the most pressing issues of our time. www.droppingknowledge.org

- **Geonet** is an online geography game. Play to learn how politics interconnects with place. www.eduplace.com/geonet
- **Headline Spot** offers a directory of children's media with updates by wire, magazine, newspaper and radio. www.headlinespot.com/for/kids/
- **Our Courts** is a site offered by Sandra Day O'Connor with civics games, action projects, news and more. www.ourcourts.org
- **Perry-Castañeda Library Map Collection** offers political, geographic and historical maps of all regions of the world. www.lib.utexas.edu/maps/
- **Pulse of the Planet** tracks nature and culture with sound portraits of life on earth. Featured stories include video, photos and interviews. http://pulseplanet.nationalgeographic.com
- **Survival International** is dedicated to self-determination. Information and advocacy regarding eighty tribes in thirty-four countries. www.survival-international.org
- **The New York Times Learning Network** provides news, lesson archives, word of the day and more. www.nytimes.com/learning
- **Tolerance** addresses conflict resolution, multiculturalism and justice through games, news and information. www.tolerance.org
- **United Nations Cyber School Bus** presents information about countries of the world, plus lessons and videos. www.un.org/Pubs/CyberSchoolBus
- **World Wise Schools** links youth with current Peace Corp volunteers to exchange emails, letters and artwork. www.peacecorps.gov/wws

- **World Affairs Councils (WACA)** offers programs promoting foreign policy awareness:

Great Decisions are focused discussions used by high schools, colleges and adult organizations. Foreign policy and international issues are chosen for intensive discussion. Participants add their views to a national opinion survey, which is presented to the Secretary of State and other key officials in the US government. This opinion poll helps to shape US foreign policy choices. There are currently about 300,000 participants in the Great Decisions program. www.greatdecisions.org

Academic WorldQuest is a team game testing competitors' knowledge of international affairs, geography, history and culture.

WACA also sponsors **Model United Nations**, **Model Arab League** and **Model Organization of American States** programs. www.worldaffairscouncils.org 202-833-4557.

Books

- *Children from Australia to Zimbabwe: A Photographic Journey Around the World* (Charlesbridge, 2006) by Maya Ajmera and Anna Rhesa Versola.
- *Hands Around the World: 365 Creative Ways to Encourage Cultural Awareness and Global Respect* (Williamson, 1992) by Susan Milord
- *How People Live* (DK, 2003) by Dena Freeman.
- *How to Build Your Own Country* (Kids Can, 2009) by Valerie Wyatt.
- *Hungry Planet: What the World Eats* (Material World, 2007) by Peter Menzel.

CHAPTER SIXTEEN

Volunteerism, Ethics & Spirituality

Volunteerism

"How wonderful that no one need wait a single moment to improve the world."—Anne Frank

One of the highest measures of humanity is empathic behavior. When we make volunteer work a normal part of our lives we don't simply teach our children strong core values, we demonstrate these values in action. As author Marc Ian Barasch writes in *Field Notes on the Compassionate Life: A Search for the Soul of Kindness,* "I know that compassion's a grace of sorts, inhering in the nature of things, but is brought forth by a certain exertion, as butter emerges from milk by the labor of the churn."

Just as children's interests pull them in certain directions, so do their concerns. They may be drawn to the suffering of animals on factory farms or worried about the effects of climate change. But as they see the scope of the problem they may lose any hope of making a difference. It's normal to be overwhelmed by seemingly insurmountable issues. And because we feel helpless to change these things it's also normal to feel anger. Anger at ourselves for not being powerful enough to make a difference, anger at the people or conditions we blame. We can channel these powerful emotions into action, becoming part of the solution. Service work is an excellent response. As Mahatma Gandhi once wrote, "As heat conserved is transmuted into energy, even so our anger controlled can be transmuted into a power which can move the world."

What tugs at your child's heart? If he is worried about water pollution, perhaps he can help with efforts to restore a local watershed. That may require networking with local environmental groups, writing letters to legislators or slogging in wetlands to remove trash. He may want to learn about the factors contributing to water pollution and research what is being done elsewhere to reverse the problem.

If your child is saddened by news reports about hunger she may want to volunteer at a community soup kitchen. She may decide to raise funds with her own creative project to donate to a food bank. She may want to study the political, social and economic roots underlying hunger and use what she's learned to advocate for better job training in the area, or write letters to government officials or contact banking institutions with ideas about micro loans for youth entrepreneurs.

Not all volunteering is uplifting. The work may provide little more than a view of the problem's magnitude. That doesn't need to stop us. If we don't teach our children that the efforts of caring people make a difference, they learn cynicism and despair.

The biggest driving force behind my career choice and my largest commitment over the last four years has been an organization called Youth Challenge, where I was able to participate in sports and activities with physically handicapped youth.

Youth Challenge is probably the best thing that's ever happened to me. Not only did I discover my passion through it, I found friends and a great environment to be in. There are few things as precious to me as my time at Y.C. Nothing compares to be able to help a child swim, play hockey, climb a rock wall, or something else they couldn't previously do, and see the huge smile on their face as they accomplish these goals. Youth Challenge helped me to grow to be outgoing & confident, be all I can be, have compassion towards others, and courage to do anything I put my mind to.

—Kate Steven, 19

What are some other ways a young person can gain from volunteer experience?

- Volunteering allows youth to give of themselves. It puts their enthusiasm to use. Although they may expect nothing in return, often they get back much more—new friends, increased knowledge and the sort of fulfillment they may not have expected.

- Volunteer positions may be the first time that homeschoolers are supervised by other adults. These relationships provide a way for young people to learn about themselves in an entirely new context. Later on these adults can also be asked to serve as job references or to write recommendations.

- Through volunteering, young people can develop important relationships with mentors. This provides more than career guidance, it can give them role models for adulthood.

- Community service teaches new skills in a purposeful manner. Tasks such as planning the church group travel route, assisting with a dog therapy program, writing fliers for a health fair, or raising funds for a homeless shelter are wonderfully instructive. These efforts "count" for those keeping academic record, but also in more important ways.

- Community service helps young people connect people of other races, income levels, ages and abilities. Their friendships widen and their perceptions change as their understanding grows.

- Volunteering helps develop independence and initiative. Most volunteer positions expect people to be self-starters able to take on new tasks, even if their efforts take place in the familiar surroundings of a local library or theater. These roles can be empowering.

- Community service gives homeschoolers a chance to deal with new situations. As they handle different circumstances their self-confidence grows, helping them deal more easily with changes in the future.

- Volunteering offers young people work experience in different fields. Too often people prepare for a career without any direct knowledge of what it means to be a county prosecutor, art therapist, mechanic or field biologist. After volunteering they may learn that their talents are best suited for other fields. Or they may have their fascination with this line of work confirmed.

• Acting out of compassion has long-term benefits. Teens who volunteer have better physical and emotional health than those who don't volunteer. The effect is still found sixty years later.

At ages eight through eleven, Cassidy went to Yale's Peabody Museum of Natural History with Luz, his mother. Together, they volunteered to sort and catalog insect specimens with one of the scientists who work in the attics of the museum. Over several months, he learned the names and habits of beetles and other bugs, while gaining the respect and trust of the scientists. Later, he was trusted to be the "Information Officer" (white coat, name tag, keys to closets, etc.) in the Great Hall of Dinosaurs at the museum on days when it was crowded with families, giving info about the dinosaurs and other fossils on display there. You can imagine his pride in such a job.
— Ned Vare, Connecticut

Often volunteering isn't "official." A family does yard work and errands for a housebound neighbor. Or they compile information and pass out fliers to get a safety initiative passed through city council. Or they put on a garage sale and donate all the proceeds to benefit a local shelter. They are making the community a better place through their own efforts. The side effect? They give their children a wonderful dose of can-do attitude.

When families reach out to help others, their children learn that this is a natural response. After all, the word "humane" is a variant of the word "human." The definition of "humane" includes *demonstrating better aspects of the human character such as kindness and compassion* and *showing respect for other people's views*. The word used to define us also describes the qualities essential to forging a society based on mutual regard.

The kids are too little at ages 3 and 6 for any volunteering just yet. We're having fun taking a "guerrilla compassion" approach. Here are some things we like to do:

At the holidays we buy a hot chocolate or coffee to give to the Salvation Army bell ringer with our thanks and a donation too!

In the summer we keep a cooler in the van. It's easy to hand a bottled drink to a traffic cop or garbage truck guys and tell them they deserve a break.

We keep a supply of umbrellas we've bought at thrift stores in the van. On a few occasions we've been able to give the gift of an umbrella to a stranger when rain starts.

Like a lot of small kids, mine draw all the time. We use some of their drawings as wrapping paper and tuck candy inside with a note that says "thanks for making our day" and then we keep these in my backpack when we go out. Then when we want to thank a helpful librarian or nice cashier we wait till we're ready to walk out and hand that person one of our little surprise thank you packages. In fact I've noticed that having a thank you package along with us puts us on the lookout for nice people—what a great way to be!

We're thinking about making pies this weekend now that strawberries are in season and if we make enough we'll take a few pies up to the sheriff's department.

—Ben, Emma and Olivia's Mom

There are many creative ways to volunteer based on local needs and the child's interests:

- Regularly visit a "grandfriend" at a nursing home, assisted living facility or in the neighborhood.
- Provide children's programs at a library, daycare or community center as storytellers, puppeteers or craft instructors.
- Knit or crochet warm hats, scarves, gloves and baby blankets to donate.
- Send letters and/or care packages to members of the military stationed far from home.
- Pick up litter in a wildlife area, beach or neighborhood.
- Clean cages, prepare food and provide animal care at a shelter, rescue center or veterinary clinic. Also consider donating food, cleaning supplies, kitty litter and other items.

- Do errands, cook for or otherwise help out a housebound person.
- Tutor.
- Raise awareness of an issue by writing, speaking out or forming a group to promote the cause.
- Serve as unofficial welcoming friends for immigrants who could use help navigating unfamiliar streets and who need assistance learning the customs and colloquialisms that aren't in any handbook.
- Repair and donate such items as toys, bikes or computers.
- Grow vegetables and offer extra produce to a hunger center.
- Develop a website for a local non-profit.
- Take photos, such as pets available for adoption or local landmarks, for an online community quiz.
- Work with a local cause to research, make phone calls or speak at meetings.

Young people can also seek out volunteer positions with area organizations. First, check into established volunteer programs. Health care centers, historical societies, libraries, museums, food or clothing banks, churches, park systems and service groups are often looking for volunteers. If your children are younger than the age requirements, offer to go through the training along with your child and serve volunteer hours as a pair or family unit. This will not only increase the number of volunteer hours for the organization, it will aid your child's ability to do an effective job. At some point it will be clear to those who supervise that your assistance along with your child is no longer needed although you may wish to continue. Working side by side with your child on these shared tasks can foster memorable experiences.

Youth may also inquire about volunteering where no volunteer program is established, such as in a veterinary clinic, community arts program or research facility. It takes time and money to develop a volunteer program. Your youth may need to make many phone calls before finding an organization willing to take on a volunteer. He or she may need to prove interests and abilities that will be valuable to the organization. Again, you may need to proffer some parent time at least initially if there are concerns about the lack of adult supervision.

We volunteer alot! My son volunteers through the Youth Volunteer Corps— this summer he logged 48 hours volunteer time at two different weeklong projects. He and my oldest daughter volunteer through the "school year" with our homeschool group as well. They have assistance finding volunteer projects through the YVC coordinators. As a family we volunteer with Meals On Wheels deliveries once a week, as well as various other things throughout the year. Last year one memorable volunteer time was ringing Salvation Army bells at Christmas. One man stopped and gave us a large donation saying that as a child he had nothing. His parents often weren't home and one year he got a favorite toy from the Salvation Army. He didn't realize who brought it until he was an adult and now he donates whenever he sees a bell ringer. It brought tears to all our eyes, even my then 6 year old.

—Angie Beck, Kansas

I look at my personal core values and find an opportunity to be of service to

Many schools now require teens to log a certain number of volunteer hours. Homeschool volunteering is more likely to be self-initiated. The difference is that you won't have a school official acting as a liaison on your behalf, so you may have to make more concerted efforts to get a coveted community service position. Are you having difficulty landing the volunteer spot you want? You may need to be proactive. There are ways to prove one's potential. First gather evidence:

- **Why do you want to volunteer?** Amass some talking points about your interests and concerns. Imagine yourself answering questions as if you were in a job interview.
- **Do you have skills to offer?** What you consider ordinary abilities may be special talents to a particular agency. For example, you may find it easy to explain to seniors how to load an iPod or you may find it fun to walk dogs. Tailor the abilities you are offering to the type of organization you want to help.
- **Who can vouch for you?** Consider asking your scout leader, piano teacher, religious leader or other adult to attest to your reliability.
- **When are you available?** Remember that you may have more favorable hours to offer than youth in school if you can help during the weekday.
- **Are you eager to help in any way?** Emphasize your willingness to pitch in with any reasonable task.

Now find a way to communicate this evidence when you request a volunteer position. You may be ready to go in for an interview once you've thought through these topics. You may want to go a step farther. You can write up a resume and enclose letters of recommendation. You can film a promo video starring you, featuring the benefits of taking you on as a volunteer. Or find a way to help out the organization such as writing about them in a letter to the local newspaper, then approach them for a volunteer position.

something that is in line with the values I am instilling in my children. I feel passionate about being there and helping our elderly citizens and enriching their lives—as they have so much to offer to younger people as well. We found a wonderful local organization called Love Is The Answer where you are matched with a senior citizen who is in a nursing facility but has few or no visitors who come to see them. This was a perfect opportunity for my kids to learn compassion for people and to learn about another person's life.

—Tamara Markwick, California

We live in a small, rural county with less than 7,000 people. My granddaughters have done a lot of community service activities here. They have volunteered at the local historical society, a local museum, the library, hospice, and other groups.

—Karen Pennebaker, West Virginia

I liked the emphasis recommended by the late Raymond and Dorothy Moore which is 1/3 work, 1/3 "schooling," and 1/3 service. It took a long time to find a place where my young children and I could serve together but we currently try to make it to a local thrift store/food pantry a couple times a month to help out. They also come with me to donate blood and we regularly think up ways to serve other people.

—Karen, Texas

Resources

Service Ideas Based on a Young Person's Interests.

Alleviating hunger
- Second Harvest www.secondharvest.org

Animals
- American Society for the Prevention of Cruelty to Animals www.aspca.org
- The Humane Society www.hsus.org
- Therapy Dogs International www.tdi-dog.org

Austin, Kesley and Sunny White found a commitment to service in an unusual way. As siblings do, they got into arguments with each other. As mothers do, Jenn White turned a problem into a learning opportunity.

"We sat down with our Mom one day and did the math. Our Mom would take five minutes each time we would bicker, and multiply that by each week, and then multiply that by each month, and then again by each year. We found that we would spend 448 hours of our childhood bickering in a year. When we heard that number we were shocked! We said to ourselves, 'What have we done for other people in that amount of time?' 'What have we done for ourselves in that time?' 'What have we done for the world in that time?'

So our mom gave us an assignment. An assignment to change our priorities. An assignment to be selfless. And an assignment to make up for the 448 hours we have spent bickering. However long it takes, we will be giving back to our community, our world, 448 hours worth of service."

Jenn White says there's "overwhelming humanitarian aid right here in the US ... from the souls of other families who care ... So we pray, we fundraise, we ask, we seek, we knock, so that we can help ... In doing so we realize our own potential, our own tools, our own way of helping."

Athletics
- Special Olympics www.specialolympics.org

Business
- Kiva http://kiva.org

Community Service
- Kids Care Clubs www.kidscare.org

Conservation
- National Park Service Youth Conservation Corps
- www.nps.gov/gettinginvolved/youthprograms/index.htm

Ecology
- Keep America Beautiful www.kab.org

Health and Human Service
- Red Cross Youth Services www.redcross.org
- Ronald McDonald House http://rmhc.org

Housing
- Habitat for Humanity www.habitat.org
- National Alliance to End Homelessness www.endhomelessness.org

Literacy
- Reading is Fundamental www.rif.org

Seniors
- Meals on Wheels www.mealcall.org

Volunteer Clearinghouses to Search for More Ways to Get Involved
- Charity Guide www.volunteerguide.org
- United Way www.unitedway.org
- Volunteer Match www.volunteermatch.org
- Youth Service America http://ysa.org
- Youth Volunteer Corps www.yvca.org

Background Information and Further Volunteering Ideas
- **Center for a New American Dream** helps make informed choices to promote social justice and protect the environment. www.newdream.org
- **The Congressional Award** recognizes initiative by American youth in four self-determined goals areas: Volunteer Public Service, Personal Development, Physical Fitness and Expedition/Exploration. The award is earned

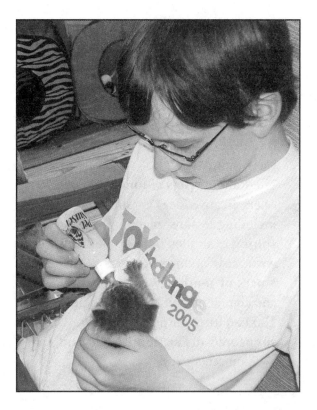

individually or with friends, at one's own pace. www.congressionalaward.org
- **Do Something** networks teens working on causes. Also provides action guides, lessons, project ideas and information. www.dosomething.org
- **Free Child** empowers youth-led social change in the arts, leadership development and community planning with resources and information. www.freechild.org
- **Global Youth Action Network** promotes youth participation in international decisions. Also offers Youth Action Awards, Global Youth Service Day. www.youthlink.org
- **Idealist Kids and Teens** provides resources enabling youth to carry out positive ideas, plus examples of those who have already made a difference www.idealist.org
- **Oxfam** offers background information about social and economic injustice as well as opportunities to make a difference. www.oxfam.org
- **Peace Jam** applies Nobel Peace Prize winners' ideas to current day issues. This worldwide organization offers clubs

conferences, curricula and local projects. www.peacejam.org

- **President's Volunteer Service Award** enables volunteers to track hours toward a certificate. www.presidentialserviceawards.gov You can log volunteer hours on the site and search for volunteer opportunities through Serve America www.serve.gov
- **The Random Acts of Kindness Foundation** offers creative ideas for spreading kindness including lessons, planning guides and inspiring examples from around the world. www.actsofkindness.org
- **Voices of Youth** develops global awareness and community-building. Young people from 180 countries participate in these UNICEF sponsored discussion boards and chats. www.unicef.org/voy

Books
- *It's Our World, Too!* (Farrar, Straus and Girous, 2002) by Phillip Hoose.
- *It's Your World—If You Don't Like It, Change It: Activism for Teenagers* (Simon Pulse, 2004) by Mikki Halpin.
- *The Teen Guide to Global Action: How to Connect with Others (Near and Far) to Create Social Change* (Free Spirit, 2007) by Barbara A. Lewis.
- *The Kid's Guide to Service Projects: Over 500 Service Ideas for Young People Who Want to Make a Difference* (Free Spirit, 2009) by Barbara A. Lewis.

Ethics & Spirituality

"There are simply no answers to some of the great pressing questions. You continue to live them out, making your life a worthy expression of leaning into the light."—Barry Lopez

At times delightfully silly, children are also attuned to the profound. They ponder matters touching on philosophy, religion and cosmology. They ask unanswerable questions. Conversations with a child who is searching for answers are difficult to hold off until you are ready with the "right" approach, especially when the concepts go deep. Children want to explore the biggest questions: "Is there an end to the universe?" "Why do people do bad things?" "What will happen to me when I die?" When these matters come up we can start by asking our children what they think. That helps us recognize how the child sees himself and the world around him.

When a young person talks about what has personal significance it's time to listen and respond from the heart. Paying attention mindfully means we don't judge or overreact. This honors the individual's search for truth, even if that truth is not as we perceive it. When an adult is open to a child's perceptions it assures the child that his feelings merit attention. This approach elevates the inner life as worthy of consideration. This is no mean feat when our popular culture skims over such matters with glib clichés or jaded mockery. We live in a time when most people are unwilling to accept doubt, difficulty and struggle as valuable lessons, let alone to look inward for guidance. Certainly most adults don't recognize that children prompt us to look at our own truths more closely. But clear-eyed children, unafraid to speak about what is true within them and around them, remind us to look beyond surface assumptions.

> We don't have to have all the answers. In fact supplying too many ready-made answers can impair the search that remains perennial even for fervent believers. Each of us longs for a personal understanding of our place in the world and the purpose of our own existence. This yearning can be particularly intense in the teen years, a time of doubt and self-scrutiny. Doubt itself is an important part of growth. Those who have gone through prolonged periods of doubt have often discovered stronger faith or deeper meaning as a result.

Psychologist Tobin Hart spent years interviewing children and adults in an effort to understand children's spiritual lives. He writes in *The Secret Spiritual World of Children*, "The evidence overwhelmingly suggests that children have a rich and formative spiritual life. From the adults with whom I have spoken, we will see that childhood moments serve as touchstones for their entire lives." He acknowledges that it's difficult for adults to teach virtues without becoming overly repressive or moralistic. He notes that when we insist on compliance with external authority but don't bring forth true understanding, we encourage moral immaturity, something that Ralph Waldo Emerson called "arrested growth." Our challenge as parents is to preserve children's wonder and joy while providing guidance as they grow into spiritually whole adults.

Many children don't translate the awe they experience into questions. Or, as they get older, they seek answers in other ways. They pay attention to the adults in their lives, hoping to find that the actions of people they admire are consistent with the beliefs these people espouse. Chances are they will find some hypocrisy along with consistency, but as they observe human nature they also learn something important about vulnerability and the value of forgiveness.

Children are often drawn to mythic themes. Epic quests, superhuman powers, unimaginable courage, tragedy and sacrifice are common elements in their favorite movies, books and video games. Such elements evoke archetypes that help young people face longings and fears. Archetypal characters such as the hero, orphan and trickster are found across cultures and may stem from what Carl Jung called the collective unconscious. Many times parents try to block children from reading books or seeing films that depict tragedy, despair or violence. As children's authors know, when this material is presented purposefully it's exactly what young people desperately seek.

Meaning is also found in the kind of personal expression that transcends effort. A child may enter that zone while running a race, painting a picture, playing the cello or dancing alone in the backyard; losing personal identity while gaining a feeling of oneness. At that moment the child feels he or she was born to do this. This state is not reserved for certain rare people, it's a gift found in the state of flow.

There are many ways to help children as they search for answers. First among them are our own beliefs. Many parents have a strong belief system with regular rituals of worship and prayer. Others look to rationality, humanism and the beautiful happenstance of finding oneself alive. Whether a family takes a religious or secular approach, it is important in our wondrously diverse world that we understand the ways people honor what is sacred to them. It need not shake our own foundations to explore the belief systems of the world's religions. Instead, as we comprehend how others approach what is beyond human comprehension we get a sense of shared search for meaning. Learn together. Find commonalities among religions. See what is joyful and celebratory in each. Notice that each has a way of calming and centering, such as prayer or meditation. Each faith also has ways of developing awareness of a higher purpose and aligning one's life with a moral code.

An adult might share his or her own search for meaning with a child. This honors the child's desire to make that connection as well. Such sharing need not be a lengthy sermon. It can be rooted in stories about the child and the parent's childhood. Remember to touch on those times when heightened feeling linked with experience. Talk about the insight gained when you noticed how bare winter branches against the sky resembled the fragile network of veins in your newborn's closed eyelids. Mention the inexplicable peace that settles over you when you are near the ocean. Tell your child you want to remember the moment you are in right now, forever.

Upon his or her wakening, ask your child to share a dream. These little stories woven in our sleep are not trifles. They can help us understand ourselves better. Listen carefully. Ask about the characters and settings in the dream. Details are where the meanings lie. For example, if your child has a nightmare about being unable to get up from a chair when a lion was at the door and she woke just as the door opened, ask her to describe the chair. It might be one used for time-out punishment or her old highchair from infancy. Ask her to tell you about the door. What did it look like? How did it open? Ask her to describe the

lion, the sounds it made and why it was at the door. If the dream was particularly distressing, ask her to imagine it again but this time changing the scenario, running it over again in her head until the frightening parts are reworked into a better outcome. The child can turn the chair into a high speed vehicle and zoom away. Or pick up a tranquilizer dart for the lion, who was at the door with a nasty toothache. Or the lion may turn from the door, step on a plane and fly back to his family waiting on the savannah. Sharing dreams helps us to have better recall of dreams in subsequent nights. Reworking dreams helps us to be aware that we can be present in our dreams as active players, observing and making storylines change, a valuable practice called lucid dreaming.

The need to belong exerts a powerful influence. We surround ourselves with a "tribe" of people made up of our family, friends, neighbors, co-workers and others. They serve as a comfort zone for us. The desire to belong, to be accepted within a group, goes back to the earliest periods in our development when being alone or an outsider was a threat to survival. Hence, we may harbor a lingering distrust of those who are different even if we don't acknowledge this response. The threat of "us" and "them" has changed, however. We don't live in isolated clans. We see people unknown to us every day. Culturally, our tribe includes those with diverse ethnic, racial and religious backgrounds. It isn't unusual to help a member of one's own group or, by extension, *someone like* those in our group, but the motivation behind reaching out to befriend someone outside our tribe requires a higher level of ethical maturity. It also takes strength to stand for one's values when others don't seem to care. Children do this all the time. They may argue to save a tree from being chopped down, tell a bully to leave a smaller child alone, plead the case for adopting a rescue dog. We need to recognize the elevated moral reasoning behind these actions. Young people can be ethical giants, willing to take on the troubles of the world. They need adults to help them see that they don't face these problems alone. They also need help understanding that many issues are more complex than right and wrong, with multiple aspects to consider. This way, each generation's tribe grows in understanding.

Learning about individuals who have followed a higher path, despite difficulties and frustrations, helps our children find role models worth emulating. The media would have us believe that crime and greed rule. But the uncelebrated daily lives of people who operate on principles of compassion and justice form the bedrock of human existence. These people are everywhere: in your home, next door and around the world. Unselfish acts performed billions of times a day weave us together as a caring species. We care for the helpless, rescue the needy, comfort the sorrowful, share knowledge, create happiness. In fact parents of young children do this on a minute by minute basis!

We can help our children exemplify moral behavior with greater ease. In particular we can pay attention to good deeds in our own homes. This alters the typical preoccupation with negative behavior. It's easy to notice children squabbling for five minutes and ignore two hours of peace. That doesn't mean disregarding unsafe or unkind behavior. It does mean that we can be mindful of where we put our parenting energy. What we consistently notice is amplified. When we habitually respond to the best in a person we are calling forth those qualities. On the other hand, if we regularly notice the worst in a person, even though we are trying to bring about improvement, we unwittingly reinforce these negative behaviors. For a child whose self-image is forming, this principle is even more important. What we recognize, persists. Noticing when a child has done something

right helps to strengthen not only that behavior, but also the motivation behind the behavior. It's simple to say, "Thanks for scooting over on the couch to make room for your brother; that was really considerate of you." Or "I'm so glad you make time to play with the dog. That really makes her day."

Young children look to us. Their dreams are formed of the words we use and the stories we tell. Their body memories are made by the way we touch them, playfully and gently or impatiently and harshly. Each generation of children brings fresh hope to this planet. The young among us are creative, compassionate and ingenious. They are plucky enough to insist on being themselves. They have extraordinary abilities to share, the exact abilities needed to bring forth the best possible future.

Starting Places
- **Explain.** Children don't necessarily agree with your judgments even though they do need to abide by your rules. It helps to talk about ethical rationale. You may think your family's underlying values are obvious to your children, but subtleties aren't easily recognized.
- **Demonstrate by example.** We know our children are watching as we gossip, swear at other drivers or mangle the truth. We show our children how we expect them to act with our own behavior. Oftentimes children help us walk a more honest ethical path through their unwavering attention.
- **Encourage higher-level thinking.** Respond to children's questions with deeper inquiries. Ask them about the reasoning they use when they make daily choices. Discuss the balance between rights and responsibilities. Talk about what might motivate people's behavior.
- **Ask the philosophical questions** such as "How can we know for sure?" "Would thinking that way change something else?" "Is

truth different from one person to another?" and "How do we decide what is good?" Don't shut down the investigation of ideas with presumptions or ready answers. Check out *Philosophy for Kids: 40 Fun Questions That Help You Wonder ... About Everything!* (Prufrock, 2000) by David White and *Philosophy for Teens: Questioning Life's Big Ideas* (Prufrock, 2006) by Sharon Kaye and Paul Thomson.

- **Cultivate internalized values.** Gradually children learn to behave ethically because it's the right thing to do, not because they'll be punished for doing the wrong thing or rewarded for behaving well. Developing a strong inner compass is a slow process. Many mistakes are made throughout life even when we try to live up to our highest ideals. When children err, correct them without making character judgments. Mistakes are natural steps in learning. Talk about the missteps; and when it's safe, don't rescue them from the outcome but rather allow the consequences to fit the circumstances.

  Show unconditional positive regard for your children, which means assurance of your love and support regardless of their behavior. At the same time expect them to act out of respect for other people's feelings and rights.

Don't offer rewards such as treats or money for good behavior, such bribes tend to foster selfishness rather than develop character.

- **Teach civility.** Politeness is simply a social code that allows us to preserve one another's comfort and dignity. Children old enough to tie their shoes can understand basic standards of civility such as adjusting their behavior to fit the situation, demonstrating respect and apologizing.

- **Find springboards to conversation.** Current events bring up concerns about fairness, justice, equality and moral responsibility. These topics link naturally to conversations about virtue, free will, trust and values.

  The dilemmas faced by characters in books, plays and movies can lead to discussions about ethical decision-making. There are common recurring themes—Do the means justify the end result? How important is winning? Is there a personal price to popularity? What does it mean to be true to yourself?

- **Tell stories.** Talk about your own life experiences. Those times when you suffered or struggled reveal ethical dilemmas to your children in a way that abstract examples cannot. Young people recognize that it's safe to share their own concerns because you have been where they are now; confused, humiliated, unsure, sometimes wrong and sometimes thankfully in the right.

- **Recognize the importance of role models.** It's a powerful motivator when a child realizes, "That's the kind of person I want to be." This person may be someone the child admires but has never met, but more likely it is a person in the child's life such as a neighbor, music teacher or coach who demonstrates compelling character. We may never know who our children quietly admire, but we can make a habit of pointing out the finer qualities in people around us. We can also expose our children to movies and books about exemplary people. These examples inspire especially when they are attainable and not exaggerated out of proportion.

Talk about people who have inspired you. What qualities do you draw forth from yourself to live up to those role models? Who in day-to-day life demonstrates character traits you want to exemplify? Can you talk to them about these qualities and how these people developed their strengths? Check out *Dare to Dream!: 25 Extraordinary Lives* (Prometheus, 2005) by Sandra McLeod Humphrey.

- **Brainstorm values and beliefs** your family regards as important. How do we uphold those on a daily basis? How can we do better? Children are often more exacting than adults, so prepare for rough questions if they observe some blurred distinctions.
- **Become familiar with beliefs around the world.** Visit a temple, mosque, synagogue and cathedral. Attend a worship service, children's program or cultural event there. Prepare by reading about the background and beliefs of the faith.

  Listen to creation stories from all parts of the world. Talk about how the story might affect a culture's worldview. Read literature with main characters of different faiths, watch children's movies made in other countries, learn about differences and similarities in religious practices.

- **Form a circle of parents and children** who wish to explore meaning together. You might share stories, songs and dreams in each session. It may be time for *kirtan*, ecstatic dance, spiritual art-making or reverent contemplation. Some find a great deal of meaning in a drumming circle, others in taking time together in nature. Remain flexible so the circle can expand with new ideas.
- **Exercise forgiveness.** Avoid holding grudges, judging others and remaining bitter. Allow forgiveness to ease the pain of small hurts and it will be a well-developed skill when larger trials loom. Learn about the value of forgiveness when applied to personal as well as political suffering. Explore stories of reconciliation and conflict resolution at The Forgiveness Project www.theforgivenessproject.com.
- **Talk about the ethical dilemmas presented by technology.** Digital technology forces us to reconsider plagiarism, privacy, intrusive advertising, slander, intellectual freedom, piracy and more. What other new developments challenge our values?
- **Consider what your children value.** Conversations about what is valued helps us see each other's perspective. What five things would you take along if you had to move? If extraterrestrials asked about life on planet Earth, how would you describe it? If all world leaders had a meeting what should they discuss? What would you like on your tombstone?
- **Encourage writing.** Putting thoughts and feelings down in a private journal promotes reflective thinking. There a young person can consider beliefs, ideas and problems freely. The act of writing itself extends the process of contemplation. It also helps the journal writer find personal meaning in experiences.

RESOURCES

Online

- **My Hero** provides glimpses of real-life heroes from around the world. The site offers stories, news, lessons plus the opportunity to submit a hero story. www.myhero.com
- **Speaking of Faith** is a public radio show about religion and ethics. Check out the archives, newsletter and slideshows. http://speakingoffaith.publicradio.org
- **The Global Oneness Project** features video interviews from those engaged in such disciplines as education, health care, ecology and more. www.globalonenessproject.org
- **This I Believe** offers thousands of statements of faith from around the world. http://thisibelieve.org

Books

- *Above All, Be Kind: Raising a Humane Child in Challenging Times* (New Society, 2003) by Zoe Weil.
- *Building Moral Intelligence: The Seven Essential Virtues that Teach Kids to Do the Right Thing* (Jossey-Bass, 2002) by Michele Borba.
- *One World, Many Religions: The Ways We Worship* (Knopf, 1996) by Mary Pope Osborne.
- *What Do You Stand For? For Kids: A Guide To Building Character* (Free Spirit, 1999) by Barbara A. Lewis and Marjorie Lisovskis.
- *What Do You Stand For? For Teens: A Guide To Building Character* (Free Spirit, 2005) by Barbara A. Lewis.

CHAPTER SEVENTEEN

Welcoming the Renaissance

A Greater Good

"If we are to achieve a richer culture ... we must recognize the whole gamut of human potentialities, and so weave a less arbitrary social fabric, one in which each diverse human gift will find a fitting place."—Margaret Mead

The word "educate" stems from the Latin roots *e* and *ducere* meaning "to lead forth" or "to draw out from within." The word itself acknowledges that the process is unique to each learner. What is whole and beautifully interwoven with an individual's experiences is truly educational. Standardizing education actually diminishes more sophisticated understanding and trivializes the learner in the process.

As we've seen, narrow approaches to education presuppose that conventional schooling is necessary for life long success. But those assumptions are wrong. Long hours of class work and homework leave insufficient time for free play, purposeful work, encounters with nature or deeply fulfilling relationships. These are key elements in building self-awareness, sustaining imagination and finding patterns within larger, complex systems.

Learning of the highest value extends well beyond measurable dimension. It can't be fit into any curriculum or evaluated by any test. It is activated by experiences which develop our humanity such as finding meaning, expressing moral courage, building lasting connections, channeling anger into purposeful action, recognizing one's place in nature, acting out of love. This leads to comprehension that includes and transcends knowledge. It teaches us to be our best selves.

We are blessed to live at a time when we are free to embrace what has truth and meaning for our families. In doing this we connect our actions to what we truly value. That reconnection is profoundly restorative for our families, but also resonates well beyond our own lives. Why? Because it's a step toward healing much greater divides.

We've grown accustomed to divisions. Early on we learn to regard our physical selves by little more than appearance, turning to doctors to manage the symptoms our neglected bodies develop. We ignore inner promptings guiding us toward more authentic lives, then expect the resulting misery can be resolved by assigning blame, seeking distractions or ingesting comfort. We cede our true authority to experts until we no longer recognize it in ourselves.

Our lifestyles tend to separate us from nature. Food is processed, garbage hauled away, the passages of birth and death largely hidden. We go about our daily activities without taking part in processes intrinsic to the natural world so we don't think about how completely everything is connected.

We're led to believe that personal values and beliefs are separate from the dictates of work, education and commerce. That leads to one set of ethics at home, with another set of more expedient guidelines for the world at large. We may treat our children tenderly yet buy products made by other children in sweatshops. We may insist on eating organic food yet carry out polluting corporate policies at work.

Separation between our beliefs and actions creates a schism that is profoundly unhealthy for the world around us, just as it is for our bodies and spirits. It takes significant inner work to act with integrity. But when we do, we begin to usher in a mighty personal peace.

Our world struggles with religious intolerance, a deep gulf between rich and poor, ecological devastation, injustice and greed. We're torn farther apart when political leaders foster fear, religious leaders preach condemnation, CEOs mandate greed as a business policy and political pundits spew vitriol. Separation does not solve our

most challenging issues. It accelerates them. This global struggle brings meaning and purpose, even transcendence at times. That's because struggle can wake us up.

Struggle can cause us to react with fear, vengefulness and judgment. That tends to create new problems, new lessons, until we gradually awaken to greater understanding. Oftentimes it takes significant difficulty before people break through limitations, identify with higher ethical standards and act in alignment with these core values.

The headlong pursuit of what is newer, more expedient and profitable has led many of us to ignore the separations that have brought us to this point. Especially what is separate within us. But denying the fullness of who we are doesn't allow us to be complete. When we acknowledge that each of us has the capacity for good and evil, for greed as well as generosity, for lies as well as truth—then we build bridges of understanding between us. We can see beyond divisions within us as well as divisions between us. There's less need to fall back on blame or fear. We can begin to fully awaken the boundless energy found in the real choice to tell the truth, to act with compassion, to do what is best for all concerned. That provides an endless wellspring of hope.

Today's challenges are proving transformative. We've shown increasing willingness to reach out to one another, to share ideas, to find meaning and value in common pursuits. We've risen up in hundreds of thousands of movements to create positive change. That's enormously powerful. As Albert Einstein said, "We can't solve problems by using the same kind of thinking we used when we created them." Our words, actions and yes, even thoughts are creating the world anew for our children.

The way we nurture our children is one of the most profound ways we align with our values in this transforming world. Every day we face powerful questions that serve as boarding passes to more intentional living. What can I attend to fully right now? What does my life teach?

How do I replenish my own wellspring of enthusiasm? What is important? What can I learn from my child?

When we change our own conditioned beliefs about what constitutes education we open up to a way of being that affects everything around us. We see what learning looks like when it flowers of its own accord. It's a purposeful, innovative and sacred process. This recognition affects the way we relate to ourselves and to the rest of the world.

We begin to understand the deeper truths taught us by nature. Our families, our cultures, our ecosystems exist in a mutual dance of interdependence and we are co-creators in this unfolding reality.

We recognize that a caring touch and the beat of a loving heart has a beneficial effect on others. We understand that the way the youngest are raised shapes the resulting society. We know, whether by taking a long view of humanity or an intuitive glimpse of ourselves, that we have the capacity to be clever, cooperative and amazingly adaptable.

We endure painful experiences, individually and collectively, that wake us up to what is more generous, wise and compassionate. This means that we are aware, right now, of the power imbedded in our daily choices. That doesn't make the choices easier. It does make them more conscious.

Homeschooling doesn't erase our doubts and worries. It doesn't guarantee success. It certainly doesn't make us "right." It does, however, affirm that children are not determined by what pressure and conformity can make of them. They are complete beings right now. As we step back from imposing any one particular destiny upon our children, we welcome who they are. We remain open to the mystery, turmoil and wonder of each person's creative response to life.

Homeschooling often unfolds in the same way that curiosity does, leaping ahead and falling back in a rhythm unique to the individual. It has everything to do with the moment, the place, the person. When we follow compelling needs and interests, not only the child's but of the family and community, we find that learning tends toward completeness, just as each part of a hologram contains all the information of the whole.

What might seem like quiet personal decisions have a ripple effect. Laughing off adversity, working together as a family, seeing the best in our loved ones, choosing what our hearts tell us—these unheralded actions are already making a significant difference.

Mohandas Gandhi said, "We must be the change we wish to see." In that case, a renaissance is in the works. The world is created every day, every moment, by each one of us. What awe-inspiring potential we have. What kind of tomorrow will today's curious, spirited, wondrous children generate?

Notes & Bibliography

Introduction

Knowles, J. Gary. Phone interview Sept. 17, 2007.

Swanbrow, Diane. "Study: Home-educated children not disadvantaged," The University Record News and Information Services, 12 April, 1993 http://www.ur.umich.edu/9293/Apr12_93/16.htm (accessed January 24, 2007).

Chapter One: Natural Learning Happens Everywhere

Natural Learning

Holt, John. *How Children Learn* (New York: Da Capo Press, 1967) Page 287, quote.

Wilson, Frank R. *The Hand: How Its Use Shapes the Brain, Language and Human Culture* (New York: Pantheon Books, 1998) Page 13, author's comments about interview subjects' attitudes towards school. Page 280, author sums up research of Seymour Sarason.

"Paying Double: Inadequate High Schools and Community College Remediation." Alliance for Excellent Education, Issue Brief, August 2006. "http://www.all4ed.org/files/archive/publications/remediation.pdf (accessed January 23, 2009).

Bridgeland, John, Dilulio, John Jr., and Karen Burke Morison. "The Silent Epidemic: Perspectives of High School Dropouts." Civic Enterprises in association with Peter D. Hart Research Associates for the Bill and Melinda Gates Foundation, March 2006. http://www.gatesfoundation.org/nr/downloads/ed/TheSilentEpidemic3-06FINAL.pdf (accessed July 23, 2008).

"Education at a Glance 2007," Organisation for Economic Co-Operation and Development, Directorate for Education. http://www.data360.org/dsg.aspx?Data_Set_Group_Id=1653 (accessed September 14, 2008).

Swanson, Christopher B. "Cities in Crisis: A Special Analytic Report on High School Graduation," Editorial Projects in Education Research Center, 1 April, 2008. http://www.edweek.org/media/swansoncitiesincrisis040108.pdf (accessed July 23, 2008).

Olfman, Sharna. "What About Play?" *Rethinking Schools* online. Volume 19, No. 3, Spring 2005. http://www.rethinkingschools.org/archive/19_03/play193.shtml Data on Finnish schools. (accessed January 8, 2007).

Ratey, John J. and Hagerman, Eric. *Spark: The Revolutionary New Science of Exercise and the Brain* (New York: Little, Brown and Company, 2008) Page 35 quoted, other pages referenced.

Madigan, Jean Blaydes. "New Study Proves Physically Fit Kids Perform Better Academically." National Association for Sport & Physical Education, California Department of Education Study, 10 December, 2002. http://www.actionbasedlearning.com/article02.shtml (accessed February 2, 2007).

Walker, Casey. "An Interview with Joseph Chilton Pearce." *Wild Duck Review*, 1998, Vol. IV, Number 2, http://www.wildduckreview.com/journal/Issue%2017-Education/Pearce/Pearce.pdf Page 2, quoted. (accessed January 9, 2007).

Lang, Susan. "CU researcher: Green space is beneficial to children." *Cornell Chronicle* online. 24 January, 2002. http://www.news.cornell.edu/Chronicle/02/1.24.02/green_space.html (accessed February 3, 2007).

Kuo, Frances E. and Taylor, Andrea Faber. "A Potential Natural Treatment for Attention-Deficit/Hyperactivity Disorder: Evidence From a National Study." *American Journal of Public Health*, September 2004, Vol. 94, No. 9, 1580-1586. http://www.ajph.org/cgi/content/full/94/9/1580 (accessed February 3, 2007).

Wells, Nancy M. "At Home with Nature Effects of 'Greenness' on Children's Cognitive Functioning." *Environment and Behavior*, Vol. 32, No. 6, 775-795, 2000. http://eab.sagepub.com/cgi/content/abstract/32/6/775?maxtoshow=&HIT S=10&hits=10&RESULTFORMAT=&searchid=1118184101225_219&stored_search=&FIRSTINDEX=0&minsc ore=5000&journalcode=speab (accessed February 2, 2007).

Glausiusz, Josie. "Is Dirt the New Prozac?" *Discover* online, 14 June, 2007. http://discovermagazine.com/2007/jul/ raw-data-is-dirt-the-new-prozac (accessed September 18, 2007).

Patterson, Karen. "Studies find natural settings help both kids and adults shrug off stress." *The Dallas Morning News*, 5 May, 2004. http://aeoe.org/resources/diversity/green_power.htm Soil bacteria linked to serotonin. (accessed September 18, 2007).

Blakeslee, Sandra. "Cells That Read Minds." *The New York Times*, 10 January, 2006. http://www.nytimes. com/2006/01/10/science/10mirr.html?pagewanted=1&_r=1&incamp=article_popular_2 Mirror neurons. (accessed May 15, 2007).

Education as Life, for Life

Olfson, Mark, Marcus, Steven C., Jensen, Peter S., and Myrna M. Weissman. "National Trends in the Use of Psychotropic Medications by Children." *Journal of the American Academy of Child & Adolescent Psychiatry,* May 2002 41(5):514-521. http://www.jaacap.com/pt/re/jaacap/abstract.00004583-200205000-00008.htm;jsessionid=Hq2 drpzn9nyM2mRYnpNdjQHX2TQnrNmH7jpWv7GF1pQQ1p2Ph9DX!1609592453!181195628!8091!-1 (accessed April 12, 2007).

Ingersoll, R. Elliott, Bauer, Ann and Burns, Laura. "Children and Psychotropic Medication: What Role Should Advocacy Counseling Play?" *Journal of Counseling and Development*, Summer 2004, Vol. 82. http://psych.umb.edu/faculty/ kogan/files/SB780%20Articles%20in%20Syllabus%202009/Ingersoll,%20r.%20Advocacy%20in%20Use%20of%20 Medications.pdf (accessed April 12, 2007).

Jukes, Ian, McCain, Ted D. E. *Windows on the Future: Education in the Age of Technology* (California: Corwin Press, 2000) Page 80, quote.

Pink, Daniel H. *A Whole New Mind: Why Right-Brainers Will Rule the Future* (New York: Riverhead Books, 2006) Pages 57 and 58, reviewing Daniel Goleman's discussion of IQ and career success. Quote taken from introduction, unnumbered page.

Kao, John. *Innovation Nation: How America is Losing Its Innovation Edge, Why It Matters and What We Can Do to Get It Back* (New York: Free Press, 2007) Page 100, quote.

Sutton, Jennifer. "Homeschooling Comes of Age." *Brown Alumni Magazine*, January/February 2002. Joyce Reed quote, general references. http://www.brownalumnimagazine.com/january/february-2002/homeschooling-comes-of-age.html (accessed February 22, 2007).

Ray, Brian D. "What Research Shows Us." *Journal of the National Association for College Admission Counseling.* Number 185, Fall 2004. http://homeschooling.gomilpitas.com/graphics/Fall04Journal.pdf College admissions officers' perceptions of homeschooled students, cited from pages 10 and 12. (accessed February 22, 2007).

Knowles, J. Gary. Phone interview Sept 17, 2007.

Tienken, Christopher H. "Rankings of International Achievement Test Performance and Economic Strength: Correlation or Conjecture?" *International Journal of Education Policy & Leadership*, April 25, 2008. Vol. 3, Number 4. http:// journals.sfu.ca/ijepl/index.php/ijepl/article/view/110/44 (accessed August, 30 2009)

Baker, Keith. "Are International Tests Worth Anything?" *Phi Delta Kappan*, Oct 2007, Vol. 89 Issue 2, p101-104, 4p http://web.ebscohost.com.ezproxy.cpl.org/ehost/pdf?vid=12&hid=5&sid=003b3792-1922-49fd-aed4-3b8a23f6de88%40sessionmgr11 (accessed 8-30-09) Page 102, quote.

"National Education Testing: A Debate." Cato Policy Report. July/August 2001. http://www.cato.org/pubs/policy_ report/v23n4/education.pdf Alfie Kohn quote page 11, emphasis on testing results in shallow thinking. (accessed January 21, 2007).

Heath, Douglas H. "Academic Predictors of Adult Maturity and Competence." *The Journal of Higher Education,* Ohio State University Press, 1977. http://ezproxy2.cpl.org/login?url=http://www.jstor.org/journals/ohio.press.html Grades and test scores do not necessarily correlate to later accomplishments in such areas as social leadership, the arts or the sciences, citation page 615. (accessed February 9, 2007).

Baird, Leonard L. (1985). "Do grades and tests predict adult accomplishment?" *Research in Higher Education.* 23(1), 3-85. 1985.

Medlin, Richard G. "Home Schooling and the Question of Socialization." *Peabody Journal of Education,* 2000. Lawrence Erlbaum Associates (Taylor & Francis Group. http://ezproxy2.cpl.org/login?url=http://www.jstor.org/journals/lebtaylorfrancis.html Pages 112-115. (accessed March 10, 2007).

Mendizza, Michael and Pearce, Joseph Chilton. *Magical Parent, Magical Child: The Art of Joyful Parenting* (California: North Atlantic Books, 2003, 2004) Page 27.

Innate Gifts

Hillman, James. *The Soul's Code: In Search of Character and Calling* (New York: Warner Books, 1997) Page 13, quote.

Duckworth, Angela L. and Seligman, Martin E.P. "Self-Discipline Outdoes I.Q. in Predicting Academic Performance of Adolescents." Vol. 16, number 12, 2005. Blackwell Publishing http://www.ingentaconnect.com/content/bpl/psci/2005/00000016/00000012/art00006 Pages 939-944. (accessed June 18, 2007).

Chapter Two: Nurturing the Learner

Trust

Benezet, L. P. "The Teaching of Arithmetic I: The Story of an experiment." Originally published in the *Journal of the National Education Association,* Volume 24, Number 8, November 1935. http://www.inference.phy.cam.ac.uk/sanjoy/benezet/1.html (Provided by Benezet Centre) Pages 241-244. (accessed July 6, 2007).

Benezet, L. P. "The Teaching of Arithmetic II: The Story of an Experiment." Originally published in the *Journal of the National Education Association,* Volume 24, Number 9, December 1935. http://www.inference.phy.cam.ac.uk/sanjoy/benezet/2.html (Provided by Benezet Centre) Pages 301-303. (accessed July 6, 2007).

Benezet, L. P. "The Teaching of Arithmetic III: The Story of an Experiment." Originally published in the *Journal of the National Education Association,* Volume 25, Number 1, January, 1936. http://www.inference.phy.cam.ac.uk/sanjoy/benezet/3.html (Provided by Benezet Centre) Pages 7-8. (accessed July 6, 2007).

Grolnick, Wendy S. *The Psychology of Parental Control: How Well-Meant Parenting Backfires* (New Jersey: Lawrence Erlbaum Associates, 2003) Pages 119-121. Learning for test diminishes recall.

Bretherton, Inge. "The Origins of Attachment Theory: John Bowlby and Mary Ainsworth." *Developmental Psychology* 28, 759-775, 1992. http://www.psychology.sunysb.edu/attachment/online/inge_origins.pdf Page 17. (accessed March 22, 2007).

Baumrind, Diana. "Effects of Authoritative Parental Control on Child Behavior." *Child Development,* 37(4), 887-907, 1966.

Steinberg, Laurence, Lamborn, Susie D., Darling, Nancy, Mounts, Nina S. and Sanford M. Dornbusch. "Over-Time Changes in Adjustment and Competence among Adolescents from Authoritative, Authoritarian, Indulgent, and Neglectful Families." *Child Development,* 1994 Society for Research in Child Development. http://ezproxy2.cpl.org/login?url=http://www.jstor.org/journals/srcd.html Page 769 (accessed March 19, 2007).

Walters, James and Stinnett, Nick. "Parent-Child Relationships" A Decade Review of Research." *Journal of Marriage and the Family*. vol. 33, no. 1, decade review part 2. Feb., 1971. http://links.jstor.org/sici?sici=0022-2445%28197102%2933%3A1%3C70%3APRADRO%3E2.0.CO%3B2-U Pages 70-111. (accessed March 20, 2007).

Grolnick, Wendy S. *The Psychology of Parental Control: How Well-Meant Parenting Backfires.* (New Jersey: Lawrence Erlbaum Associates, 2003) Pages 15, 16. Study of mothers and babies at play.

Glenn, H. Stephen and Nelsen, Jane. *Raising Self-Reliant Children in a Self-Indulgent World: Seven Building Blocks for Developing Capable Young People* (California: Prima Publishing, 2000) Quotes from pages 52, 63.

Einstein, Albert. "A Friendly Universe." *Ortholog.* Hanley, Zac. http://www.ortholog.com/archive/compleat_scientist/a_friendly_universe.php Einstein quote about friendly universe. (accessed August 5, 2007).

The Nature of Interests

Wilson, Frank R. *The Hand: How Its Use Shapes the Brain, Language and Human Culture* (New York: Pantheon Books, 1998) Page 281, author's discussion of Benjamin S. Bloom's research.

Anderson, Lorin W. "If You Don't Know Who Wrote It You Won't Understand It: Lessons Learned From Benjamin S. Bloom." *Peabody Journal of Education*. 1996. Lawrence Erlbaum Associates.

"According to Habitat Heroes Study, Children Fear the End of the Earth," RedOrbit.com. Monday, 20 April 2009, 07:00 CDT source: Habitat Heroes, source: PR Newswire http://www.redorbit.com/news/business/1673194/according_to_habitat_heroes_study_children_fear_the_end_of/ (accessed May 2, 2009).

Gillham, Jane and Reivich, Karen. "Cultivating Optimism in Childhood and Adolescence." *Annals of the American Academy of Political and Social Science*, 2004. http://ezproxy2.cpl.org/login?url=http://www.jstor.org/journals/sage.html Page 147. (accessed July 21, 2007).

Brown, Jr., Tom. *The Tracker* (California: Berkley Books, 1978). Page 1, quote.

In the Flow

Csikszentmihalyi, Mihaly. *Finding Flow: The Psychology of Optimal Experience* (New York: Basic Books, 1998).

Free Range Learning

"Media Multi-tasking Changing the Amount and Nature of Young People's Media Use." Report by the Henry Kaiser Family Foundation, press release. http://www.kff.org/entmedia/entmedia030905nr.cfm Total amount of screen time reported as 8 ½ hrs. (accessed August 11, 2007).

Gosselin, N. "Age difference in heart rate changes associated with micro-arousals in humans." *Clinical Neurophysiology*. Volume 113 , Issue 9 , Pages 1517-1521 http://linkinghub.elsevier.com/retrieve/pii/S138824570200189X (accessed July 23, 2007).

Interests in Perspective

Elkind, David. *The Power of Play: Learning What Comes Naturally* (New York: Da Capo Lifelong Books, 2008) Page 77, quote. No transfer of responsibility from one type of activity to another.

Chapter Three: Work, Play and other Essentials

Meaningful Work, Authentic Roles

Seligman, Martin E. P. *Authentic Happiness: Using the New Positive Psychology to Realize Your Potential for Lasting Fulfillment.* (Free Press, 2002) Page 224. Original research reported in by Vaillant, G. and Vaillant, C. "Work as a Predictor of Positive Mental Health." *American Journal of Psychiatry*, Vol. 138, 1981, pp. 1433-1440. Chores as predictor of positive mental health later in life.

Wolf, Liz. "Chore Wars: Researcher Finds that Involving Young Children in Household Chores Pays off Later." *Minnesota Parent,* March, 2003. http://nfb.org/Images/nfb/Publications/fr/fr14/fr04se09.htm Marty Rossmans's research on chores. (accessed June 1, 2007).

Savage, Jon. *Teenage: The Creation of Youth Culture* (New York: Viking, 2007).

Challenges

Dweck, Carol S. *Self-Theories: Their Role in Motivation, Personality, and Development* (New York: Psychology Press, 2000).

Bronson, Po. "How Not to Talk to Your Kids: The Inverse Power of Praise." *New York Magazine* 12 Feb, 2007. http://nymag.com/news/features/27840/ (accessed August 8, 2007).

Mischel, Walter, Shoda, Yuichi and Monica L. Rodriguez. "Delay of Gratification in Children." *Science* 1989. American Association for the Advancement of Science http://ezproxy2.cpl.org/login?url=http://www.jstor.org/journals/aaas.html (accessed July 17, 2007).

Creativity

Moss, Robert. *The Three Only Things: Tapping the Power of Dreams, Coincidence and Imagination* (California: New World Library, 2007).

Slowing Down

Honore, Carl. *In Praise of Slowness: Challenging the Cult of Speed* (New York: HarperCollins Publishers, 2004) Pages 251, 252, quotes.

Stillness

de Becker, Gavin. *Protecting the Gift: Keeping Children and Teenagers Safe* (New York: The Dial Press, 1999).

Simplicity

Chaplin, Lan Nguyen and Deborah Roedder John. "Growing up in a Material World: Age Differences in Materialism in Children and Adolescents." *Journal of Consumer Research.* December, 2007. http://carlsonschool.umn.edu/assets/93681.pdf Deleterious effects of materialism. (accessed January 8, 2008).

"What Do Kids Really Want That Money Can't Buy?" Poll commissioned by the Center for a New American Dream, conducted in February 2003 by Widmeyer Communications. Information based on a nationally representative telephone study of 746 American children ages 9-14. http://www.newdream.org/publications/bookrelease.php (accessed January 8, 2008).

Fromm, Erich. *To Have or to Be?* (New York/London: Continuum International Publishing Group; rev. ed., 1996).

The Importance of Play

Wenner, Melinda. "The Serious Need for Play," *Scientific American,* February 2009, http://www.scientificamerican.com/article.cfm?id=the-serious-need-for-play (accessed February 26,2009). Children's free-play time dropped by a quarter between 1981 and 1997.

Ginsburg, Kenneth R. and the Committee on Psychosocial Aspects of Child and Family Health. "The Importance of Play in Promoting Healthy Child Development and Maintaining Strong Parent-Child Bonds." *American Academy of Pediatrics* 9 Oct., 2006. http://cgood.org/assets/attachments/October_2006_AAP_Report.pdf (accessed June 14, 2007).

Louv, Richard. *Last Child in the Woods: Saving Our Children From Nature-Deficit Disorder* (North Carolina: Algonquin Books, 2005) Page 97, quote.

Chudacoff, Howard. *Children at Play: An American History* (New York: NYU Press, 2007).

Elkind, David. *The Power of Play: Learning What Comes Naturally* (New York: Da Capo Lifelong Books, 2008)

Fisher, Richard. "Ever Decreasing Span." *New Scientist Magazine* Dec 15-21, 2007. Page 30. Atention span shortened by early exposure to TV.

Technology and Learning

Gorlick, Adam. "Media multitaskers pay mental price, Stanford study shows." *Stanford Report,* August 24, 2009 http://news.stanford.edu/news/2009/august24/multitask-research-study-082409.html (accessed November 12, 2009).

Ramin, Cathryn Jakobson. *Carved in Sand: When Attention Fails and Memory Fades in Midlife* (New York: HarperCollins, 2007) Thumb tribe quote, page 32.

"Is Technology Producing a Decline in Critical Thinking and Analysis?" Science Daily Jan 29, 2009. Adapted from materials provided by University of California-Los Angeles http://www.sciencedaily.com/releases/2009/01/090128092341.htm Technology changing learning. (accessed February 11, 2009).

Johnson, Steven. *Everything Bad is Good for You: How Today's Popular Culture is Actually Making Us Smarter* (New York: Riverhead Books, 2005). Page 196. quote.

Beck, John C. and Wade, Mitchell. *Got Game: How the Gamer Generation Is Reshaping Business Forever* (Massachusetts: Harvard Business School Press, 2004).

Marks, Kevin. "Internet Regeneration." *Epeus Epigone* 24 February, 2006. http://epeus.blogspot.com/ (accessed March 25, 2006).

Brown, John Seely. "Learning in the Digital Age." http://www.johnseelybrown.com/learning_in_digital_age-aspen.pdf Online transcript based on a talk given at the Aspen Forum. Pages 16-17. (accessed January 10, 2007).

Empathy and Cooperation

Vedantam, Shankar. "If It Feels Good to Be Good, It Might Be Only Natural." *Washington Post* 28 May, 2007. Page A01. http://www.washingtonpost.com/wp-dyn/content/article/2007/05/27/AR2007052701056.html (accessed June 24, 2007).

Blakeslee, Sandra. "Cells That Read Minds." *The New York Times*, 10 January, 2006. http://www.nytimes.com/2006/01/10/science/10mirr.html?pagewanted=1&_r=1&incamp=article_popular_2 (accessed June 27, 2007).

Childre, Doc, Martin, Howard and Donna Beech. *The Heartmath Solution* (New York, HarperCollins, 1999).

Ehrenreich, Barbara. *Blood Rites: Origins and History of the Passions of War* (New York: Henry Holt and Company, 1997). Page 47, quote.

Fry, Douglas P. *Beyond War: The Human Potential for Peace* (New York: Oxford University Press, 2007).

Tomasello, Michael. *Why We Cooperate* (Massachusetts: MIT Press, 2009). Research on infant helpfulness.

Mendizza, Michael. "Allowing Human Nature To Work Successfully." Interview with Jean Liedloff, originally published in the Fall/1998 issue of *Touch The Future*. The Liedloff Society for the Continuum Concept, http://www.continuum-concept.org/reading/human-nature.html (accessed July 11, 2007).

Robinson, B.A. "Shared belief in the 'Golden Rule'" *Religious Tolerance,* 7 August, 2007. http://www.religioustolerance.org/reciproc.htm (accessed September 19, 2007).

Chapter Four: Connecting with Others

Learning Communities

Miller, Ron. *Creating Learning Communities* online book at www.creatinglearningcommunities.org (accessed June 17, 2007).

Reaching out through Technology

Friedman, H.S. "Paradoxes of Nonverbal Detection, Expression, and Responding: Points to Ponder." Hall, J.A. and Bernieri, F. J. (eds.). *Interpersonal Sensitivity: Theory and Measurement.* (New Jersey: Erlbaum, 2001). Pages 351-362.

Dalrymple, David. "Technology in Education." *Edge: World Question Center.* http://edge.org/q2007/q07_index.html#contributors (accessed July 7, 2007). Author's permission via email.

Chapter Five: Collaborating Benefits Everyone

Wider Collaboration

Putnam, Robert, Feldstein, Lewis and Don Cohen. *Better Together: Restoring the American Community* (New York: Simon & Schuster, 2003).

Smith, Christian, and Sikkink, David. "Is Private Schooling Privatizing?" *First Things: A Journal of Religion, Culture and Public Life.* No. 92, 16-20 April, 1999. http://www.firstthings.com/article.php3?id_article=3137&var_recherche=%29.+Is+private+schooling+privatizing (accessed June 23, 2007).

Underhill's Games. www.underhillsgames.com Phone interview with Lee McLain, 5 February, 2008.

Hampton, Virginia Youth Services. www.areyouinthegame.com Phone interview with Whitney Dunlap-Fowler, assistant program manager, 5 February, 2008.

Chapter Six: Homeschooling Changes Everything

Homeschooling as a Harbinger of Educational Change

Hawken, Paul. *Blessed Unrest: How the Largest Movement in the World Came into Being and Why No One Saw It Coming.* (New York: Viking, 2007).

Esterl, Mike. "German Tots Learn to Answer Call of Nature." *The Wall Street Journal.* 14 April, 2008; Page A1. http://online.wsj.com:80/article/SB120813155330311577.html?mod=hpp_us_personal_journal (accessed July 8, 2008).

Cameron, Brent and Meyer, Barbara. *Self Design: Nurturing Genius Through Natural Learning* (Colorado: Sentient Publications, 2006).

Gladwell, Malcolm. *The Tipping Point: How Little Things Can Make a Big Difference* (Back Bay Books, 2002).

Homeschooling as a Right

"Homeschooling in the United States: 2003 Statistical Analysis Report," Institute of Education Sciences, U.S. Department of Education, http://nces.ed.gov/pubs2006/homeschool/ (accessed January 7, 2007).

Kaseman, Larry and Susan. "The Fraser Study: Puffing Up Homeschooling and Selling Our Freedoms." *Home Education Magazine.* Jan-Feb 2008, Vol. 25, no. 1, page 24.

"2007-2008 NEA Resolutions: Annual Meeting." http://64.233.169.104/search?q=cache:psyFVHyEIAQJ:www.nea.org/annualmeeting/raaction/images/2007-2008Resolutions.pdf+National+Education+Association+parent+choice+homeschooling&hl=en&ct=clnk&cd=4&gl=us#45   (accessed April 10, 2007)

Homeschooling as Self-Correcting

Daly, James. "Future School: Reshaping Learning from the Ground Up." *Edutopia* interview with Alvin Toffler, author of *Revolutionary Wealth* http://www.edutopia.org/future-school (accessed January 8, 2009).

Homeschooling as Collective Intelligence

Kohn, Alfie. *The Homework Myth: Why Our Kids Get Too Much of a Bad Thing* (New York: Da Capo Press, 2007).

Homeschooling as Strengthening Families, Friendships and Communities

Pearce, Joseph Chilton. *The Biology of Transcendence: A Blueprint for the Human Spirit* (Vermont: Park Street Press, 2002). Page 251, quote.

Watters, Ethan. "DNA Is Not Destiny: The new science of epigenetics rewrites the rules of disease, heredity, and identity." *Discover* online. 22 November, 2006. http://discovermagazine.com/2006/nov/cover (accessed February 19, 2007).

Anthes, Emily. "Stretch Marks for Dad: What Fatherhood Does to the Body and the Brain." *Slate* online. 14 June, 2007. http://www.slate.com/id/2168389/ (accessed September 1, 2007).

Prescott, James W. "Body Pleasure and the Origins of Violence" *The Bulletin of The Atomic Scientists.* November 1975, pp. 10-20. http://www.violence.de/prescott/bulletin/article.html (accessed August 24, 2007).

"Breastfeeding Practices—Results from the National Immunization Survey." Centers for Disease Control and Prevention http://www.cdc.gov/breastfeeding/data/NIS_data/data_2004.htm (accessed September 1, 2007).

"CASA Report Finds Teens Likelier To Abuse Prescription Drugs, Use Illegal Drugs, Smoke, Drink When Family Dinners Infrequent." National Center on Addiction and Substance Abuse at Columbia University. 20 September, 2007. http://www.casafamilyday.org/PDFs/reportIV.pdf (accessed September 6, 2007).

Anderson, Lorin W. "If You Don't Know Who Wrote It You Won't Understand It: Lessons Learned From Benjamin S. Bloom." *Peabody Journal of Education.* 1996. Lawrence Erlbaum Associates.

Bloom, Benjamin S. "Innocence in Education." *The School Review.* 1972, The University of Chicago Press. Page 127, "… repeated failure in coping with the demands of the school appears to be a source of emotional difficulties and mental illness." Page 338, relates this to the judgments and marks of the teachers, the people in the lives of the students more than the tests taken by the youth. Page 10, teaching info rather than complexities.

"Response Statement JAMA article on the Adolescent Health Study." National Institute of Health. 9 September, 1997. http://www.nih.gov/news/pr/sept97/chda-09.htm Teens feeling a sense of "connectedness" and who spend key times of day with parents are much less likely to engage in risky behaviors. (accessed February 23, 2007).

Ray, Brian D. "What Research Shows Us." *Journal of the National Association for College Admission Counseling.* Number 185, Fall 2004. http://homeschooling.gomilpitas.com/graphics/Fall04Journal.pdf Page 11. (accessed September 7, 2007).

Homeschooling as Re-envisioning Success

Kao, John. *Innovation Nation: How America is Losing Its Innovation Edge, Why It Matters and What We Can Do to Get It Back* (New York: Free Press, 2007). Page 159, quote.

Gladwell, Malcolm. *Outliers: The Story of Success* (New York: Little, Brown and Company, 2008). Pages 35 to 42.

Chapter Nine: Full Spectrum Learning

Finding Your Own Way

Aldort, Naomi. *Raising Our Children, Raising Ourselves: Transforming Parent-child Relationships from Reaction And Struggle to Freedom, Power And Joy* (Aldort, 2006).

Glenn, H. Stephen and Nelsen, Jane. *Raising Self-Reliant Children in a Self-Indulgent World: Seven Building Blocks for Developing Capable Young People.* (California: Prima Publishing, 2000).

DeGrandpre, Richard. "Is Your ADHD Support Group a Front Organization for the Pharmaceutical Industry?" The National Alliance against Mandated Mental Health Screening and Psychiatric Drugging of Children. http://www.ritalindeath.com/Front-Group.htm (accessed September 21, 2007).

Chapter Ten: Science & Nature

Nature

Cornell, Joseph. *Sharing Nature with Children* (California: Dawn Publications, 1998). Pages 103, 139.

Chapter Eleven: Math, Business & Critical Thinking

Math

Eglash, Ron. *African Fractals: Modern Computing and Indigenous Design.* (New Jersey: Rutgers University Press, 1999).

Greenberg, Daniel. "And 'Rithmetic." Excerpt from *Free At Last.* (Massachusetts: Sudbury Valley School Press). http://www.mountainlaurelsudbury.org/Rithmetic.asp (accessed June 14, 2007).

Antonelli, Paola and Mandelbrot, Benoit. "The Curator and the Mathematician Discuss Fractals, Architecture and the Death of Euclid," *Seed Magazine,* March 24, 2008 http://seedmagazine.com/content/article/paola_antonelli_benoit_mandelbrot/ (accessed May 29, 2009).

Wasley, Paula. "Abstract Math Produces Tangible Learning, Study Finds." *The Chronicle of Higher Education* news blog. 24 April, 2008 http://chronicle.com/news/article/4364/abstract-math-produces-tangible-learning-study-finds (accessed July 11, 2008)

O'Neil, John. "Vital Signs: Mental Abilities: Peering Into a MathWhiz's Brain," *The New York Times,* 13 April, 2004.

Ferguson, Robert C. "Teacher's Guide: Research and Benefits of Chess." United States Chess Federation. http://www.quadcitychess.com/benefits_of_chess.html (accessed July 11, 2008).

Business

Dominguez, Joe and Robin, Vicki. *Your Money Or Your Life: Transforming Your Relationship With Money And Achieving Financial Independence* (Penguin, 1999).

Milliken, Bill. *The Last Dropout: Stop the Epidemic!* (Hay House, 2007)._

Critical Thinking

"Brain network linked to contemplation in adults is less complex in children." Physorg.com 7 March, 2008. Washington University http://www.physorg.com/news124110190.html (accessed July 11, 2008).

Wenner, Melinda. "Bad Decision-Makers Lack Reasoning Skills." Live Science.com 22 May, 2007. http://www.livescience.com/health/070522_decision_making.html (accessed July 11, 2008).

Chapter Twelve: Physical Education & Health

Physical Education

Ratey, John J. and Hagerman, Eric. *Spark: The Revolutionary New Science of Exercise and the Brain* (New York: Little, Brown and Company, 2008).

Health

Lu, Chensheng, Toepel, Kathryn, Irish, Rene, Fenske, Richard A., Barr, Dana B. and Roberto Bravo. "Organic Diets Significantly Lower Children's Dietary Exposure to Organophosphorus Pesticides." *Environmental Health Perspectives* 2006 February, 114(2): 260—263. Published online 1 September 1, 2005. http://www.pubmedcentral.nih.gov/articlerender.fcgi?artid=1367841 (accessed December 15, 2007).

Nestle, Marion. "Ethical dilemmas in choosing a healthful diet: vote with your fork." *Proceedings of the Nutrition Society* 2000, 59, 619—629. http://64.233.169.104/search?q=cache:IxWf43CV5s8J:www.foodpolitics.com/pdf/ethdilem.pdf+energy+expenditure+from+farm+to+fork&hl=en&ct=clnk&cd=7&gl=us (accessed December 15, 2007).

Paddock, Catharine. "Organic Food Is More Nutritious Say EU Researchers." *Medical News Today,* 29 Oct 2007 http://www.medicalnewstoday.com/articles/86972.php (accessed December 15, 2007).

Jones, Diane Carlson. "Body Image and the Appearance Culture Among Adolescent Girls and Boys An Examination of Friend Conversations, Peer Criticism, Appearance Magazines, and the Internalization of Appearance Ideals." *Journal of Adolescent Research.* 2004, Vol. 19, No. 3, 323-339.

Nichter, M. "Listening to girls talk about their bodies." *Reclaiming Children and Youth.* 9(3), 182–184, 2000.

Poirot, Carolyn. "High-fructose corn syrup fueling obesity epidemic, doctors say." *The Seattle Times.* 4 December, 2005. http://seattletimes.nwsource.com/html/health/2002658491_healthsyrup04.html (accessed December 15, 2007).

"U.S. Government Facts: Children's Chemical Exposure via Food Products." Organic Consumers Association. Data assembled in July 2005. http://organicconsumers.org/organic/wic-faq.pdf (accessed December 15, 2007).

Chapter Thirteen: The Arts

Hodges, Donald A. "Implications of Music and Brain Research." *Music Educators Journal,* 2000. National Association for Music Education. http://ezproxy2.cpl.org/login?url=http://www.jstor.org/journals/menc.html (accessed August 20, 2007).

Fiske, Edward B. "Champions of Change: The Impact of the Arts on Learning." The Arts Education Partnership. The President's Committee on the Arts and the Humanities. http://www.aep-arts.org/files/publications/ChampsReport.pdf (accessed August 20, 2007)

Gazzaniga, Michael. "Learning, Arts, and the Brain: The Dana Consortium Report on Arts and Cognition 2008." http://www.dana.org/uploadedFiles/News_and_Publications/Special_Publications/Learning,%20Arts%20and%20the%20Brain_ArtsAndCognition_Compl.pdf (accessed July, 2009).

Rettig, Perry R. and Rettig, Janet L. "Linking Brain Research to Art Education." *Art Education,* 1999 National Art Education Association. http://ezproxy2.cpl.org/login?url=http://www.jstor.org/journals/naea.html (accessed August 20, 2007).

Chapter Fourteen: Language Arts

Barks, Coleman. *A Year with Rumi* (New York: Harper Collins, 2006).

Amergin's Song was a poem "passed down in the oral tradition for almost three millennia until it began to be written down in various forms about 1100 A.D." Page 409.

Moore, David W. "About Half of Americans Reading a Book." Gallup News Service. 3 June 2005. http://www.gallup.com/poll/16582/About-Half-Americans-Reading-Book.aspx (accessed January 13, 2007).

National Endowment for the Arts, "Reading on the Rise: A New Chapter in American Literacy." http://www.arts.gov/research/readingonRise.pdf (accessed January 10, 2010).

Shand, Michael A. "An Annotated Bibliography of Vocabulary-Related Work Produced by the Johnson O'Connor Research Foundation," Center for the Study of Reading. Technical Report No. 605. November 1994. http://www.eric.ed.gov/ERICDocs/data/ericdocs2sql/content_storage_01/0000019b/80/13/6c/18.pdf (accessed January 20, 2007).

Boone, Jon. "Native English speakers face being crowded out of market." VII International Investment Forum Sochi 2008. *The Financial Times* 14 Feb, 2006. http://search.ft.com/ftArticle?queryText=english+worldwide&page=2&aje=false&id=060214011594&ct=0 (accessed January 26, 2007).http://technorati.com Technorati tracking 112.8 million blogs as of April 11, 2008

"Public Library Use: ALA Library Fact Sheet Number 6." American Library Association. 2008. http://www.ala.org/ala/alalibrary/libraryfactsheet/alalibraryfactsheet6.cfm (accessed April 11, 2008).

Elkind, David *The Hurried Child: Growing Up Too Fast Too Soon* (New York: Perseus, 2001), pages 36, 37. Citing study from the 1930s by Carleton Washburn, Evanston, Illinois, educator.

University of Otago, "Research finds no advantage in learning to read from age five." Monday, 21 December 2009. http://www.otago.ac.nz/news/news/otago006408.html (accessed January 6, 2010).

Keys, Karen and Crain, William. "Parental Patience and Children's Reading: A Pilot Study of Homeschooled Children." *Encounter: Education for Meaning and Social Justice,* Volume 22, number 4, winter 2009. https://great-ideas.org/Encounter224/Keys-Crain224.htm (accessed December 28, 2009).

Aamodt, Sandra and Wang, Sam. "Tighten Your Belt, Strengthen Your Mind." *The New York Times.* 2 April, 2008. http://www.nytimes.com/2008/04/02/opinion/02aamodt.html?em&ex=1207454400&en=0ca7a89030aadb0d&ei=5087%0A (accessed April 11, 2008).

Foreign Language

Abbott, Martha G., Caccavale, Therese Sullivan and Ken Stewart. "Cognitive Benefits of Learning Language." *Duke Gifted Letter:* Volume 8, Issue 1, Fall 2007. The Duke University Talent Identification Program Online Newsletter for Parents of Gifted Youth. http://www.discoverlanguages.org/i4a/pages/index.cfm?pageid=4724 (accessed December 15, 2007).

Wolff, Robert. *Original Wisdom: Stories of an Ancient Way of Knowing* (Vermont: Inner Traditions International, 2001). Pages 192, 193.

Chapter Sixteen: Volunteerism, Ethics & Spirituality

Volunteerism

Barasch, Marc Ian. *Field Notes on the Compassionate Life: A Search for the Soul of Kindness* (Rodale Books, 2005).

Cauldwell, K. "The Science of Altruism? Researchers Discover Brain Patterns Associated with Selflessness." *Associated Content*. 31 Jan 31, 2007   http://www.associatedcontent.com/article/130960/the_science_of_altruism_researchers. html (accessed December 15, 2007).

Flora, Carlin. "Field Guide to the Do-Gooder: Earth Angels." *Psychology Today Magazine*, Jan/Feb 2008 http://psychol-ogytoday.com/articles/index.php?term=20080118-000003&page=1 (accessed July 11, 2008).

Ethics & Spirituality

Hart, Tobin. *The Secret Spiritual World of Children*. (Hawaii: Inner Ocean, 2003). Pages 7, 172.

Chapter Seventeen: Welcoming the Renaissance

The Shift. 2007 Lighthouse Films Inc. www.theshiftmovie.com "Global Healing Activities: Over 250,000 initiated in the last two years."

Hawken, Paul. *Blessed Unrest: How the Largest Movement in the World Came into Being and Why No One Saw It Coming*. (New York: Viking, 2007).

Index

interests (*continued*)

See also, arts; current events; history; language arts; mathematics; nature; physical education; science; volunteerism

intuition, 73, 78

I.Q., 14, 21, 55

L

language arts

activities and resources, 234-243

holistic learning of, 228-243

See also, reading

learning

active, 173-186, 187-206, 207-218, 223-227, 228-243, 244-246, 247-254, 254-258

delayed, 11-13, 24-26, 187-188, 230-232

diet, effect on, 214

direct, 4, 9, 70-71

hands-on, 4, 79, 173-176, 188-189

heart-centered, 83-85, 259-261

through conversation, 43, 49

through imitation, observation, 9, 34, 112, 156-158

through meaningful participation, 4, 54-59, 109-117, 124, 162, 169, 259-272

inquiry-based, 173-176, 203-206, 266-272

interest-led, 5, 19-22, 32-39, 43, 46-47, 96-98, 168, 266-272

lifelong, 19-22, 48

mirror neurons and 9-10, 82

motivation, 3, 11-15, 26, 32-35, 41, 50, 59, 133-134, 207-208

natural, 2, 11, 18, 38-39, 44-45, 59, 124, 171

new interests, 46-50, 88, 110-118, 173-176

readiness, 24-27, 133-134, 187-189, 230-232

restrictive, 11-13, 18, 26, 29, 39-42, 171, 273-274

technology and, 79-82, 105-108, 118

travel and, 151-155

learning communities, 97-98

M

materialism, 54, 62-65, 75-77

mastery, research on, 60-61, 143

See also, goals; growth mindset; learning

mathematics

activities and resources, 189-196, 198-202, 204-206

brain hemisphere and, 189,

delayed, 24-26

holistic learning of, 187-206

readiness, 133-134, 187-189

remedial rates, 5

media, 203-206, 215, 229-230, 254-258

messages and, 34, 44, 141, 269

mental health, 12, 75-76, 86-87, 139-140, 214-218

mentor(s), 34, 112, 198, 260-266

elders as, 90-92

interest-based, 102-103

older youths as, 87-88

organizations, 104

See also, business and finance; work

mirror neurons, 9-10, 82

motivation, learning and, 3, 11-15, 26, 32-35, 41, 50, 59, 133-134, 207-208

See also, boredom; creativity; readiness

multitasking, 80

N

nature

activities and resources, 182-186, 209-213

benefits of being in, 7-9,76-77

holistic learning, 181-186

metaphor for learning, 44-45, 62, 171

vs unnatural stimuli, 7

Other Titles of Interest from Hohm Press

In the Best Interest of the Child
A Manual for Divorcing Parents

by Nadir Baksh, Psy.D. and Laurie Murphy, R.N., Ph.D.

This book will help parents save their children unnecessary anguish throughout the divorce process. Written by a licensed clinical psychologist, and a nurse and counselor, the authors have a private practice with families and also work as court-appointed evaluators in child-custody disputes.

Paper; 144 pages, $16.95, ISBN: 978-1-890772-73-4

You Don't Know Anything …!
A Manual for Parenting Your Teenagers

by Nadir Baksh, Psy.D. and Laurie Murphy, R.N., Ph.D.

This book offers immediate and clear help to parents, family members and teachers who are angry, confused, frustrated, sad, or at their wit's end in dealing with their teenagers. Beyond advice for crisis situations, *You Don't Know Anything …!* informs parents of the new stresses their kids today must cope with, and suggests ways to minimize these pressures for both adults and teens.

Paper; 188 pages, $12.95, ISBN: 978-1-890772-82-6

8 Strategies For Successful Step-Parenting

by Nadir Baksh, Psy.D. and Laurie Murphy, R.N., Ph.D.

No matter who you are, and how much experience you've had with kids, becoming a step-parent, and "blending of families," is difficult work. The book presents 8 strategies, in the form of action steps, to maximize anyone's chances of success in this endeavor.

Paper, 188 pages, $14.95, ISBN: 978-1-935387-08-4

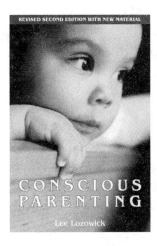

Conscious Parenting
Revised Edition with New Material

by Lee Lozowick

Any individual who cares for children needs to attend to the essential message of this book: that the first two years are the most crucial time in a child's education and development, and that children learn to be healthy and "whole" by living with healthy, whole adults.

Paper, $19.95, 336 pages, ISBN: 978-1-935387-17-9

Parenting, A Sacred Task
10 Basics of Conscious Childraising

by Karuna Fedorschak

Moving beyond our own self-centered focus and into the realm of generosity and expansive love is the core of spiritual practice. This book can help us to make that move. It highlights 10 basic elements that every parent can use to meet the everyday demands of childraising. Turning that natural duty into a sacred task is what this book is about. Topics include: love, attention, boundaries, food, touch, help and humor.

Paper, 158 pages, $12.95, ISBN: 978-1-890772-30-7

The Active Creative Child
Parenting in Perpetual Motion

by Stephanie Vlahov

This book provides specific hints for coping, for establishing realistic boundaries, and for avoiding labels and easy judgments where any child is concerned. Written in a simple, journalistic style, the author draws from her experience with her two active/creative sons, and those of others, to present a handbook of encouragement and genuine help.

Paper, 105 pages, $9.95, ISBN: 978-1-890772-47-5

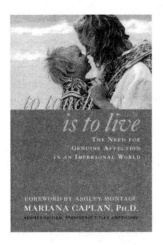

To Touch Is To Live
The Need for Genuine Affection in an Impersonal World

by Mariana Caplan

Foreword by Ashley Montagu

The vastly impersonal nature of contemporary culture, supported by massive child abuse and neglect, and reinforced by growing techno-fascination are robbing us of our humanity. This uncompromising and inspiring work offers positive solutions for countering the effects of the growing depersonalization of our times.

Paper, 272 pages, $19.95, ISBN: 978-1-890772-24-6

When Sons and Daughters Choose Alternative Lifestyles

by Mariana Caplan

A guidebook for families in building workable relationships based on trust and mutual respect, despite the fears and concerns brought on by differences in lifestyle. Practical advice on what to do when children join communes, go to gurus, follow rock bands around the country, marry outside their race or within their own gender, or embrace a religious belief that is alien to that of parents and family.

Paper, 264 pages, $14.95, ISBN: 978-0-934252-69-0

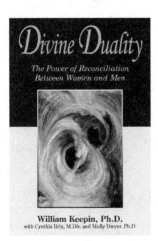

Divine Duality
The Power of Reconciliation between Women and Men

by William Keepin, Ph.D.,
with Cynthia Brix, M.Div. and Molly Dwyer, Ph.D.

This book demonstrates a revolutionary type of healing work between men and women, known as "gender reconciliation." Based on 15+ years of development, *Divine Duality* describes what can happen when a transpersonal/spiritual dimension underlies such work. No other book currently deals with this subject with the depth of insight and proven results presented here.

Paper; 320 pages, $16.95, ISBN: 978-1-890772-74-1

We Like To Live Green
English Language Edition

Nos Gusta Vivir Verde / We Like To Live Green
Spanish / English Bi-Lingual Edition

by Mary Young
Design by Zachary Parker

This Earth-friendly book provides an introduction to vital environmental themes in ways that will appeal to both young children and adults. We can all recycle and reuse, conserve water or grow a garden! Lively full-color photo montages demonstrate how to make a difference in a world threatened by pollution and ecological imbalance.

Children / Environment, ISBN: 978-1-935387-00-8 (English), ISBN: 978-1-935387-01-5 (Bi-Lingual), 32 pages, paperback, 8 ½ X 6 inches, $9.95

We Like To Eat Well
English Language Edition

Nos Gusta Comer Bien
Spanish Language Edition

by Elyse April
Illustrations by Lewis Agrell

What we eat is vitally important for good health … but so is *how* we eat … *where* and *when* we eat … and *how much* we eat … especially in reducing obesity and diabetes II, which have reached epidemic proportions in the U.S. This book encourages young children and parents to develop the healthy eating habits that can last for a lifetime.

Children / Nutrition, ISBN: 978-1-890772-69-7 (English), ISBN: 978-1-890772-78-9 (Spanish), 32 pages, paperback, 8 ½ X 6 inches, $9.95

We Like To Help Cook
English Language Edition

Nos Gusta Ayudar a Cocinar
Spanish Language Edition

by Marcus Allsop
Illustrations by Diane Iverson

All the young children in these brightly-colored picture books are helping adults to prepare healthy and delicious foods — all in accordance with the Healthy Diet Guidelines illustrated by the USDA Food Pyramid. Children help themselves or assist the adults by performing many age-related tasks, like pouring, shaking, washing, mashing and mixing — actions that most young children love to do.

Children / Health and Nutrition; ISBN: 978-1-890772-70-3 (English); ISBN: 978-1-890772-75-8 (Spanish); 32 pages; paperback; 8 ½ X 6 inches; $9.95

We Like To Move
Exercise is Fun
English Language Edition

Nos Gusta Movérnos
El Ejercicio Es Divertido
Spanish Language Edition

by Elyse April
Illustrations by Diane Iverson

The children in these brightly-colored picture books (available in English or Spanish) are engaged in many different forms of physical activity. The book also presents multicultural characters — including African, Hispanic, Caucasian and Asian children and adults, along with varied locales from a busy city street scene to a country landscape.

Children / Fitness ISBN: 978-1-890772-60-4 (English), ISBN: 978-1-890772-65-9 (Spanish), 32 pages; paperback 8 ½ X 6 inches; $9.95

We Like Our Teeth

English Language Edition

Nos Gustan Nuestros Dientes / We Like Our Teeth

Spanish / English Bi-Lingual Edition

written and illustrated by Marcus Allsop

These picture books (English language and English/Spanish editions) for children and parents will encourage them to care for their teeth. Bright, whimsical images show baby and adult animals caring for their own strong, healthy teeth. The clever, rhyming text spells out the basics of good dental hygiene: brushing, flossing, dental visits, healthy foods, etc.

Children / Dental Health, ISBN: 978-1-890772-86-4 (English), ISBN: 978-1-890772-89-5 (Bi-Lingual), 32 pages, paperback 8 ½ X 6 inches, $9.95

We Like To Play Music

English Language Edition

Nos Gusta Tocar Música / We Like To Play Music

Spanish / English Bi-Lingual Edition

by Kate Parker
Design by Zachary Parker

Human communication skills are helped by exposure to music at an early age—even before birth! Infants and young children need music as a way to rhythmically organize sounds, and to express emotions and messages. *We Like to Play Music* is an easy-to-read picture book full of photos of children playing music, moving to a beat and enjoying music alone or with parents or peers. The rhyming text, using the simplest vocabulary, says how everyone can play music.

Children / Music, ISBN: 978-1-890772-85-7 (English), ISBN: 978-1-890772-90-1 (Bi-Lingual), 32 pages, paperback 8 ½ X 6 inches, $9.95

We Like To Read

A Picture Book for Pre-Readers and Parents

English Language Edition

Nos Gusta Leer / We Like To Read

Libro Ilustrado Para Pequeños Y Padres

Spanish / English Bi-Lingual Edition

by Elyse April
Illustrations by Angie Thompson

Providing a new look at how to teach and encourage reading by using play and "attachment parenting" — i.e., lots of physical closeness and learning by example — the upbeat rhyming format provides cues on how to provide a foundation for reading while enticing children with game-like activities.

Children / Reading, ISBN: 978-1-890772-80-2 (English)
ISBN: 978-1-890772-81-9 (Bi-Lingual), 32 pages; paperback
8 ½ X 6 inches; $9.95

The Rainbow Feelings of Cancer

A Book for Children Who Have a Loved One With Cancer

by Chia & Carrie Martin

Children need to share what they feel, and ask what they want to know, when someone in their family has cancer. This book is a valuable resource in encouraging this conversation between children and parents or other caregivers.

Children / Cancer; ISBN: 978-1-890772-16-1; 32 pages; hardcover; $14.95

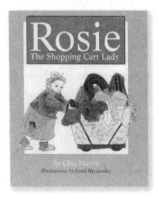

Rosie, The Shopping Cart Lady

by Chia Martin
illustrations by Jewel Hernandez

This book addresses neither the global questions of injustice nor a specific solution to the problem of homelessness in the U.S. today. Rather, it is about one direct act of kindness — from one human being to another.

Children/Homelessness; ISBN: 978-0-934252-51-5; 32 pages; hardcover; $15.95

About the Author

Laura Grace Weldon is a widely published author who writes for national publications about learning, sustainability and spirituality. She is also a poet and long-time columnist with *Home Education Magazine*. Laura lives on a small farm with her husband and their homeschooled children. Although she has deadlines to meet she "often wanders from the computer to preach hope, snort with laughter, cook subversively, observe chicken behavior, discuss life's deeper meaning with her patient offspring, sing to bees, feed cows, walk dogs, concoct tinctures, watch foreign films and make messy art." Visit her at http://lauragraceweldon.com

About Hohm Press

Hohm Press is committed to publishing books that provide readers with alternatives to the materialistic values of the current culture, and promote self-awareness, the recognition of interdependence, and compassion. Our subject areas include natural health, parenting, children's health, religious studies, women's issues, the arts and poetry. We are proud to offer the acclaimed *Family Health /World Health* series for children and parents, covering such themes as nutrition, dental health, reading, and environmental education. Hohm Press presents the work of contemporary spiritual teachers, including Lee Lozowick, Arnaud Desjardins, Dr. Robert Frager, Philippe Coupey and J. Krishnamurti, and books by authors distinguished in their fields: Georg Feuerstein (Yoga and Tantric Studies), Will Keepin and Cynthia Brix (Gender Studies), Laurie Murphy and Nadir Baksh (Marriage and Family Counseling), and Redhawk and Vraje Abramian (Poetry and Poetic Translations), among others.

Additional Contact Information

Visit our website at www.hohmpress.com

Hohm Press
PO Box 4410
Chino Valley, Arizona 86323
800-381-2700